State Capitalism and Development in East Asia Since 1945

Historical Materialism Book Series

The Historical Materialism Book Series is a major publishing initiative of the radical left. The capitalist crisis of the twenty-first century has been met by a resurgence of interest in critical Marxist theory. At the same time, the publishing institutions committed to Marxism have contracted markedly since the high point of the 1970s. The Historical Materialism Book Series is dedicated to addressing this situation by making available important works of Marxist theory. The aim of the series is to publish important theoretical contributions as the basis for vigorous intellectual debate and exchange on the left.

The peer-reviewed series publishes original monographs, translated texts, and reprints of classics across the bounds of academic disciplinary agendas and across the divisions of the left. The series is particularly concerned to encourage the internationalization of Marxist debate and aims to translate significant studies from beyond the English-speaking world.

For a full list of titles in the Historical Materialism Book Series available in paperback from Haymarket Books, visit: www.haymarketbooks.org/series_collections/1-historical-materialism.

State Capitalism and Development in East Asia Since 1945

Edited by
Owen Miller

Haymarket Books
Chicago, IL

First published in 2023 by Brill Academic Publishers, The Netherlands
© 2023 Koninklijke Brill NV, Leiden, The Netherlands

Published in paperback in 2024 by
Haymarket Books
P.O. Box 180165
Chicago, IL 60618
773-583-7884
www.haymarketbooks.org

ISBN: 979-8-88890-322-3

Distributed to the trade in the US through Consortium Book Sales and
Distribution (www.cbsd.com) and internationally through Ingram
Publisher Services International (www.ingramcontent.com).

This book was published with the generous support of Lannan
Foundation, Wallace Action Fund, and the Marguerite Casey Foundation.

Special discounts are available for bulk purchases by organizations and
institutions. Please call 773-583-7884 or email info@haymarketbooks.org
for more information.

Cover art and design by David Mabb. Cover art is a detail from *Construct
21, Morris (Kersey), Arbutus / Malevich, Fabric Ornament No. 12*. Paint on
paper mounted on canvas (2005).

Printed in the United States.

Library of Congress Cataloging-in-Publication data is available.

Contents

Acknowledgements

This book has had a very long period of gestation. So much so that it seemed at times the world might have changed unrecognisably by the time it was finished. The world certainly has changed, but although economic, environmental, social and even epidemiological catastrophes come and go, I am sad to say that the central subjects of this book – capitalism and the state – have endured. Hence, I will venture to say that the relevance of this book will be assured for a while longer.

This volume was first conceived around 2010, inspired in part by reading Lee Jeong-goo's work on state capitalism in China. The authors gathered together as a group to discuss the project and present our work at Gyeongsang National University in Jinju, South Korea in May 2011 and again at SOAS in London in November 2012. Eleven years have now passed since then and various obstacles that seemed insurmountable at the time have been overcome, one way or another.

As with any project of this kind there are many people who have contributed in large and small ways. Firstly I must thank the contributors to this volume, not only for their chapters that have made this book but for their almost infinite patience in waiting for this book to actually be completed and appear in print. I would like to thank Jeong Seongjin for hosting us in Jinju way back in 2011 and always being helpful and enthusiastic about this project. I also have deep gratitude for Kim Ha-young, whose work on state capitalism in North Korea has inspired me since the early 2000s when I first translated parts of her book *North Korea from an Internationalist Perspective*, and who has always responded to my endless queries about correct citations of Kim Il Sung quotations with alacrity and patience. I'm grateful to both Lee Jeong-goo and Tobias Ten Brink for sticking with this project through the years and helping to give the book a timely analysis of contemporary Chinese capitalism, alongside the more historical chapters on the two Koreas and Mao's China. This book would not be what it is without the contribution of Kim Yong-uk, who agreed to fill a big gap and write a chapter on Mao's China quite late in the project. I'm immensely grateful to Yong-uk for turning in a highly original piece of work and putting up with my frequent nagging. Mike Haynes has been another stalwart, who, despite apparently having an unfathomable number of research interests and projects on the go, has provided various updates to his concluding chapter, which plays a crucial role in broadening out the insights developed in the rest of the book to show how East Asian state capitalisms are significant for understanding the totality of global capitalism in the twenty first century.

Finally, I'm deeply thankful for the support and friendship of Gareth Dale, with whom I co-wrote the introduction. Gareth's contribution to this book has gone far beyond that task, with helpful advice and encouragement at all stages of the project, along with the occasional prod in the back to get a move on. More than anything Gareth has shaped my understanding of state capitalism and helped to give this book the solid theoretical foundations that it needed.

Others who have aided this book by commenting on drafts, participating as discussants at our seminars and giving valuable scholarly advice include Jamie Allinson, Chang Dae-oup, Jamie Doucette, Vladimir Tikhonov and Nik Howard. I would also like to express my gratitude to Justin Choi, who was responsible for translating parts of Chapter 2, and to Choi Youngchan who translated Chapter 6.

This book received important support from an Academy of Korean Studies grant that the SOAS Centre of Korean Studies received between 2011 and 2016, which allowed us to hold a workshop at SOAS in 2012 and also helped to pay for some of the translation work. I'm grateful to my colleague Professor Jaehoon Yeon who administered the grant and has always been very supportive of this project and my work in general.

On a personal level, the most fundamental support of all has come from my family: Becky, Raya and Ellis, the last of whom only arrived on the scene halfway through the development of this book. Thank you for continuing to believe that I am doing something worthwhile.

Owen Miller
April 2023

Notes on Contributors

Tobias Ten Brink
Professor of Chinese Economy and Society, Jacobs University, Bremen

Gareth Dale
Senior Lecturer in Politics and International Relations, Brunel University, London

Michael Haynes
Professor of International Political Economy, University of Wolverhampton

Jeong Seongjin
Professor of Economics, Gyeongsang National University, South Korea

Kim Ha-young
A writer and activist based in Seoul, Kim Ha-young is a member of the South Korean organisation Workers' Solidarity, which is part of the International Socialist Tendency

Kim Yong-uk
Researcher based in Seoul, a member of the South Korean organisation Workers' Solidarity

Lee Jeong-goo
Research professor based in Seoul

Owen Miller
Lecturer in Korean Studies, SOAS, University of London

Note on Romanisation of East Asian Words

This book uses the Pinyin Romanisation system for transcribing Chinese words, the McCune-Reischauer system for Korean and the Hepburn system for Japanese. As ever, there are exceptions and these are principally for well-recognised conventional spellings of certain personal names, such as the former South Korean president Syngman Rhee or the Guomindang leader Chiang Kai-shek. This book also adheres to the East Asian convention of placing the surname before the given name in personal names, although again there are a few notable exceptions where a person's name has been deliberately 'Westernised', as in the case of the above-mentioned Syngman Rhee.

CHAPTER 1

The Emergence and Development of Capitalism in East Asia: the State Capitalist Approach

Owen Miller and Gareth Dale

1 Setting Out the Problem: the Rise of Capitalism in East Asia

In the second half of the twentieth century the East Asian region[1] underwent one of the most profound human transformations in history. It was a transformation that moved hundreds of millions of people from rural life to cities, from agricultural work to industrial and office work and from premodern village society to the modern urban world of apartments, mass consumption and the nuclear family. Between 1953 and 1987 the population of North Korea shifted decisively from rural peasant farming to urban industrial and office work; in 1953, fewer than one in five people lived in towns; by 1987 it was three in five.[2] A similar and equally dramatic story can be told of South Korea where, between 1945 and 1985, the urban population rose from 14.5 percent to 64.9 percent of the total population.[3] In Japan too, although the transformation had started considerably earlier, from the 1950s onward tens of millions of people have moved from village life to apartment living in huge cities and the daily rigours of office and factory work.[4] In China the scale of the shift may be vastly greater, but the basic picture is the same: a movement of people from rural villages to industrial cities and from the western interior to the eastern coasts that has been billed as humanity's greatest ever migration, involving 250 million people.[5] Along with this great human shift have come all the other elements of

---

1 There are of course differing definitions of 'East Asia' and which countries should be included. For the purposes of this book the region is defined as encompassing China (PRC), Taiwan (ROC), North Korea, South Korea and Japan.

2 Official North Korean statistics give an urbanisation rate of 17.7 percent for 1953 and 59.8 percent for 1987. See: Central Statistical Board 1961; Eberstadt and Banister 1992, p. 21.

3 See United Nations 2018. Since the 1980s South Korea's urban population has continued to rise at a fast rate, reaching a peak of 81.9 percent in 2010.

4 Japan started from a much higher postwar base of 53.4 percent urban population in 1950. However, it also urbanised rapidly in the postwar boom, reaching 76.7 percent in 1985 and then growing again to 90.8 percent by 2010. (United Nations 2018).

5 On Chinese rural-urban migration, see for example: Lu and Xia 2016.

capitalist modernity: class formation, exploitation, mass consumption, mass media, the destruction of old ways of life, and the intervention of the state and business into everyday life on a hitherto unheard of scale. This transformation has a deeper history, stretching back into the late nineteenth century and the Meiji Restoration in Japan, but its roots also lie in two world wars and multiple regional wars; in the colonial experience; and in the wave of revolutions-from-above that followed the Second World War. In short, while the countries of East Asia became part of the capitalist world system in the late nineteenth century, it was in the second half of the twentieth century that they were completely transformed by capitalist modernity. This volume begins from the premise that this transformation occurred with the deep involvement of the state, in countries stretching right across the political spectrum, from 'communist' China and North Korea to 'capitalist' Japan and South Korea. This book is a contribution to understanding the origins and nature of this great transformation experienced by almost one-quarter of the earth's population.

There is now a widespread belief that East Asia represents the future of global capitalism, but the region's road to capitalist preeminence is not so well understood or uncontroversial. In fact, the emergence and development of capitalist societies in East Asia has long been a source of confusion and contention for economists, historians and mainstream commentators.[6] This is demonstrated amply by the great variety of approaches and assessments that are made of capitalist development in the region. In the past much praise has been lavished on Japan's Toyota capitalism, the Tiger economies of the 1970s and 1980s and China's emergence as the industrial powerhouse of the world since its economic reforms began in 1978. But, equally, East Asian capitalism, almost since its initial emergence in Japan in the late nineteenth century, has frequently been understood as abnormal or substandard. Marxists debating Japan's backwardness in the 1930s saw Japanese capitalism as somehow 'distorted',[7] while neoliberals seeking explanations for the Asian financial crisis of 1997 castigated East Asia's statism and 'crony capitalism' in the 1990s, seeing it as inherently inferior to 'Anglo-Saxon capitalism'. Meanwhile, some parts of the story of East Asian economic development have been considered so abnormal that they have been consistently excluded from most accounts, in particular the 'miraculous' growth of North Korea's industrial economy in the 50s and 60s and the PRC's economic development prior to 1978.[8]

---

6 Perhaps the most famous debate in the English language has been that over the developmental state concept outlined by Chalmers Johnson, among others. See Johnson 1999.

7 For the Japanese debate see: Hoston 1986; Walker 2016.

8 In 1965 the economist Joan Robinson wrote of the [North] 'Korean Miracle' (Robinson 1965).

In one sense the cause of the confusion that has beset observers of East Asian development, from Marxists to neoliberals, can be laid at the door of Eurocentrism. Or rather, the tendency to build our models of 'normal' capitalism based on those parts of the world – Western Europe in particular – where the system first emerged. This has meant that both the transition to capitalism in the non-European world and its subsequent development have consistently been seen through the European experience, which determines what is normal/abnormal. A large dose of (neo)liberal ideology has also abstracted capitalism from the state, as a purely economic market-based system, and this tendency has clearly influenced Marxist analyses too. From our current vantage point in the early twenty-first century, however, there is little sense in viewing the development of capitalism in East Asia as abnormal, or somehow 'less capitalist' than the preceding phases of capitalist development, centred on the North Atlantic region. The development of capitalism in East Asia has, of course, been firmly situated within the particular phases of global capitalist development during which it has occurred, as well as the geopolitical configurations of that period (Japanese imperialism, Cold War, post-Cold War/Washington Consensus) and the specificities of the regional context. However, as this book will argue, it has nonetheless produced an authentically modern, capitalist world, albeit one that has been rent by vicious ideological divisions and produced a variety of different capitalist economies and political regimes.

This raises the question of how best to construct an integrated account of the emergence and development of capitalism in East Asia that can explain in a coherent way industrialisation both during and after Japanese colonial rule; Chinese capitalism both pre- and post-1978; and the economic miracles of both North and South Korea. This is the central question addressed in this book. The authors provide answers that are firmly rooted in the classical Marxist analysis of capitalism but at the same time build on it in order to understand the burgeoning role of the state in the functioning of capitalism since the early twentieth century. What binds together the analyses found in the chapters of this book and gives them their explanatory power is the idea of state capitalism.

2   Theories of State Capitalism

In general journalistic and academic usage, state capitalism is used loosely to refer to regimes in which states own or control a sizeable proportion of the business sector. During the Great Recession 2007–2009, the weakening of neoliberal confidence coincided with a flurry of interest in state capitalism among mainstream business publications. In 2012 *Business Week* ran a report on 'The Rise of Innovative State Capitalism', and *The Economist* published a dossier entitled 'The Rise of State Capitalism: The Emerging World's New Model'. 'Across much of the developing world', *Business Week* warned,

> state capitalism is replacing the free market. From 2004 through 2009, 120 state-owned companies made their debut on the Forbes list of the world's largest corporations, while 250 private companies fell off it. State companies now control about 90 percent of the world's oil and large percentages of other resources – a far cry from the past, when BP and ExxonMobil could dictate terms to the world.[9]

'State capitalists' in economies such as China and Brazil, it added, 'have shattered the idea that they can't foster innovation to match developed economies'. They could even 'push multinationals out of some markets entirely'.[10] Equally, China demonstrated that state capitalism and globalisation are not antithetical. Roughly two-thirds of Chinese FDI, it was reported in 2012, stemmed from state-owned firms, and of the 61 Chinese firms on the Fortune 500 list in 2011, no fewer than 59 were state owned.[11]

The Economist struck a similar note; raising the spectre of geo-economic regime change. The current crisis of 'liberal capitalism', it lamented,

> has been rendered more serious by the rise of a potent alternative: state capitalism. ... Elements of state capitalism have been seen in the past, for example in the rise of Japan in the 1950s and even of Germany in the 1870s, but never before has it operated on such a scale and with such sophisticated tools. ... State capitalism is on the march, overflowing with cash and emboldened by the crisis in the West. State companies make up 80% of the value of the stock market in China, 62% in Russia and 38% in Brazil. ... Add the exploits of sovereign-wealth funds to the ledger, and it begins to look as if liberal capitalism is in wholesale retreat. ... State capitalism increasingly looks like the coming trend.[12]

The usage to which the term is put in this volume draws upon a more complex and encompassing theory, from within the Marxist tradition. Broadly put, this theory holds that the state is always an integral part of the capitalist system:

---

9   Kurlantzick 2012.
10   Kurlantzick 2012.
11   Nagel 2012, pp. 641–57.
12   *The Economist* 2012, pp. 3–18.

capital accumulation cannot occur without the state and the capitalist state cannot exist without capitalism.[13] However, capitalist societies can vary greatly according to the degree of direct involvement by the state in the process of capital accumulation. At one point on the spectrum there are states that avoid any direct involvement in business, although they will inevitably be intervening in capitalist society in myriad other ways. Far down the other end are states that become so involved in capital accumulation that they completely eclipse private capital and act within their own borders as though they were a single huge conglomerate, the former Soviet Union being only the most well-known example. While societies on this spectrum may vary hugely in the character of their economies and their political regimes, state capitalism theory holds that they are all subject to the same underlying capitalist dynamics identified by Marx in *Capital*. Those dynamics are the capital-labour relation that underpins most production under capitalism and the drive for competitive accumulation that keeps it in constant motion.

Perhaps the best-known originator of this theory is the Jewish-Palestinian Trotskyist Tony Cliff, but it has roots stretching back well before the 1940s. When Marxists in the 1920s and 1930s – such as Gavril Miasnikov, Friedrich Adler and Ryan Worrall[14] – began to develop a critique of the Soviet Union they were to some extent recapitulating debates in nineteenth-century social democracy between Marx/Engels and advocates of the 'developmental state': Lassalle and the *Kathedersozialisten*. Lassalle had imagined the modern state to be a class-neutral structure, an instrument of justice that could be re-engineered by the labour movement to implement a socialist programme. The *Kathedersozialist* Adolf Wagner analysed a tendency to increasing statification of the economy, *en route* to comprehensive state intervention, which he termed 'state socialism'. Marx and Engels were dismissive of these ideas. Lassalle, in Marx's paraphrase, was proposing that socialism arises not 'from the revolutionary process of transformation of society' but from aid that 'the state gives to the producers' co-operative societies'. Marx scoffs at Lassalle for this notion – as if 'a new society can be built through state loans, much as the building of a new railway!'[15] A couple of years later, Engels developed the point. 'The modern state, whatever its form', he wrote,

> is an essentially capitalist machine, the state of capitalists, the ideal collective capitalist. The greater the productive forces it takes ownership of

---

13   Barker 1978, pp. 16–42.
14   Van der Linden 2007, pp. 49–63.
15   Marx 1875 (Translation by GD).

and the more that it in reality becomes a collective capitalist, the greater the number of citizens it exploits. The workers remain wage workers, proletarians; the capital relation is not *aufgehoben*; rather, it is intensified.[16]

In the 1940s these ideas were exhumed by theorists such as C.L.R. James, Raya Duneyavskaya, and Tony Cliff who broke from the Trotskyist tradition to label the Soviet Union and its satellites as capitalist. James and Dunayevskaya described the USSR as a 'single capitalist society'[17] – in other words, a society dominated by a single capitalist (the state) – while Cliff described it as 'bureaucratic state capitalism'.[18] James, Dunayevskaya and Cliff were by no means the only Marxists to come to this conclusion in the postwar period. Within the Soviet Union itself dissident thinkers developed their own theories close to that of state capitalism,[19] while in China too Trotskyist dissident Zheng Chaolin developed a theory of state capitalism to explain the nature of Chinese society under Mao and was rewarded with a life spent behind bars.[20]

However, it was Cliff's 1955 book *Stalinist Russia. A Marxist Analysis* that developed the most detailed analysis of state capitalism in the Soviet Union. In it, Cliff argued that after the social movements that had brought the Bolshevik-led government to power subsided, the chief proprietor of Russian industry, the Communist Party, under pressure from military and economic competition, came to subordinate society to the exigencies of competition with capitalist states. The producing classes were divorced from the means of production and obliged to sell their labour power, while consumption was suppressed in the interest of maximising investment in the productive sector and the arms industry. The government now occupied, in relation to the national economy, 'the position which a capitalist occupies in relation to a single enterprise', as Trotsky portrayed the Soviet Union in the 1930s.[21] Trotsky didn't draw the con-

---

16   Engels 1894 [1878], p. 260 (Translation by GD).

17   See James, Dunayevskaya & Lee 1950 and also Dunayevskaya 1958.

18   Cliff 1948, chapter 6. On earlier theories of state capitalism see Ciliga 1940; Fernandez 1997. There were also those on the right who articulated forms of state capitalism theory, including ex-communists, conservatives and even fascists. For example, Michael Polanyi, Oswald Mosley and Arthur Koestler. Koestler wrote in the early 1940s, for example, that 'Economically the Soviet Union represents State Capitalism. The State owns the means of production and controls the production of goods' (Koestler 1945, p. 188).

19   See, for example, the work of Yuri Semenov, who used the concept of 'industrial-statism' to describe the fusion of politics with economics in the process of late industrialisation. Semenov 1993.

20   Zheng 2023, pp. 152–76. On Zheng's life and thought, see: Zheng and Benton 1997.

21   Trotsky 1972, p. 43.

clusion that the system had become state capitalist, but Cliff did. In his reading the Soviet Union operated as a unit of capital – albeit with internal differentiation, not unlike a multi-divisional enterprise. The *nomenklatura*, the caste of functionaries that controlled Soviet society, had come to act as a capitalist ruling class. Although focused on Soviet Russia, Cliff's book carried implications for theorising capitalism and the states system. In the following sections we bring these to the fore, before outlining in detail the approach to Soviet Russia that Cliff originated and then shifting geographical focus to East Asia.

3   From Capitalism to State Capitalism

In its method, the theory of state capitalism draws inspiration from Marx's approach in *Capital*, with its movement from the commodity form, considered abstractly, towards the capitalist mode of production in its concrete reality. A central feature of this method is that it attempts to wrestle with the way in which, as capitalism evolves, the concepts with which we understand it are transformed.[22] By way of example, consider Jairus Banaji's discussion of wage labour. The concept can be used as a 'simple category', i.e. one that has purchase in various modes of production, but with the advent of capitalism it becomes conceivable as a 'historically determinate abstraction' – specifically, in Marx's usage, as 'capital-positing, capital-producing labour'.[23] The character of wage-labour as a 'specifically bourgeois' relation of production did not come about through the mere generalisation of commodified labour-power. Rather, in interaction with a set of interrelated social processes – competitive state-building, changes in lord-peasant relations, development of trade and cities, emergence of the world market, differentiation of the peasantry, bourgeois revolutions, etc. – the capital-wage-labour relation began to take shape as the fulcrum of surplus extraction.[24] A second example is capital, considered in its ownership aspect. As the system evolved, historically, private property in the means of production tended to transform from a personal into an impersonal form, thanks to institutional innovations such as the joint stock enterprise. In the process, capital came to appear in corporate form – in a sense in a 'purer' guise as a social power rather than as the personal property of 'private' individuals. The corporation itself is staffed by 'organisation men', and women, turned

---

22   Haynes 1983, p. 79.
23   Banaji 1977; Marx 1993 [1857], p. 463.
24   Banaji 1977.

out by the business schools and applying the latest scientific management techniques to the task of making profit. In such environments, in Marx's prescient words, 'only the functionary remains, the capitalist disappears from the process of production'.[25] The relation of functionaries to their enterprise is not one of ownership – or if it is, as Colin Barker has put it, 'it *owns them* rather than the reverse', in much the same way that (as Marx remarked) 'the Prussian estate *inherited* the eldest son'.[26]

State capitalism theory applies this historico-analytical method to a set of concepts central to the analysis of capitalist society, including the law of value, capital, and competition.

When we say capitalism, we are using it, as Marxists, to refer to a system of value in expansionary motion. Value, for Marx, is the alienated form of wealth in commodity-producing societies. Through being exchanged, commodities 'acquire a socially uniform status as values, which is distinct from their sensuously varied objectivity as articles of utility'.[27] Any economy in which commodity production occurs to a significant degree knows value, and indeed the 'law of value' – and ethical critiques of forms of economic behaviour that set value (in the form of money) as an end in itself go back to Aristotle, if not before. Unique to capitalism is that it is a system of formally independent economic entities each of which must exchange in order to exist. Social labour in capitalism takes, to borrow Patrick Murray's term, a 'practically abstract' form: i.e. it is productive of commodities, with acts of production socially validated through the exchange of products for the universal equivalent (money).[28] The social basis of generalised commodity production is thus a systematic separation through which interdependent producers assume the form of atomised units governed by relations of competitive antagonism. The coordination of producers' activities occurs 'behind their backs', through exchange. Such interaction is based upon interdependence – the need of independent producers for one another's products – and it is coercive, with competition obliging all producers to conform to prevailing prices or risk returning from the marketplace with their commodities unsold. Regulation of this activity is not direct, by custom or planning, but indirect, via the outcome of the relations between the units, between their products. To sell a commodity it must not only satisfy a perceived need, but also be produced and distributed within the socially necessary labour-time – or 'value'. (Put differently, it must aim to secure at least the

---

25   In Chattopadhyay 1994, p. 26.
26   Barker 1998, p. 38.
27   Marx 1990, p. 21.
28   Murray 2000.

'socially necessary' price.) Competition among producers of a particular commodity establishes a standard input requirement, which Marx called 'socially necessary labour'. Prices, ultimately, are regulated by socially necessary labour time, as established through the process of competition. Competition is not an addition to the concept of value but immanent in it. What Marxists refer to as the 'law of value' is not simply a description of the principles that operate in commodity-producing society, it is also 'a coercive force operating on all producers'.[29]

The imperative of value expansion, in this analysis, flows from two structural features of capitalist society. Firstly, production is based largely on free wage labour, with labour power sold as a commodity – the mass of producers, separated from the means of production and the means of subsistence, are compelled to sell their labour power in order to survive. Secondly, the owners of the means of production exist in a competitive relationship with one another. Competition compels them to perpetually seek ways to increase profitability – essentially, by reducing the 'socially necessary labour time' required to produce and distribute goods and services. In harness, these features give rise to the peculiar collective purpose of capitalist societies: the self-expansion of capital. For capitalists, as Marx put it, 'Accumulate! Accumulate!' is the alpha and omega; competition compels them to 'reconvert the largest possible proportion of surplus value or surplus product into capital'.[30]

The self-expansion of capital rests on the exploitation of wage-labour, which, compelled by need to enter into a contract under which it submits to the will of capital for the period of its hire, produces the means ('surplus-value') for capital's reproduction, for its expanded domination of society to continue.[31] Alongside wage labour, of the social relations and institutions that define and organise an economy of this type, money – the fulcrum of almost all commodity exchange – and markets occupy centre stage. Markets, as Patrick Murray puts it, 'belong to the social arrangements that render labour abstract; they function as a sort of "labour-processing" plant'.[32] But they are not by any means the only such arrangement. Inter-capital competition does not take place only through market exchange. Other, non-market modalities of competition include 'spending surplus value on ways of manipulating the market, advertising goods, creating a "product image", bribing buyers in firms and

29   Barker 1999–2000.
30   Marx 1990, p. 654.
31   Barker 1999–2000.
32   Murray 2000, p. 45.

state agencies'.[33] In an earlier era, Nikolai Bukharin identified 'the struggle for spheres of capital investment' as an example of capitalist competition by other means.[34] A regime of practical abstract labour, moreover, depends upon a panoply of social practices: the design and enforcement of contractual transactions, regimes of measurement, standardisation, benchmarking and performance indicators, the disciplining, regimenting and social reproduction of workers, and the construction of material infrastructures and social organisations (factories, firms, state agencies, bureaucracies) that invent, supervise and enforce these processes,[35] not to forget the army of 'Weberian spirits' – instrumental rationality, the work ethic, utility, status competition – that justify, legitimise, activate and animate them. Moreover, given that the realm of commodity production is a realm of property, of relations of ownership, with the inevitable threats of appropriation by others and coercive responses to those threats, an additional and essential aspect of the capital relation is the production of means of violence and exclusion. Police and soldiers, fences, walls and alarm systems, guns, bombs and warplanes, as Colin Barker has argued, 'are all part of the real economic necessities of commodity production' in its capitalist form.[36] 'The "moment of coercion" (the state)', in Peter Burnham's formulation, is 'present in every economic act built on the commodification of social relations'.[37]

The capital relation, then, is necessarily mediated through states. States fulfil several functions indispensable to the capitalist order. On this, Neil Davidson has provided a useful three-fold distinction. Firstly, capitalist states impose 'a dual social order: horizontally over competing capitals so that market relations do not collapse into "the war of all against all"; and vertically over the conflict between capital and labour so that it continues to be resolved in the interest of the former'. Second, they establish '"general conditions of production" which individual competing capitals would be unwilling or unable to provide, including some basic level of technical infrastructure and welfare provision'. Third, they 'represent the collective interests of the "internal" capitalist class "externally", in relation to other capitalist states and classes'. This includes the realm of 'international relations' ('geopolitics', 'foreign policy', etc.). In none of these cases does a direct and functional relationship exist between the interests of capital and the actions of states. At all levels the field is criss-crossed with con-

---

33   Harman quoted in Davidson 2012.
34   Bukharin quoted in Davidson 2012.
35   Moore 2014, Lampland 1995.
36   Colin Barker 1999–2000.
37   Burnham 1995, p. 153.

tradictory pressures: between the interests of capitals and those of citizens (as expressed for example in social movements or at the ballot box); among capitals, each of which lobbies political authorities to represent their interests; between the common interests of states in upholding capitalist order at the global level (the 'liberal' emphasis in IR theory) and their separate interests in supporting 'their' capitals against rivals (the 'realist' emphasis); and so on. Such contradictions, in addition to the institutional materialisation of states themselves, give state managers considerable autonomy. Nonetheless, if they fail to back 'their' capitals in the world market, and still more if they fail to secure capitalist property relations, the limits of that autonomy will be forcefully revealed.

The competition of capitals, we are suggesting, is threaded into the states system, and the world market is organised politically. Important in this regard is states' constitution, through national currencies, of 'nationally delimited spheres of circulation' (to borrow Hannes Lacher's term). This ensures that the law of value operates differently in the national and the international spheres – because national values are mediated internationally by exchange rates, the law of value cannot mediate the allocation of socially necessary labour time on a global scale in any direct way.[38] Competition between capitals, in short, is 'mediated by state boundaries'; the border mechanisms of territorial states function as 'offensive weapons in the struggle for world market shares and profits', as states 'organize the external projection of national class interests through foreign policy, diplomacy and military force'.[39] Tariffs, exchange rates, export subsidies, foreign aid, and influence within international organisations, are the sorts of policies and programmes that can be applied by states to boost the competitiveness of 'their' capitals, and to tilt geo-economic rules and regimes in their interests. Capitalism, in other words, is not a system simply of economic competition. Capitals require from states not simply infrastructure, they need them to ensure that the effects of competition are experienced as far as possible by rivals. They want competition, as Davidson puts it, 'to take place on their terms; they do not want to suffer the consequences if they lose'.[40]

In mediating and organising the international competition of capitals, states become drawn into that competition, as active elements, and this imbues geopolitics with a capitalist character. Geopolitical rivalry acts as a transmission mechanism, compelling states to ensure that the systems and institutions they control are competitive, economically and militarily, with rivals. On pain of fragmentation or demotion in the emerging world hierarchy (and until the

---

38   Lacher 2006, p. 114.
39   Lacher 2006, p. 114.
40   Davidson 2012.

twentieth century of outright colonisation), states find themselves coerced, in part through geopolitical pressures, to intervene in, consolidate, and generally reshape society in the interests of capital. Geopolitical interaction in a capitalist world, as Andrew Wright summarises it, 'imposes subservience of states to the law of value'.[41]

What does it mean, to subordinate *states* to the law of value? Does that 'law' not apply strictly to market-mediated competition, with socially necessary labour expenditure determined only *a posteriori*, after goods have exchanged and sales numbers and prices have signalled the degree to which the labour time expended on each item was in fact socially necessary? At the core of the theory of state capitalism is a negative response to this question. It is a response that few have explored more insightfully than Barker. Socially necessary labour time, he begins, is indeed only adjudicated *a posteriori*, 'but that doesn't mean producers don't have to take account of it, in anticipation. They know it very well, even if they don't express it in those terms. If they get it wrong, the punishment can be severe'. The question then is: does essentially the same 'law' also apply to arms production and means of 'defence'? And in addition, 'is the necessary "unproductive" labour expenditure associated with the maintenance of private property relations also subject to the same principles (or "laws")?' Surely the same *a posteriori* and 'anticipation' issues arise in respect of the defence of private property and the state as they do in respect of selling shampoo or soap. People and firms invest in equipment to defend their premises against burglars – at a particular 'socially necessary' cost – in 'anticipation of the possibility of being burgled'. They find out, after the fact, whether they had done enough. Likewise, Barker continues, military commanders and ministers of defence invest in their armed forces 'in anticipation of what they may need to do; they find out after the fact if their anticipations were accurate. Hitler anticipated that he could conquer Stalin's Russia, with what he had thought would prove to be a satisfactory mixture of good tactics, military morale and superior productive-cum-military strength. After the fact, he was proved wrong'.[42]

Does this line of argumentation risk broadening the scope of the 'law of value' such that it loses all precision and purchase? Does it imply that *all* geopolitical rivalry is cut from the same cloth as capitalist geopolitical competition? For, surely, all such competition involves anticipation, consideration of means and ends, and the use of manufactured instruments of war. Consider for example Russia's pre-capitalist history. Russian social life, Trotsky poin-

41   Wright 1997, p. 14.
42   Barker 1999–2000.

ted out, 'has *all the time* been under the influence, even under the pressure, of its external social-historical milieu'.[43] The earliest incarnation of the Russian state, indeed, originated in commercial and military rivalries and interactions through which Scandinavian merchants (the 'Rus') gained sway over East Slav peoples. The state, centred on Kiev, was oriented initially towards Constantinople, was then conquered by the Mongols and fragmented into rival principalities, one of which, Muscovy, eventually rose to hegemony.[44] Throughout Russia's early evolution, geopolitical and geo-commercial interactions and rivalries played a major determining role, whether in the unhinging of Kiev's development 'by the geo-commercial impact of the Crusades' or Muscovy's emergence from Mongol domination – 'hugely assisted by the otherwise unrelated assault of Timur on the Golden Horde', or the emergence of a *Pax Ottomana* which provided a security umbrella under which commercial routes flourished that linked Russia and Central Asia with Europe via the Black Sea.[45] At every step of the way, Justin Rosenberg argues, 'the evolving Russian social formation was a hybrid, a changing amalgam of pre-existent "internal" structures of social life with "external" socio-political and cultural influences. From the Viking north to the Byzantine south, from the Mongol east to the European west, a succession of external pressures (and opportunities) of radically varying cultural form all left their mark on the inner shape of the Russian state'.[46]

In what ways did these patterns alter with the rise of capitalism – initially in the United Provinces, England and their imperial extensions, then in the other Western European empires? Distinctive about the new system was that (i) its organisation of social extraction, pivoting as it does on the capital-wage-labour relation and with complex systems of money and finance, tends to be relatively abstracted from territory (when compared to other modes of production); (ii) it is conducive to the institutional separation of economy from polity – and therefore, to the rise of the 'political state'; (iii) as a consequence of the previous two points, it promotes specifically the development of nation states, and leads ultimately to the replacement of looser archipelagos of empires and city states with a regimented and institutionalised universal nation-state system; (iv) it consistently outperformed other systems in raising productivity and hence (v) enabling the construction of infrastructurally powerful and consistently well-funded states – it tends, in other words, to facilitate (or compel) the augmentation of the 'infrastructural' capacities (to use Michael Mann's term)

---

43   Trotsky 1931. Emphasis added.
44   Rosenberg 2006, p. 321.
45   Anievas and Nisancioglu 2015, p. 322; Rosenberg 2006, p. 322.
46   Rosenberg 2006, p. 325.

of states, alongside their despotic power; (vi) it is inherently expansionary, with expansion transmitted along economic and political channels.

Confronted with the rise of the United Provinces, England, and the rest, non-capitalist states increasingly faced a choice: replicate the institutions that were enabling the amassing of power in these capitalist centres, or risk subjugation. For Russia, the new set of pressures emanating from Western Europe prompted the state, under Peter the Great, to attempt the 'modernisation' of its governmental and military administration, and political culture more generally, a project that saw Russia survive the eighteenth century with a strengthened state but without a transformed civil society. Trotsky's assessment of Russia's post-Petrian history is instructive. 'Under the influence and the pressure of its more differentiated Western milieu, a pressure that was transmitted through the military-state organization, the State in its turn strove to force the development of social differentation on a primitive economic foundation'.[47] Staffed with landlords, ingrained with absolutist traditions and values, and overseeing a still heavily feudal agricultural empire, the attempts of the Tsarist state to stimulate capitalist development in agriculture in order to swell the surplus available to industry were stumbling, half-hearted, and prone to relapse. And yet, in part in response to geopolitical competition – Napoleon's march on Moscow was an early warning; 1855 and 1905 were alarming defeats – the Tsarist autocracy did eventually abolish feudal serfdom and delegated senior positions of state to modernisers. Above all during Count Witte's stints in high office (1892–1905), the government, rather than allow the stalled agrarian revolution to block industrialisation, succeeded in coupling a traditional method of surplus extraction, the taxation of peasants, with large-scale borrowing from external sources of finance in order to push through a panoply of measures aimed at, as Witte himself put it, 'removing the unfavourable conditions which hamper the economic development of the country and at kindling a healthy spirit of enterprise'.[48] Witte presided over rafts of reforms: savings banks were encouraged, state banks was established to funnel domestic savings and foreign capital into industry; steamship companies and nautical and engineering schools were founded, corporate law was reformed and the ruble made convertible.[49] Capitalism, in Trotsky's summary, 'seemed to be an offspring of the State'.[50] If geopolitical mechanisms helped ensure the subservience of states such as Russia to the law of value in the nineteenth century, how did this play out in the aftermath of the 1917 Revolution?

47　　Trotsky 1931.
48　　Witte, quoted in Dale 2004.
49　　Trotsky 1971, p. 33.
50　　Trotsky 1931.

4   State Capitalism in Russia

The Bolsheviks' wager in 1917 was that despite the inevitable assault by capitalist states, Russia's revolutionary trajectory could be consolidated if similar
gambles paid off elsewhere, undermining the number and power of enemy
states. (It's no coincidence that Trotsky was the theorist identified most closely
with the theory of geopolitics as capitalist transmission mechanism *and* with
the notion that defence of workers' power would require its replication internationally.) The predicted world-revolutionary wave did occur, but without the
hoped-for revolutionary breakthroughs. The inherent difficulties faced by a
revolution in a backward country intensified. That socialist revolution could
occur in Russia was, as Victor Serge summed up the case, in part due to the
Bolsheviks' 'intransigence' but also 'because the system here was weakest ...,
because the socialist revolution benefited from a bourgeois revolution which,
though necessary, was feeble and tardy, unable to complete itself; because on
the ruins of the tsarist regime the Russian proletariat found itself faced only
with an inexperienced, disarmed bourgeoisie'.[51] The same factors, however, that
account for the occurrence of the revolution also determined the fragility of
the regime to which it gave rise. If bourgeois weakness and the military defeats
suffered by the Tsarist armies were both, ultimately, consequences of Russia's
relative economic and technological weakness, this same weakness enlarged
the difficulties confronted by the revolutionary regime: a small working class,
low living standards, poorly developed economic and cultural infrastructures,
and a military that was poorly equipped in comparison to those that invaded
in 1918–21. Then, as the global revolutionary wave ebbed over the course of the
1920s, the dilemma that Lenin had posed in 1919 grew starker: 'We are living not
merely in a state, but in a system of states, and it is inconceivable for the Soviet
Republic to live alongside the imperialist states for any length of time. One or
other must triumph in the end'.[52]

The decisive *direct* imperialist intervention was the invasion of over a dozen
powers – unmistakeably a 'geopolitical mechanism' – in the attempt to crush
the revolutionary regime. The attempt failed in a formal sense but did suc-
ceed in ravaging Russia's economic substance and social fabric. War and its
henchmen (famine, disease, poverty, and so on) scythed through the population. Military invasion, economic embargo and capital flight combined with
the consequences of civil war to reduce economic output to less than one third

---

51   Serge 2017, p. 416.
52   Lenin 1919.

of its pre-war level.[53] As a result of war and economic evisceration, the social basis of the communist cause – the politically mobilised working class – haemorrhaged. The regime found itself hollowed out from within; the Communist Party had been swept to power by social movements that then dissolved. As the working class was whittled away, the ranks of the Party were swelled by the officials on whom it increasingly relied. The democracy of the soviets expired and was replaced by a one-party state. Alienated from the working class, much of the Party began to lean towards those forces which recommended the strengthening of private capitalism in agriculture or to those, concentrated within the party and state bureaucracies, which advocated a programme of national modernisation: the build-up of state power as an end in itself. Trotsky's 'left opposition' retained a significant presence until the late 1920s; its destruction owed more than a little to the 'geopolitical mechanisms' of which he had warned.

The programme of national modernisation that came to be known as 'socialism in one country' had to confront the legacy of revolution and war. The post-1917 regime had acted to lessen social inequalities and, where possible, improve workers' and peasants' living standards. This, together with the depletion of foreign capital and technology imports that had been vital to industrialisation under Tsarism, sharply curtailed the resources available for investment. Although the regime succeeded in stabilising the postwar economy, and in some respects more successfully than some rival powers, notably Britain, its GDP per capita continued to lag behind most other large economies, at around one-fifth of that of Britain and one-sixth of the US during the 1920s. If the emergent strategy of national modernisation was to entertain a chance of success, therefore, the obstacles to rapid capital accumulation, above all the legacy of the 1917 revolutions as embodied in the control of land by the peasantry and in the Communist Party's commitment to raising workers' living standards, would have to be overcome. The destruction of this twin legacy, although a necessary consequence of the policies of Stalin's faction, was not planned in advance. Rather, the new system arose in an unpremeditated manner, as the emerging strategy of sections of the *nomenklatura* linked to Stalin responded to a set of interconnected crises that arose toward the end of the 1920s.

The crises of 1927 unfolded in several dimensions: international relations, the economy, workers' and peasants' discontent, and non-Russian republics chafing against Moscow's rule. Policymakers reacted with short-term expedients. Nonetheless, the measures taken indicate in their general direction a clear set of underlying priorities. The first and most important of these was the

---

53   Nove 1992, p. 62.

assumption that external invasion threatened again. The militarisation imperative connected with a second priority, industrialisation. Even in 1926–8 the *pace* of industrialisation, measured against the meagre surplus released from agriculture, was fairly intense. By the yardstick of modern warfare, however, its *level* remained inadequate. The growing conviction of sections of the Communist Party around Stalin that rapid industrialisation was required at any cost explains why resort was made, in 1927–8, to *forced* procurements of grain, and why brute repression was meted out to those who resisted. The programme wasn't planned in advance. Rather, through haphazard responses to short-term crises, the faction around Stalin stumbled upon what became their defining cause: forced industrialisation, with the aim of re-arming. It required, moreover, the sidelining and eventual routing of those political forces that championed the interests of private agriculture and the working class, expressed within the Party by the left and right opposition. It was here, in the concatenation of repressive moves that flowed from the imperative to accelerated industrialisation – triggered by a security scare – that the distinctive structures of bureaucratic state capitalism began to take shape. In 1927, concern for the Soviet Union's security escalated into full-blown war fever when the crushing of the most militant section of the Chinese labour movement by Moscow's putative ally, Chiang Kai-shek,[54] in the final defeat of the revolutionary wave of the 1920s, was followed by the abrogation by Britain's Conservative government of relations with Russia. Stalin's faction exploited the war scare. Their invocations of an external threat were deployed wholesale to justify internal repression: against peasants resisting requisitioning and collectivisation, against labour unrest, and against internal party opposition. Moral panics were concocted to threaten and cajole, to turn the population against the enemy within: the 'kulak menace', the 'saboteur in foreign pay', the 'right-wing appeaser', the 'Trotskyist', and the other stock miscreants and evildoers of the Stalinist imaginary. Meanwhile, the hoarding that the war scare elicited exacerbated food shortages. By the end of the year the country was sliding toward economic crisis.

Policymakers reacted with short-term expedients, notably the arbitrarily-enforced procurements of grain in 1927–8 – but this only deterred the *muzhik* from sowing. Renewed signs of economic crisis prompted the government to expedite industrialisation and redesign its relations with the peasantry. In this compressed period much of the previous social fabric – including protective institutions such as the traditional peasant community, trade unions and factory committees – was either torn up or stitched into the state bureaucracies.

---

54   In pinyin transliteration: Jiang Jieshi.

This enabled a dramatic rise in the rate of exploitation. Net investment soared from 1928 to 1937, rising from 10 percent to 23 percent of net national product, while household consumption fell from 82 per cent to 55 percent.[55]

In this analysis, Stalin's industrialisation drive was an embodiment of counter-revolution, through which the social and cultural gains of 1917 were pushed back, civil liberties and intellectual freedoms were stamped out, workers' organisations subordinated to the party-state, and oppositionists sidelined, exiled or murdered. Its specific form was not a return to feudalism but a radical imposition of capitalist relations, in which these did not merely 'seem' to be the offspring of the state, as in Trotsky's depiction of the Russian economy under Nicholas II, but materially were. Within a few years, a traditional agricultural arrangement consisting largely of petty production was subordinated to a single capitalist landlord. This was no feudal fusion of economics and politics, nor did it resemble the exaction of tribute from peasant smallholders by such empires as Ming China or Mughal India. It was, rather, the sundering of peasants and their means of production into absolute property, on one hand, and a proletariat, on the other. No longer did the state need to batten upon the peasantry, as feudal landlords or tributary tax collectors had done. Rather, it inserted itself *between* the means of production and the agricultural labour force, assuming coercive command of the former as well as direct control over the labour process. This gave it an unparalleled ability to appropriate agricultural surplus and to funnel it directly into industry and the military, without the need to engage in the delicate task of squeezing tribute from private landholders.[56]

Had the functionaries who implemented the collectivisation programme been readers of Marx, they could have gained stimulating insights from the chapters on agriculture in *Theories of Surplus Value*. The 'only requirement' of the capitalist mode of production, in respect of land, Marx writes, is that

---

55   Resnick & Wolff 2002, p. 266. For the subordination of consumption to accumulation, see
      also: Binns 1975.
56   We do not have space to go into the question of free wage labour here. Capitalism requires
      a level of general labour mobility and market competition; it is to this extent based on
      free wage labour. But it is compatible with forced labour too – slavery, prisons, inden-
      tured labour, and so on. In the case of the bureaucratic state capitalist societies, forced
      labour was a significant component in some (notably the Soviet Union in the 1930s). But
      there was on the whole a considerable degree of labour mobility. In East Germany, for
      example, although firing workers was usually, in practice, difficult, labour contracts were
      very similar to those in Western market economies, and levels of wages and bonuses was
      determined to a considerable extent by inter-firm competition for labour power. See e.g.
      Zander 1974; Huinink and Mayer, 1993.

it 'should not be common property, that it should confront the working class as a condition of production, not belonging to it'. This purpose will be 'completely fulfilled' if land 'becomes state-property'. The 'radical bourgeois' therefore aspires to 'a refutation of the private ownership of the land, which, in the form of state property, he would like to turn into the common property of the bourgeois class, of capital'. In practice, he 'lacks the courage, since an attack on one form of property – a form of the private ownership of a condition of labour – might cast considerable doubts on the other form'.[57] However, in the peculiar circumstances of counterrevolution in 1920s Russia this is indeed what came into being – the 'radical bourgeois' appearing in the guise of the Stalinist state. In this analysis, the agent of the accumulation drive arose not, as Trotsky had forewarned, from petit-bourgeois layers but rather, as some of his fellow oppositionists proposed and as Cliff later traced in detail, from within the party-state bureaucracy, which began to act as the 'personification of capital'.[58]

The penetration of state into society that occurred during Stalin's counterrevolution should thus be understood as a precisely and eminently capitalist moment. Just as in Britain the road to the free market was opened and kept open by an enormous increase in continuous, centrally organised state intervention, so too, in the Soviet Union the mobilisation of society behind the drive to catch up with Western market economies occurred through an enormous increase in state ownership but also, simultaneously, the 'economisation' of the state – and of the Communist Party. The Party, as Lewin has described, underwent a process of 'depoliticisation'. Its cells 'became brokers in the service of their branch of the economy, sometimes even of just one enterprise. ... The economy was declared to be the most important "front", to use the martial terminology of the times'.[59] That battle, moreover, was prosecuted in the workplaces through techniques of individual competition, via income and status. What Martha Lampland has identified in the case of Soviet Hungary applied equally to Russia: the 'pageantry of enforced collectivity' (mass rallies and so on) notwithstanding, the Stalinist era saw an 'intensive individuation of persons', the goal of which was to create 'a mass of individuated workers unfettered by the drag of an antiquated collectivity'.[60]

'Stalin's revolution', in this light, involved the conversion of the Soviet party-state, spurred by geopolitical competition, into an agent of wholesale prolet-

---

57   Marx 1858.
58   Cliff 1974, p. 165.
59   Lewin 1985, p. 32.
60   Lampland 2016.

arianisation and capital accumulation. The party-state could project political power throughout society with such determination and resolution precisely because it was itself undergoing a process of 'economisation'. The fusion of state and economy implied a particularly direct geopolitical transmission of the law of value, and enabled the central state bureaucracy, in command of all channels of international competition, to prioritise the military sector. That imperative – of geoeconomic and geopolitical competition – underpinned the programmes of breakneck industrialisation and forced collectivisation, as well as the extreme repression that these called for. In short, the same historical transformation that 'married the state and capital', in Mike Haynes' description, also 'completed the subordination of the Soviet economy to the world economy'.[61] In the process, it elevated the Soviet Union into a major force in the world system. By the 1940s Moscow was proving itself as a great power; its T34 and KV tanks outnumbered and outperformed their German rivals,[62] enabling it to conquer most of Eastern Europe and to reign for half a century as the planet's second most powerful imperialist state, with nuclear weapons, a permanent seat on the UN Security Council, allies across four continents, and legions of imitators. And not only was this an imperialist state, it also rescued the pre-Soviet imperial form. That is to say, in an age of declining empires (the Ottoman, Habsburg Austro-Hungary, Wilhelmine Germany, and, in the mid-twentieth century, imperial Japan and the West European empires), the Soviet Union under Stalin succeeded in replicating – albeit in ostensibly national form – the Tsarist imperium (with Russia dominating the non-Russian periphery), just as that form of political arrangement was, globally, experiencing its final and convulsive demise.

5   Theoretical Implications

Let us step back now to consider what the above argument implies for the question of the international transmission of capitalist competition (or the 'law of value'). It does not propose that capitalist economic and geopolitical competition operate in identical ways. All capitalist states command soldiers and arsenals whereas only a few private businesses do. A miscalculation of risks in the geopolitical arena can result in thermonuclear war, unlike in the arena of private business competition (at least at time of writing). Competitive

---

61   Haynes 1985, p. 110.
62   Bonwetsch 1997 and Sapir 1997.

defeat tends to be managed differently, too. Businesses that suffer existential losses are generally forced by lenders to make structural adjustments, or they merge with others, or go into administration – they 'go out of business'. States, given their command of armies and hence their ability to appropriate resources come what may, in addition to (in the modern period) the hold of the national idea and its material manifestation in the interstate system, tend, even in the course of precipitous economic decline, to soldier on. They do not go bankrupt in the same way as businesses – although the disappearance of some, such as the GDR in 1990, and the bankruptcy and debt bondage of others, such as the dozens of countries subject to IMF structural adjustment programmes or Greece following the crisis of 2008, do bear comparison with the administration of bankrupt businesses. What the above argument does propose, however, is that states must be able to defend themselves, that this requires the mobilisation of resources (a mobilisation that must be as effective as that of competitors), and, moreover, that in a capitalist world system geopolitical competition operates to transmit and enforce capitalist imperatives, including pressure to reduce socially necessary labour time to the global benchmark, on pain of sliding down the global political-economic hierarchy or, at the extreme, facing the prospect of military occupation or economic evisceration by powerful rivals.

The argument we are making is not transhistorical. 'International relations', including war and diplomacy (in the broad sense of 'the negotiated management of inter-societal relations'),[63] have been an institutionalised feature of all forms of class-state society, but the inter-state system that emerged in and with global capitalism possesses unique features. One is the tendency for capitalist polities to become organised in the form of nation states, and, simultaneously, to take interest in affairs beyond their borders. The framework of the international system mediates commodity relations that are inherently transnational in potential. In Rosenberg's formulation, insofar as 'capitalist relations of surplus extraction are organized through a contract of exchange which is defined as "non-political"' it becomes possible 'in a way that would have been unthinkable under feudalism, to command and exploit productive labour (and natural resources) located under the jurisdiction of another state'.[64] Each state is imbricated in a world society and economy whose movements it can influence but not control. Not only, then, do capitalist states exist in relations of interdependence with and antagonism to external powers, compelling each to stake forceful claims to definite forms of control over territories and the people

---

63   Rosenberg 2006, p. 320.
64   Rosenberg 1994, p. 129.

and things within them. That is the case with any states-system. In capitalism, however, 'the state's own stability and health are dependent upon social processes beyond its borders ... Therefore in order to play the role of the state the national state must strive to burst through its own national character'.[65] States' interests in maintaining power and supporting the processes of accumulation upon which they depend entail intervention not only within but beyond their home territories. Not only must they counter threats from other states, but they are compelled to seek influence over property and populations beyond their home territories – massaging and manipulating external frameworks of rights, defending investments, and partnering and clashing with other states. States are inherently international, not simply through their mutual relations but because they depend on and are threaded into transnational economic circuits. As with the evolution of global capitalism, those circuits intensify and intertwine across borders, states are drawn into denser interconnections. The internationalisation of capital, in short, developed in tandem with the globalisation of the nation-state system, the ramping up of the infrastructural and coercive power of states, and the amassing of permanently mobilised military machines. This means that war, between capitalist powers, has the potential to become total war in a specific sense: capitalist states are capable of mobilising a colossal proportion of society's resources. Here too, we are highlighting the potential *immediacy* and *intensity* of the geopolitical transmission of the law of value in global capitalism.

If global capitalism is a system in which each capital is governed by a law of value that competitively commensurates acts of production against prevailing norms, competitiveness varies greatly among capitals and territories. On one hand, the operation of even 'free' international trade unleashes powerful spatially-polarising tendencies, as well as opportunities to 'catch up'. Economic unevenness accompanies and reinforces the power asymmetries of the states-system: states with a strong fiscal base are able to project power where others cannot. On the other, the ploughing of capitalist relations into all corners of the globe stimulates the emergence of countervailing tendencies, whereby the economic consequences of, or the political means of dealing with, 'backwardness' stimulates the development of the technological or military muscle required to appropriate a greater proportion of global surplus value. Thus, the early capitalist powers were joined by second and third waves, and recent decades have witnessed several regions of the 'Third World' approaching economic comparison with those at the top.

---

65   Wright 1997 p. 12.

These processes provide a window through which we can study the historical emergence of state capitalist regimes. The one on which we have concentrated up to this point is the Soviet Union, with its unique brand of bureaucratic state capitalism forged in a peculiar crucible: state-led counter-revolution in a land without a bourgeoisie. But what of the many other forms of state capitalism? What of Rákosi's Hungary and Tito's Yugoslavia? What of Germany and Turkey in the 1930s? Britain and Japan in the 1940s? India, China and North Korea in the 1950s? South Korea and Egypt in the 1960s, Vietnam and Peru in the 1970s – and so on. These all had in common a high degree of state ownership and control, particularly of 'strategic industries'. Common to most of them was a weak (or weakened) domestic bourgeoisie, a drive to steep-ascent industrialisation (involving central planning, a bias towards heavy industry and a large arms sector, and relative autarky), and rule by a single party that lashes all social institutions into a national corporate unity subordinated to the goal of rapid economic growth and military might.

What accounts for the shared state-capitalist cast of these (and many similar) regimes? Several factors can be discerned. One is the scale of production, and the scale of organisation, of leading industries. To caricature only a little, the principal scale of ownership, production and marketing in most industries in the eighteenth was local; in the nineteenth and early twentieth centuries it was national, and thereafter global. (Think for example of wheat, beer, iron, furniture and home furnishing, road vehicles, and earth-moving equipment.) Specifically 'national' variants of state capitalism – including the 'bureaucratic' type in which most (or all) of the formal economy is taken into state ownership – flourished in the historical period when capital concentration reached a stage where major sectors of the economy could be organised at nation-state level without unduly impairing competitiveness.[66]

A second factor is geopolitics and war. In partial contrast to market competition, the *intensity* of geopolitical competition varies dramatically. As we have shown above, geopolitical competition, including arms races, tend to draw states into a muscular economic coordination role, notably of the arms industry and other strategic sectors. The features of state capitalist economies – relative autarky, an emphasis on heavy industry, a high savings ratio, allocation by administrative decision and the extensive use of political incentives and ideological appeals geared to increasing output – are typical of war economies (either of states actually at war, or states engaged in arms races and

---

66   The period where this applied varies by industry and region.

other forms of heightened military preparation).[67] It is no accident therefore that the most extreme forms of state capitalism emerged during the era of the two world wars. The form of competition shifts from market-oriented to military-oriented, although in reality there can be no 'pure' market or military competition.[68]

A third factor is uneven development and 'catch-up' industrialisation. Outside wartime, capitalist 'heartland' economies have tended to be liberal, with relatively small state-capitalist elements.[69] Because the liberal heartlands became home to the most profitable forms of capital accumulation, a self-reinforcing dynamic ensued: these areas expanded their global influence, winning allies by dint of their economic and cultural pre-eminence or directly extending the liberal heartland through imperial conquest, and these processes, in turn, fuelled the profitability of heartland businesses as well as their independence from state power. Other powers, confronting the international success of the liberal heartland (the Netherlands, Britain, the US), in their attempts to overcome relative backwardness tended to rely heavily upon centralised administration. In the early modern period this primarily took the form of absolutist regimes adopting mercantilist methods in imitation of the Dutch.[70] In the nineteenth century it involved an internalisation of capitalist structures, via state-led reforms (and 'passive revolutions') that encouraged the expropriation of the peasantry and facilitated the growth of market-oriented agriculture and industry. Where success was achieved, as with France, Germany and Japan, assimilation into the liberal heartland was usually the eventual outcome. For weaker economies, the disadvantages of backwardness could outweigh advantages. This was particularly so where a relatively late development of capitalism combined with political domination by imperialist states, entailing not only plunder, conquest and the undercutting of local industries but also the denial or limitation of sovereignty. For post-colonial developing countries, funds for accumulation had to come essentially from savings out of current consumption of the domestic population, 'and if the level of current livelihood of the population is low, and the political and administrative machine weak', in Nigel Harris's words, any surplus is likely to be meagre, such that 'only a very powerful army and police force can snatch the surplus for national

---

67   Lange 1969, p. 171. For earlier treatments of state capitalism as war economy and vice versa, see Nikolai Bukharin 1982 [1916]; Cliff 1964.
68   As Chapter 3 in this volume shows, Chinese state administrators in the 1950s were acutely concerned with comparing China's labour productivity with that of other countries.
69   Van der Pijl, 1993, 1995, 1998.
70   Arrighi 1994, pp. 140–1.

investment between the peasant's hand and mouth'.[71] Heightened repression (which enhances the role of the state), in turn, tends to breed wider military conflict, which further cements the centrality of the state.[72] Typically, it is linked to a strategy of import-substitution industrialisation (ISI – which, again, accords a key role to the state), and, in many cases, revolutionary upheavals. The latter may be anti-imperialist, e.g. in opposition to colonial rule or to the undermining of ISI development strategies by the liberal great powers or to comprador bourgeoisies, and are invariably fought under the banner of emancipation. However, because revolutions by their nature focus the attention of political entrepreneurs and social movements on the gaining of state power, they tend to facilitate the notion that the state is the key lever through which to achieve economic goals (e.g. ISI; capital concentration). In such cases, too, the result tends to be conducive to state capitalism – at any rate, this was the case for much of the twentieth century. In his development of Trotsky's theory of permanent revolution, Cliff termed this process 'deflected, state capitalist, permanent revolution' and highlighted the role of particular class layers such as the intelligentsia, bureaucracy and military officers in carrying out such revolutions. He argued that 'Mao's and Castro's rise to power are classic, the purest, and most extreme, demonstrations of "Deflected Permanent Revolution"' but 'Other colonial revolutions – Ghana, India, Egypt, Indonesia, Algeria etc. – are deviations from the norm' where a 'Simon-pure state capitalism' (i.e. bureaucratic state capitalism) was unable to develop for various reasons.[73]

   In combination, these factors help explain the phases of étatisme that individual states – Britain, for example, during the Napoleonic wars and the Great Depression – and the world system as a whole pass through. Mike Kidron identifies three phases. In the 'Liberal, or entrepreneurial-capitalist, phase', from the mid-eighteenth century to 1914, the dominant tendency was the clearing away of protectionist regulation (privileges granted to monopolies and corporations, the regulation of production by craft guilds, trade protection measures, and so on). The early-phase state also assumed a commanding role in creating and maintaining physical infrastructure and consolidating market-enabling institutions (legal system, stable currencies, etc). But its direct economic involvement was relatively slight, outside wartime and imperial conquest. The middle phase lasted until 1989. The typical state in this phase 'went farther than its

---

71   Harris 1971, p. 140.
72   Wendt and Barnett 1993.
73   Cliff 1963. The authors of this chapter would however take issue with the idea of a 'normal' state capitalism as implied by Cliff here.

predecessor in providing a physical infrastructure for the market. It came to dominate the so-called commodity inputs in industry: steel, energy, water and other utilities'. This was the case not only in Eastern Europe, China and most newly-independent countries but also in Western Europe. States in this period embraced nationalisation 'not only of the classic infrastructural services and the broad-spectrum inputs into modern production, but also the specific differentiated products that usually remained in private hands in the hub countries'.[74] Although the bureaucratic state capitalisms of this period may be largely consigned to the history books, state capitalism theory still has much to offer when it comes to understanding contemporary capitalism. In the neoliberal era the state has not retreated so much as involved itself in capital accumulation and competition in new and different ways. As Chris Harman wrote in 1991, at the time of the Gulf War:

> The world may no longer be made up of capitals fused one hundred percent to states. But it is not, and cannot be, a world in which capitals float free of states. It is a hybrid world, in which each capital increasingly spreads beyond state boundaries but at the same time depends as much as ever on its state (or, sometimes, its states).[75]

Taken together, these factors explain why state capitalism predominates at certain times and in certain places. It is found disproportionately in particular economic sectors: where natural monopolies exist (e.g. transport), and which are deemed strategic (e.g. oil, or electricity, but not banking). It thrives where states are attempting to punch their way to the top of the world-economic hierarchy.[76] It thrives at times of war and in societies geared to war – which is why Germany 1914–18 was a critical example (inspiring the work of Otto Neurath on administered economies, and Bukharin on the tendency toward state capitalism). And it thrives in conditions of de-globalisation, when international trade and capital networks collapse, prompting states to intervene (the 1930s is the paradigm here).

---

74   Kidron (n.d.).
75   Harman 1991.
76   It is no accident that state capitalism received its early theorisation by writers of the German Historical School such as Adolf Wagner. See Pollard 2011.

6   Developmental State Theory and State Capitalism in East Asia

In recent decades the most prominent explanation for East Asia's remarkable development in the second half of the twentieth century has been developmental state theory (DST). This approach, advocated initially by Chalmers Johnson, Alice Amsden and Meredith Woo, posits that the state in East Asian countries, beginning with the Japanese state as model, has been able to place itself above individual corporations and capitalists and play the key role in encouraging and coordinating economic development. Johnson contrasts this model of capitalism favourably with both the laissez-faire capitalism of North America and Western Europe and with the 'state socialism' of the former Soviet Union or pre-reform China.[77] Johnson's version of DST centres around the particular state bureaucracy embodied in Japan's Ministry of International Trade and Industry (MITI) and its 'perfection of market-conforming methods of state intervention in the economy' through such means as financial institutions, tax incentives, economy-wide planning, and government funded R&D.[78] Meanwhile, Amsden and Woo applied DST to the South Korean case, the former focusing on the state's role in the industrialisation learning process (combined with low wages and state subsidies) and the latter on the state's mobilisation and allocation of financial resources.[79] More recently, a number of scholars have sought to apply DST to post-reform China, particularly since its economic take-off in the 1990s, arguing, for example, that the PRC represents a new form of 'dual developmental state' in which there is both a centralised developmental state and regional developmental or 'entrepreneurial' states.[80]

Developmental state theory has been criticised by Marxists from a number of angles. Addressing the case of South Korea, Dae-oup Chang has targeted two aspects in particular: the idea of state autonomy that is embedded in DST and the historical misreading of the formation of the South Korean state that serves to mystify its character.[81] In this volume, Lee Jeong-goo presents similar criticisms of the application of DST to the case of post-reform China, arguing that the state in China is not autonomous from capital accumulation, but in fact acts as a 'collective capitalist'. He also argues that rather than the state standing above capital, state and capital are bound together by structural interdependence.

---

77   Johnson 1999.
78   Johnson 1999.
79   Woo 1991; Amsden 1989.
80   For a detailed discussion of developmental state theory and China see Chapter 6 of this book.
81   Chang 2009.

Unsurprisingly, Marxists have also criticised DST for lacking a serious analysis of the role of class in capitalist society. So, for example, DST explanations of East Asian development have tended to overlook the importance of suppressing wages and consumption in the 'Asian miracles' and thus, also, the key role of state violence and coercion in creating the conditions for industrialisation and catch-up development.[82] This is another illustration of the many ways in which the state, far from being autonomous from capital, is closely entwined with it and in fact essential for the process of capital accumulation in any society, but particularly in those at the earlier stages of industrialisation.

Applications of DST to East Asian countries have certainly not been blind to the specific historical and geopolitical conditions that facilitated development, perhaps most obviously their relationship with the US during the Cold War.[83] However, there has been a tendency to downplay geopolitical factors, such as inter-bloc competition, and to maintain a form of methodological nationalism that assumes the nation state as the fundamental unit of analysis and, by extension, the potential of any state, with the right institutional apparatus, to achieve capitalist development, abstracted from the global capitalist system. Jeong Seongjin provides a corrective to this tendency in Chapter 4 of this volume by showing how the Cold War and its hot wars in Korea and Vietnam were crucial to both the recovery of Japanese capitalism in the 1950s and the take-off of South Korean capitalism in the 1960s. In the South Korean case, close ties with the US and an inflow of capital from the Vietnam War allowed Park Chung-hee's repressive state capitalism to 'internationalise', turning decisively away from the inward-looking path of other Third World state capitalisms like India or North Korea.

Finally, DST explicitly maintains a 'two worlds' framework for analysing East Asian development in the twentieth century, supporting a fundamental division of the world into 'capitalist' and 'communist' (or often 'state socialist'). The most obvious problem with this way of dividing the economies of the world is that there is little attempt made in DST to define what 'capitalism' and 'state socialism' actually are or how they differ fundamentally from one

---

82   Campling, Miyamura, Pattenden and Selwyn 2016.

83   A number of different scholars have noted the importance of geopolitics and security concerns in the formation and viability of developmental states in East Asia. Woo for example, notes that this 'security environment showers benefits on the guaranteed state in the form of bilateral aid or multilateral loans, and enhances Korean maneuverability' Woo 1991, p. 8. [also: Amsden 1989; Johnson, Cumings]. However, these scholars have tended to see military competition and security as an important factor that is external to the process of capitalist development, rather than something constitutive of that development. The latter approach is one that will be taken in this volume.

another, other than in the extent of state property. Studies of the actual functioning of global political economy in the twentieth century also tend not to
support this division, showing instead how closely interrelated the two Cold
War blocs were through trade, economic competition and military rivalry. As
stated at the beginning of this chapter, it is the intention of this volume to
treat this conceptual division as profoundly unhelpful and to contribute to
the development of a historical political economy that overcomes it on the
basis of state capitalism theory. Such a critique is by no means new, and has
previously been clearly articulated by Colin Barker in his article on the Meiji
Restoration:

> ... if we consider the 'development problem', we find reasons to doubt
> that these two countries [China and Japan] do really represent widely
> different systems. Rather, there is an important sense in which they can
> be comprehended, not as two distinct 'systems' but as 'parts' of a more
> encompassing single 'system' from which they both derive common char-
> acteristics.[84]

More recently, Oscar Sanchez-Sibony's book *Red Globalization* has made a similar and equally forceful point, from a somewhat different angle. Based on
extensive new research into archival materials he demonstrates that the Soviet
Union was, during much of the twentieth century, a vastly weaker rival to the
US, *within* the world capitalist system.[85]

The chapters in this book no doubt owe much to the scholarship of those
in the tradition of developmental state theory, but this book also constitutes a
conscious critique of DST. The authors here seek to integrate the DST insight
that there is not one 'normal' form of capitalism, but also to go beyond this
and concretise in Marxist terms what forms state capitalism can take. Crucially,
it sets its sights beyond simply explaining 'successful' cases of Asian development to understanding both the 'capitalist' and 'communist' countries of East
Asia as parts of the same global capitalist system, all shaped and driven by
the same logics of capital accumulation, military competition and class conflict.

---

84   Barker 1982, (unpaginated).
85   Sanchez-Sibony writes that: 'The Soviet economy became first autarkic and then global-
        ized in roughly the same measure and on roughly the same timetable as the world first
        became autarkic in the interwar period and then globalized in the postwar'. Sanchez-
        Sibony 2014, p. 6.

7   East Asian Development and State Capitalism: the Japanese Model

The Japanese model looms large when examining state capitalism in twentieth century East Asia. Indeed, Japan's significance as a role model went far beyond East Asia; the Meiji Restoration was a model of independent development for colonised elites and aspiring bureaucracies all over the world. In East Asia itself, Japanese-style capitalism was not only a model to be emulated but a structure that was directly imposed – to one extent or another – in places like Manchuria, Taiwan and Korea, via Japan's colonial empire. A digression into the history of state capitalism in Japan is thus unavoidable here. To talk of Japanese state capitalism in the singular would be somewhat misleading as Japan at different times in its modern history (since the Meiji Restoration of 1868) established quite different varieties of state capitalism. Broadly speaking we can talk of two periods and two types of state capitalism: the mixed system of state support and large conglomerates established in the first decades after the Restoration and then the wartime state capitalism of the period 1937–45 that came close to usurping private capital altogether and instituting a form of bureaucratic state capitalism. The historical outline here will therefore focus on these two periods.

Whatever else it may have been, there can be little doubt that the Meiji Restoration of 1868 was a social revolution from above, carried out in order to create the conditions for the independent establishment of capitalist social relations, and, by extension a modern state and industry. The basis of this was the abolition of the lordly domains (*han*) and samurai stipends (*karoku*) and the systematic introduction of a new land tax that provided the state with capital to build the country's first modern infrastructure: harbours, lighthouses, telegraph, postal system, and railways.[86] In addition to infrastructure, the Meiji state from the very beginning involved itself directly in production and capital accumulation, by setting up model enterprises in areas such as ship-building, mining, munitions and textiles. As Andrew Gordon writes, 'the Meiji government played an unusually direct role in building and operating industrial enterprises. Government leaders were convinced that private investors lacked the initiative and the knowledge to run modern factories'.[87] Effectively, in the first couple of decades after 1868, the Japanese state substituted itself for a capitalist class that had not yet emerged. It acted as an ignition for the capitalist system, creating a small industrial working class and training the first generation of

---

86   Gordon 2003, p. 70.
87   Gordon 2003, p. 71.

industrial managers and engineers. Private investment in capitalist enterprises then began to take off in the 1880s and 1890s, led by a railway boom, but the state continued to play an important role in the economy, both encouraging and subsidising private enterprise and more directly in its continued control of some mines and rail lines as well as its establishment of the Japanese steel industry in the 1890s. The bureaucrats of the Meiji state understood well that multi-faceted state involvement in the economy was necessary for catch-up development and based their ideas in part on those of the German economist Friedrich List, rather than on the laissez-faire economists of England.[88] These ideas thus became part of the common sense of Japanese capitalism and have continued to be a major influence on both the thought and practice of Japanese capitalism and statecraft ever since.[89]

In the 1870s and 1880s another distinctive and long-lasting feature of Japanese capitalism began to coalesce: the large monopolistic conglomerates usually called *zaibatsu*. Two of the earliest conglomerates were Mitsui, centred around banking, mining and trading, and Mitsubishi, which had an early focus on shipping, shipbuilding and railways, both of which are still massive combines today. The *zaibatsu* began to thrive in the late nineteenth century through their close relationship with the state bureaucracy and lucrative preferential government contracts.[90] Thus, the particular form taken by Japanese state capitalism was a hybrid, in which state support, direction and involvement in production mixed with huge conglomerates that were themselves closely linked to the state.[91] The *zaibatsu* also proved to be a feature of Japanese state capitalism that would have a profound influence on the country's East Asian neighbours and today the same word is used in Korea (pronounced *chaebŏl*) to refer to huge family-owned conglomerates like Samsung and Hyundai.

In the first decades of the twentieth century Japan's fledgling capitalist economy prospered through the achievement of regional hegemony and acquisition of colonies after wars with China and Russia, and most spectacularly through the great windfall of WWI.[92] But in the 1920s and 1930s the Japanese economy faced tougher times, not least as a result of the global depression that dragged down most of the world after the crash of 1929. This changed economic

---

88   On List's importance in Japan see: Fallows 1994, pp. 179–80; Gordon 2003, p. 72.

89   See: Morris-Suzuki 1989.

90   For example, the agreement between Mitsui and the government to sell coal from a government mine, as described by Andrew Gordon (Gordon 2003, p. 97).

91   The exact nature of Japanese capitalism was something that perplexed Japanese Marxists in the 1920s and 1930s. See: Hoston 1986 and Walker 2016.

92   Crawcour 1997, pp. 101–9.

environment, along with a ramping up of military competition and a drive for imperialist expansion led to a second, quite distinct, period of Japanese state capitalism that brought it much closer to the bureaucratic state capitalism of Stalin's Soviet Union. In addition to the prevailing conditions that pushed Japan – and in fact, much of the rest of the world – towards a more profound form of state capitalism, there was, argues Nakamura, direct influence from Marxist thought, which had influenced many intellectuals in 1920s Japan who would later go on to become either bureaucrats or pro-government scholars.[93]

However, the biggest impetus for a push towards a deeper form of state capitalism undoubtedly came from the start of the Second Sino-Japanese War in July 1937 and then the Pacific War in 1941 and the concomitant increase in the army's political influence. The government had begun to increase its control over production and investment in certain industries as early as 1934, but this accelerated greatly after 1937, with the introduction of a Five-Year Plan for Key Industries. In September 1937 a series of new economic control laws were passed that brought greater state control over distribution of raw materials, imports and exports and company finance. Between 1938 and 1940 the Japanese state along with the army continued to increase its control over various aspects of the economy with such measures as the 1938 National Mobilisation Law. These measures also included greater control over wages and labour. Nakamura writes of the Japanese state's wartime economic planning: 'These plans were similar in structure to those initiated by the Soviet Gosplan. The Resources Agency (*Shigen kyoku*), established in 1928, had secretly made careful studies on the Soviet plans'.[94]

During this stage of wartime state capitalism, the Japanese government still claimed that the measures it was undertaking to control the economy were temporary, but at the same time a debate was taking shape over whether the changes should be taken even further and made permanent. This debate centred around the concept of the 'New Economic Order' outlined by the Showa Research Association in its 'Tentative Plan for the Reorganisation of the Japanese Economy' (1940), which proposed to separate ownership from management of capital and shift decisively away from profit maximisation as the primary motive of industry. Under the plan there would need to be a wide-ranging programme of nationalisation and enterprises 'were regarded as production units to achieve targets set by the state ... closely resemb[ling] a Soviet

---

93   Nakamura 1999, pp. 10–1.
94   Nakamura 1999, p. 14.

planned economy model'.[95] Although the government of prime minister Konoe did try to implement this plan, it was stymied by strong opposition from the business sector. However, the situation would change again with the outbreak of the Pacific War in December 1941.

After the war began three further laws were passed which aimed to deepen state control over material resources and labour and to consolidate small and medium-sized firms. In 1943 the Munitions Companies Law allowed the state to designate certain enterprises as munitions companies which basically brought them under state control and required their managers to achieve government-set production targets. The workers of these 600 'munitions companies' as well as many thousands of workers in Korea and Manchuria were conscripted and forced to stay in their posts.[96] So, in effect, the onset of the Pacific War allowed the Japanese state and military – for a brief period at least – to achieve the sort of bureaucratic state capitalism that had previously been advocated in the Showa Research Association's 'Tentative Plan'.[97]

If there was a clear shift in Japan in the 1930s and 1940s towards a 'purer' form of state capitalism, then this was perhaps even more true of its colonies in Korea and Manchuria, which were seen as strategically important territories and places where a well-developed lobby of private capitalists simply did not exist. In Korea, for example, the Government-General (colonial administration) strongly supported the entrance of *zaibatsu* capital into the colony and played an important role in providing, maintaining and repressing a large pool of cheap industrial labour.[98] This led to the establishment of large and very advanced heavy industrial complexes concentrated mainly in northern Korea. These modern company towns that arrived in the midst of predominantly agrarian 1930s Korea, included Ch'ŏngjin, where Mitsubishi built a huge steel complex and Hŭngnam, where Chisso established a massive nitrogenous fertiliser plant. North Korea's initial industrial growth, described by Kim Ha-young in Chapter 2 of this volume, was built directly upon this legacy of Japanese colonial state capitalism. A similar story can be told of the PRC's early industrial heartland in the northeast, much of which had previously belonged to Japan's puppet state of Manchukuo. During the 1930s and early 1940s this state became an experiment in Japanese state capitalism under the control of the Kwantung Army. The Japanese state and its closely allied business conglomerates invested a huge amount of money in Manchukuo to

---

95   Nakamura 1999, p. 16.
96   Palmer 2013, p. 145.
97   Nakamura 1999, pp. 18–9.
98   Miller 2016.

establish modern steel and chemical industries, along with the massive hydro-electric dam at Suiho that still produces power for China and North Korea today.[99]

The experiment with a form of bureaucratic state capitalism would come to an abrupt end with Japan's defeat in August 1945, but it left a very significant legacy across post-war East Asia. In Japan itself, US occupation and intervention in the economy as well as the Korean War led to a new accommodation between state and capital that created the developmental 'miracle' described by Chalmers Johnson and others. Other parts of East Asia on the other hand often stayed closer to Japanese wartime state capitalism, or even attempted to emulate the state intervention of the Meiji period. The next section will outline the central topic of this book: namely, how North Korea, South Korea and the People's Republic of China have achieved capitalist growth – often very rapid growth – through varied and evolving forms of state capitalism.

8   State Capitalism, Industrialisation and War in East Asia Since 1945

The remaining chapters of this book illustrate the way in which, for most of East Asia, varieties of state capitalism were the normal way of organising capitalism and pursuing catch-up development in the decades after the Second World War. The authors also show how, rather than representing a route towards an idealised form of national autarky, state capitalisms emerge from and are constantly shaped by geopolitical competition. Nor can state capitalism be counterposed in any simple sense to the internationalisation of capital. Rather, it has always been bound up closely with interstate economic and political competition and with international flows of capital in various forms. Interstate competition most obviously takes the form of large-scale imperialist rivalries: the striving for regional and global hegemony by the great powers through alliances, territorial expansion and wars. But within the broader framework of post-war imperial rivalry (the Cold War), smaller, often critical, rivalries were taking place, like that between North and South Korea. It is also clear from the following chapters that war – the most extreme form of geopolitical competition – has been decisively important in East Asian capitalist development. Any account of the region's capitalist development since the late nineteenth century must therefore incorporate the series of international wars that beset

---

99   Eckert 2016, pp. 216–17; see Young 1998, p 183 for an estimate of Japanese investment in Manchuria.

the region from the 1890s to the 1970s (First Sino-Japanese war, 1894–5; Russo-Japanese War, 1904–5; Second Sino-Japanese War, 1937–45; Pacific War, 1941–5; Korean War, 1950–3; Indo-China Wars, 1955–75) as key moments in this process.[100]

Thus, the three polities examined in detail in this volume – South Korea, North Korea and the People's Republic of China – all emerged in the late 1940s out of the wreckage of Japanese imperialism and the Pacific War and were forged in the furnace of a new clash of imperialisms: the Cold War. The South Korean state was created not by a revolutionary or democratic movement from below – although such a movement had appeared in embryo soon after liberation in August 1945 – but by US partition and military occupation (1945–8). Subsequent state formation was decisively shaped by the violent struggle to suppress popular left-wing forces as well as by the mass mobilisations and massacres of the Korean War. In the 1950s the government of Rhee Syngman established a corrupt form of authoritarianism based on anti-communist and nationalist ideology.[101] However, it was General Park Chung Hee and his 1961 coup that established a new form of authoritarianism more suited to fast-paced state capitalist development, spurred by competition with the North.

Park and his co-conspirators termed their coup a 'military revolution' and saw themselves as 'revolutionaries'. Indeed, this could legitimately be understood as a form of 'revolution from above' that sought to establish a new form of state capitalism in the Republic of Korea, and with it, a new accumulation regime. Thus, after coming to power Park and his comrades brought the economy more firmly under state control, nationalising the financial sector and disciplining the nascent capitalist class (sometimes physically).[102] In the 1960s Park's government also created a biopolitical regime of discipline and mobilisation that drew every member of society into the task of rapid capital accumulation, sending many young men to fight in Vietnam, while at the same time encouraging large-scale emigration and birth control and suppressing popular consumption.[103]

---

100   East Asian capitalism was also profoundly affected by the two World Wars fought mainly in Europe.

101   Hwang S. 2016.

102   Kim H. 2004.

103   The Park regime's policy of family planning – including sterilisation – was quite explicitly geared towards accumulation. In the early 1960s the government estimated that the enforcement of family planning and the subsequent lowering of population growth could yield $2 billion for the state, which could then be invested in the productive economy. See: Moon 2005, pp. 81–9.

As Jeong Seong-jin argues in Chapter 4 of this volume, the South Korean state capitalist economy was established initially in the crucible of war and then deepened through the inflow of capital that was part of the US-led permanent arms economy[104] in the 1950s and 60s. While the Korean War itself had restarted the global permanent arms economy, triggering the long boom, the post-war period saw billions of dollars of US aid pour into the Republic of Korea to prop up a key American ally, helping to give birth to the *chaebol* conglomerates that have become synonymous with South Korean capitalism. The import substitution industrialisation strategy pursued under Rhee and the early years of Park Chung hee's government achieved moderate growth but ultimately failed to create the economic take-off that South Korea became known for. Again, Jeong argues that it was war and the arms economy that was crucial to that eventual take-off, which began in the late 1960s and accelerated in the 1970s. As Jeong shows, it was South Korea's geopolitical internationalisation through its deep involvement in the Vietnam War that paved the way for its economic internationalisation as an export-oriented economy (and some time later its shift away from authoritarian state capitalism). Specifically, it was a combination of new inflows of capital from Vietnam War special procurements and military salaries and South Korea's embedding in the triangular political-economic relationship with Japan and the US that led to the internationalisation of Korean capitalism. This internationalisation combined with the authoritarian state's subordination of labour (including reproductive labour) as well as the shift to a defence industrial complex in the 1970s (the so-called HCI policy) to create South Korea's economic take off, later dubbed the 'Miracle on the Han River'.

The trajectory of North Korea's state capitalist development had much in common with that of the South, although the two parted ways dramatically in the 1970s, ironically at the moment that they first attempted political rapprochement. The Democratic People's Republic of Korea was formally established as a nation in 1948 after three years of Soviet occupation and tutelage, but one of the decisive moments in the country's revolution from above had already come with the land reform and sweeping nationalisations of spring-summer 1946. Unlike South Korea, the emerging North Korean state faced no significant internal opposition and an authoritarian state on the Soviet Stalinist model was established swiftly in the late 1940s.[105] The Korean War brought near

---

104   On the theory of the permanent arms economy, see: Vance 1951; Kidron 1967; Pozo-Martin 2010.

105   On the early years of North Korea see: Armstrong 2004; Lankov 2002; Kim S. 2013; Miller 2016.

ruin, but after the armistice wartime mass mobilisation segued into a permanently mobilised state capitalism, with Kim Il Sung increasingly able to position himself as unchallenged supreme leader from the late 1950s. As Kim Ha-young shows in her chapter, Kim Il Sung used the extensive post-war Soviet aid to set out on a path of primitive accumulation and rapid heavy industrialisation, building also on the industrial legacy left by the Japanese. So focused was Kim Il Sung on heavy industrialisation that in the first five-year plan (officially 1957–61, although it was said to be complete in 1959) 83 percent of industrial investment went to heavy industry, despite the misgivings of his Soviet backers about such an autarkic developmental strategy.[106] As with South Korea under Park Chung Hee, North Korea's strategy of high-speed primitive accumulation was marked by the subordination of popular consumption to industrial investment, with investment rising from 21 percent of GNP in 1960 to 35 percent in 1984, while at the same time wages rose far more slowly than GNP. This was overwhelmingly driven by the need to compete militarily with the South and its superpower backer, the US. Kim Il Sung himself saw securing the fledgling North Korean nation state as a prerequisite for economic and social development. Indeed, lacking military aid on anything like the scale received by South Korea from the US, the DPRK began to spend astronomical amounts on defence, and from the 1960s began to turn the entire country into an enormous garrison, devoting around 30 percent of GNP to defence in certain periods.

This is the first significant way in which North Korea's state capitalist political economy diverged from that of the South. Whereas the ROK could build its military on US aid and its industrial economy by taking advantage of the international redistribution of dollars through the permanent arms economy, the North suffered from a sort of inverted permanent arms economy in which military spending became parasitic on the rest of the economy. As South Korea began its take off phase in the late 1960s and early 1970s North Korea also tried to internationalise its state capitalism by turning to Japan and European countries such as France and Sweden to upgrade its technology and seek an infusion of new capital, financed by debt secured on future mineral exports. Unfortunately for North Korea, without the geopolitical advantages enjoyed by its southern rival and with some spectacularly bad timing (specifically the Oil Shock of 1973), its tentative foray into internationalisation ended in disaster and a huge debt burden. It is therefore no surprise that it was precisely in the mid-1970s that the South Korean economy overtook that of the North (in fact

---

106   Van Ree 1989.

1976 was the year according to the CIA).[107] North Korea's 'Juche' thought, which came to prominence in the late 1960s and 1970s, was therefore largely a rhetorical device, whose aim was to obscure the very real dependence of the DPRK on both its imperial benefactor – the USSR – and, to a lesser extent, international trade. Once North Korea became more isolated in reality, from the 1980s onward, Juche did the vital ideological work of turning a necessity into a virtue. Ultimately however, as Kim Ha-yong argues in Chapter 2, the DPRK's long-term economic crisis, which had its roots in the 1960s and 70s, was a crisis of capitalist accumulation, shaped both by geopolitics at the international level and class dynamics at the domestic level.

After the victory of the communists in the Chinese Civil War and the establishment of the People's Republic of China in October 1949, China set out on a path of developmental bureaucratic state capitalism much like that of the Soviet Union and its other near neighbour, North Korea. However, as has been pointed out on a number of occasions before, this was by no means the starting point of state capitalist development in China. On the contrary, the Republic of China, under Chiang Kai-shek's Guomindang, had already exhibited strongly state capitalist tendencies, as had parts of China – such as Manchuria – which were formerly under Japanese control during the 1930s and 40s.[108] Two chapters in this volume analyse the Chinese state capitalist economy, looking at both the Mao Era of the 1950s and 60s and the mutation of the system after 1978.

In Chapter 3 Kim Yong-uk examines the condition of the working class in the early Mao period, thereby aiming to understand more clearly the character of the system as a whole and link the domestic class dynamics of Chinese society with the international dynamics of capitalist economic and geopolitical competition. He shows that the conventional view of employment security under Mao is greatly exaggerated and that there was considerable flexibility in the employment system, as the state used various forms of insecure employment, mass layoffs and other means to reduce labour costs and increase surplus value extraction. The key factor driving this subordination of labour under Chinese state capitalism was very much the same as that driving state capitalist accumulation in North and South Korea during the same period: international capitalist competition in its economic and geopolitical forms. However, in contrast to Jeong Seong-jin and Kim Ha-young, Kim Yong-uk focuses on how the Chinese bureaucratic ruling class consciously tied themselves to global eco-

---

107   CIA National Foreign Assessment Center 1978, p. iii.
108   Gluckstein [Cliff] 1957, pp. 188–90.

nomic competition, without actually participating on any significant scale in the global market. Thus, the CCP bureaucrats were constantly comparing not only the quantity of their production but also its quality with the advanced capitalist countries. As Kim Yong-uk argues, the senior bureaucrats were trying to calculate socially necessary labour time on an international scale and determine whether the productivity of Chinese workers under their state capitalist model had reached the level of rival capitalist countries. Already in the 1950s this led them to study very closely the per capita productivity of Chinese industrial workers and then look for ways to raise this productivity through such means as introducing piece rates and continuously changing the employment structure in order to increase the turnover of workers and the number of temporary positions. In other words, the Chinese bureaucracy were deeply influenced by the broader capitalist world and attempted to introduce a form of Taylorist capitalist regime in China's industrial sector. This reveals a labour system under China's developmental state capitalism that is a far cry from the supposed Maoist 'workers' state' invoked nostalgically by Wang Hui and other contemporary leftist critics in China.[109]

As in North Korea, the principal driving force behind rapid industrial accumulation in Mao's China was international military competition, mainly with the US, which backed the nationalist regime in Taiwan. This was further compounded by the Sino-Soviet split, which gave China a second major enemy and even led to physical confrontation with the Soviet Union in the late 1960s. Symbolic of this military industrialisation was Mao's Third Front initiative of the late 1960s where the Chinese state attempted to create an entirely new, clandestine industrial base in the mountainous western interior of the country, with the aim of making the country resilient to foreign invasion.[110] Such a project must have been hugely costly but was entirely consistent with the logic of capitalist accumulation driven by geopolitical competition.

While this analysis helps us to confirm that China prior to 1978 was a capitalist country,[111] it does open up another question: what exactly was the nature of the change that occurred in China after 1978 when Deng Xiaoping's process of 'reform and opening' began? Political economists, both mainstream and otherwise, have made considerable efforts to define the political economy of the PRC since reform and opening. As Tobias ten Brink points out in Chapter 5, while there have been a variety of approaches, most of them have held in common

109   Werner 2012.
110   Naughton 1988.
111   Kim Yong-uk is not the first to argue this. See, for example, Zheng 2021 [1950], Gluckstein 1957, Harris 1978.

the idea that contemporary China is either not capitalist, or not fully capitalist. There has been a strong tendency to see China after 1978 either as a unique type of social formation or as a hybrid of capitalism and socialism. From a Marxist perspective this is problematic in a number of ways, particularly in terms of its lack of clarity about what actually constitutes capitalism or socialism. Ten Brink argues that after 1978 China transitioned from a centrally-planned state capitalist economy – or more accurately an economy characterised by 'plan anarchy' – to a 'variegated state-permeated capitalism'. To put this another way, China has, since 1978, gradually transformed from a bureaucratic state capitalism with a minimal role for the market to a 'regionalised state capitalism' in which domestic competition and the market are crucially important. The 'variegation' of Chinese capitalism is expressed in different ways: through the variety of state-owned, local-government-owned and private enterprises; through the differing roles of domestic and foreign capital; and through a finance sector that has diversified but is still dominated by the state-owned banks. That the state sector retains a major presence does not mean China is in any respect less-than-capitalist. If anything, it appears ultra-capitalist. As Martin Wolf has observed, 'China is, in a sense, the most capitalist economy ever'.[112]

China's 'reform and opening' transformation has of course meant changes in the labour regime, but taken together Kim and ten Brink's chapters demonstrate that this transition was by no means from a Maoist 'workers' state' to a new Chinese capitalism. The last 20 years has seen an explosion in the size of the Chinese working class, symbolised by the historic rural to urban migration of 250 million workers, referenced at the start of this chapter. However, the contemporary labour regime has many fundamental features in common with the regime of the Mao period, in which a weak and fragmented working class, lacking its own independent organisations, faces a hegemonic state-capital. Of course, the nature of that hegemonic bloc has changed quite significantly with private Chinese capitalists, foreign capital and the local and national state all operating somewhat independently, but tied together by the central state and the CCP. The old ways of controlling workers and providing them with social security through the work unit (*danwei*) have also been eroded and to some extent replaced with more European-style structures. It also seems likely that in the current era the segmentation and flexibilisation of employment that already existed under Mao have been taken to new levels, creating what some have called a 'neoliberal utopia'.

---

112   Wolf 2010.

China's opening has of course coincided with the global era of neoliberal capitalism in which the transnational nature of capitalism has come increasingly to the fore and the intense international military-political competition of the Cold War era has eased somewhat (although China's defence spending still amounted to just under two percent of GDP, or $147 billion in 2016). As South Korea did in the late 1960s and early 1970s, China has been able to successfully internationalise its state capitalism. This has happened in rather different ways in the two countries for a variety of reasons, not least of these being the vastly different scales of their economies and the central role of the Chinese Communist Party in the Chinese case. Contemporary China now provides a rather clear demonstration of the fact that under capitalism there is no simple opposition between state and capital, public and private. State-run institutions are not only acting as capital, they compete with each other at a variety of levels, creating a complex new form of capitalist economy, and yet still one that emerged gradually from the earlier form of Chinese developmentalist state capitalism, without a corresponding political upheaval. Both pre- and post-1978 Chinese capitalism have been 'competition-driven', but the form of competition has changed, along with the country's economic relations with the outside world. China's capitalism is now driven less by a developmental imperative born out of Cold War geopolitical rivalries and far more by the complex web of global and local capitalist rivalries that drive competitive accumulation of a more 'traditional' form. Of course, capitalism is constantly mutating and as this book goes to press in 2023 there is much talk of a new era of decoupling in global supply chains and a new Cold War between China and the US. How far this set of geo-political-economic processes might work to dismantle the current form of export-oriented, state-permeated capitalism in China and replace it with something else remains to be seen.

9   Conclusion

This introductory chapter has sought to lay the groundwork for the rest of this volume in two ways. First, by elaborating the Marxist theory of state capitalism, and second, by demonstrating its relevance and utility when applied to understanding the development of capitalist relations of production in twentieth-century East Asia. The first part was felt necessary partly because the term state capitalism has been used in a great variety of different ways, and partly because its particular incarnation as a Marxist theory of the former Stalinist states has seen little development in recent decades and is often thought of as either a theoretical dead-end or, at best, a useful idea whose time has passed. By discussing the theoretical foundations of state capitalism we have attempted to put the concept on a firmer basis and show how the bureaucratic state capitalism described most coherently in the 1950s by Tony Cliff is only one specific application of the theory.

It should be clear from the foregoing discussions of state capitalism theory that it is not intended to be part of a typology of capitalisms. Rather it is a theory that describes a tendency inherent to the capitalist mode of production itself, that finds a greater or lesser degree of expression in different times and places. This is not to say that there isn't something particular about the bureaucratic state capitalism described by Cliff and others, but rather that such an 'extreme' form of state capitalism is still on the spectrum of societies founded on the capitalist mode of production, made possible in particular historical and political conditions. Those conditions can be summarised as catch-up industrialisation in circumstances of intense military and geopolitical rivalry, usually in postcolonial or otherwise newly-established nation states. However, while these conditions were sometimes conducive to bureaucratic state capitalism, in the absence of other factors such as a Stalinist-style party-state or a moment of state capitalist revolution from above, they could also lead to 'milder' forms of state capitalism, as we have seen in cases such as South Korea.

The analyses of East Asia's headlong capitalist development during the twentieth century presented in this volume demonstrate precisely the value of state capitalism theory. It is particularly successful as a tool for understanding East Asia's epic social transformation – the urbanisation and industrialisation that has changed hundreds of millions of lives in only one or two generations – exactly because it cuts across the conventional conceptual boundaries of 'socialism' and 'capitalism' that have long stymied our understanding of this process. By focusing our attention on the geopolitical pressures that have forced the pace of capital accumulation and fostered strong states – states-as-capital even – in East Asia, the theory expands our understanding of how the mechanisms of capitalism operate, revealing how crucial the Cold War was in East Asia as a driver of industrialisation. At the same time, state capitalism theory has much to offer us in terms of understanding how such processes of industrialisation driven by geopolitical competition in turn drove particular dynamics of class formation and class struggle. Thus, the creation of 'mobilised societies' and the close control of the workforce, alongside the draconian suppression of popular consumption, should be understood in the global context of capitalist competition (military and economic) rather than simply the development strategy of autonomous governments and their bureaucracies.

In contemporary East Asia, the over-arching importance of geopolitics and imperialism has by no means disappeared, states still play key roles in economic affairs, and labour is still subjected to regimes of strong coercive discipline. However, the state capitalisms studied in this book have changed and mutated in a variety of ways. While South Korea was successful in internationalising its state capitalism at the time of the Vietnam War and has since embraced many aspects of neo-liberalism, the cases of China and North Korea are more complicated. China, as noted above, has mutated into a novel hybrid, while North Korea has transitioned away from bureaucratic state capitalism in a completely different manner. Whereas the marketisation of state capitalism in China was a ruling class strategy, introduced through the policy of 'reform and opening', marketisation in North Korea has come about in an ad hoc manner, driven partly from below and partly from above, in response to the collapse of the state economy in the 1990s after the withdrawal of Soviet subsidies. Almost a quarter of a century after North Korea's economic collapse, its economy seems to be in a new phase: on the surface the state tries to maintain the appearance of an omnipotent bureaucratic state capitalism, while simmering just below that surface is a vigorous market system of private trading companies and even manufacturers, usually disguising themselves as state enterprises. North Korea's marketised state capitalism is no longer simply an ad hoc survival mechanism of small marketplaces and predominantly women traders. It has now been captured to a large extent by sections of the bureaucratic ruling class and a new entrepreneurial middle class (called *tonju*) who run large swathes of the economy for their own profit, while of course paying their dues to either the Korean Workers' Party or particular offices within the state apparatus. As in China, the boundaries between state and private capitalism have become blurred, and perhaps in some cases meaningless, but the general tendency is clearly towards further marketisation and the control of the economic heights by an oligarchical group with strong links to the party-state.[113]

While the era of 'pure' bureaucratic state capitalisms may be over, the intertwining of state and capital is intrinsic to capitalist societies and will only disappear with the end of capitalism itself. Hence the insights of state capitalism theory will remain useful and relevant for understanding our contemporary societies and for helping us to decipher whatever novel forms the state/capital nexus takes in the future. With the particular hybridity of forms found there, this seems especially true of contemporary East Asia.

---

113   Lankov 2013; Park I.H. 2017.

CHAPTER 2

The Trajectory of North Korean State Capitalism: from Formation to Crisis, 1945–90

Kim Ha-young

1 Introduction: a New Approach to Understanding North Korea[1,2]

The enigmatic character of the Democratic People's Republic of Korea (DPRK, or North Korea) has become a cliché of both popular and scholarly discussions of the country. The country appears as inherently reclusive, isolated and sui generis, separated from the rest of the world system or even from the flow of history itself. Alternatively, the DPRK is given a plethora of different descriptive labels that often do little to further our understanding of the country: state socialist,[3] Stalinist,[4] communist, corporatist,[5] feudal[6] or even fascist.[7] The confusion over the character of North Korea stems from both the DPRK state itself,

---

1   Editor/translator's note: there are a large number of quotations from Kim Il Sung in this chapter and I decided for the sake of consistency and the convenience of readers to cite the English edition of the collected works of Kim Il Sung, which is referenced as *Works*, along with the volume number. I also decided to use the English translations found in the *Works*, rather than translating directly from the original Korean edition, even though there are occasionally idiosyncratic translations in the English edition. When referencing the speeches and other works of Kim Il Sung I have given the full title of the speech along with the relevant volume and page number. Although this is inconsistent with the general style of footnote citations in this book I felt it would be of greater utility to the reader than citing each speech or article of Kim Il Sung individually in the bibliography (OM).

2   Various Korean-language versions of this chapter have been published previously, the first version in 2005 in the Korean journal *Chinbo p'yŏngnon* and a fully revised and expanded version in 2014 in a pamphlet entitled *Pukhan kukka chabonjuŭi ŭi hyŏngsŏng kwa wigi – marŭk'ŭsŭjuŭi punsŏk* [The formation and crisis of North Korean state capitalism – a Marxist analysis]. The author previously dealt with the early formation of the North Korean state and the Soviet military occupation in her 2002 book *Kukchejuŭi sigak esŏ pon hanbando* [The Korean peninsula from an internationalist viewpoint]. The analysis of North Korea presented in this chapter and in Kim's other works is based on Tony Cliff's theory of state capitalism.

3   Hart-Landsberg 1998.

4   Lankov 2013.

5   Cumings 1982.

6   Derr and Kelly 2018.

7   Myers 2010. Myers actually writes in his book *The Cleanest Race* that he does not 'intend to label North Korea as fascist' because the term is too vague, but he frequently compares North

with its desire to closely control information about the country and substantial capacity for historical mythmaking, and from the preconceptions and narrow concerns of media and academia in the English-speaking world. It is also the case that surface aspects of North Korea give rise to particular – often mutually conflicting – perceptions. The country's nationalised command economy fits with popular conceptions of what constitutes 'socialism' while its highly controlled, authoritarian society of ubiquitous surveillance looks much like 'high Stalinism'. At the same time however, the state has now passed down power through three generations of the same family, projecting the image of a monolithic, monarchic polity.

In keeping with the other chapters in this book, the analysis of the DPRK's history presented here will go beyond superficial descriptions of the North Korean political system to examine the socio-economic basis of the country during the first 45 years of its existence. In the Marxist analysis of North Korea that follows, the analytical toolkit developed for the study of capitalism – in its varying forms – will be applied to North Korea's development from its founding to the end of the Cold War. There are three basic pillars to this analysis of North Korea as a state capitalist society. The first of these is that North Korean society and economy were shaped by geopolitical competition, from the state's very inception as a product of the emerging Cold War in the 1940s, through the crucible of the Korean War and the ensuing decades of fierce North-South rivalry that turned both countries into 'garrison states'.[8] This geopolitical competition drove the Soviet Union to provide extensive aid to North Korea but it also shaped and constrained the economic decisions that the new ruling class of the country made and forced it to concentrate on heavy industry and military spending. The second is that North Korea is a class society with a bureaucratic ruling class and an exploited working class that was formed rapidly during the course of the 1950s and 1960s as the country pursued heavy industrial growth. Finally, the third pillar of this analysis is that the North Korean economy has been subject to the same fundamental crisis dynamics as other capitalist economies, including a falling rate of profit and a declining rate of productivity growth.

In order to pursue this analysis and trace the trajectory of North Korea's social and economic development over more than four decades of its history,

---

Korean ideology to fascist ideology and writes that 'the country has always been ... ideologically closer to America's adversaries in World War II than to communist China and Eastern Europe' (p. 10).

8 The term 'garrison state' derives originally from a 1941 article by Harold D. Lasswell: 'The Garrison State'.

this chapter will examine three periods. The first is the establishment of the North Korean state capitalist system in the 1940s, initially under Soviet military occupation and in the image of Stalin's Soviet Union. The second is the post-Korean War period from 1953 to the 1960s when the country's economy grew at breakneck speed on the basis of economic plans that prioritised heavy industrial growth. The third period to be examined is that of crisis and decline that began in the mid-1960s with the slowdown in North Korea's economic growth and became worse in the 1970s and 1980s as the DPRK's economy fell decisively behind that of South Korea under Park Chung Hee.

2   The Soviet Occupation and the Formation of North Korean State Capitalism

The origins of the North Korean system can be traced back to the Soviet occupation of northern Korea in August 1945. From the first decade of the twentieth century until 1945 Korea was a Japanese colony. Although Koreans struggled continuously against Japanese rule, both within Korea itself and in places like Manchuria – where many Koreans had migrated – liberation was not achieved by their own efforts. At the end of the Second World War the fate of Korea now fell into the hands of the 'liberating' Allied armies.

Only when the direction of the war had shifted decisively in favour of the Allies after the US had dropped the first atomic bomb on Hiroshima, did the Soviet Union actually join the Pacific War. After that it was only a week before Japan announced its unconditional surrender and by that time the Soviet Army had already passed through Manchuria and pushed into the northern part of Korea. This created a situation in which the USSR could have a say in the future of postwar Northeast Asia. Stalin wanted to regain the influence held by Tsarist Russia in Northeast Asia before the Russo-Japanese War of 1904–1905.

As the Soviet army advanced quickly southward, the US began to worry that the USSR would swallow Korea whole and it hastily attempted to draw a line between the two countries' occupation zones. The US therefore proposed General Order No. 1, under which the Soviet commander would accept the Japanese surrender in Manchuria, the Korean peninsula north of the 38th parallel and the island of Sakhalin, while in Japan, the Philippines and the Korean peninsula south of the 38th parallel it would be US General MacArthur. The Soviet Union accepted this proposal.

After suffering for 36 years under Japanese colonial rule, the Korean people were barely able to enjoy their liberation before the country was divided into north and south with the two halves placed respectively under the control of the Soviet military and the US army. The division was not yet finalised and the Allies were still negotiating the post-war settlement, but with the global Cold War getting under way and both the US and Soviet Union attempting to construct their own systems in their respective occupation zones, the division line became steadily more entrenched.

The Soviet Union made efforts to secure its own national interests and from the very beginning of its occupation pursued a policy of establishing a pro-Soviet regime in Korea, even if only in the northern part of the peninsula. Stalin spoke quite brazenly about his policy for the Soviet occupation zones, saying, 'The character of the Second World War is different to previous wars. Now the victorious countries have the right to force their own system on the countries that they occupy, as far as their armies have the power to do so'.[9]

Some progressive South Korean researchers claim that the Soviet Union's 'socialist' occupation policy was in line with the Korean people's aspirations for change and the two could thus create a virtuous circle. Immediately after Korea's liberation people's hopes for a better society were soaring. According to one survey made straight after liberation, some 77 percent of the Korean people answered that they 'preferred left wing ideology'. However, the Soviet occupation authorities had absolutely no intention of accommodating Korean desires.

To take an example, immediately after liberation Korean workers chased Japanese managers from the factories and formed factory committees to requisition and control each factory and enterprise. The seizure of factories and enterprises by the workers began to spread to every sector. Northern Korea, with its plentiful natural resources and proximity to the continent, had been developed by imperial Japan as a base for its heavy chemical industry and therefore had many large-scale factories and in some areas a tradition of workers' struggle dating back to the 1930s. However, autonomous management by the factory committees was criticised as 'unionism' and brought to an end by the Soviet occupation authorities.

The Soviet occupation authorities also dissolved all autonomous Korean armed organisations including the red guards formed by the Korean communists. Korean-language newspapers were shut down one after another or subjected to Soviet censorship. The newspaper of the domestic Korean communists was also the subject of censorship. Any activity from below that attempted to escape from the control of the Soviet military was criticised as a 'leftist error'.

---

9 Kim H. 1995, p. 77.

War reparations were another reason the Soviet authorities rejected the self-management by the factory committees. The Soviets actually had their eyes on the heavy industrial facilities in the northern part of Korea. They requisitioned factories, raw materials and plant owned by the Japanese army or Japanese individuals and seized all rights to their storage and use. The Soviet authorities also mobilised their own experts and technicians to play the main role in the resumption of operations at factories and enterprises. This was so that factories could return to full operation as quickly as possible, thus allowing their finished goods to be shipped back to the USSR. In addition, some enterprises were shut down so that the entirety of their expensive equipment could be removed and taken back the USSR.

The Soviet removal of finished goods, factory facilities and machinery continued for a number of months from the beginning of the occupation until the middle of the following year. The Soviet removal of assets was so great that according to a report compiled by the transport chief of the Soviet civilian administration the railways of northern Korea were completely occupied with removing factory facilities and other 'war spoils' and transporting troops until the end of February 1946. Until April 1946 half of all rail transportation continued to be occupied with fulfilling the demands of the Soviet authorities. In fact, the August 1946 law to nationalise key industries could only be fully implemented in October 1946 once the Soviets had taken their 'war spoils'.[10]

Although the Soviet occupation authorities formally handed over administration to the Provisional People's Committee in February 1946[11] they did not allow them to have real authority. The 'ten administrative offices' that were formed through the meeting of the various provincial People's Committees had to unconditionally carry out the directives of the occupation authorities. The PCs originally brought together the left and right in an alliance, but the Soviets ensured that Communists – who would tend to be pro-Soviet – made up at least half of the members of the provincial PCs. At the end of 1945, when the North Korean branch of the Korean Communist Party had some four or five thousand members, the nationalist Korean Democratic Party[12] had 300,000–500,000 members, so the Communists could only come to occupy half the positions within the PCs with the help of the Soviet occupation authorities.

---

10   The exact quantity of goods and machinery removed from factories in North Korea is not known. For more details on the removals, see: Chŏn H. 1999, pp. 81–4.

11   Lankov 2002, p. 27.

12   The Korean Democratic Party (Chosŏn minjudang 조선민주당) was a nationalist political party founded shortly after liberation, in November 1945, by independence activist Cho Mansik and others in the leadership of the South P'yŏngan Province People's Committee.

Of course, the nationalists only had to serve Soviet interests and the Soviet authorities would to some extent cooperate with them. However, when the KDP took up a position of opposition to Soviet policies on the Korean peninsula (e.g., the establishment of a Korean provisional government and the decision at the Moscow foreign ministers' conference to support a four-power trusteeship over Korea for up to five years), the Soviet Army immediately imprisoned the KDP leader Cho Mansik in the Koryŏ Hotel. They then installed a puppet leadership in the KDP and eventually dissolved the party altogether. The PCs continued, formally at least, to be coalitions, but no parties were able to hold independent political positions that diverged from those of the Soviet authorities or the North Korean branch of the Korean Communist Party.

The person that the Soviets most strongly supported in order to establish a pro-Soviet system in northern Korea was of course Kim Il Sung. Along with the ethnic Korean Soviet Communists (the so-called 'Soviet Faction') who were sent from the USSR, Kim Il Sung's 'Manchurian Faction' played the decisive role in setting up a pro-Soviet Communist Party, government and army in northern Korea. Kim Il Sung was well-known for his activities as an anti-Japanese partisan.[13] He had been involved in the anti-Japanese guerrilla struggle in Manchuria and in the China-Korea border region during the 1930s, but toward the end of the decade, when large-scale counter-insurgency operations mounted by the Japanese police made guerrilla activities increasingly difficult, he fled to the USSR. The guerrillas who escaped to the USSR were reorganised into the 88th Special Brigade under the Soviet 25th Army in the Far East. This is where Kim Il Sung was given the rank of captain in the Red Army.

Later the North Korean authorities would claim in their propaganda that Kim Il Sung led the Korean People's Revolutionary Army and returned to Korea carrying out a joint military operation with the Soviet Army. But this is not true. Kim Il Sung actually returned to Korea on a Soviet battleship called the Pugachev and at that time his title was deputy commander of the Soviet Army Garrison in Pyongyang. From the Soviet point of view, Kim Il Sung – who was already a captain in the Soviet Army – was far more trustworthy than the domestic communists who had set up their headquarters in the southern part of Korea. As Major-General Lebedev, the political commissar of the 25th Army, confirmed, 'that Captain Kim Il Sung was chosen from among the main Korean leaders and brought to northern Korea is a historical fact that can't be hidden'.[14] With his weak domestic support Kim Il Sung was only able to emerge as the

---

13   Suh 1988, chapters 2 and 3.
14   *Pirok Chosŏn minju juŭl inmin konghwaguk – sung*, p. 289.

most powerful figure after his return to Korea due to the backing of the Soviet occupation authorities.

After the Moscow Conference of Foreign Ministers' in December 1945, the left-right confrontation within Korea became more prominent and the conflict between the US and the Soviet Union also increased. The two powers fought to compose a Korean provisional government that would be friendly to them and the US-Soviet negotiations (the first meeting of the Joint Commission in May 1946) ended in failure. From this point onward the division became gradually more entrenched. The trend toward establishing independent governments in both the north and south of Korea gained strength.

Already in December 1945 Colonel-General Iosif Shikin – chief political commissar of the Soviet Army – stated in a report that, 'We have not yet been able to secure a sufficiently stable economic and political position [in Korea] that will guarantee the interests of the [Soviet] state even after our troops withdraw'. He also insisted that centralised administrative organs must be established and land reforms carried out.[15]

The Provisional People's Committee was formed in February 1946 against this background and in February 1947 the 'Provisional' part of the name was removed and it became simply the People's Committee of North Korea, meaning that in reality a separate government had been established. The North Korean branch of the Korean Communist Party saw this as 'an administration led by our party' and Kim Il Sung consolidated his hegemony within the party.

The Provisional People's Committee did pursue speedy land reform measures and the nationalisation of key industries, measures which have led many to argue that North Korea was being remodelled along socialist lines. While the 'People's Democracy Reforms' of 1946 established a socio-economic structure similar to that of the Soviet Union in the northern part of Korea, this was far from being a socialist revolution in the Marxist sense. Central to Marx's concept of revolution was the self-emancipation of the working class; the idea that through revolution the working class would organise themselves as the ruling class and take control of the means of production. In northern Korea however, the self-activity of workers was suppressed from the beginning of the Soviet occupation and the 'People's Democracy Reforms' were a revolution from above, carried out not by the working class but by the North Korean Communist Party (later renamed the Korean Workers' Party) with the support of the occupying Soviet Army. The aim of the North Korean Communist Party was to

---

15   Kim S. 1995, p. 63.

establish an independent national economy by following the Stalinist development model, which meant using the state to carry out primitive accumulation and achieve rapid industrialisation.

The strategy of state-led high-speed industrialisation was not only followed by Stalinist countries. Although there may have been differences of degree, the tendency toward putting the whole economy under the control of the state was developing across global capitalism. During the period stretching from the depression that began in 1929 to the 1970s this tendency arose repeatedly, particularly in relatively weak national economies. This did not mean a transformation to a new mode of production but rather a particular stage of capitalist development – state capitalism.[16] Because the fragile new countries that now appeared were faced with competing with the already developed capitalist companies and states, they had no option but to use the coercive power of the state to concentrate all the resources that they could use. It was only via this method that they could lay the foundation for the development of industry. In fact, in the Third World the economic success stories of that period were not those countries that left everything to the market, but those where there was strong state intervention. It was only natural that the North Korean bureaucracy followed this path.[17]

The land reforms were completed swiftly in only 20 days by confiscating land belonging to landlords and collaborators without compensation and distributing it to the peasants for free. The farmers received not only cultivation rights but actual ownership rights.[18] By fulfilling the long-held desire of the Korean peasants, the North Korean branch of the Communist Party was able to reap considerable political support. At the same time, around 87 percent of the landlords who had their land confiscated moved to the South. One of the aims of the land reform was the 'complete purging of the economic base of anti-communist and anti-Soviet elements'.

However, a more important objective of the land reform was the extraction of surplus from the agricultural sector for the sake of rapid industrialisation. Above all, it was necessary to provide a stable supply of food for urban workers. Although the reforms had made it possible for North Korean peasants to own land, they were not able to sell, mortgage or rent their land and they had

---

16   For a description of this historical period of global state capitalism, see Harman 1991.

17   The introduction of strong state planning in South Korea – which had lagged behind the North economically in the 1950s – after Park Chung-hee's 1961 coup should also be understood in this context.

18   For an English translation of the Law on Agrarian Reform see: Kim Il Sung, *Works* 2, pp. 93–5.

to bear a heavy burden in the form of the high tax-in-kind. This tax amounted to around a quarter of the grain harvest. According to the Provisional People's Committee, 'among the peasants there was a tendency to confuse the tax-in-kind with the grain requisitions carried out under the Japanese colonial government', and this gave rise to 'tax avoidance and false reporting of yields and area under cultivation'. The state bureaucracy also aimed to gain control of the remainder of peasants' grain, after the tax-in-kind had been paid, through their grain purchasing operations. Through this system peasants sold their grain to the government at low prices and were provided with daily necessities in return. However, the rice price was fixed by the state at least 30 percent lower than the market price, while the everyday commodities supplied in return were only around 20 percent cheaper than market prices and were usually in short supply. Rice purchasing by the state therefore ran up against major resistance from peasants.

The nationalisation measures of 1946 have long been a key basis for viewing North Korea as a socialist country. Due to the fact that under Japanese colonial rule most factories were owned by Japanese and therefore fell under the control of the Soviet Army in the north immediately after liberation, it was not at all difficult for the North Korean government to carry out a sweeping nationalisation of industry. Almost 100 percent of railways, ports, communications and mines as well as 90 percent of the key industries (1,034 companies) were nationalised under these measures. The nationalised sector therefore accounted for 72.4 percent of GDP in 1946, 83.2 percent in 1947 and 90.7 percent in 1949.

However, although the state owned the means of production, the state was certainly not under workers' control. The people who controlled the state – and therefore production too – were the Communist Party bureaucrats, with the support of the Soviet occupation authorities. The North Korean authorities claimed that the means of production were 'owned by all the people', but Korean workers were not able to own or control the means of production and neither did they have any say in the planning of production or distribution. If the workers had actually been in control of production then the needs of the people would have been prioritised, but the concerns of the bureaucracy were completely different. The aim of the bureaucracy was rapid industrialisation and they therefore poured all of North Korea's resources into this. Popular consumption was subordinated to accumulation. From 1946 until the start of the Korean War in June 1950 the production of means of production grew far faster than the production of consumer goods.

TABLE 2.1   Comparison of growth in means of production and consumer goods (1946–9)[a]

Year	Total industrial production	Means of production	Consumer goods
1946	100	100	100
1947	154	176	130
1948	218	254	180
1949	337	375	288

a   Figures taken from Central Statistical Board 1961.

TABLE 2.2   Ratio of production of means of production to consumer goods
as a proportion of total industrial production (1944–8)[a]

	1944	1946	1947	1948
Means of production sector	84.9	72.0	74.4	77.3
Consumer goods sector	15.1	28.0	25.6	22.7

a   This table originally appears in: Chŏn H. 1999, p. 111.

The ratio of production of means of production to consumer goods also reveals a similar trend, with consumer goods recovering from a wartime low of 15.1 percent under the Japanese to 28 percent of total industrial production in 1946 but then falling back to 22.7 percent by 1948. Under Japanese colonial rule northern Korea was developed as a production base for war materiel, focusing on heavy and chemical industries. But as can be seen in Table 2.2, after liberation, under the rule of the Korean Communist Party / Workers' Party the basic economic structure remained largely unaltered and continued to overlook popular consumption. In fact, for the North Korean bureaucracy, who were keen to pursue a heavy-industry-first strategy, the economic structure they inherited from the Japanese colonial administration offered a perfect base.

The North Korean bureaucracy chose the single manager system as its way of managing enterprises and, as the North Korean authorities themselves recognised, this ensured the 'obedience of all workers to a manager appointed by the state'.[19] Immediately after liberation factory committees had been created in order to implement workers' self-management, but by this time not even

---

19   Ri Chongdŭk 1955, *Inmin* 3, p. 96.

the shell of these committees remained. The North Korean People's Committee minister for labour, O Kisŏp, insisted on the importance of independent trade unions and workers' rights but he was severely criticised for this within the Party.[20] O had participated in the Wonsan General Strike of 1929 and spent 14 years in jail under the Japanese. Now the only thing that was demanded of workers was that they increase production, or, in other words, that they work longer and harder.

At that time, as they greeted their liberation from Japanese rule, we can assume that the Korean people were indeed enthusiastic to work harder in order to construct a new country. However, this is not enough when it comes to driving workers to work ever harder. Thus, in order to establish firmer labour discipline the North Korean bureaucracy introduced coercive measures and new punishments. They also introduced a system of labour passports that recorded information about an employee's employment status and served to limit their mobility as a worker. Workers who broke labour regulations could be detained and absence or lateness could be punished with reductions in food rations. The bureaucracy also used a variety of incentives to encourage productivity. Kim Il Sung argued in 1954 that 'we must eradicate equalitarianism in wages, and increase the workers' material incentives so that they raise their skill levels'[21] but already in the late 1940s a differential wages system was implemented and from 1947 a piece rate wage system was introduced. A movement to encourage competition over production among workers was also widely promoted in order to achieve production targets. Workers who exceeded the production targets were named 'model workers' and touted as leaders of the socialist competition movement. They also received material rewards from the state. This was closely modelled on the Soviet Stakhanovite Movement of the 1930s and Stalin's socialist competition movement of the 1940s.[22]

The fact that the North Korean bureaucracy strove for rapid industrialisation and made the production of means of production the priority of their economic planning reflects the way in which North Korea was subordinated to the demands of the Soviet Union in its competition with the West. But at the same time it reflected the fact that the North Korean ruling class could not avoid being aware of its competitors in the South. In relation to the establishment of economic planning in North Korea, the commander of the Soviet maritime

---

20   On O Kisŏp, see: Armstrong 2004, pp. 88–9.
21   Kim Il Sung 1954, 'On Shortcomings Revealed in the Industrial and Transport Spheres and Measures to Rectify Them', *Works 8*, p. 280.
22   On the disciplining and mobilisation of North Korean workers see Kim Y. 2012 and Kwon O. 1997.

military district, Kirill Meretskov, emphasised, 'North Korea's industry must develop in a manner that is beneficial for us [the USSR]'.[23] The Russian actually in charge of the Soviet occupation, Colonel-General Terentii Shtykov, also asserted that 'the development of a series of sectors of Korean industry must take into account the demands of our [Soviet] industry in the far east'.[24]

Demonstrating the superiority of the North Korean system by achieving faster economic growth than the South continued to be the ultimate goal of the North Korean bureaucracy in the future. At the same time they were locked in a military confrontation with their competitors in the South, who were under the protection of the US Army. In the late 1940s, the North Korean regime openly shouted about crushing the 'treacherous [South Korean] puppet government' and 'uniting the nation's territory'.[25] At the time, members of the government believed that the side that has overwhelming superiority in the production of engines would be victorious in a future war, showing that North Korea's heavy industry first strategy was closely connected to its preparations for war in the late 1940s.

The Korean War broke out on 25 June 1950 and it quickly expanded to become a war between imperialist powers, with first the US joining the war and then China (the Soviet Union also participated secretly). However, although the war continued until 1953, killing untold numbers of ordinary people and ruining the whole Korean peninsula, in the end neither North nor South Korea were able to reunite the country. The war left only wounds, hatred and a new ceasefire line that was little different from the old 38th parallel that had divided the country before the war.

3   After the Korean War: Geopolitical Competition and Industrial Accumulation

The Korean War left North Korea in a state of ruin. The commander of the US-led United Nations Command (June 1950–April 1951), General Douglas MacArthur, went as far as to claim in his May 1951 testimony to the US Congress that he had 'never seen such devastation' as he saw in Korea.[26] During the war the US military dropped a quantity of bombs on North Korea equivalent to what it

---

23   Chŏn H. 1999, p. 112.
24   Chŏn H. 1999, p. 112.
25   Of course, at that time the South Korean president Syngman Rhee was exclaiming the same things, arguing for the need to 'go north' and unite the country.
26   United States Congress 1951, *The Military Situation in the Far East vol 1*, p. 82.

had deployed in the whole theatre of the Pacific War. According to one North Korean source, the war destroyed some 8,700 factories, 600,000 houses, 5,000 schools, 10,000 hospitals and clinics and thousands of cultural and welfare facilities. At the height of the war in 1951 industrial output had already fallen to half its 1949 level while production of means of production had collapsed to one-third of the 1949 level.[27]

Faced with this situation, for the North Korean bureaucracy economic reconstruction was the paramount issue. Although the fundamental direction of economic planning prior to the war was rapid industrialisation, this now had to be greatly accelerated. The post-war recovery policy proposed by Kim Il Sung was one of prioritising heavy industry. For the sake of rapid industrialisation he insisted that all resources should be poured into heavy industry in particular. This was achieved by sacrificing the consumption of the ordinary people, but Kim Il Sung was prepared to proceed along this path remorselessly.

> The havoc wrought by the war upon our economy is beyond description. Therefore, overall, simultaneous reconstruction in every branch of the national economy is quite impossible ... If we do not determine correctly what should be done first in industrial reconstruction, this will retard the rehabilitation and development of the national economy as a whole and lead to the waste of a vast amount of funds, materials and labour or to their remaining idle. We must, therefore, start with the building of basic industrial facilities which will expedite the overall rehabilitation and development of the economy.[28]

The 'basic industrial facilities' that Kim Il Sung enumerated included steel manufacture, machine manufacture, ship building, mining, manufacture of electrical equipment, chemicals, and the construction materials industry. Light industry was mentioned occasionally, but then only on an equal footing as individual industries within the general field of heavy industry. In official terms this was called the 'Heavy industry first, with simultaneous development of light industry and agriculture'.[29] In reality, Kim Il Sung's economic development line

---

27   The figures here are from: Ch'oe Chunggŭk 1992, *Widaehan choguk haebang chŏnjaeng kwa chŏnsi kyŏngje*, quoted in Yang M. 2001, pp. 61–2.

28   Kim Il Sung, 'Everything for the Postwar Rehabilitation and Development of the National Economy', August 5, 1953, *Works 8*, p. 17.

29   To a certain extent this expression was used to please the Soviet Union, which was providing aid to the DPRK. In the post-Stalin Soviet Union, the balanced development of heavy industry with light industry and agriculture (the Malenkov Line) was being advocated.

was that everything should go to support the production of means of production. 'We cannot talk about an independent economy unless we have a metal
machine industry capable of producing with our own effort the means of production that we need'.[30]

Not everyone was happy with this situation. Conflict even developed within
the Korean Workers' Party over the priority for investment. Dissatisfaction
among sections of the party leadership (specifically from the Soviet faction and
the Yan'an faction) at the heavy industry-first development line was a reflection of the atmosphere in the Soviet Union after the death of Stalin. At the
time Krushchev was keen to rectify the contradictions arising from the unbal-
anced growth strategy of the Stalin era and this position of the Soviet communist party was also reflected within North Korea by the formation of an
anti-heavy industry first grouping within the KWP, composed of figures such as
Pak Ch'ang-ok, Ch'oe Ch'ang-ik and Yun Kong-hŭm. At the same time, underlying this opposition was the dissatisfaction that the North Korean people felt
about their standard of living. At the August 1956 plenum of the KWP central committee, minister of commerce Yun Kong-hŭm insisted that the people's
discontent was rising because the party had focused on heavy industry and neglected to raise the living standards of ordinary people. He also criticised the
fact that the workers and farmers were treated so harshly, while the salaries of
officers in the People's Army were excessively high.[31]

However, Yun Kong-hŭm was pulled from the platform before he could even
finish his speech. He was expelled from the party on the spot. Having slipped
out of the violent atmosphere of the meeting hall, Yun Kong-hŭm, Sŏ Hwi and
others fled to China. At one stage some of the figures who were opposed to Kim
Il Sung's line were able to return to the central committee with the help of the
Soviet Union and China, but after the Hungarian Revolution was crushed by
Soviet intervention in 1956, the wave of purges began in earnest. This was the
so-called 'August Factional Incident', and it led to the almost complete elimination of the Soviet and Yan'an Factions within the Korean Workers' Party. Some
one thousand figures from the Yan'an Faction escaped to China to avoid the
'Anti-Factional Struggle'.[32]

The result of this struggle within the party was that the heavy industry first
line became more firmly entrenched. The position of the party was summed
up thus: 'Industrialisation means that before anything else we must establish

---

30   Kim H. 1953.
31   Sŏ T. 2005.
32   Kim S. 2004, p. 141.

TABLE 2.3   Structure of GNP expenditure[a]

GNP	Consumption	Investment	Inventory increase	Net overseas transfers
1960	100.0	79.7	21.1	0.1	-0.9
1970	100.0	67.3	29.7	4.6	-1.7
1977	100.0	63.0	30.0	5.0	-2.0
1984	100.0	58.0	35.0	5.0	-2.0

a   Yang M. 2001, p. 83.

a heavy industrial sector that can produce means of production and within that sector the rapid development of the machine building industry has particular significance'.[33] According to the legal promulgation of the first five-year plan that was formally passed at the third meeting of the second session of the Supreme People's Assembly, of the total amount of industrial investment, the proportion going into heavy industry would be around 83 percent. Rapidly raising the rate of accumulation was now seen as the supreme good. If North Korean society had actually been managed according to socialist principles, then accumulation would have been under the control of the people's consumption demands. However, the consumption of the North Korean people was completely ignored and subordinated to accumulation. An official North Korean source revealed that the principle here was that 'people's consumption level could only be decided after the necessary accumulation had been deducted'.[34] Table 2.3 shows how investment as a proportion of GNP grew continuously between 1960 and 1984 while consumption consistently fell.

The North Korean state encouraged the production of mass consumer goods by means of utilising idle resources and labour power in local areas and by the use of handicraft manufacturing methods as a way of reducing investment in the consumer sector and guaranteeing the priority growth of heavy industry. As a result, there was both insufficient quantity of consumer goods and their quality fell. To make matters worse, the distribution of goods to working-class areas in the immediate post-war period was so poor that workers could barely spend 50 percent of their wages on consumption goods.[35] Focusing investment on

33   Chŏn Y. 1958, 'Urinara kwadogi kyŏngje palchŏn ŭi t'ŭksŏng', quoted in: Kim Yŏnch'ŏl 2001, p. 86.
34   Sahoejuŭi kyŏngje kwalli munje e taehayŏ, vol 3, (Chosŏn nodongdang ch'ulpansa).
35   Kim Y. 2001, pp. 83–4.

TABLE 2.4   Composition of basic construction investment by the
state in the industrial sector

	Total industrial investment	Investment in heavy industry	Investment in light industry
1954	100.0	81.0	19.0
1956	100.0	83.3	16.7
1958	100.0	85.0	15.0
1960	100.0	80.6	19.4
1962	100.0	63.7	36.3
1964	100.0	73.8	26.2
1966	100.0	84.7	15.3
1970	100.0	88.8	11.2

TABLE 2.5   Ratios of means of production and consumer goods as proportions of total industrial production

	1953	1954	1956	1960	1964	1970	1975	1984
Means of production	38	47.1	54	55	52	63.9	66.5	65.4
Consumer goods	62	52.9	46	45	48	36.1	33.5	34.6

heavy industry resulted in a rapid change in the ratio of production of means
of production to production of consumer goods. Tables 2.4 and 2.5 illustrate
clearly how mass consumption was consistently and thoroughly subordinated
to accumulation.

The source of North Korea's high rate of accumulation was the squeezing
of the working class and peasants. The situation of intense conflict between
North and South immediately after the war provided the atmosphere in which
this could be rationalised. First of all, in order to achieve rapid industrialisation
the North Korea bureaucracy had to extract more surplus from the agricultural
sector than they had done before. The Korean Workers' Party therefore began to
pursue forced collectivisation immediately after the war, which could be seen
as a sort of 'socialist primitive accumulation' aimed at securing state control
over food resources and labour power in order to achieve industrialisation. As
Kim Il Sung wrote in his 'Theses on the Socialist Rural Question in our Country',
'a formerly backward agrarian country like ours has no other way but to draw

a certain amount of funds for socialist industrialization from the countryside for some time following the victory of the revolution'.[36]

The Korean War had caused an increase in the quantity of land that was uncultivable and expanded the ranks of the poor peasants; in turn, this meant that the state was able to push ahead very quickly with its programme of collectivisation. However, it did not proceed without opposition. Peasants hid their grain, slaughtered their livestock and even began a campaign to withdraw from the cooperatives. The peasants who were found to have taken part in these actions were punished as spies and counter-revolutionaries.

The extraction of surplus from agriculture was achieved mainly through the tax-in-kind and government procurement of grain. The tax-in-kind, which was set at 25 percent of the harvest, played a key role in state control of the food supply from the time it was introduced with the land reform of 1946 right up until its abolition in 1966. It meant that the government could monopolise the overwhelming majority of the surplus agricultural product in the form of tax, without paying for it. In addition to this the state was able to absorb the remainder of the surplus through procurement. After the abolition of the tax-in-kind the procurement system became more coercive and usually after the farm workers were given their rations the rest of the surplus foodstuffs were forcibly purchased by the state. The procurement price was set very low. Although North Korea did not publish figures on its procurement of agricultural goods we can make informed assumptions about the level of the purchase prices by looking at articles in sources such as the journal *Kyŏngje kŏnsŏl*. For example, one such article notes, 'At the current stage the procurement price is fixed lower than the actual value because a portion of the net income produced by the peasants needs to be transferred into the development of industry'. Another article in *Kŭlloja* insisted that, 'From now on it will be possible to continually reduce the procurement price of agricultural goods. It is not possible to permit the tendency of agricultural procurement prices to continually rise without taking into account the situation of government finances, or current developmental conditions within industry'.[37] We can assume that this represents well the position of the North Korean bureaucracy, who were concerned with providing a supply of cheap surplus grain to the working-class population of the cities.

The forced collectivisation drove large numbers of peasants into the cities in search of work. According to North Korea's official statistics, immediately after

---

36   Kim Il Sung, *Works 18*, p. 173.
37   Nam Ch'unhwa 1957, quoted in: Sŏ T. 2005, p. 743.

TABLE 2.6   Trend of labour productivity and real wages, 1949–64[a]

	1949	1953	1956	1958	1960	1962	1964
Labour productivity rate in the industrial sector	100	78	153	n.a.	214	241	282
Real wages of manual workers and office workers	100	n.a.	98	159	203	211	218

a   Yang M. 2001, p. 163.

the Korean War in 1953 the agricultural population constituted 66.4 percent of the total employed population, but in 1960, only a few years after collectivisation had begun, the farming population had fallen to 44.4 percent and by 1987 it was only 25 percent.[38]

The main resources for accumulation in the North Korean economy came from the industrial sector. One of the key tools to this end was the low wage policy. In a workers' state, increases in the productivity of workers would have to be achieved by improving workers' living standards. However, in North Korea the real income of workers did not keep pace with increases in labour productivity. Table 2.6, which is based on North Korea's official statistics, confirms this. We can also confirm this from the following words of Kim Il Sung: 'Originally in the seven-year plan (1961–1967) it was predicted that per capita production would be increased by 220 percent. We calculated accordingly that the wages of manual and office workers should be increased by around 30– 35 percent'. In other words, he was saying that wage increases would only reach one-sixth or one-seventh of the level of the projected productivity increase during this period. However you look at it, this was a low wage policy.[39] When inflation of consumer goods prices is taken into account, even this nominal increase in wages had little actual effect. For example, 'Although between 1960 and 1964 the cash wages of workers and office workers increased on average 8.6 percent on a per person basis and 14 percent per household, since the prices of retail goods index rose 20.5 percent the result was that the real income of individuals actually fell by around 10 percent while that of households dropped by 5 percent'.[40] As we can see in Figure 2.1, while the wealth of the country was increasing, for a long time workers' real wages did not rise and this indicates that over time a larger proportion of the wealth being created by workers was being returned to accumulation.

38   Eberstadt and Banister 1992. See Table 28, p. 83.
39   Yang M. 2001, p. 162.
40   Yi S. 2004, p. 423.

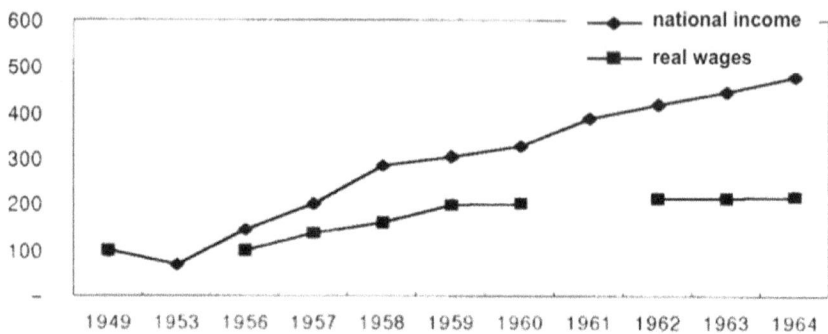

FIGURE 2.1 Growth trends for national income and real wages, 1949–64
         Note: Yi Y. 2000, p. 216.

In addition, high rates of turnover levies[41] also served to support the consumption-suppressing accumulation mechanism. As a form of indirect taxation on consumer goods, the turnover levy was a source of state income that could be used for investment. Adding this levy to the original manufacturing cost of consumer goods had the effect of greatly increasing the cost of commodities. The North Korean authorities explained this by arguing that they needed to use such a mechanism to control the demand for goods with a limited supply, such as luxury items and luxury foods. However, if we examine North Korean documents we can find that a high sales levy was imposed on mass consumption items too. In a 1969 speech, Kim Il Sung pointed out that 'We must do away once and for all with the idea of trying to increase state revenue by raising the prices of high-cost fabrics by the addition of large turnover levies ... I am told that even foodstuffs for daily consumption including sugar and eggs, in addition to textiles, do not sell well because they are too expensive'.[42]

The process outlined above reveals how the North Korean bureaucracy threw itself fanatically into the accumulation of means of production. However, according to Marx, this sort of compulsive accumulation is only a categorical imperative within capitalist society. As he wrote in *Capital*, 'Fanatically bent on making value expand itself, he [the capitalist] ruthlessly forces the human race to produce for production's sake'.[43] On the other hand, Marx

---

41   The 'turnover levy' (Korean: *kŏrae suipkŭm* / 거래수입금) was a type of sales tax introduced in the DPRK based on the pre-existing system used in the Soviet Union since 1930.

42   Kim Il Sung, *Works 23*, p. 117.

43   Marx, *Capital 1*, chapter 24, section 3.

made it absolutely clear that such compulsive accumulation could not exist within communism as he conceived it. 'In bourgeois society, living labour is but a means to increase accumulated labour. In communist society, accumulated labour is but a means to widen, to enrich, to promote the existence of the labourer'.[44]

However the North Korean bureaucracy chose to describe the character of North Korean society, it was a fact that 'living labour [was] but a means to increase accumulated labour', and that the bureaucrats were 'ruthlessly forc[ing] the human race to produce for production's sake'. Just as Tony Cliff described the Soviet bureaucracy after 1928, the North Korean bureaucracy can be understood as the purest form of the personification of capital in their control over the process of accumulation. North Korea is a bureaucratic state capitalist society with no resemblance to real socialism at all. The reason that the North Korean bureaucracy threw themselves so enthusiastically into the task of accumulation for accumulation's sake was precisely because the North Korean economy was not separated from the world system. At the beginning of the twentieth century, capitalism moved toward the use of state intervention in order to reduce domestic competition, but far from bringing an end to competition, this actually stimulated greater economic and military competition between states. This sort of global inter-state competition – especially the competition with South Korea – had a very strong influence on the functioning of the North Korean economy. External competitive pressures were the primary factor determining the economic planning of the North Korean ruling class.

While North Korea lacked internal competition between capitalists the level of military competition demonstrates that it existed within the world system and was on the receiving end of serious competitive pressures which exerted significant influence on the economy. In order to catch up with the level of US armaments that were entering South Korea, North Korea had no choice but to devote even more of its resources to securing a heavy industrial base. North Korea's military spending was very high and this became a big burden on the economy. According to a report from Kim Il, first vice-premier of the cabinet, at the fifth Korean Workers' Party conference, 'Spending on the defence sector made up 19 percent of the total government budget in 1960, and then in 1967–1969, after the Second Conference of the Korean Workers' Party [October 1966], 31.1 percent went into strengthening the nation's defence capacity, and over the last nine years the huge sum of almost 8 billion *won* has been spent on building our defences'.[45]

---

44   Engels and Marx, *Manifesto of the Communist Party*, Chapter 2.
45   Kim Il 1998, p. 114.

Although it has not been a competitor in the global market, North Korea was never economically cut off from the other nations of the world either. In fact, the scale of the country's international trade grew steadily from the 1960s through to the 1980s and in the 1970s trade with European countries and Japan increased sharply. The North Korean economy's dependence on foreign trade increased from 20.5 percent in 1965 to 29.4 percent in 1975, returning to 20.5 percent in 1985.[46] The scale of foreign trade exerts an influence on the management of the domestic economy. The reason for this is that the people managing industry have no choice but to constantly compare production costs in their own economy with those in other economies in order not to fall behind. This imperative was reflected in the pages of North Korean theoretical journals, where the industrial sector was urged to raise the quality of consumer goods and the productivity of the consumer goods sector by making equipment and facilities conform to global standards. This was precisely the reason why the North Korean bureaucracy were frantically trying to increase the level of investment, maintain low wages and raise the speed of factory work.

4   The North Korean Working Class and State Capitalist Accumulation

The North Korean working class and peasantry were the victims of the process of accumulation. While the North Korean bureaucracy constantly stressed that 'the people are the masters of the state', the opinions of the workers and the mass of ordinary people were never reflected in the state's planning. The state owned the means of production, but the state power was not in the hands of the workers and people.

North Korean workers were 'free labourers' in the sense that they did not own or control the means of production, but neither were they tied to them. In return for selling their labour power, they received the minimum amount necessary to reproduce that labour power in wages (or 'living costs' as they are called in North Korea); aside from these 'living costs' paid to the workers, the remainder (of their surplus labour time) was monopolised by the state and the ruling class. Whatever the North Korean bureaucracy did, their aim was to expand their accumulated resources by reducing the share returning to the workers.

---

46   Korean National Statistical Office 1996, *Nambukhan kyŏngje sahoesang pigyo*, pp. 98–100.

The number of North Korean workers increased very rapidly along with economic growth. Immediately after the Korean War North Korea was exhausted by the shortage of workers. To solve this problem, measures were implemented to increase the number of women workers and move the population of workers in rural villages into the cities.[47] The population of women workers increased from 169,000 in 1956 to 780,000 in 1964. Male workers made up 80.1 percent of the workforce in 1956, but this had dropped to 62.7 percent by 1964. At the same time, the urban population increased from 17.7 percent in 1953 to 47.5 percent in 1965, making it almost on a par with the rural population.[48] By 1987 the urban population had overtaken that of rural areas with a ratio of 60 percent to 40 percent.[49]

With the large-scale influx of unskilled novice workers who were unaccustomed to factory work, factory discipline weakened and the labour movement tradition that had existed under Japanese colonialism all but died out. In the heavy industry sector, workers with experience of more than 10 years made up less than four percent of the total workforce by 1953. Kim Il Sung pointed out that many workplaces 'are without order or discipline, in a state of anarchy'. He also reflected negatively on the tendency of managers to get work done more quickly simply by increasing labour inputs: 'Even when more than 20 workers work in unison and finish in half a day the job which a worker takes a day to finish, they shout hurrahs, claiming they have done their work ahead of schedule. And again when over a hundred workers spend a day to complete a task which is to be done by five or six workers in two or three days, they shout hurrahs, saying that they have over-fulfilled the plan'.[50]

The bureaucracy thus attempted to administer the workers with very strict labour laws and factory discipline. For example, 'it was within the authority of the person responsible for a workplace to force the workers to work 2–4 hours overtime when considered necessary, and to defer giving permission for workers to take both fixed and supplementary holidays', meaning that this measure legalised overtime work.[51] Although this was a decision made during wartime, it was not repealed after the war had ended. In addition, 'workers who arrived late for work, left early or were absent without any good reason, broke the rules concerning lunchtime or did not observe working hours could be given a 'cau-

47   Kim Y. 2012, p. 390.
48   Central Statistical Board 1961, p. 18.
49   For North Korean urbanisation statistics 1953–87 see: Eberstadt and Banister 1992, p. 21.
50   Kim Il Sung, 'On Shortcomings Revealed in the Industrial and Transport Spheres and Measures to Rectify Them', March 21, 1954, *Works 8*, pp. 257–97.
51   Kim Y. 2012, p. 394.

tion', 'warning', 'severe warning' or have their wages docked or even be demoted or sacked. If a worker neglected their work during working hours and lost more than 30 minutes working time, this was considered as an absence from work and their food rations could be cut ... If a labourer or clerk produced substandard goods during the course of their work, according to the law they would be made to bear material responsibility, regardless of whether they were actually punished or not'.[52] There was also a law that forbade workers from moving jobs in an attempt to stop the frequent changing of jobs by workers. A 1953 ordinance of the Supreme People's Assembly stipulated that 'any worker who wishes to leave their workplace or move workplace must have the permission of their manager', and that 'a person who voluntarily deserts their workplace will be referred to the People's Court and can receive a punishment of 6 months to a year of reformative labour'.[53]

However, it is not the case that North Korean workers were completely forbidden from changing workplaces and were essentially like slaves. In fact, even with these very strict labour laws the North Korean authorities were unable to prevent labour mobility. On the contrary, in the postwar conditions of labour shortage, workers were able to enjoy de facto freedom of choice in terms of workplace. There was a tendency for factories and enterprises to hoard labour in order to deal with changes in the plan coming from higher up that would suddenly increase production targets, but this caused an ongoing labour shortage. Factories that were short of hands were able to overlook the labour regulations and workers were able to leave one workplace and search for a new one.[54]

North Korean workers certainly suffered from long working hours and every intense work. While touring a production site, Kim Il Sung commented to the factory workers, '... we are still in a difficult situation, and we should advance faster than others to ameliorate our position as soon as possible; why should we make it a point to stick to Soviet norms [a standard for the quantity of labour inputs]? What is wrong if we Koreans produce twice as much as the Soviet people? I told them not to lag unnecessarily behind the Soviet norms'.[55]

---

52 Yi S. 2004, pp. 409–10.
53 Chosŏn chung'ang t'ongsinsa, *Chosŏn chungang yŏn'gam 1954–55*, p. 50.
54 Kim Il Sung himself discussed the problems of labour turnover in some detail in the early 1950s and it continued to be a common theme in North Korean journal articles during the rest of the decade. See: Kim Il Sung, 'On Shortcomings Revealed in the Industrial and Transport Spheres and Measures to Rectify Them', 21 March 1954, *Works 8*, pp. 274.
55 Kim Il Sung, 'On Some Immediate Tasks of the City and County People's Committees', August 9, 1958, *Works 12*, pp. 349–70.

The 'mass line' was used in order to squeeze out more labour power. This took its most well-known form in the Chollima Movement, a movement of collective innovation which was initiated by a speech in which Kim Il Sung argued for 'the creation of a revolutionary high tide in socialist construction'.[56] What was stressed in this movement was the exhortation to increase production by increasing production efficiency and the utilisation rate of existing facilities rather than by increasing either labour power or facilities inputs. This approach reflected the more difficult conditions that North Korea found itself in by the end of the 1950s, when even Soviet aid was beginning to slow down and the country was being forced to stand on its own to a greater extent.[57] In this process examples of 'speed' production were stressed and widely publicised, just as they had been in the Stakhanovite Movement of the USSR in the 1930s. So, for example, Kangsŏn Steel Mill's blooming mill was able to produce 120,000 tons of rolled steel even though it had a nominal capacity of only 60,000 tons.[58] Another widely publicised 'miracle' was the case of the railway workers who built the Haeju-Hasŏng broad gauge railway in only 75 days, when it should have taken 3–4 years to complete. In this process a variety of competitive movements were created such as the '500 shovels movement' and the 'one thousand shovels movement'.[59]

Party leaders organised all-worker meetings and 'zealots' meetings' in every factory and enterprise at which workers resolved to complete the five-year plan 1.5 years or more under the target. In any case, production targets were gradually increased by the party or the on-site 'zealots' meetings'. This was closely linked to criticism of managers who were considered to be conservative or half-hearted in their pursuit of production targets and engineers who stressed the importance of technology. Resolutions to complete the five-year plan ahead of schedule appeared in the pages of the newspapers on a daily basis. Regional factories were encouraged to produce daily necessities and other manufactured goods without state investment. For example, it was widely reported that in Kaech'ŏn-gun and Kangsŏ-gun, South P'yŏngan Province, small blast furnaces had been produced by piling firebricks inside drums and these were used to make pig iron. Meanwhile, in Sunch'ŏn-gun and Sŭngho-gun success was

---

56   This was Kim Il Sung's 13 December 1956 'Concluding Speech to the Plenary Meeting of the Central Committee of the Workers' Party of Korea', *Works 10*, pp. 352–61.

57   According to van Ree, Soviet aid and trade to North Korea began to slow quite drastically in the early 1960s, van Ree 1989, pp. 61–7.

58   Kim Il Sung, 'On the Tasks of the Cabinet in Implementing the Ten-Point Political Programme of the Government of the Republic' December 18, 1967, *Works 21*, pp. 503–4.

59   Kim Y. 2001, p. 208.

reported in manufacturing cement using small brick kilns. These cases won high praise as representative examples of the defeat of 'technological mysticism'.[60]

Those workers who enthusiastically put into practice these innovation movements were called 'innovators' (*hyŏksinja*) or 'zealots' (*yŏlsŏngja*) and the 'model' that they achieved was introduced to their whole work team or to the entire factory and applied to the rest of the ordinary workers. However, these 'model' cases were actually achieved by assembling teams of the best workers or by guaranteeing particularly excellent conditions for production. These zealots and innovators were often able to escape the ranks of the working class, receiving the political reward of upward mobility. Often they became factory managers or members of the Supreme People's Assembly. In the second term of the Supreme People's Assembly in 1957, 12 'Heroes of Labour' and 3 'Meritorious Miners' were elected as representatives, making up 7 percent of the total number of representatives. But by the third term of the assembly in 1962, during the period of the Chollima Movement, their number had increased markedly. There were now 62 'Heroes of Labour', 17 'Meritorious Miners' and 23 Chollima Movement section chiefs, making up a total of 27 percent of the representatives.[61] However, the majority of workers were not able to climb the ladder of social mobility and suffered from continuous tiring labour and low living standards.

While Kim Il Sung promoted the 'mass line' and emphasised the importance of political ideology while criticising those who stressed only material incentives as 'revisionists', North Korea certainly did not disregard material incentives. In fact, Kim Il Sung himself criticised the 'tendency towards equalising wages' and proposed instead the principle of distribution according to quantity and quality of labour.[62] In the North Korean constitution it states that, 'Distribution according to the quantity and quality of labour is a socialist economic principle, it is also a powerful means of raising workers' will to produce and the level of technology and skills as well as pushing forward productive development'.[63] In North Korea the grade and wages of a particular job were decided by

---

60   This brings to mind the Great Leap Forward (1958–62), when China attempted high-speed industrialisation. In fact, Kim Il Sung visited China during the Great Leap Forward and actually observed the 'manufacture of iron' using a small-scale 'backyard furnace'. However, the iron manufactured in these furnaces was poor quality and useless. See: Sŏ T. 2005, p. 829.

61   Kim Y. 2001, p. 400.

62   See footnote 19 above.

63   Ch'oe Chongt'ae, Kim Kangsik 2003, p. 86.

a number of different factors including the level of complexity of the work, differences in labour conditions, the level of skills and technology, the importance of the sector to overall economic development and workers' qualifications. And in terms of payment, both the flat rate system and the *togŭpche* or 'contract system' were used. This latter system was a type of piece rate system under which workers were paid according to the results of the work they carried out within a fixed period of time. This system actually came in two forms: the simple contract system and the progressive contract system (in the latter the wage was calculated on the basis of a piece rate that would increase progressively according to how far the production norm was exceeded) demonstrating clearly that the North Korean authorities relied on the use of economic compulsion to make workers work harder. Aside from this, a cash incentive system was also used. However, the piece-work payment system fostered competition between workers and led to the atomisation of the working class. On this subject Tony Cliff quoted Franz Neumann, who wrote of the use of piece rates under the Nazis: 'The preponderance of the performance wage brings the problem of wage differentials into the forefront of social policy. It is essential that this problem be understood not as an economic question but as the *crucial political problem of mass control* ... Wage differentiation is the very essence of National Socialist wage policy ... the wage policy is consciously aimed at mass manipulation'.[64]

While the North Korean bureaucracy drove workers to work harder and systematically subordinated consumption to accumulation, they also strengthened repression in order to prevent workers from organising to express their dissatisfaction. North Korean workers did not enjoy either the right to organise to defend their collective interests nor democratic rights more generally. Although North Korea did have workplace unions called 'occupational leagues', these were not independent organisations protecting the interests of workers. Originally, North Korea's 1946 Labour Law gave considerable power to the occupational leagues, talking of 'collective bargaining' and stipulating that 'Labour disputes between employers and workers shall be settled by the employers and the trade unions'.[65] However, after the Korean War the character of collective agreements themselves changed completely and they were replaced by 'agreements on the duty to compete' as part of the competitive production movement. At one stage Sŏ Hwi, national chair of the Occupational League, did attempt to strengthen the authority of the unions, arguing that 'the com-

---

64   Cliff 1988, p. 31. The quotation is originally from Neumann, *Behemoth*, p. 353.
65   An English translation of the 1946 labour law can be found in Kim Il Sung, *Works* 2, pp. 247–
      51.

petitive production movement shouldn't be carried out at all costs',[66] but he was purged in the August Factional Incident of 1956 and after that the occupational leagues were under the firm control of the party leadership.[67]

Vice-chair of the Occupational League Pak Sang-hong stressed that it was not 'an organisational form that had some sort of "autonomy" outside of the leadership of the party', but rather an organisation 'under the leadership of the party'. He also emphasised that if the management side took a 'bureaucratic attitude, unconcerned with the lives of the workers', the workers would have to respond 'with positive principles of cooperation and solidarity, rather than confrontation'. It seems as though he was demanding that workers should be completely unconcerned with their own lives. Now collective agreements were focused on guaranteeing that production plans were exceeded and stressing the duties and responsibilities of workers to that end. At a central committee plenary meeting in June 1964, even the collective bargaining system – that had continued to exist only as a formality anyway – was finally abolished. At this meeting, Kim Il Sung declared that 'it is irrational for managers to make production agreements with the Occupational League'. Since the interests of the administrators and the League were completely identical, production agreements were as 'meaningless' as workers making agreements with themselves and were just 'old forms of trade union activity current in capitalist society'.[68] By looking at the 'Socialist Labour Law' enacted in 1978 we can confirm that collective bargaining itself is completely absent from North Korea.

Under North Korea's penal code those that are found guilty of 'obstructing managers in the execution of their duties by acts of violence, threats or insults'[69] are to be given terms of reformative labour, revealing the sorts of actions used by workers in conditions where they are unable to take collective action like strikes. In addition to this, North Korean workers are not able to enjoy freedom of thought and expression. In North Korea there can only be one system of thought, that is, the ideology of the leader. Neither is there freedom to hold rallies or demonstrate (freedom of association). The North Korean penal

---

66   Sŏ Hwi 1956, 'Che 3ch'a tangdaehoe kyŏlchŏng silhaeng ŭl wihan chigŏp tongmaeng tanch'e ŭi kwaŏp', quoted in Sŏ Tongman 2005, p. 653.

67   For more on the transformation of the North Korean trade unions between 1945 and 1950 see: Kwon O-yun 2004.

68   Kim Il Sung, 'On improving and strengthening the work of the working people's organizations', June 26, 1964, *Works 18*, p. 337.

69   'Interference with the Execution of Duty', DPRK Criminal Law Code chapter 7, section 1, article 220. An English translation of the DPRK Criminal Law Code can be found here: https://www.hrnk.org/uploads/pdfs/The%20Criminal%20Law%20of%20the%20Democratic%20Republic%20of%20Korea_2009_%20(1).pdf (Accessed January 2020).

code stipulates that persons participating in riots or demonstrations with 'anti-state aims' or inciting others to do so can be sentenced to life in a labour camp or the death penalty, along with the confiscation of property.[70] Even if there is no 'anti-state aim', collectively defying the directions of a state institution can land a ringleader with a maximum sentence of more than 10 years of reformative labour.[71]

The fact that the independent activity of workers is completely prohibited in this way is clear evidence that the interests of North Korean workers and bureaucrats are quite different from one another. If that were not the case there would be no reason for the North Korean bureaucracy to systematically curtail and repress the demands and participation of workers from below. In contrast, for a true dictatorship of the proletariat the working class and its independent activity would be the real source of its power

5   The Contradictions of Economic Growth and the Onset of Crisis

During the decade following the Korean war the DPRK achieved astonishing rates of growth. During the Three-year Plan (1954–6) an average annual rate of 30 percent was recorded; and during the first Five-year Plan (1957–60) the growth rate was still over 20 percent. It is well known that the left-wing British economist Joan Robinson visited North Korea in 1964 and returned with great praise for the country and its 'economic miracle'.[72] However, as North Korea entered the 1960s its growth rate began to slow considerably (although it still maintained a level of around 10 percent annual growth), and eventually it was announced that the Seven-year Plan that began in 1961 and had been scheduled to finish in 1967 would have to be extended by three years. In the early 1970s the growth rate recovered temporarily but during the second Seven-year Plan (1978–84) it collapsed to the 3–4 percent level. Already the North Korean government had lapsed in some years in their annual reporting of growth rates, but from 1983 they stopped publishing industrial growth figures altogether. The North Korean economy stagnated for the whole of the 1980s and the growth rate for the third Seven-year Plan (1987–93) dipped into negative figures with an average annual growth rate of –2.9 percent.[73]

---

70   DPRK Criminal Law Code, chapter 3, section 1 – Crimes Against the State.
71   'Collective Disturbance', DPRK Criminal Law Code, chapter 7, section 1, article 219.
72   Robinson 1965.
73   This figure is from the Bank of Korea's annual estimates of North Korea's growth rate: *Pukhan kyŏngje sŏngjangnyul ch'ujŏng kyŏlgwa.*

Many scholars have pinpointed the economic problems of the North Korean economy as being inefficiency and waste. It is certainly true that there are huge inefficiencies and waste in the economy. For example, as Kim Il Sung himself pointed out, there was a tendency for managers to 'keep excessive reserves of manpower, materials and equipment in an attempt to make things easier for them'.[74] Because they do not know when production targets might increase or the supply of materials might cease, factory managers will keep hold of more materials and machinery than they need while avoiding cooperation with other industrial sectors. This meant that materials that were urgently needed by one factory could be piled up unused at another. Even more seriously, 'when an order comes from the materials supply office to send the remaining materials to another sector this is not carried out'.[75] The situation was exactly the same for labour, as Kim Il Sung once again pointed out: '... many of the newly built factories cannot work because of the shortage of labour. However, manpower is being wasted everywhere, particularly because of self-centredness on the part of factories and other enterprises'.[76] Factories and enterprises would always underreport their production capacity to higher bodies while requesting more materials and machinery than they actually required. The State Planning Commission was well aware of this practice and took it into account when receiving reports from enterprises, always sending less materials and labour than were asked for. The result was that the authorities could not know accurately about the productive capacity of industry or the actual demand for labour and materials. Kim Il Sung called this 'direct[ing] economic affairs without scientific calculation', or in other words, 'working by rule of thumb'.[77]

To give another example, in their striving to complete or exceed the plan from a monetary point of view, factories and enterprises would concentrate on producing easy products or products with the highest monetary value and neglect the production of other types of needed goods, a problem that Kim Il Sung himself recognised. This meant that some products were being overproduced and piling up in warehouses while other products were in short supply, causing major problems for production in related factories and enterprises. Essentially

---

74   Kim Il Sung, 'On Shortcomings Revealed in the Industrial and Transport Spheres and Measures to Rectify Them', *Works 8*, p. 287. Quoted in Kim Y. 2001, p. 279.

75   Kim Il Sung, 'On Some Problems for the Improvement of the Management of the Socialist Economy', February 1, 1973, *Works 28*, pp. 116–17. Quoted in Kim Y. 2001, p. 301.

76   Kim Il Sung, 'For Enterprising Ideological, Technical and Cultural Revolutions in the Light Industry Sector', January 31, 1973, *Works 28*, pp. 95.

77   Kim Il Sung, 'On Some Problems for the Improvement of the Management of the Socialist Economy', February 1, 1973, *Works 28*, pp. 116–17. Quoted in Kim Y. 2001, p. 296.

it meant that the distribution of resources between factories could not function properly. Kim Il Sung raised examples such as the factory that encountered problems with its production of electric motors because the smelting factory was not producing enough copper, and the tractor factory where production was held up because a machine-building factory was not supplying the necessary crankshafts. Kim described this as 'departmental selfishness' and criticised the tendency for factory managers to 'take no interest in whether other factories fulfil their plans or not; these people think that they need worry about nothing, so long as they carry out their own plans and receive bonuses'.[78]

Other examples might include overly rushed production aimed at fulfilling the plan, or the problems associated with the mass innovation movements such as damage and wear and tear to machinery, waste of raw materials and labour and the huge expenses that they consumed. For example, at the Kangsŏn Steel Works, where the Chŏllima Work Team Movement began, rushed production caused plant to be overworked meaning that 'the long-term tasks of the plan were not fulfilled and they were unable to overcome the disturbance caused to production'.[79] In addition, while the 'innovation' that was emphasised by the mass innovation movements meant that the chosen few factories could exceed the plan, this caused bottlenecks for the economy as a whole. Making concentrated use of limited resources and materials for a fixed period of time would actually cause stoppages during other periods. Also, the fact that this gave rise to differences in the tempo of production between different factories, or between different production processes within a single factory, brought about bottlenecks in particular sectors and this led to bottlenecks in the economy as a whole.[80]

This sort of inefficiency and waste is widely understood as one of the contradictions of socialist economic planning. However, Tony Cliff's point concerning the Soviet Union can equally be applied to the North Korean economy:

> If ... by the term 'planned economy', we understand an economy in which all component elements are adjusted and regulated into a single rhythm, in which frictions are at a minimum, and, above all, in which foresight prevails in the making of economic decisions – then the Russian economy is anything but planned.[81]

---

78   Kim Il Sung, *Works 21*, p. 67. Quoted in Yang Munsu 2001, p. 216.
79   *Rodong Sinmun* editorial, 21.7.1959, quoted in Kim Yŏnch'ŏl 2001, p. 248.
80   Kim Y. 2001, p. 249.
81   Cliff 1988, p. 95.

And, as in the Soviet Union, in North Korea too, 'instead of a real plan, strict methods of government dictation are evolved for filling the gaps made in the economy by the decisions and activities of this very government'.[82]

Inefficiency and waste were so prevalent in North Korea's economy not because it was a planned economy but because it was subordinated to the competitive logic of the world system. The direct reason that the various forms of waste arose was that the economic planners set the production targets excessively high. In order to protect themselves from this sort of pressure [from above] factory managers would underreport their productive capacity and over request labour and materials and then hoard them. The result was the vicious circle that was described above. However, behind the excessive targets set by the North Korean bureaucracy lay factors that they could not control, such as the pressure of international competition (especially the competition with South Korea). In other words, inefficiency and waste actually originated with the system of competitive accumulation itself.

Another problem for those who seek to explain North Korea's economic contradictions through waste and inefficiency alone is that they overlook the fact that the DPRK achieved huge economic growth in the period after the Korean War. It is not sufficient to understand the North Korean economy simply as a failure. After the terrible famine and economic collapse of the 1990s many people have forgotten that during the 1950s and 1960s the North Korean economy grew at an astonishing speed and until the mid-to-late 1970s the CIA judged that it outstripped the economy of the South in almost all economic sectors.[83] Despite its severe imbalances and its ups and downs, the North Korean economy achieved very impressive results in its early decades. As Tony Cliff once again pointed out in relation to the Soviet economy, an intimate dialectical unity existed between the poor management of the bureaucracy and the great leaps made by industry. The problem was that the very methods that had ensured fantastically high-speed growth during one period – sacrificing consumption in order to achieve high and rapid rates of accumulation – gradually became an impediment to further growth.

North Korea's bureaucratic state capitalist economic system could not avoid the classic problem experienced by all capitalist systems. That is, the tendency for the rate of profit to fall as a result of general investment increasing faster than labour power investment in the process of accumulation. We can indeed confirm that the same mechanism found elsewhere under capitalism has been

---

82   Cliff 1988, p. 103.
83   CIA National Foreign Assessment Center 1978.

TABLE 2.7   Trends for North Korea's production, investment and productivity (average annual rates of increase)[a]

	1966–70	1971–7	1978–86	1987–90
GNP (A)	10.2	12.1	7.1	5.2
Capital (B)	10.1	14.3	13.4	9.9
Labour (C)	3.0	3.6	3.4	2.7
Capital productivity (D)	0.1	−2.2	−6.3	−4.7
Labour productivity (E)	7.2	8.5	3.7	2.5
Total Factor Productivity (F)	3.2	2.5	−1.9	−1.6

a   Yang M. 2001, p. 113.

operating in North Korea. Table 2.3 shows how the rate of investment as a proportion of GNP grew steadily between 1960 and the 1980s, while as we've seen, during the same period the rate of growth fell steadily. If we look at the statistics for capital productivity growth rates calculated by Yang Munsu, we can see that capital efficiency declined constantly between the 1960s and the 1980s (see Table 2.7). This indicates that in order to receive a fixed quantity of surplus it was necessary to continuously increase the amount of investment and accumulation was encroaching on accumulation itself.

This is not to say that the North Korean state made no efforts to raise productivity. The bureaucracy did in fact attempt to improve its old, inefficient methods of exploitation. In the initial conditions of North Korean industrialisation the maximum amount of resources were invested and the unskilled workers who came flooding into the cities were set to work as hard as possible using the most primitive techniques (what the North Korean authorities termed the abolition of 'technological mysticism'). The low level of labour productivity was not very important. This was because at this stage it was possible to create something out of the nothingness of the post-war ruins. In Pyongyang, where it is said that the Americans had had to stop bombing because there were no buildings left to destroy, roads were laid and factories stepped in to fill the empty spaces. However, the method of 'extensive' growth which brought rapid growth revealed its inefficiency more and more as time went on. According to Kim Il Sung, steel production in the DPRK in 1961 was using twice as much coke, 1.5 times as much power and three times as much refractory material as in the advanced countries.[84] From the early 1960s the North Korean authorities began

---

84   Kim Il Sung in 1961, quoted in Yi T. 2009, p. 135.

to emphasise the need to 'use machinery and facilities, raw materials, resources, labour power and capital in a more rational manner'. What was required now for the economy to move to the next level of growth was intensive development based on raising the productivity of both capital and labour. But in order to stimulate the workers to show more creativity and raise their productivity, they needed to be supplied with better food, better holidays and more consumer goods. In fact, in the initial stage of the First Seven-Year Plan (1961–70) the North Korean state did actually pay renewed attention to the production of consumer goods that it had previously ignored. However, this honeymoon period did not last long. Due to the international pressure of competitive accumulation, the tendency to sacrifice agriculture and consumer goods to investment in heavy industry arose once again and the plan was revised in 1962 to re-emphasise heavy industry.[85]

There were two factors in particular that meant North Korea in the 1960s lacked the leeway to pay more attention to the needs of mass consumption. First, Kim Il Sung had begun to take an independent line from Moscow. In 1962 the Soviet Union established a plan for the economic unification of the COMECON bloc. This was in effect an attempt to control the economic plans of the member countries in order to promote product specialisation and an international division of labour based on the principle of comparative advantage. Kim Il Sung opposed this move and pursued his own independent economic line (summed up in the slogan 'regeneration through one's own efforts' *charyŏk kaengsaeng*). In response the Soviet Union refused to provide aid, including machinery, causing a major blow to North Korea, which was substantially reliant on the USSR for manufacturing facilities, technology, and raw materials among other things. In order to make up for this economic blow North Korea had to divert a lot of its resources.[86]

Second, from the early 1960s onward the country's military spending increased massively. On top of the fact that the Soviet Union reduced its aid programme and the Chinese army withdrew from the country in 1958, North Korea's observation of the weak Soviet response to the Cuban missile crisis also amplified its sense of insecurity. In addition, tensions were heightened on the Korean peninsula during this period with the establishment of the Park Chunghee military government in South Korea and its pursuit of diplomatic relations with Japan. In 1962 the central committee of the Korean Workers' Party adopted the *'Pyŏngjin Line'* that called for a simultaneous emphasis on the economy and

---

85   Chung 1972.
86   For more on the deteriorating DPRK-Soviet relations in the early 1960s, see Szalontai 2005, Chapter 7.

national defence, and this brought cuts to investment in light industry (which had been increasing for a while) and regional budgets. From 1961 to 1963 investment in light industry occupied around 30 percent of all investment in industry (30.4 percent in 1961, 36.3 percent in 1962, 31.8 percent in 1963), but after 1965 it dropped back below 20 percent of investment (12.7 percent in 1965, 15.3 percent in 1966) while investment in heavy industry rose. In addition, by the late 1960s military spending was absorbing around 30 percent of the total state expenditure (30.4 percent in 1967, 32.4 percent in 1968, 31 percent in 1969).[87]

One result of this was that a section of the bureaucracy once again raised the need for reform in the mid-to-late 1960s. This issue caused the first internal struggle within the North Korean bureaucracy since the 'August Factional Incident' of 1956. It was at the time that the seven-year plan failed to achieve its targets on time and the three-year extension to the plan was introduced as a last resort. Even Kim Il Sung acknowledged that 'At the moment we are not able to increase our output on a per capita basis'.[88] To make matters worse, the new system of 'unification and subdivision of planning' that was introduced in order to boost efficiency and strengthen bureaucratic control of planning, was not effective. Hoarding and waste continued as before. The challenge to Kim Il Sung's line from members of the old Kapsan Faction, including Pak Kŭmch'ŏl and Yi Hyosun and others, centred around the problem of the speed and balance of economic development, and the utilisation of the law of value. According to official North Korean records this group opposed the Chollima Movement that symbolised high speed economic construction and propounded 'revisionist economic theory' (referring to the Liberman Theory fashionable at that time in the USSR).[89]

This group believed that because the party had pushed both people and machinery so hard during the preceding period, it needed to regulate the speed of development and find some balance. They argued that although it was true that the level of output was important, in the future the party should not simply concentrate its attention on the scale of production, but also on the quality of the goods produced. In order to raise the quality of goods, they proposed that efforts should be made to establish a founda-

---

87   Chung 1972, see especially the tables on pp. 74–5; Yang Munsu 2001, p. 118; Yi T'aesŏp 2009, p. 161 (based on budget reports of the DPRK Supreme People's Assembly 1968–70).

88   Kim Il Sung 1965, '7 kaenyŏn kyehoek ŭi kangch'ŏl koji rŭl chŏmnyŏnghagi wihayŏ', quoted in Yi T'aesŏp 2009.

89   Chosŏn rodongdang chung'ang wiwonhoe tangnŏksa yŏn'guso, Chosŏn rodongdang ryaksa 2, p. 217.

tion in modern science, and that to do this it was logical that the excessive spending on defence would have to be reduced. In general, they stated rather frankly their opinion that in order to achieve the balanced development of the economy, policy and budget priorities would have to be readjusted.[90]

In response, Kim Il Sung reiterated his point of view, emphasising high-speed growth.

These bastards [pointing to Pak Kŭmch'ŏl] went to this mine [the Kŏmdŏk Mine] and ordered the workers to 'cease bragging and do the required amount of work', preventing the workers from even saying 'we will produce more'. This sort of behaviour results from the poison of revisionism. When we have not yet united our country and we are still struggling face to face with our enemies, how can we rest content with just a moderate output?[91]

Kim Jong Il also played an important role in this controversy. According to official North Korean documents, the supporters of Pak Kŭmch'ŏl and Yi Hyosun formed a 'Group for studying the application of the law of value' and wanted to apply a method of enterprise management in the factories that would stress material incentives. Kim Jong Il responded by stressing 'autonomous factors' (*chuch'ejŏk yoin*), meaning essentially the 'high revolutionary zeal of the working masses'. He argued that,

In socialist society the decisive factors in determining the high speed of economic growth are not objective but subjective. ... Thus, in the management of the economy, one must first look at people, rather than facilities, raw materials and resources, and in order to maintain the fast development of the people's economy, one must calculate first the loyalty of the working masses to the party and the leader and their revolutionary enthusiasm rather than looking at material conditions.[92]

---

90   Yi S. 2004.
91   Kim Il Sung, *Works 22*, 'Youth must become the vanguard on all fronts of the building-up of our economy and defence to bring our revolution to final victory', April 13, 1968, p. 140. (The translation of this passage is not the one found in the English edition of Kim Il Sung's *Works* but my own translation that reflects better the strength of Kim Il Sung's language in this speech – OM).
92   Kim Jong Il 1992, *Selected Works 1*, 'On having a correct understanding of the political, moral and material incentives', June 13, 1967, pp. 208–19.

In the end this conflict within the bureaucracy ended in the defeat of Pak Kŭmch'ŏl and Yi Hyosun and they were purged from the central committee of the Korean Worker's Party. However, the need for reform soon reared its head again and the party had no choice but to take on board, to some extent, the problems that they had raised. In 1969 Kim Il Sung published his 'On some theoretical problems of the socialist economy' which included a section concerning the 'formal utilisation of the law of value' in which he seemed to acknowledge the need to make use of the law of value.[93] Later Kim Il Sung clarified that this article was written in order to emphasise that the phenomenon of disregarding price differentials or thinking that material incentives were unnecessary was wrong.[94] Also, in the early 1970s the KWP central committee pressed for the excessive unification and subdivision of the plan to be relaxed.

Despite these shifts, North Korea's insistence on sticking to the economic line of self-reliance and its pursuit of the dual development of the economy and national defence continued to place a heavy burden on the economy as a whole. In particular, the North Korean bureaucracy came to realise that it was increasingly difficult for them not to fall behind the states and corporations of the West with the very limited resources and technology they had available to them within the boundaries of one country. As the world capitalist system entered the 1970s, 'globalisation' started to become more influential than state capitalism, and thus those countries that stuck to the state capitalist road began to fall behind. Now the most successful corporations in the world were those that began to organise not just sales but also production on an international scale. As Chris Harman argued: 'Those national ruling classes that had placed all the varieties of goods dealt with in the domestic market in the hands of enterprises based in a single country began to discover that these companies were unable to mobilise the level of resources required in order to catch up with the most advanced enterprises in the world system. Production limited by narrow national borders became ever more inefficient and fell behind technologically'.[95]

The North Korean bureaucracy, which had so strongly emphasised the self-supply of industrial plant in the 1960s (during this decade the ratio of domestically supplied industrial plant reached 90.6 percent) began in the 1970s to import superior machinery from the West and actively seek to attract for-

93   Kim Il Sung, 'On some theoretical problems of the socialist economy', March 1, 1969, *Works 23*, pp. 380–404.
94   Kim Il Sung, 'On taking good care of state property and using it sparingly and further developing the fishing industry', June 20, 1969, *Works 24*, pp. 1–74.
95   Harman 1991.

eign capital. This was possible because of the changing international situation brought about by the US-China detente. At the same time North Korea began to participate in dialogue with the South and actively tried to improve diplomatic ties with Western countries. In effect they were attempting to use the changed international conditions to bring about improvements in the domestic economic situation. From 1972, North Korea imported machinery and plant on a large scale from Japan, France, Britain and West Germany, relying on loans from these countries to finance the spending. They also managed to get long-term loans from international financial institutions and it's thought that the credit and aid that North Korea managed to get from Western countries during this period totalled more than $1.2 billion.[96] In 1974 as much as 53.7 percent of the North's total overseas trade consisted of imports from Western countries, including a number in the OECD.[97]

North Korea thought that it would be able to repay its loans by exporting nonferrous metals such as lead, zinc and copper. However, when the 1973 Oil Shock caused a worldwide recession, this assumption was shown to be mistaken. From 1974 the international price of nonferrous metals collapsed as the advanced capitalist states reduced their imports of metals in the aftermath of the recession. Conversely, both the cost of the advanced plant North Korea was importing from the West and the price of oil increased steeply, raising the cost of running the machinery. North Korea could not stop its trade balance going into the red and by 1976 it faced a situation of having to default on its loans. The strategy of developing its economy by employing Western capital and technology had been a failure and the great sense of fear created by this slight opening to the world market encouraged a conservative inertia. To make matters worse, the mid-1970s saw the arrival of the new cold war globally while on the Korean peninsula North-South dialogue came to a halt and Park Chung-hee embarked on a programme of military strengthening aimed at giving South Korea an independent national defence.

However, because of the problems posed by the old state capitalist model, North Korea could not ignore the need for the introduction of advanced machinery in its industrial sector. Once North Korea was unable to import the raw materials and plant it needed due to the default on its debts, the economy quickly fell into serious difficulties. In a speech of March 1980, Kim Il Sung noted, 'Recently, because coke has not been coming into the country from abroad, the Hwanghae Amalgamated Steelworks and the Kim Ch'aek Steel-

---

96   Yi C. 2011.
97   Yang M. 2003, p. 62.

works have come to a standstill and this is causing much hue and cry'. In his new year's addresses in 1979 and 1980, Kim Il Sung spoke of the need to 'normalise production', showing that production was not running normally at the time. In addition, in his New Year speech for 1979 he argued: 'We must put great efforts into developing foreign trade' and 'prioritise the production of export goods in all sectors of the people's economy'. This demonstrated the difficult position they found themselves in where it was impossible to normalise production without increasing imports. However, the problem was that North Korea was not able to make any export products of good enough quality to guarantee its expanding imports. In the years 1978–1980 imports of machinery grew again but as before this gave rise to problems associated with foreign debt, and imports contracted again in 1981. In the mid-1980s the DPRK concluded new trade agreements with both the USSR and China and continued to trade mainly with these two countries and especially with the USSR.

Suffering from a lack of advanced means of production and a burden of defence spending that it found increasingly difficult to maintain, the North Korean economy fell into a slump in the 1980s. Already at this time the situation of the economy was serious enough that vice president Im Ch'unch'u told a group of scholars visiting from Yanbian in China that 'the people are starving'.[98] In 1984 North Korea established a joint venture law which was aimed at going beyond simply increasing foreign trade and pursuing economic cooperation with advanced foreign capital in the science and technology sector. This seemed to be a sign of economic opening and was modelled on the PRC's 'Law on Chinese-Foreign Joint Ventures' which was adopted at the early stage of China's programme of reform and opening in 1979. However, from 1986–7 this atmosphere of reform and opening rapidly cooled, perhaps because the North Korean bureaucracy had been observing how attempts at reform in the Soviet Union and Eastern Europe had given rise to demands for political reform. North Korea walked the tightrope of reform with extreme caution, trying reform measures only insofar as they did not exert any influence on the ruling system itself. Repeatedly reform measures would be put in place only to be followed by a cooling-off period. In any case, the joint venture law was unable to achieve any significant results. According to South Korea's Ministry of Unification, up to 1992 there were no more than a few dozen joint ventures in operation and of those 85 percent were formed with partners associated with the pro-DPRK Japanese-Korean organisation Ch'ongnyŏn. North Korea's first free trade zone was established in 1991 at Rajin-Sŏnbong on the northeast-

---

98   Yi C. 2011, p. 125.

ern coast in an attempt to attract foreign capital, but it too failed to achieve any significant results. North Korea's domestic economic conditions and its internal politics did not provide an attractive prospect for foreign investors. The non-committal attempts at opening by the North Korean state were not able to prevent the country's economy from falling deeper into a slump.

6   Conclusion

In the 1990s the North Korean economy began to contract in earnest. Between 1990 and 1998 the economy recorded nine consecutive years of negative growth. During this period North Korea's GDP contracted by 30 percent and the utilisation rate of industry dropped below 30 percent of capacity. The scale of government finances was also halved in the period 1994–8 and famine became endemic. Even according to the figures publicised by the North Korean authorities, some 220,000 people died of starvation between 1995 and 1998.[99] Once the real state of the North Korean economy became known to the outside world in the mid-1990s, those who had harboured illusions regarding the North Korean system got a terrible shock and began to look for the causes of the economic collapse in external factors such as the fall of the Soviet Union or the natural disasters of the 1990s. Of course, the collapse of the Eastern Bloc and the catastrophic floods of 1994–5 had serious effects. For example, from 1991 the flow of Russian crude oil into North Korea reduced drastically and it became even harder for North Korean industry to operate without sufficient energy inputs. It is also true that the floods massively worsened the food supply situation. However, the factory utilisation rate had been falling in the 1980s and there were already problems in the supply of food. The collapse of the Soviet Union and Eastern Europe was just the final straw that exacerbated a crisis that had already been brewing for some time.

In this chapter the author has attempted to show that North Korea's crisis originated with flaws that are internal to bureaucratic state capitalism, which is just one form of capitalist system. Many people believe that the reason so many people in North Korea have been pushed into destitution is the socialist system. However, the Soviet army of occupation did not lay the foundation for socialism and neither did the North Korean bureaucracy develop a socialist society, but rather the state-led rapid industrialisation model. In order to survive its

---

99   For a discussion of mortality during the North Korean famine of the 1990s, see Goodkind, West and Johnson 2011.

intense military competition with the US and the US-backed South Korea it had to grow a heavy industrial base that could support military power as fast as possible. It was this sort of external competitive pressure that was the deciding factor in North Korea's economic priorities. While the bureaucracy increased heavy industrial and armaments production it oversaw a plan that suppressed popular consumption. The workers of North Korea were forced to endure great sacrifices in order to construct the economy amidst a threat of war that was constantly exaggerated by the ruling bureaucracy. Being pushed into following a closed state capitalist economic model with insufficient domestic resources resulted in behaviour that could look quite crazy, like the extreme voluntarism of the Mass Line and the supercharged personality cult of the *suryŏng* system.

However, this economic model was not able to guarantee continued growth and productivity and return on investment declined during the 1960s and 1970s. At the same time, technological progress at a global level came more and more to rely on the transfer of resources across national boundaries. In response to this, while the Soviet Union and the states of Eastern Europe threw themselves into the free market system from the 1980s onward, North Korea retained its position of relative isolation within the global system and hunkered down. While the people of Eastern Europe and the Soviet Union subsequently suffered greatly at the hands of the global market, the North Korean people instead suffered extreme poverty as their economy crashed. Of course, the North Korean bureaucracy did want to improve relations with the West, especially with the US, on the precondition that they could maintain their firm control of North Korean society. However, the US has consistently refused to take the hand offered by North Korea because it has wanted to maintain its hegemonic position in East Asia and keep its military stationed there, thus requiring an exaggerated threat from North Korea.

Today North Korea is regularly described as a country that is almost impossible to understand. It is a country that receives food aid every year and yet also possesses nuclear weapons and fires long range ballistic missiles; a country that declares itself to be socialist but has achieved a three-generation hereditary succession; a country that can put on mass games involving the mobilisation of hundreds of thousands of people, but where corruption is rife and many basic services have broken down. However, as this chapter has attempted to show, these North Korean contradictions are not to be explained by appeals to the country's uniqueness and isolation but by paying careful attention to the particular way in which the country has been incorporated into the world capitalist system and how this has given rise to a particular set of constraints and pressures on its state and society.

CHAPTER 3

Workers in Mao's China: Labour and Capital under Chinese State Capitalism, 1949–62

Kim Yong-uk

1   Introduction: China, Capitalism and the Question of Free Wage Labour[1]

Like other chapters in this volume, this chapter starts from the position that China under Mao was capitalist, despite the state's own claims to the contrary. Of course, this view is not widely shared among scholars who study China before 1978, even among those who are Marxists. When Mao's China is described as a form of capitalist society, the most familiar objection raised by Marxists is that it was in some sense 'unlike capitalism'. They focus particularly on the question of 'proletarianisation' in their analysis of Chinese society, from the Mao period up to the present day. In Marx's theory of capitalism, wage labourers assume pride of place not only in economic analysis but also in terms of praxis. Another reason why the question of proletarianisation occupies such an important position in debates on the social character of China is that the supposedly 'unique' mechanisms for disciplining the working class, symbolised by the *hukou* (household registration) and *danwei* (work unit) systems, were thought to have made China different not only to the western capitalist world but also to the former Soviet Union and other 'socialist' countries of Eastern Europe. For those scholars who believe that Mao's China was a non-capitalist society, Deng Xiaoping's reform and opening measures meant the dissolution of the working class as a subject and its 'depoliticisation'.

In her work on the new generation of Chinese workers, Lu Tu deliberately avoids using the word working class (*gongren*), instead using the term '*min-gong*'. In her estimate the modern Chinese new working class (*xin gongren*) is different to the working class of the Maoist period (by which she automat-

---

1 Editor/translator's note: This chapter uses many primary source documents taken from a series of published anthologies that are listed in the Bibliography II. Rather than list each individual document in the bibliography I have given full references for primary sources in the footnotes to this chapter, for the convenience of the reader (OM).

ically means workers at state enterprises). Whereas in the past the *gongren* assumed the position of 'social protagonists', in the current period a worker merely means someone who is employed by someone else. The prominent Chinese new left thinker Wang Hui – who wrote the preface to Lu Tu's book – also agrees with her assessment.[2]

Here lies the crux of a continuing theoretical debate on the relationship between capitalism and free labour. In *Capital* Karl Marx defined the working class under the capitalist system as 'free wage labourers'. What he meant by this is captured in the following quotation:

> In the case of the free worker, the value of his labour capacity, and the average wage corresponding to it, does not present itself as confined within this predestined limit, independent of his own labour and determined by his purely physical needs. The average for the class is more or less constant here, as is the value of all commodities; but it does not exist in this immediate reality for the individual worker, whose wage may stand either above or below this minimum. The price of labour sometimes falls below the value of labour capacity, and sometimes rises above it. Furthermore, there is room for manoeuvre (within narrow limits) for the worker's individuality, as a result of which there are differences in wages, partly between different branches of labour, partly in the same branch of labour, according to the industriousness, skill, strength, etc, of the worker, and indeed these differences are in part determined by the measure of his own personal performance. Thus, the level of the wage appears to vary according to the worker's own labour and its individual quality. This is particularly strongly developed where a piece wage is paid. Although the latter ... does not change in any way the general relation between capital and labour, surplus labour and necessary labour, it nevertheless expresses the relation for each individual worker differently, according to the measure of his own personal performance. Great strength or special skills may increase the purchase value of the slave as a person. but this is of no concern to the slave himself. It is different with the free worker, who is himself the proprietor of his labour capacity.[3]

This 'classical' position on the relation between capitalism and free wage labour has received criticism recently.[4] Marx himself was well aware of the use of

---

2 Lu T. 2013.
3 Marx, *The Economic Manuscripts*. CW34: pp. 436–38.
4 Van der Linden and Roth 2014; Banaji 2010.

forced labour in the developmental stage of capitalism. As he described vividly in his analysis of primitive accumulation in *Capital* Volume I and *Grundrisse*, various forms of coercion were deployed in the development of capitalism and forms of subsumption of labour to capital were also diverse. For Marx, free wage labour is something that is intimately connected with the capitalist dynamic of competitive accumulation. What he meant by 'free wage labour' – as with other key concepts related to capital accumulation – is not an object with fixed characteristics but a developing tendency, forming relations with other things in movement. We have to understand this concept in the context of Marx's general method of analysing capitalism. As such, observing whether or not wage labourers are acting 'freely' in a particular period may be an important object of research, but this cannot provide a fundamental answer to the question of whether they constitute 'free wage labourers'.

As Henry Heller, Henry Bernstein, and more recently Jurgen Kocha have maintained, capitalism in its early development process could fuse with the slave system to some extent but the free wage system is more conducive to the process of industrialisation.[5] As a consequence, the claim that capitalists can freely choose between free wage labour and slave labour is exaggerated. Instead, they must make a choice based on various constraints, including the size of their capital, the level of competition from other capitalists and various international factors such as geopolitics. However, as the quotation above from Marx shows, because capital accumulation is a very dynamic process in which fixed capital is replaced by mobile capital and goes along with the rising technical/organic composition of capital, attempting to tie workers to a particular means of production or workplace as slaves or serfs, will inevitably give rise to contradictions. This does not mean that it is impossible for coercion and accumulation to coexist, but that capital accumulation at a higher level is facilitated by its combination with free wage labour. Although extra-economic coercion might be required during the early stages of the development of production, it has very obvious limitations when it comes to motivating workers to continuously produce use values. If there is no tendency to raise worker productivity through economic coercion – the pressure to work harder in order to receive higher wages – then a particular capital can fall behind in the field of international competition and come under pressure to respond. In backward countries where the state has to take the lead in capital accumulation this contradiction is even more pronounced. In backward countries lacking in capital, technology and social infrastructure, if the state wants to respond to international compet-

---

5   Kocka 2016, pp. 124–7; Bernstein 2013, pp. 320–5; Heller 2011, pp. 170–1.

ition by committing to capital-intensive production with long accumulation cycles (heavy and military industries) then it has to concentrate capital and labour and carefully plan their deployment. However, the state bureaucrats of these backward countries had to perform contradictory roles. While demanding blind obedience and loyalty to the bureaucratic hierarchy, they also had to motivate workers to increase productivity and efficiency so as to outperform their international rivals.[6]

1.1 The Working Class under Mao

If we examine studies on workers under other regimes of so-called 'actually existing socialism' we can easily find several points of similarity between those workers and workers in western capitalist societies. For instance, it is well known that during Stalin's first five-year plan, workers actively moved from one workplace to another, regardless of what the central government wanted. Donald Filtzer demonstrated that during Stalin's rule, even under the period of most severe controls on the working class, stretching from the first economic plan to the postwar 'reconstruction' period, workers could still move between jobs with ease, with the obvious exception of those in the gulags. This was because in the Soviet Union the labour shortage was more important than the law.[7] Once capital accumulation on a massive scale was under way, the ban on labour migration had no real effect, even before the internal passport system was abolished in the 1950s. The similarity with Western workers could also be observed in the differentiation of wages. According to Filtzer, in the Soviet labour system, wages were differentiated in accordance with the importance of the industry, region, skill, age and gender in a similar way to wages in western capitalist countries.[8]

In contrast, the lives of workers in Mao's China have been understood as unusual even among the 'actually existing socialist' states. Many scholars have argued that unlike in the Soviet Union, Chinese workers had almost no mobility at all. A popular account of China's economic history by Barry Naughton repeats this claim by sampling only one year (1978).[9] He also claims that even though there were eight classes of wages during this period, this wage differentiation failed to incentivise Chinese workers. In other words, the wages

---

6   Nigel Harris 2016, p. 135.
7   Filtzer 2002a, p. 165; Filtzer 2002b, Part I, Chapter 3.
8   Filtzer 2002b, pp. 234–5.
9   Naughton 2007, p. 181.

system failed to function in the same way as it did under 'normal' capitalism. Left-leaning scholars also claim that a type of social contract existed in this period, under which the CCP provided secure employment and good welfare in exchange for workers' loyalty to the party. However, more recent studies have begun to show that essentially, the CCP's labour policy was not all that different from that of the previous Guomindang government.

To put it differently, the labour control mechanisms that limited the commodification of wage workers and were thought to be unique to 'socialist' China – the distribution of labour, the *hukou* and *danwei* systems, wage controls – had already been implemented by the Guomindang government to meet wartime needs. The Guomindang state set an upper limit for wage levels and in 1938 implemented the state purchase of daily necessities, followed by a rationing system in 1942.[10] The nationalists also responded to massive wartime inflation and labour supply instability by forcing all firms to provide welfare to labourers and in return tied the workers to their workplaces. Essentially, the nationalists were ordering companies to become a complete community, or rather, a 'unit' (*danwei*). In fact, there are some scholars who claim that the term *danwei* itself was first used by the Guomindang before the CCP introduced it.[11] The Guomindang also continuously strengthened restrictions on the movement of labour, ultimately forbidding workers to move from one workplace to another, a policy that was later followed by the CCP.[12] The Guomindang even made it impossible for companies to fire workers. As such, when it came to the movement of labour, state regulation became more important than the market. As one US embassy observer noted, the political purpose of all this was to prevent solidarity between factories and forestall the influence of 'outside agitators' by fragmenting and isolating the working class in individual factories.[13] The Communist party merely rolled this out to the whole nation. This was not a phenomenon unique to China but rather, a common feature at the time of the Second World War, whereby capital sought to control workers through what Chris Harman termed 'partial decommodification'. Unlike Harman, who sought to connect this phenomenon to total war and the international competition for capital accumulation, the authors cited above sought to outline the continuity between the Guomindang and the CCP without explaining why this happened in the way it did. Consistent with Harman's point regarding 'partial decommodification', this chapter seeks to explain how the

10   Howard 2004, pp. 230–1.
11   Bian 2005, pp. 158–9.
12   Frazier 2002, p. 63.
13   Frazier 2002, p. 66.

formation of free wage labourers took place during the Maoist period through the dynamics of capital accumulation.

This chapter will examine the history of Chinese workers under the early years of Mao's rule through two discrete periods. First, the period from the civil war to the end of the First Five-Year Plan in 1957; and second, the Great Leap Forward (1958–60). In two further sections I will consider separately two of the most important questions related to capital and labour under state capitalism: primitive accumulation and geopolitical pressures as the mechanism of competitive capital accumulation. My periodisation coincides with the usual political periodisation of the early Maoist regime. This is due to the fact that in societies where investment is determined by bureaucratic commands, the cycle of capital accumulation is closely correlated with the political cycle. During the whole of this period the Chinese working class was undergoing a process of becoming free wage labourers. This process of proletarianisation took place according to the needs of the command economy and contradictory state interventions aimed to control, facilitate and sometimes reverse the process. However, there are clearly fundamental connections between competitive capital accumulation and free wage labour. This will be made clearer if one expands the scope of analysis of class formation from the narrow confines of 1949–60 to include the whole period from the start of the twentieth century up to the early twenty-first century, a point that will be addressed in the conclusion of this chapter.

2   The Chinese Working Class from the Civil War to 1957

2.1   *The Background: What Kind of Revolution Was 1949?*
In the mid-1920s there was the possibility of a real working class-led revolution succeeding in China. Of course, this position is rather different to the general line of interpretation popular among contemporary Sinologists, who insist on the heterogeneity of the Chinese working class at that time, and hence the impossibility of a successful workers' revolution:

> In the 1920s, when Communists first tried to organize coal miners and silk workers, they made little headway. These wage earners spoke different dialects, had been recruited in their native villages by different foremen or gangsters, and had different levels of skill and professional status. They simply did not see themselves as members of the same class. Even if, in Marxist terms, the Chinese working class had come to exist as a class in itself, it was far from becoming a class for itself. The Chinese Communist

Party (CCP) was a vanguard without working-class followers. After coming to power in 1949 through a peasant revolution, in which 'the villages laid siege to the cities', the CCP had to call a proletariat into being.[14]

That such a claim is touted without much scruple in a left-wing publication reveals how simplistic the understanding of the Chinese revolution in the 1920s among leftists actually is. If we examine the records of the Communists, the Comintern, the Guomindang, and bourgeois organisations from the period 1925–7, we can see that quite the opposite was actually true. The Chinese communist party and Comintern were startled by the Chinese workers' full-scale class struggle, independent of the Communist-Guomindang united front, and did their best to calm them down. This position was a result of the class-collaboration line enforced by the Comintern at that time.[15] The resulting defeat of the working-class movement in the 1920s had profound effects for the trajectory of the Chinese communist party as well as the revolution itself. The reaction and right-wing terror arising from the defeat of 1927 provided the impetus for the militarisation and bureaucratisation of the organisation, and during the period of anti-Japanese struggle and civil war, Stalinist ideology was firmly implanted in the Chinese communist movement.

As Michal Reiman argued, the transition from the Russian Revolution to the Stalinist programme of military-industrial nation-building was not something planned in advance, but rather an ad hoc process led by Stalin and the new Soviet bureaucracy in response to the aftermath of the civil war, the destruction of the working class, and various national and international contingencies in the late 1920s, including war fever and a lack of resources for investment.[16] In China however, Stalinist state-building was precisely the goal of the 1949 revolution from the start. Contrary to Slavoj Žižek[17] the departure from a worker-centred outlook entailed not merely an ideological shift but a qualitative transformation. When workers' struggle revived in 1945, the Chinese communist party sought to make use of it as part of its anti-Guomindang front, but it was consigned to a passive supporting role. Once the goal of defeating the nationalists had been accomplished, working class militancy was consciously suppressed by the party. As we will see, during the 1950s the CCP continued to put great efforts into taming a working-class movement that had been developing outside its control since the 1920s.

---

14   Hurst 2015.
15   See: Isaacs 2010, chapter 4; Chŏn I. 2002, part 4; Li D. 2016, chapter 2; Chan 2002.
16   Reiman 1987, chapter 9.
17   Žižek 2007, pp. 4–5.

While the Chinese working class played no significant role in the Chinese Revolution of 1949, it was still a transformative event that brought huge developments in China's transition to capitalism. From 1949 until the end of the first five-year plan in 1957, CCP officials succeeded in accumulating more industrial capital than Chinese bureaucrats and private business had managed in their pursuit of 'modernisation' during the whole of the previous century. But the experience of the working class was more complex. On the one hand, Chinese workers must have welcomed the prospect of stability and job-creation after a long period of war; on the other hand, in the process of capital accumulation they were made dependent on the regime as never before.

In the process of working-class formation, there were, broadly speaking, three conspicuous developments, all of which aimed at acclimatising the working class to the new regime of capital accumulation: the neutralisation of working-class militancy; the establishment of a differentiated wage system; and the flexibilisation of the workforce.

2.2 *Neutralising Working-Class Militancy*

First, the CCP sought to neutralise working-class militancy. Inspired by the CCP coming to power, Chinese workers turned to struggle, but this was completely contrary to the wishes of the communists. As labour minister Li Lisan lamented: 'Why are there so many labour disputes? ... Why are the workers unable to recognise their own overriding interest? ... The working class are making excessive demands. They seem to think there is no other way than to resort to the old methods of carrying out strikes and encircling factories and owners'. Such was the view of the so-called father of the Chinese labour movement, a man who was eventually purged for being too much on the side of the working class.[18] Other central party bureaucrats were more severe, noting that the 'current labour disputes had brought a state of anarchy ... the main cause of which is leftist deviations. As a result, the capitalists are being persecuted'.[19]

The communist party respected the interests of capitalists not so much because they still believed in a stageist conception of revolution but because

---

18   Li Lisan, 'Zai quanguo laodong juzhang huiyi shang guanyu laozi guanxi wenti de baogao' 李立三：在全国劳动局长会议上关于劳资关系问题的报告 [Li Lisan, A report on labor relations at the National Labor Directors Conference], 13 March 1950 in Zhongguo shehui kexueyuan he zhongyang dang'an guan 1994, pp. 118–19. Concerning his dismissal, see Wang L. 2013, p. 139.

19   Shanghai shi laodong ju: Yi nianlai teshu anjian de zongjie 上海市劳动局：一年来特殊案件的总结 [Shanghai Labor Bureau: Summary of special cases in the past year], 22 June 1950, in Zhongguo shehui kexueyuan he zhongyang dang'an guan 1994, p. 141.

as the rulers of a modern state they needed to stabilise industrial relations in the private sector in order to maximise production. Accordingly, when the CCP criticised the capitalists, they did not do so in the interests of the working class. For instance, in the second quarter of 1951, a Labour Ministry report censured the working class immediately after their criticism of capitalists: 'The workers are causing great concern among capitalists by demanding improvements in their welfare and conditions without mentioning production at all'.[20] An article in *Renmin Ribao* (People's Daily) of 7 July 1951 considered the three phases of labour relations during the New Democracy period after liberation, and while it criticised the workers it also judged that it had done a good job of taming their militancy:

> During the first phase, from the liberation up to early 1950, because the workers had an inaccurate understanding of the concept of ownership they made excessive demands for welfare, violated labour regulations and chose to engage in methods of struggle such as strikes against the capitalists ... This created a chaotic and abnormal situation. However, the people's government and the labour unions were able to educate the workers and the capitalists, and the situation improved. During the second phase, from March to June 1950, many workers were laid off due to problems in industry and commerce during that period and demanded their jobs back while others demanded wage increases ... The situation was well mediated and there were few strikes. In the third phase, from July 1950 onward, the number of strikes declined markedly.[21]

However, this optimism turned out to be misplaced. In 1952, at the time of the 'Five-anti Campaign',[22] the workers saw the bureaucrats criticising the private capitalists and once again entered into a large-scale struggle. Dur-

---

20   Zhongyang renmin zhengfu laodong bu 1951 nian di er jidu gongzuo qingkuang zonghe baogao 中央人民政府劳动部 1951 年第二季度工作情况综合报告, [A comprehensive report on the work of the Ministry of Labor of the Central People's Government in the second quarter of 1951], in Zhongguo shehui kexueyuan he zhongyang dang'an guan 1994, p. 82.

21   *Renmin ribao*: 'Xin minzhu zhuyi laozi guanxi de jianli he muqian cunzai de wenti' 人民 日报：新民主主义劳资关系的建立和目前存在的问题 [People's Daily: The establishment of a new-democratic labor-management relation and its problems], 11 July 1951, in Zhongguo shehui kexueyuan he zhongyang dang'an guan 1994, p. 181.

22   The 'Five-anti Campaign' was launched in January 1952. The five antis were bribery, theft of state property, tax evasion, cheating on government contracts, and stealing state economic intelligence.

ing that period one incident in particular caught the attention of the highest level of the Chinese bureaucracy.

> Amidst the 'Five-anti Campaign' certain abnormal phenomena arose ... The workers snatched the administration of the factory from the company president and then set up a 'democratic management committee'. This sort of behaviour is not good ... The 'democratic management committee' must be dissolved and the problems between workers and capitalists must be resolved through the establishment of worker-management negotiations.[23]

These were the words of premier Zhou Enlai. His comment suggests that this problem was not confined to a single enterprise. Two weeks later, the party committee of the ACFTU remarked that 'the current demands of the workers are excessive', particularly in relation to their interference in management: 'the workers do not take orders from the capitalists, and the capitalists dare not issue any'. Among the bureaucracy the fear that workers may refuse orders from the capitalists and attempt to seize control of the means of production held by private capitalists had been aroused from the very early days of the PRC government. The central officials were astonished, for instance, when the workers sought to emulate the principles of land reform within the setting of the urban factories. A 22 June 1950 report from the Shanghai labour office, for example, discusses how 'the emerging struggle in urban settings is mechanically modelled on the struggle against the feudal landowners'.[24]

The party sought to downplay this problem as farmers with land reform experience coming to the cities and making trouble. However, we can confirm that this was a bigger problem than indicated by a few short records by observing the indirect evidence that slogans of workers' control were raised as a military strategy during the Civil War but were then rejected. It was in fact Li Lisan who was deeply critical of the move to use workers' control slogans

---

23   'Zhou Enlai: Guanyu wu fan zhong chuli waishang chang dian laozi guanxi deng wenti de zhishi' 周恩来：关于五反中处理外商厂店劳资关系等问题的指示, [Zhou Enlai: Instructions on the handling of labour relations in foreign-owned factories and shops in the Five-anti campaigns], 10 May 1952, in Zhongguo shehui kexueyuan he zhongyang dang'an guan 1994, p. 86.

24   Shanghai shi laodong ju: 'Yi nianlai teshu anjian de zongjie' 上海市劳动局：一年来特殊案件的总结，[Shanghai Municipal Labor Bureau: This year's summary of special cases], 22 June 1950 in Zhongguo shehui kexueyuan he zhongyang dang'an guan 1994, p. 140.

in order to reinforce the anti-Guomindang struggle among the workers.[25] It was also reported at the time that the People's Liberation Army had already intervened in several factories to forcibly put a stop to workers' control.[26] This was another moment at which the authoritarian nature of the CCP's 'mass line' was fully revealed. According to Donny Gluckstein, this is what distinguished the labour movement that arose after the First World War from that which arose after the Second. Whereas in the aftermath of the First World War, the communist parties encouraged workers' self-management, after the Second World War, the now Stalinised communist parties everywhere were hostile to worker militancy and sought to absorb workers and their organisations into the bureaucratic party machine.[27] There was nothing unique about the Chinese Communist Party's Mass Line. As the party became hostile to workers' self-management, there was no chance for 'popular organisations' under democratic control such as labour unions or labour councils to be constructed. The All-China Federation of Trade Unions (ACFTU) was revived in 1949 but it was first and foremost a state-controlled organ to encourage increases in production and talk of workers being the masters of the factories was simply rhetoric. Li Huayin, who conducted oral interviews with the workers from the Maoist period, summarised their assessment of the popular organisations as follows:

> Both the trade unions and the workers' congress, the two major venues for workers to participate in management, were subject to the control of the factory leader and party secretary, and their functions were limited to handling issues pertaining to workers' welfare benefits rather than their rights in the workplaces; in other words, there was no institutionalized channel whereby workers could develop a real sense of being the master of state firms or strong loyalty to them.[28]

2.3   *The Wage System under Early Maoism*

Secondly, the Chinese Communist Party condemned the progress achieved in wages and working conditions during the Second Sino-Japanese War (1937–45) and the Civil War as 'feudalistic remnants' or 'equalism' and introduced instead a wage system most conducive for capital accumulation. As such, if you look at the 'Resolution on the Wage Problem' adopted at the Sixth National Workers'

25   Li S. 2009, p. 53.
26   Frazier 2002, p. 98.
27   See Gluckstein 2012, p. 96 and Conclusion.
28   Li H. 2016, p. 397.

Congress in 1948, there is an interesting passage that condemns 'the corrupt Guomindang bureaucratic wage system'. The CCP criticised the Guomindang wage system not so much for its exploitative nature as for its being unconducive to the development of heavy industry.

> During the Guomindang period wages were higher in light industry than in heavy industry, and postal and telegram businesses paid better than the railway or shipping industry ... Higher wages in light industry is an expression of the essence of the Guomindang's bureaucratic comprador capitalism, and violates the policy of new democratic Chinese economic construction ... Guomindang denigrated heavy industry and sought to encourage light capitalism as a way to make a quick return on initial investment.[29]

From the perspective of the CCP, the really unforgivable crime committed by the Guomindang was its 'equalism'. Thus the biggest wrong committed by the private enterprise wage system was not so much the exploitation as its 'equalism that reversed the importance of light and heavy industry'. 'In the current wage system private enterprises are one of the main problems ... their wage differentiation is too small'.[30] The CCP's issue with the low level of wage differentiation was two-fold: one was that low wages failed to attract skilled workers into heavy industry, where in some instances light industry actually paid higher wages; the second was the failure to implement a graduated wage system, thereby removing the incentive to increase productivity. In other words, the CCP wished to implement a wage system that was in line with the passage on free wage labour from Marx quoted above; a system that would encourage enthusiasm for labour, unlike the previous inadequate Guomindang system. In fact, there was nothing 'feudalistic' about the lack of wage differentiation under the Guomindang regime, which originated instead from wartime inflation and the subsequent reaction from the working class. At the same time, more equal pay and better working conditions were the fundamental things that labour unions and workers had struggled for. At that time many Chinese workers

---

29   Gongzi tiaoli shuomingshu (chugao) di yi zhang: Muqian qingkuang 工资条例说明
     书（初稿）第一章：目前情况, [Regulations on salary (first draft) the first chapter: the
     current situation], 12 August 1950 in Zhongguo shehui kexueyuan he zhongyang dang'an
     guan 1994, p. 465.

30   Zhonggong zhongyang guanyu gongzi wenti fu beiping shiwei dian 中共中央关于工资
     问题复北平市委电, [The Central Committee of the Communist Party of China on the
     issue of wages in Fubeiping City], 20th January 1949 in Zhongguo shehui kexueyuan he
     zhongyang dang'an guan 1994, p. 462.

saw the lessening of wage differentiation in the late Guomindang period as something they had accomplished on their own. They found it impossible to understand why the Communist Party – supposedly a workers' party – wanted to reverse those gains and create new cleavages within the working class. As one worker commented, 'the differences were never this great under Guomindang. It wasn't as if some [workers then] ate meat, while the others ate soup'.[31] In 1953 a similar issue was raised in Tianjin, as Jeremy Brown recounts: '"Since we are all members of the working class", some party members said, "might two different ration levels affect the unity of the working class?"'[32]

As a result of the CCP's forceful push for wage reforms, during the period 1950–6 wage differentiation within the working class widened significantly. In August 1951, the 8-level graduated wage system was introduced, and the 'hidden wage' persisting since the Guomindang period was eliminated, resulting in the conversion of housing rent and utilities charges to wage deductibles in accordance with the given wage class.[33]

The wage gap between the managerial and working class also widened.[34] Correlations between wages and geographical areas or industrial productivity growth also began to emerge.[35] In addition, differences in the enterprise ownership system gave rise to wage differentiation. Workers under the collective ownership system[36] always made up a significant proportion of the total during the Mao years, comprising 26.5 percent of the total in 1957, 30–33 percent in 1960 and 27–30 percent in 1970. In the case of Wuhan, workers at state-owned enterprises did not have to pay medical fees at all, while workers at collectively owned workplaces only had 50–80 percent of their fees paid for them. There were also cases where workers at collectively-owned enterprises had to fulfil a certain quota before they would be paid their wage.[37] Li Huaiyin quotes one worker as saying: 'we were a large state enterprise with good benefits and high wages ... so it was easy to find a marriage partner'.[38]

As a result, workers employed at state enterprise firms located in the big cities with newer facilities enjoyed relatively higher wages compared to other sectors. One's political position and activity as a worker was also, in a broad sense,

---

31   Howard 2004, p. 342.
32   Brown 2012, p. 35.
33   Howard 2004, p. 343.
34   Zhang J. 2011, p. 172.
35   Howe 1973, p. 65.
36   Collective owned enterprises in China were distinguished from state-owned enterprises in that they were controlled by local governments.
37   Li H. 2016, p. 390.
38   Li H. 2016, p. 392.

connected to one's wage level. In order to be promoted, one had to work hard and the promotion entailed a higher wage. There were various paths to promotion for these workers: being invited to join the CCP or the party youth organisation; being a 'leading' worker or a model worker; being given the opportunity to enter university; or being promoted as a section leader. Such provisions allowed many workers to rise up the ranks and also fostered the perception of the early Mao period as a 'golden age' for many.

The key determinant of wage levels for the CCP was not its struggle against feudalism or 'equalism' but the ratio between wages and capital accumulation, although those struggles could be deployed rhetorically as a means of boosting capital accumulation. However, throughout the Mao period it was never questioned that the sum-total of wages had to be subordinate to capital accumulation. This dramatically reveals how the aim of the new labour regime created by the CCP was to fix the direct producers as exploited wage labourers, thus periodically leading to heightened conflict and contradictions between the party and the working class. The area where this tension was brought most sharply to a head was in the private sector, where the level of workers' struggle was relatively high. And of course, it was Li Lisan who was first to express his criticism of the workers. On 1 May 1949, citing the 'excessive demands' of the working class, Li argued that 'if private firms spent all their gains on improving the living conditions of the working class, how could they accumulate capital and expand industrial capacity? ... Some portion of it ought to be preserved as profit so as to inspire them to re-invest'.[39]

Such an idea enjoyed widespread currency among the bureaucratic class across the nation; one report from Tianjin branch of the ACFTU in 1952 strongly attacked some workers for demanding 'profit-sharing' with private capitalists as an 'irrational and feudal system left over from the old society'.[40] Such demands from Chinese workers were labelled 'economism' and it was argued that the central problem was that these demands would eliminate 'the capitalists' appetite for investment by disrupting commercial capital accumulation'. A government report from 1951 bears witness to the party officials' widespread perception that urban workers were 'backward' and '[lacked] revolu-

---

39   Li S. 2009, p. 109.
40   Tianjin shi zong gonghui: Siying shangye yingye, gongzi, gongshi, fuli qingkuang diaocha
      baogao 天津市总工会：私营商业营业，工资，工时，福利情况调查报告,
      [Tianjin Federation of Trade Unions: wages, working hours, and welfare in private com-
      mercial business: a survey report], 3 October 1952 in Zhongguo shehui kexueyuan he
      zhongyang dang'an guan 1994, p. 585.

tionary consciousness'.[41] This, they contended, was a consequence of their 'economistic mentality'. Even while CCP bureaucrats labelled the workers the leading class, they continued to hold them in contempt when they demanded their share. In 1957, for example, party officials in Shanghai lambasted the '"extremely strong economism among workers" and argued that a "narrow economistic tendency was the principal issue in the labour movement in Shanghai"'.[42] Thus, long before the term economism gained notoriety during the Cultural Revolution, it was already frequently used as the antithesis of capital accumulation.

The Communist Party unambiguously declared their 'long-term interest' or 'national interest' more important than Chinese workers' 'private interest' or 'short-term interest'. The gap between the two was to be determined by the rate of accumulation. But how exactly to express or justify the gap between accumulation and wages was a constant source of disagreement among the Chinese bureaucracy. One of the disagreements focused on how to interpret the meaning of the wage system under the new regime. Li Lisan maintained that workers in the new China were still wage labourers, although the antagonistic character of the wage system had now disappeared. However, Li Fuchun, representing the national planning committee, believed that even using the term 'wages' was unsatisfactory, since the word continued to imply exploitation, even if the level of exploitation was lessened.[43]

From the bureaucratic perspective, the total purchasing power of the working class had to be fixed at a level that would not impede capital accumulation, which at the time was quite low. The problems were aggravated by so much capital being concentrated in heavy industry, leading to very low levels of productivity and overall production in light industry and agriculture. For instance, at end of the First Five-year Plan (1953–7) the Chinese premier Zhou Enlai had to release the state's reserve goods so as to meet demand created by the increased purchasing power of the working class. In the final stages of the First Five-year Plan at the end of 1956, the central party bureaucrats were beginning to discuss the idea of a 'rational low-wage system' as a desperate measure to tackle this problem. The aim of this policy was to lower the total wage of Chinese workers in order to satisfy the contradictory goals of increasing the labour productivity of workers in a backward country while at the same time focusing on accumulating capital in heavy industry. In other words, the aim was

---

41   Chen F. 2014, p. 508.
42   Chen F. 2014, p. 508.
43   Gao A. 2008, pp. 50–1; Li S. 2009, p. 206.

to reduce the total wage bill as far as possible without sacrificing the capital-ist wage system. Reading the articles written in support of this policy we can see the extent to which the central bureaucrats were vexed by their attempts to resolve this intractable problem.

The author of one such article (Song Ping) argued that the set wage will merely be a nominal figure rather than reflecting real purchasing power: 'If an increase in wages does not have the guarantee of the production of con-sumer goods, then it will only be a nominal, not a real wage increase ...'. But he nonetheless maintained that because China is a backward country its real pur-chasing power would have to be limited: 'because of the backward state of our economy, our very poor foundations and our excessive population, the value of the consumer goods actually available for consumption by the people only increased by about 4 *yuan* per head per annum ... all we can do is to implement a rational, low wage system'.[44]

Frankly acknowledging the negative relationship between consumption and capital accumulation, Song argued the wage level and its rise have to be subor-dinate to capital accumulation:

> [W]e are at present faced with the immense and formidable tasks of con-struction ... Construction requires capital and we can only depend upon our domestic accumulation for this capital. Consequently we must eco-nomize on consumption and resolutely uphold the policy of building the country through hard work and thrift ... this concept of the wage level having to correspond to the level of production by no means implies that by however much production increases, wages must be increased accordingly. Because, if this were the case it would affect national capital accumulation ... In the future wages must still be increased in line with the development of production, but, when we compare the two, the wage increase will be smaller and slower than the increase in production.[45]

Without actually using the word 'exploitation' this describes precisely the func-tioning of exploitation. As the expression 'we can only depend upon our do-mestic accumulation for this capital' shows, the CCP's strategy of capital accu-mulation was to scrape up as much domestic capital as possible by establishing antagonistic relations of exploitation domestically in order to triumph in its inter-state competition internationally. The party and its bureaucratic machine

---

44   Howe 2016, p. 337.
45   Howe 2016, pp. 338–9.

were built atop this goal and formed special interests in line with this. Despite the chaos and ceaseless conflicts among bureaucrats during the Mao period, the bureaucratic class as a whole never failed to maintain this exploitative stance. Barry Naughton describes the situation thus:

> Even during the 1950s, industrial workers had created a 'surplus' (total profit and tax) for the state greater than their own wage. But, during the 1960s, the surplus created by each worker climbed to a much higher level and in 1965 surpassed four times the value of his total wage for the first time. In that year, state-owned industry produced a total profit and tax of 30.92 billion yuan – virtually all of which was turned over to the government – or slightly over 2,500 yuan per worker. By comparison, the annual industrial worker wage in that year was 633 yuan. Through 1978, state-owned industry more than doubled in size, and more than doubled its labor force, but the basic financial relationship remained unchanged. In 1978, each state industrial worker created total profit and tax of just over 2,500 yuan, and the average industrial wage was 631 yuan. Throughout this period, the typical state-owned enterprise (SOE) was generating a surplus for the government equal to about four times what it paid to the enterprise workers.[46]

Of course, one may argue that this is merely surplus and not 'surplus value'.[47] Before one determines whether this amounts to capitalist exploitation or not, the suggestion that the state 'furnished welfare' or that 'state-enterprise workers enjoyed socialist privileges', often shared by leftist scholars of China, effectively accepts uncritically the propaganda of the Chinese bureaucracy that attempted to hide the underlying exploitative relations. All Chinese workers, including workers at state enterprises, received less in total wages than the total wealth they created. The Chinese wage system therefore reflected this exploitative relationship.

2.4   Establishing Discipline and Flexibility

Thirdly, between 1949 and 1957, another characteristic of the CCP's central labour policy was the pursuit of flexibility in the allocation of labour, based on strict central control. On the one hand, the party wanted to discipline labour, and on the other hand to expand labour productivity, reduce the 'surplus work-

---

46   Naughton 1997, p. 174.
47   This problem will be addressed further below.

force', and at the same time increase the flexibility of employment. Centralised allocation was emphasised because the central bureaucracy had to allocate resources and labour according to their investment priorities. But this did not mean that the CCP was simply eliminating the previously existing labour market.

First, as pointed out earlier with regard to the continuity between Guomindang and CCP regimes, there was never a textbook labour market in China prior to 1949. Like other less advanced countries setting out on the path of industrialisation and suffering a shortage of both skilled and unskilled labour, there existed in China a wide range of non-market means to employ and retain workers. Furthermore, even in the railway sector – a high-tech sector that had been built by foreign capital – it was difficult to buy sufficient labour power in the labour market and as a result a variety of non-market employment systems functioned, including indentured labour (*baogongzhi*) and apprenticeship systems (*xuetuzhi*). Under these various systems restrictions were placed on the movement of workers from one workplace to another.[48]

Given the retardation of the development of the Chinese labour force, with the rate of illiteracy at over 90 percent, the skilled and educated labour force had to be carefully identified and allocated. Another reason why labour had to be centrally allocated was due to the concern that competition in hiring might be harmful to the prioritisation of heavy industry and the nationalised sector, or that it would bring about a rise in the total wage bill. If enterprises and work units (*danwei*) had to compete for the same limited labour force, then that would 'create havoc for the average wages as [firms] would have to improve offers on wages and benefits'.[49] On the other hand, in order for Chinese industry to reach the level of the more advanced competitors, China would have to employ advanced technology and machinery so as to improve productivity. In other words, the central bureaucracy understood that it would have to produce more with less labour. However, as less workers were required to do the same work, this necessarily entailed the creation of a 'surplus workforce', thus requiring that workers either be allocated to new production processes or new places found for them. Due to the dynamics of capital accumulation, as China geared towards long-term industrialisation, the process of production was in constant need of tweaking. Thus the meaning of 'permanent' or 'fixed' (*gudinggong*) labour was relative. The central bureaucrats sought to bring the relationship between wage labourers and capital accumulation under their strict super-

---

48   Sun Z. 2013, pp. 39–42. For the case of Shanghai before 1949, see Chŏn I. 2002, p. 150.
49   Howe 1973, p. 57.

vision. This system of labour control instituted by the CCP bureaucracy was completely different both in motivation and dynamics to the prohibitions on movement found under feudalism and slavery. Defining the Mao period as a sort of 'state feudalism', as some scholars do,[50] is therefore highly problematic, especially when you consider that the Chinese bureaucracy also pursued labour flexibility. Prior to the Great Leap Forward, the bureaucracy struggled to meet its contradictory demands for both fixity and flexibility in labour supply.

It was only in the mid-1950s that the central government implemented a universal system of labour allocation across the board; prior to that the Chinese 'labour market' had been very fluid. In the case of private enterprises a report by the labour dispute resolution agency under the Ministry of Labour noted that 'the free movement of private enterprise workers ... must be suppressed effectively',[51] which leads us to suspect that movement between jobs was relatively unconstrained. Nor does it seem that this phenomenon was restricted to the private sector. A report from 1952 criticises that 'Not only is labour allocation highly irrational under the current situation but flows of labour are governed by the spontaneous capitalistic regulation, with a great deal of movement between factories and workplaces'.[52] Similarly, it was common for workers to refuse the workplace allocated to them under the centralised allocation system. Newly employed young workers were criticised for easily switching jobs and thus ignoring the central plan. The most extreme case was reported in Wuhan, where 34 steel workers moved 5,000 kilometres in search of easier jobs.[53]

On 5 August 1953, which marked the start of the First Five-year Plan, a joint report from the Labour Ministry, Interior Ministry and the Central Employment Commission continued to point out the limitations of the centralised labour allocation system: 'to secure the workforce necessary for industrial development, universal labour allocation has to be pursued in stages ... However, in the current circumstances it is premature to allocate universally, and pub-

---

50   Gabriel, Resnick & Wolff 2011.

51   Laodong bu laodong zhengyi chuli si: 1954 Nian shang ban niandu laodong zhengyi tiao-chu gongzuo de qingkuang he women de yijian 劳动部劳动争议处理司：1954 年上半年度劳动争议调处工作的情况和我们的意见, [Ministry of Labour, labour dispute resolution agency: The situation of labour dispute mediation in the first half of 1954 and our opinion], September 1954 in Zhongguo shehui kexuewon he zhongyang dangan guan 1998a, p. 303.

52   Laodong bu dangzu: Guanyu laodongli diaopei gongzuo de chubu yijian 劳动部党组：关于劳动力调配工作的初步意见 [The party committee in the Ministry of Labour: Preliminary Opinions on Labour Redeployment], 11th December 1952, in Zhongguo shehui kexuewon he zhongyang dangan guan 1994, p. 267.

53   Gipouloux 1986, p. 86.

lic/private firms and institutions ought to place restrictions on their hiring of manpower and focus on narrowing the path to individual employment'.[54] All that the central government could achieve under these trying circumstances was to secure as far as possible the workforce it needed for its priorities in the heavy industry and national defence sectors.

A report by the northeast labour bureau claimed that 'national defence, heavy industrial production, and infrastructure construction are the primary objectives of labour force allocation', and argued that not prioritising labour allocation in these sectors is 'a form of equalist thought that refuses to distinguish between what is most important and what is of secondary importance'.[55] However, even during the First Five-year Plan, when this system was in the midst of being implemented, there were still limitations on the extent to which the universal allocation system could suppress the unauthorised movement of labour even at state enterprises. This was because the bureaucratic system built by the CCP was a competitive system in which individual units were assigned production-related quotas.

For example, according to a report of the Guangdong People's Committee in December 1956, '[Enterprises] are not going through the Labour Ministry but instead directly hiring the peasants who are flowing into the city. Some work units (*danwei*) are even recruiting workers from the villages by sending out managers or using recruiters'.[56] The March 1957 issue of *Laodong tongxun* also claimed that, 'In Zhangjiakou 29 factory, mine and construction work units have privately recruited some 2,850 workers and the city bureau of construction even posted a sign outside its second factory site reading "you can register directly today"'.[57] Recruitment by individual enterprises became such a serious

54   Zhongyang laodong jiuye wciyuanhui, neiwu bu, laodong bu guanyu laodong jiuye gong-zuo de baogao 中央劳动就业委员会，内务部，劳动部关于劳动就业工作的报告 [Labour Ministry, Interior Ministry and Central Employment Commission joint report on labour and employment], 5th August 1953, in Zhongguo shehui kexuewon he zhongyang dangan guan 1998a, p. 5.

55   Dongbei xingzheng weiyuanhui laodong ju: Dongbeiqu 东北行政委员会劳动局：东北区劳动力统一调配工作总结 [The northeast labour bureau: Summary of unified labor distribution work in Northeast China], 14 August 1953, in *Zhongguo shehui kexuewon he zhongyang dangan guan* 1998a, p. 269.

56   Guangxi xing renmin weiyuanhui: Guanyu tuoshan chuli nongmin mangmu liuru chengshi de zhishi 广西省人民委员会：关于妥善处理农民盲目流入城市的指示 [Guangdong People's Committee: Instructions for properly handling farmers' blind inflows into cities], May 1957, in Zhongguo shehui kexuewon he zhongyang dangan guan 1998a, p. 350.

57   Laodong tongxun zonghe baodao: Nongmín mangmu liuru chengshi de xianxiang fei-chang yanzhong 劳动通讯 综合报道：农民盲目流入城市的现象非常严重

problem that in 1957 the PRC State Council had to promulgate a 'notice relating to prohibition of the reckless recruitment of labourers and employees and the effective regulation of workforce increases by enterprises and work units'.[58] The central government understood the severity of this problem and carried out a survey of the labour recruitment situation in the regions, discovering many interesting facts in the process. Principally they discovered that the local managers were the at the root of this problem through their efforts to attract workers to their own factories with promises of higher wages and positions as permanent workers.

According to a joint report of the Labour Ministry and Ministry of Supervision dated 2 July 1957, the results of a survey of 12 provinces, including Jiangsu, Beijing, Anhui, Liaoning, Gansu and Qinghai, showed that 66,340 people had been employed directly by work units without the permission of central government. The majority of them were temporary workers but 534 people were employed from the start on a 'long-term' basis and around 1,500 people had been converted from temporary workers to permanent workers, showing that workers could be given additional economic rewards, according to their skill level or technique.[59]

Some firms went so far as to visit rural areas to recruit with the promise of higher wages. Even those with a minimal level of skills were highly valued, so much so that in Huangshi city, Hubei Province, four agricultural cooperatives filled all of their important staff positions that way, including accountants.[60] The central government was highly critical of this practice and periodically ordered city authorities to send migrants in search of work back to their hometowns. As a result, the city of Tianjin sent 100,000 people in search of jobs

---

[Laodong Tonxun: Peasants blindly flowing into cities is a very serious phenomenon], March 1957 in Zhongguo shehui kexuewon he zhongyang dangan guan 1998a, p. 353.

58   Guowuyuan guanyu youxiao de kongzhi qiye, shiye danwei renyuan zengjia, zhizhi mangmu zhaoshou gongren he zhiyuan de xianxiang de tongzhi 国务院关于有效地控制企业，事业单位人员增加，制止盲目招收工人和职员的现象的通知 [State Council notice relating to the prohibition of the reckless recruitment of labourers and employees and the effective regulation of workforce increases by enterprises and work units], 1957, in Zhongguo shehui kexuewon he zhongyang dangan guan 1998a, p. 169.

59   Jiancha bu, laodong bu guanyu muqian qiye, shiye, jiguan sizi zhaoshou renyuan de qingkuang ji chuli yijian xiang guowuyuan de baogao 监察部，劳动部关于目前企业，事业，机关私自招收人员的情况及处理意见向国务院的报告, [The Ministry of Supervision, Ministry of Labour report on the current situation of enterprises, undertakings, and institutions privately recruiting personnel and handling opinions to the State Council], 2nd July 1957, in Zhongguo shehui kexuewon he zhongyang dangan guan 1998a, p. 172.

60   Zhongguo shehui kexuewon he zhongyang dangan guan 1998a, p. 173.

back to rural areas in 1955–6. Interestingly, those already in employment, even if unlicensed, were exempt from the forced deportations.[61] Thus, despite the emphasis on central control of labour, increasing production was always the priority.

While the cases cited up to now show the central government criticising flexibility in the employment system, we cannot ignore the fact that the centre itself consciously pursued labour flexibility, in the broadest sense of hiring and firing, wages, and working conditions. The objective of the central government in its First Five-year Plan was not so much banning layoffs and wage fluctuations as planning them as far as possible. The central authorities, from the founding of the PRC in 1949, included 'layoffs' as part of state labour policy, and they were not only confined to particular groups of workers like temporary labourers. For instance, a commentary in the *Tianjin Daily* dated 1 September 1949 noted that 'the growth and prosperity of national industry and commerce ought to dictate what constitutes legitimate grounds for hiring and firing and the right of companies to do this must be protected ... otherwise the growing cost of supporting surplus labourers will force factories to stop functioning if not close ... and the capitalists will no longer employ people'.[62] As the next quotation shows, even when the central bureaucracy was carrying out its 'increase production and save resources' (*zengchan jieyue*) campaign at state-owned enterprises, labour power was included as a target for savings and savings in labour were openly related to the expansion of funds for accumulation: 'Let's struggle to accumulate in excess of the plan, by achieving savings in the total factory workforce, workers, workshop technicians and metals'.[63]

On 29 December 1955, the PRC State Council insisted that layoffs amount to a 'saving on wages so that infrastructure capital can be accumulated'.[64] The government also emphasised the importance of piece rates (*jijianzhi*) and other forms of wage flexibility. Piece rates became a complex phenomenon, closely related to the problem of dealing with 'surplus manpower'. If workers worked hard because of the piece rate system it also became a way of working out who could be laid off. For example, according to a report by the Northeastern Bureau

---

61   Brown 2012, p. 44.

62   Tianjin ribao duanping: Jianli zhengchang de laozi guanxi, 天津日报短评：建立正常 的劳资关系 [Tianjin Daily: to establish normal labour relations], 1 September 1949, in Zhongguo shehui kexuewon he zhongyang dangan guan 1994, p. 114.

63   Zhongguo shehui kexuewon he zhongyang dangan guan 1994, p. 114.

64   Guoweyuan guanyu guojia jiguan jingjian gongzuo de zhishi 国务院关于国家机关 精简工作的指示 [The State Council's instructions on the layoffs [jingjian] in state organs], 29 December 1955, in Zhongguo shehui kexuewon he zhongyang dangan guan 1998a, pp. 180–1.

of the CCP, dated 14 February, 1951, in a situation where labour productivity had been raised by the introduction of the piece rate system, a surplus of employees would arise who should be disposed of in a timely fashion.[65] Likewise, a report from the Labour Ministry, entitled 'The current situation of piece-rate wages at state enterprises nationally', noted that after the piece-rate system was introduced at Mine No. 13 in Ankang, Shaanxi Province, the workers were reorganised and their numbers could be reduced from 128 to 76.[66]

The CCP bureaucracy took particular care to implement employment flexibility at heavy industrial plants where the latest machinery was installed. It was at these core workplaces that they strove to eliminate 'surplus labour' as far as possible. For instance, the Fushun Aluminium Plant, built by Soviet technicians and operated with Soviet machinery, had an actual workforce of 6,000, although its target workforce was only 1,700. The central planning authorities quickly issued a corrective order that the plant begin a campaign to improve its productivity per capita, which by 1956 had eliminated 2,742 workers and increased productivity by 23.5 percent above the planned target. This was considered such a significant example that it drew a comment from Li Fuchun, who at that time was vice premier of the State Council and head of the State Planning Commission. Directing his remarks specifically at those factories with Soviet machinery, he ordered that 'you must struggle to reduce the actual number of workers to a level below the planned number'.[67] Another case of layoffs at a major industrial site was the Shijingshan Iron and Steel Works in Beijing,

---

65 Dongbei ji guanyu zai dongbei gongying jinyezhong shixing jijian gongzi zhidu gei zhonggong zhongyang de qingshi baogao 东北局关于在东北公营金业中实行计件工资制度给中共中央的请示报 [The Northeast Bureau's report for the Central Committee of the Communist Party of China, on the implementation of the piece-rate wage system in the state owned industries in the Northeast], 4 February 1951, in Zhongguo shehui kexuewon he zhongyang dangan guan 1994, p. 518.

66 Laodong bu: Muqian quanguo guoying qiye jijian gongzi jiben qingkuang 劳动部：目前全国国营企业计件工资基本情况 [Ministry of Labour: The current situation of piece-rate wages at state enterprises nationally], November 1952, in Zhongguo shehui kexuewon he zhongyang dangan guan 1994, p. 519.

67 Zhonggongye bu guanyu jingji jishu huodong fenxi: Fushun lu chang yijiuwuliu nian dingyuan jiejin sulian sheji dingyuan shuiping 重工业部关于经济技术活动分析：抚顺铝厂一九五六年定员接近苏联设计定员水平 [Analysis of economic and technological activities of the Ministry of Heavy Industry: workforce numbers in Fushun Aluminum Plant in 1956 are close to the Soviet Union's level], 7 May 1956, in Zhongguo shehui kexuewon he zhongyang dangan guan 1998a, pp. 128–9; Lifuchun pi zhuan zhonggongye bu guanyu 'fushun lu chang 1956 nian dingyuan jiejin sulian sheji dingyuan shuiping' de baogao 李富春批转重工业部关于《抚顺铝厂 1956 年定员接近苏联设计定员水平》的报告 [Li Fuchun's report to the Ministry of Heavy Industry on 'workforce numbers in Fushun Aluminum Plant in 1956 which are close to the Soviet Union's level'], in Zhongguo shehui kexuewon he zhongyang dangan guan 1998a.

where around 3,600 workers or a quarter of the 15,000 workers in three work units were laid off. In the same report it was reported that among 120,000 workers at factories and mines attached to the Beijing city government, 20,000–30,000 workers had been laid off.[68]

So where did these laid off 'surplus' workers go? Orders from the central government typically advised that 'laid off workers be re-assigned with care', and cases where skilled workers with sought-after skills were sent off to rural areas and left the industrial sector would have been rare. Nonetheless, some permanent workers did get dismissed and found themselves forced back to the rural areas, showing that not all workers were re-assigned.

For example, if we look at the May 1955 Beijing report already quoted above, it relates that when permanent workers were laid off and moved back to their villages they would 'constantly send letters demanding jobs'.[69] The pressure for labour flexibility became even more intense as the First Five-year Plan began to overheat in 1956. According to a 1956 report on 17 Beijing city enterprises, the number of employed was 61,254 persons, of which 4,518 or 7.35 percent were judged to be 'surplus' to requirements and were laid off.[70] Another report, this time from April 1957, noted that the Tian Sheng bureau of forest industry had cut as much as half of its total workforce.[71]

There are various other pieces of evidence showing that the cases of lay-offs cited above were far from unusual and in fact formed a part of the everyday experience of Chinese workers in the 1950s. Important recent research by Feng Chen, dealing with workers' struggle during the First Five-year Plan,

---

68 Renmin ribao shelun: Juti di lingdao zhigong qunzhong de jieyue yundong 人民日报社论：具体地领导职工群众的节约运动 [People's Daily editorial: concretely leading the saving movement of the workers and the masses], in Zhongguo shehui kexuewon he zhongyang dangan guan 1998a, p. 178.

69 Zhonggong beijing shiwei guanyu changkuang, qiye jingjian wenti de qingshi baogao 中共北京市委关于厂矿，企业精简问题的请示报告, [Report of the Beijing Municipal Committee of the Communist Party of China on the issue of layoffs [jingjian] in factories and mines], 20 May 1955, in Zhongguo shehui kexuewon he zhongyang dangan guan 1998a, p. 177.

70 Beijing shi laodong ju beijing shi 17 ge qiye laodongli qingkuang de diaocha baogao 北京市劳动局北京市 17 个企业劳动力情况的调查报告, [Beijing Municipal Labor Bureau: Investigative Report on the Labor Situation of 17 Enterprises], May 1957, in Zhongguo shehui kexuewon he zhongyang dangan guan 1998a, p. 188.

71 Yangguoliang: Renyuan jianle yiban, gongzuo da you gaijin tian sheng sen gong ju zenyang jinxing keshi dingyuan gongzuo 杨果良：人员减了一半，工作大有改进田升森工局怎样进行科室定员工作, [Yang Guoliang: The number of personnel has been reduced by half, and the work has greatly improved, how Tiansheng Forest Industry Bureau carried out the departmental staffing work], April 1957, in Zhongguo shehui kexuewon he zhongyang dangan guan 1998a, pp. 195–6.

demonstrates the ease with which factory managers in the Maoist period could threaten workers' job security with layoffs and other means. One manager at the famous Anshan Iron and Steel Plant allegedly remarked to the workers, 'You can't go home before the job is done; otherwise, you'll be fired or your salary will be reduced'.[72] In November 1956, when labourers in construction complained of their workload, the managers told them they had to choose between fulfilling their quotas or being sacked.[73] Then, in January 1957, 190 dock workers in Wuxi staged a hunger strike, demanding job permanence after observing that workers were being dismissed as their productivity increased. Similar actions spread across the whole city as temporary workers at other workplaces were inspired by the dockers.[74] In Harbin, where one-third of the workers at 35 factories had temporary status, 2,900 workers also mobilised into collective action against threatened redundancies. A construction worker speaking at a CCP conference at Qingdao in July 1956 condemned the managers who had 'laid them off arbitrarily'.[75] When workers were dismissed in 1956 as a result of the socialist reforms, workers in Tianjin sarcastically noted that 'this [policy] is not to reform capitalists, but workers'.[76]

Faced with the need to increase employment flexibility and resistance from workers, one response from the CCP bureaucrats was paradoxically to imitate their sworn enemies, the Guomindang. The reason the term *gudinggong* (permanent/fixed worker) came to be officially used to mean 'regular worker' was the introduction of the 'total employment / total allocation' policy for labour power in 1955–7. The old distinction between 'long-term worker' and 'temporarily employed worker' that had existed under the Guomindang was effectively revived under slightly different terms.

Under the Guomindang, temporary workers in state-managed factories had largely been employed in dangerous jobs such as construction and handling of raw materials. From the point of view of the employers, they were able to use temporary workers to suppress wage increases for permanent workers and under the Guomindang such temporary workers made up 3–15 percent of all employment.[77] However, from the point of view of employment flexibility the Communist Party was far more ambitious than the Guomindang. The CCP further subdivided temporary workers into different groups, including *hetonggong*

---

72   Chen F. 2014, p. 501.
73   Chen F. 2014, p. 502.
74   Chen F. 2014, p. 503.
75   Chen F. 2014, p. 504.
76   Chen F. 2014, p. 504.
77   Howard 2004, p. 9.

(contract workers, mostly from the countryside), temporary workers (including those from an urban background), seasonal workers and worker-peasants[78] and during the period from the latter part of the First Five-year Plan to the Great Leap Forward this sort of flexible employment became as important a form of employment as permanent employment. This sort of policy made it possible for the Department of Metallurgy to openly demand in an ordinance of March 1957 that 'each enterprise has the authority to increase or reduce its personnel, as long as it does not exceed the labour plan'. The flexibilisation of labour became a foundation for high levels of accumulation, and that was, of course, the intended outcome. For example, the Labour Ministry explained its introduction of the 'worker-peasant' system in 1958 as intended to 'conserve state funds' and 'expedite construction by increasing state accumulation in conjunction with the low wages policy and the implementation of the part wage, part ration system'.[79] As one bureaucrat who supported this system put it very plainly:

> The fact that large numbers of staff and workers are flowing rapidly into the cities with their families, not only changes them from workers into pure consumers, and causes a loss of labour force in the villages but, moreover, gives the cities numerous new difficulties ... If, according to the calculations, 60 percent of staff and workers require family hostels ... the sum of at least 4.488 billion to 5.615 billion *yuan* is required. This is equivalent to between 70 and 80 per cent of China's industrial investment in the year before.[80]

Instead, he claimed that labour force waste could be avoided if temporary workers are hired and can be sent back to the villages when they are not needed. This would also, he insisted, mean that funds would not need to be used to build accommodation and other facilities for workers but could instead go

---

78   Gao A. 2008, p. 156.

79   Mawenrui zai laodong bu tuixing xin laodong zhidu sichuan xianchang huiyi shang de zongjie fa yan 马文瑞在劳动部推行新劳动制度四川现场会议上的总结发言 [Ma Wenrui's concluding remarks at the on-site meeting of the Ministry of Labor: How to promote the new labour system in Sichuan], 9th November 1958, in Zhongguo shehui kexuewon he zhongyang dangan guan 2011a, p. 99; Laodòng bu dangzu guanyu ruhe tuixing yi nong yi zhidu de yijian gei zhonggong zhongyang de baogao 劳动部党组关于如何推行亦农亦制度的意见给中共中央的报告 [The Party Committee of the Ministry of Labour's report on how to implement the 'worker-peasant system'], 29th December 1958 in Zhongguo shehui kexuewon he zhongyang dangan guan 2011a, pp. 100~101.

80   Zhang Qingwu, 'Why must we reduce urban population?' *Gongren Ribao* (Workers' Daily), 4 January 1958, quoted in Howe 2016, p. 349.

into accumulation. Once the idea of labour flexibility had been foregrounded so explicitly, its extension was unavoidable. Once the Great Leap Forward was fully underway this practice was massively expanded. A Ministry of Labour official commented on 29 December 1958 that 'converting numerous manual labourers into permanent workers costs too much and produces too little profit'.[81] The importance of this report cannot be overstressed since it offers an answer as to why the Ministry of Labor sought to make use of the temporary worker system: 'of course where skilled workers are in demand, frequent movement of labour is undesirable for production'. However, the report also noted that it was not desirable if workers could only enter a workplace but not leave and recommended that 'low skill workplaces must utilise this system'.[82]

'Saying that we should convert workers to "permanent" status because they feel insecure is to deny the principle of *nengjin nengchu* [workers can enter and also leave a workplace, e.g. labour mobility]. Their sense of insecurity could be done away with by enhancing political propaganda and treating them properly'.[83] The term *nengjin nengchu* captures how the temporary labour system developed during the Maoist period. This term was deployed in a similar way to what is now called 'labour market flexibility' and its use became widespread among the CCP bureaucracy during the 1950s. For example, beginning in 1955 Liu Shaoqi[84] used a similar term when criticising the rigidity of the permanent worker system, while in November 1958 Labour Minister Ma Wenrui shared this view, emphasising that workers should be able to move between workplaces (*nengjin nengchu*). According to Ma Wenrui, this system had the advantage of 'transforming the [current] situation where workers are shackled to a single type of occupation for their whole lives'.[85] A report by the Ministry of Labour issued prior to this in June 1958 also criticised the worker-trainee system, point-

81   Laodong bu dangzu guanyu ruhe tuixing yi nong yi zhidu de yijian gei zhonggong zhongy-
        ang de baogao 劳动部党组关于如何推行亦农亦制度的意见给中共中央的报
        告 [Report of the Party Committee of the Ministry of Labour on how to implement the
        'worker-peasant system'], 29th December 1958 in Zhongguo shehui kexuewon he zhongy-
        ang dangan guan 2011a, p. 103.

82   Zhongguo shehui kexuewon he zhongyang dangan guan 2011a, p. 101.

83   Zhongguo shehui kexuewon he zhongyang dangan guan 2011a, p. 103.

84   At that time Liu was 1st Chairman of the Standing Committee of the National People's
        Congress and 1st Vice Chairman of the CCP.

85   Mawenrui zai laodong bu tuixing xin laodong zhidu sichuan xianchang huiyi shang de
        zongjie fa yan 马文瑞在劳动部推行新劳动制度四川现场会议上的总结发言
        [Ma Wenrui's concluding remarks at the on-site meeting of the Ministry of Labour: How
        to promote the new labour system in Sichuan], 9th November 1958, in Zhongguo shehui
        kexuewon he zhongyang dangan guan 2011a, pp. 98–9.

ing out that workers 'entering a workplace but not leaving ... is a serious problem' that requires addressing, going so far as to call for the destruction of the
'iron rice bowl'.[86] This damning expression – describing a rigid employment
system – derived not from the period of Deng Xiaoping's reforms after 1978,
but precisely from the Great Leap Forward period. In fact, Mao never opposed
the expansion of labour regime flexibility and when the Central Employment
Commission, Ministry of Internal Affairs and Ministry of Labour collectively
submitted their report to Mao in August 1953, he approved it, on the basis
that 'a substantial number of temporary workers could be employed depending on the local situation'.[87] Mao also enthusiastically supported the rational
low wage.[88]

The temporary worker system was put forward as a means to increase labour
flexibility and capital accumulation, but at the same it time posed a tremendous headache for central bureaucrats. What concerned them was not so much
the suffering of workers as the risk of not achieving greater flexibility and thus
weakening their efforts at raising productivity or increasing the total wage bill.
Thus in August 1953 the Ministry of Labour had demanded that 'once their
assigned work has been completed [temporary workers] should be dismissed
immediately and when the time needed to complete the job becomes lengthy
they should not be converted to permanent workers'.[89] Looking at a subsidiary
report from the Labour Bureau of Gansu Province, we can see that these sorts
of layoffs had already been occurring to a significant extent, as it noted that,
'In order to reduce expenditure, many enterprises are not converting temporary workers to permanent status and are easily dismissing them'.[90] Towards the

---

86   Zhonggong zhongyang zhuanfa Laodong bu dangzu dangqian gongye qiye buchong lao-
     dongli wentí xiang zhongyang de qīngshi baogao 中共中央转发劳动部党组当前工业
     企业补充劳动力问题向中央的请示报告 [The Central Committee of the Commun-
     ist Party of China forwarded the report to the Central Committee: the report to the Party
     Group of the Ministry of Labour on the problems of the supplementary labor force in the
     industrial enterprises], 1958. 6. 29, in Zhongguo shehui kexuewon he zhongyang dangan
     guan(1998a), p. 161. Iron rice bowl = 铁碗 (tiewan).
87   Zhongyang laodong jiuye weiyuanhuì, neiwu bu, laodong bu guanyu laodong jiuye gong-
     zuo de baogao 中央劳动就业委员会，内务部，劳动部关于劳动就业工作的
     报告 [The Joint report of the Central Labour and Employment Committee, the Ministry
     of Internal Affairs, and the Ministry of Labour on Labour and Employment], 1953. 8. 5, in
     Zhongguo shehui kexuewon he zhongyang dangan guan 1998a, p. 5.
88   Howe 1978, p. 191; Meisner 2004, volume 1, p. 255.
89   Laodong bu: guanyu linshi gong wenti de chuli 劳动部: 关于临时工问题的处理 [Min-
     istry of Labor: Handling of temporary workers] 1953. 8. 6, in Zhongguo shehui kexuewon
     he zhongyang dangan guan 1998a, p. 137.
90   Gansu sheng laodong ju zhì zhongyang laodong bu han 甘肃省劳动局致中央劳动部

end of the First Five-year Plan in 1957, when there were signs that the total cost of wages would exceed the plan, the central government tried to take remedial measures by fixing the period of employment for temporary workers at one month. If they were employed for more than one month then 'workers have to renew their contracts each month and when the job is completed they must be dismissed, in accordance with the stipulations of their contract'.[91] The warnings of the central government on this point were so strong that a May 1957 report on labour power from the Ministry of Electric Power Industry went as far as to use the very rare and rather plain term 'dismissal' (*jiegu*) rather than a euphemism.[92] However, this treatment of temporary workers – worse even than the conditions of casualised workers under neoliberalism – came as a huge shock to the workers themselves. In a report of April 1957, the labour minister changed his position, arguing that the monthly contract system was 'making temporary workers suffer insecurity and is having a negative influence on productivity' and therefore contracts should be made to match the length of the job workers are employed for, 'as long as they step down at the end of the contract period'.[93] However, even this proposal represented a major retreat from the original temporary worker policy of the CCP. For example, on 20 October 1949, provisional regulations in the city of Shanghai stipulated that temporary workers had to be converted to permanent workers without question if the work they were employed for went on for longer than six months.[94]

In the case of temporary workers, labour flexibility was not entirely a one-sided affair on the part of employers. Temporary workers also chose to move from one workplace to another in search of better wages. According to a report

---

函 [Letter sent to the Central Labour Department by Gansu Provincial Labour Bureau], 1957. 7. 3., in Zhongguo shehui kexuewon he zhongyang dangan guan 1998a, p. 138.

91   Guowuyuan guanyu linshi gong guyong qixian de jieshi de tongzhi 国务院关于临时工雇用期限的解释的通知 [Notice of the State Council on the interpretation of the term of employment of temporary workers], in Zhongguo shehui kexuewon he zhongyang dangan guan 1998a, pp. 138–9.

92   Dianli gongye bu zhao yong linshi gongren de buchong guiding 电力工业部招用临时工人的补充规定 [Supplementary regulations for the recruitment of temporary workers by the Ministry of Power Industry], 1957. 5. 18, in Zhongguo shehui kexuewon he zhongyang dangan guan 1998a, p. 139.

93   Ma Wenrui: 1957 Nian de laodongli diaopei gongzuo xiang ti 马文瑞： 1957 年的劳动力调配工作向题 [Ma Wenrui: The problem in labour force allocation in 1957], 1957. 4. 23, in Zhongguo shehui kexuewon he zhongyang dangan guan 1998a, p. 140.

94   Shanghai shiwei: Shanghai shi siying qiye guyong linshi gong zhanxing banfa 上海市委：上海市私营企业雇用临时工暂行办法 [Shanghai Municipal Committee: Interim measures for temporary employment at private enterprises in Shanghai], 1949. 10.20, in Zhongguo shehui kexuewon he zhongyang dangan guan 1994, p. 290.

from December 1956, one particular construction site recruited 255 new temporary workers, of whom some 88, or 34 percent, left their posts.[95] In addition, it is not the case that temporary workers were completely lacking in bargaining power. It was the rule that workers who had migrated from the country to the city without permission should be sent back to their villages, however, in this situation too, productivity came before the regulations. When these migrant workers were considered to be essential for production they could be granted urban residence. According to a May 1957 report from the Ministry of Public Security, 'when they are engaged in a fixed piece of work within a particular work unit or enterprise, permission can be granted to add workers to the city register (*hukou*)'.[96] In the Xinjiang and Heilongjiang regions, where there was a labour shortage, it was also permitted for workers who had migrated from outside the area to be settled as permanent workers. According to the same document, this could also be the case even when migrant workers didn't have employment: 'if there are positions available then they can be permitted to gain urban residence. There is no need to forcefully return them to their places of origin'.[97]

In contrast to other countries that were suffering from a shortage of labour in the 1950s, the Chinese communist party was preoccupied mainly with how to deal with surplus labour and how to secure a supply of temporary workers. The clear wage-gap between urban and rural areas meant that without any specific coercive measures or large-scale enclosures, many peasants migrated to cities to become an urban proletariat.[98] As with today's *nongmin gong*, the CCP in the 1950s was most concerned with ensuring that Chinese peasants did not become fully urban workers. Chuang has applied the concept of 'proto-proletarianisation' to these temporary workers in a similar way to

---

95 Neimenggu zizhiqu laodong ju guanyu linshi gongren de dongyuan he gonggu gongzuo de jingyan 内蒙古自治区劳动局关于临时工人的动员和巩固工作的经验 [The Inner Mongolia Autonomous Region Labour Bureau's experience in mobilising and consolidating temporary workers], December 1956, in Zhongguo shehui kexuewon he zhongyang dangan guan 1998a, p. 147.

96 Gong'an bu guanyu gedi zhixíng liuru chengshi he fan suo chengshi renkou gongzuo zhong fasheng de wenti ji jiejue yijian xiang guowuyuan de baogao 公安部关于各地执行流入城市和繁缩城市人口工作中发生的问题及解决意见向国务院的报告 [Ministry of Public Security report sent to the State Council: issues arising from population inflows into cities, the problems from implementing their reduction and how to solve them], 1957 5. 27, in Zhongguo shehui kexuewon he zhongyang dangan guan 1998a, p. 364.

97 Zhongguo shehui kexuewon he zhongyang dangan guan 1998a, p. 365.

98 This is not to say that there was no coercive mobilisation or slave labour involved in the Chinese process of proletarianisation. This will be addressed in the Great Leap Forward section.

Pun Ngai's use of 'semi-proletarianisation' in her analysis of *nongmin gong* in today's PRC.[99] Chuang contends that, much as workers at state enterprises had not been commercialised at all, temporary workers were not in a real sense proletarianised as their basic livelihoods were still guaranteed by rural production brigades and urban work units (*danwei*).[100] However, contrary to Chuang's evaluation, it is possible to explain the issue of partial employment using the concept of the 'reserve army of labour'. But the really contentious part of Chuang's argument is not only that workers at state firms were not true proletarians, but that they comprised a 'privileged' group who were in opposition to temporary workers. Thus, in the conflict between temporary workers and the CCP bureaucrats Chuang claims that the state enterprise workers were on the same side as the bureaucrats, because they enjoyed ideological, or perhaps even material, benefits in comparison to temporary workers. According to Chuang, state enterprise workers were beneficiaries of the Communist Party's 'rural sacrifice policy' and could thus be 'rice-consumers' rather than 'rice-producers'.

It is true that the bureaucrats discriminated between state enterprise workers and temporary workers. For instance, in 1957 the central government ordered differential hiring systems for permanent and temporary workers in new state enterprises. Factory managers also discriminated against temporary workers on a daily basis. A report from the Inner Mongolia autonomous region is laced with comments such as 'not a single decent human being among temporary workers', and 'half of them [temporary workers] are hooligans', which seem to be aimed at fomenting prejudice against temporary workers among the permanent workers. The same report also notes that managers are 'not interested in temporary workers' suffering and preferential treatment given to permanent workers is common in the work units'.[101]

However, this does not automatically mean that the permanent workers were in an exploitative relationship with the temporary workers, nor does it provide evidence that they benefitted from this arrangement. For example, from 1956 (the year of the last national wage increase by wage level modification) till the end of Mao's rule in 1976, state enterprise workers received no

---

99   Chuang Collective 2016, p. 72; Pun 2016, pp. 66–8.
100   Chuang Collective 2016, p. 80.
101   Neimenggu zizhiqu laodong ju guanyu linshi gongren de dongyuan he gonggu gongzuo de jingyan 内蒙古自治区劳动局关于临时工人的动员和巩固工作的经验 [Inner Mongolia Autonomous Region Labor Bureau's experience in mobilizing and consolidating temporary workers], December 1956, in Zhongguo shehui kexuewon he zhongyang dangan guan 1998a, p. 147.

increase in their wages and in fact saw their perks and welfare benefits either reduced or lose value due to inflation. And of course, this period coincides with the expansion of the temporary labour workforce. In his research on the relationship between the temporary worker system and wages, Yamamoto Tsuneto has argued that 'there is no doubt that the existence of a low-paid workforce would have suppressed wage increases for the medium and higher-paid workforce'.[102] For instance, issue 22 of *Laodong* in 1958 carried a 'model' case of a particular workplace in Qingdao where temporary contract workers complained that permanent workers were receiving 170–180 *yuan* while they only received 44–52 *yuan*; the factory manager then used this as an opportunity to reduce the pay of permanent workers.[103] In another example, the report assessing the First Five-year Plan noted that 'new workers increased by 790,000 in 1957 and their average wage was so low that the wages of existing workers stagnated. As a result, the wages of existing workers increased only by 4.8 per cent, achieving only 98.2 per cent of the targeted increase in average wages for workers'.[104]

Regardless of whether they were permanent or temporary workers, the efforts to expand capital accumulation by increasing employment flexibility during this period resulted in sharp rises in both working hours and industrial accidents. For example, according to a March 1956 report from the Ministry of Railways, the extension of working hours was very serious and as the primary cause the report noted that 'under the influence of capitalistic management ideology and right-wing conservatism, many of the managers believe that the extension of working hours is unavoidable'.[105] However, in the midst of the central government's drive to exceed the plan targets, far from being curtailed this 'capitalistic management ideology' was being spread more widely.

According to internal documents, in 1953 industrial accidents in Shanghai had doubled compared to the previous year.[106] In Hunan Province, in 1954 the rate of fatal industrial accidents leapt by 225 percent, and the majority

---

102   Yamamoto 2000, p. 91.

103   Yamamoto 2000, p. 103 note 34.

104   Guojia tongji ju: Wuqi nian gongye laodong jihua zhi hang qingkuang baogao 国家统计局：五七年工业劳动计划执行情况报告 [National Bureau of Statistics: Report on the implementation of the industrial labour plan in 1957], 28 January 1958 in Zhongguo shehui kexuewon he zhongyang dangan guan 1998b, p. 1047.

105   Tiedao bu guanyu yange xianzhi jiaban jiadian de zhishi 铁道部关于严格限制加班加点的指示 [Ministry of Railways' instructions on strict restrictions on overtime], 9th March 1956, in Zhongguo shehui kexuewon he zhongyang dangan guan 1998a, p. 975.

106   Chen F. 2014, p. 500.

of those were in mining. The internal documents also reveal that the rise in industrial accidents at this time was entirely due to managers becoming careless about safety in order to fulfil production quotas. In the case of one factory in Shandong Province, while it made a profit of 1.2 million yuan in a year, it spent only 3,000 yuan on safety equipment. According to one report, some 42 percent of industrial accidents were the result of a lack of even the minimal level of safety equipment.[107] In 1955, in the middle of the First Five-year Plan as workers' fatigue accumulated, many of them showed worrying signs of health problems. In a report released by the heavy industry section of the ACFTU in July 1955 it was stated that the health of workers nationwide was being damaged. It reported that at one particular mine, after working hours were extended the sickness rate increased by 23.5 percent in a month and then by 94 percent the following month. Workers' health was so badly damaged that some of them were constantly coughing up blood.[108] In another case, at a Northern Manchu steel construction company, after the workers had been working continuously for 40 hours a worker in a half-conscious state fell into a six metre deep well and was seriously injured.[109] An internal report composed in 1957, with the title 'Instructions on the problems facing industrial workers', expressed criticism that industrial accidents were continuing to occur regularly as a result of managers' negligence.[110] The problem was so serious that in May 1957 even Zhou Enlai raised the issue of the rising numbers of industrial accidents in a report.[111] In the mining industry, where demand greatly outstripped supply, unbelievable incidents occurred one after another. Between December 1956 and April 1957 there were workplaces where some 42 percent of workers experienced some sort of accident and 53 percent caught a work-related illness. The result was that among workers at mines around two-thirds quit their jobs within two years and after nine years only one in five workers remained in their jobs.[112] Inevitably there must have been strong opposition from Chinese workers to these conditions, but the early response from the central government was extremely cynical. For instance, an editorial in the People's Daily (*Renmin*

---

107   Chen F. 2014, pp. 499–500.
108   Zhongguo zhonggongye gonghui quanguo weiyuanhui guanyu jiaban jiadian qingkuang de baogao 中国重工业工会全国委员会关于加班加点情况的报告 [Report of the National Committee of the heavy industry section of the ACFTU on overtime work], July 25, 1955, in Zhongguo shehui kexuewon he zhongyang dangan guan 1998a, p. 974.
109   Zhongguo shehui kexuewon he zhongyang dangan guan 1998a, p. 974.
110   Gao A. 2013, p. 56.
111   Gipouloux 1986, p. 148.
112   Gipouloux 1986, p. 150.

Ribao) on 16 January 1957 criticised workers for fetishising safety equipment in order to avoid doing hard work and insisted that 'it is a fantasy to expect labour conditions to change within a short space of time'.[113]

2.5   Women Workers under Early Maoism

Finally, the segment of workforce most marginalised by the CCP bureaucrats' efforts to accumulate the maximum amount of capital were women workers. Women workers, numbering 2.44 million in total, comprised 12.6 percent of the total workforce in 1956. The discrimination they faced stemmed not just from traditional views regarding gender roles. The main source of the problem was rather modern and was rooted in production costs. For instance, a 1957 report from the Wuhan city labour bureau reveals how traditional gender discrimination was combined with the contemporary problem of maximum capital accumulation.

> [S]ome factories do not hire female workers with children. In some cases when women workers got pregnant they were sent home ... [responding to this criticism a manager replied as follows]: 'Do you even think about the national wealth? Not only do we have to give women 56 days maternity leave when they get pregnant, it is also disadvantageous for production. If a child gets sick, the factory must foot the bill ... this is all just waste ...'[114]

The factory managers prioritised the cost saving above all else and took little care for the welfare of women workers. As such, illness among women workers was extremely frequent.

> Various sorts of illnesses are a serious problem among women at many factories. At four work units, including Wuhan Sand Mine, of 2,490 women workers 2,007 have contracted women's diseases of various kinds. In the case of Wuhan Woollen Mill, 98.4 percent of the total female workforce are suffering from disease.[115]

---

113   Gipouloux 1986, p. 151.
114   Wuhan shi laodong ju: Wuhan shi ge gongchang nugong baohu gongzuo qingkuang diaocha baogao 武汉市劳动局：武汉市各工厂女工保护工作情况调查报告 [Wuhan Municipal Labor Bureau: Investigation report on the work of women workers in various factories in Wuhan], August 1957, in Zhongguo shehui kexuewon he zhongyang dangan guan 1998a, pp. 991–2.
115   Zhongguo shehui kexuewon he zhongyang dangan guan 1998a, pp. 992–3.

Since managers often did not make any special allowances for pregnant workers and forced them to continue with physically demanding work, miscarriages were frequent occurrences. It was reported that in Shenyang, for example, pregnant women and women who had given birth less than four months before were being forced to work,[116] while in the textile sector generally, the miscarriage rate rose from 10 percent to 30 percent and the rate was said to be even higher in some jobs.[117] Most shocking of all, some textile factories and other light industrial workplaces in Shanghai, Qingdao, Wuhan, as well as the northeastern and southwestern regions required women to submit dead fetuses in order to be granted sick leave.[118]

Despite the central government's efforts to flexibilise the labour force, the bureaucrats appear to have felt that they had not achieved their aims. For instance, reports from Beijing city's mining enterprises and other firms are full of negative assessments.

> There has been no serious effort to improve labour organisation, aside from in cases where there was a political problem. There has been a lot of noise but little has been put into practice and layoffs have been limited. We are simply achieving higher production by using the 'human wave strategy' [i.e. by using large numbers of workers].[119]

Some studies, basing their evidence on these cases, suggest that the Chinese labour regime was somehow different from the 'normal' capitalist one. An important recent study by Yiching Wu on the Cultural Revolution, for example, applies Robert Brenner's version of the theory of bureaucratic collectivism to the Maoist period.[120] Despite the central bureaucrats' criticism of excess employment and surplus labour accumulation at provincial and work unit levels, the Chinese urban industrial labour process between 1949 and 1957 does not differ from the 'general' pattern of capital accumulation described in Marx's *Capital*.[121]

---

116   Chen F. 2014, p. 501.
117   Gipouloux 1986, p. 81.
118   Gipouloux 1986, p. 82.
119   Zhonggong beijing shiwei guanyu changkuang, qiye jingjian bianzhi wenti de qingshi baogao 中共北京市委关于厂矿，企业精简编制问题的请示报告 [Report of the Beijing Municipal Committee of the Communist Party of China on the issue of layoffs (*jiangjian*) in plants and mines], 1955. 5. 20, in Zhongguo shehui kexuewon he zhongyang dangan guan (1998a), p. 177.
120   Wu Y. 2015, see chapter 2 and epilogue.
121   If agriculture were included this would be a completely different picture. This issue will be discussed later in this chapter.

The most significant and fundamental transformation during this period was the steadily rising technical composition of capital during the ceaseless efforts to expand capital accumulation. Per capita productive assets for each worker were worth 3,525 RMB in 1952, increasing to 5,138 RMB in 1957. This increase was not simply an illusion created by price rises, but reflected a real advance in the technical composition of capital.[122] During the same period electricity usage per person increased from 1,386 watts to 2,469 watts, and from 1.73 horsepower to 3.1 horsepower respectively.[123] Naturally, as time went on, the role played by rising per capita productivity in production increases became greater than that played by the increasing size of the workforce.

The rate of contribution from the increasing of the workforce in the increase in the total value of industrial output fell from 52.4 percent in the 1949–52 period to 41.4 percent during the period of the First Five-year Plan. On the other hand, the rate of contribution from labour productivity rose from 50.3 percent in the first period to 64.8 in the second period.[124] However, as we have seen above, this acceleration of the labour process did not reduce the burden on workers. On the contrary, during this period working hours became longer and work more intense. That contemporary capital accumulation was aimed at responding to external competition, not to fulfil the needs of labour or the citizenry more generally, supports the overall contention of this chapter. This assertion will be even clearer once we have analysed the period of the Great Leap Forward.

As can be seen, from the perspective of labour the First Five-year Plan was a period of heightening contradictions. The underlying social conflicts that had been suppressed since 1949 erupted in the 'Hundred Flowers Campaign'[125] of 1957. This campaign had similar origins to the revolutionary upheavals of the same period in Eastern Europe: divisions among the ruling elites and changes

---

122   Gongye qiye laodong jishu zhuangbei shuiping 工业企业劳动技术装备水平 [Technological level of industrial production (collective ownership firms are not included)], in Zhongguo shehui kexuewon he zhongyang dangan guan 1998b, p. 1134, table 1.

123   Gōngyè gōngsī rénjūn hào diàn liàng 工业公司人均耗电量 [Electricity usage per person in industrial production], in Zhongguo shehui kexuewon he zhongyang dangan guan 1998b, p. 1136, table 4.

124   Tigao laodong shengchanlu dui fazhan gongye shengchan de zuoyong 提高劳动生产率对发展工业生产的作用 [The effect of improving labor productivity on the development of industrial production], in Zhongguo shehui kexuewon he zhongyang dangan guan 1998b, 1957, p. 1127, table 6.

125   The full name of this movement came from a February 1957 speech by Mao in which he quoted from a poem saying: 'Let a hundred flowers bloom; let a hundred schools of thought contend'.

in the Soviet party line after the death of Stalin that emboldened intellectuals
and students. According to Shen Zhihua, already in 1956 the Chinese workers
were 'attempting to do a "Hungary"'.[126] However, by the time labour struggles
erupted seriously in 1957, for the most part the demands of Chinese workers
were no different than those of workers in other capitalist states. For instance,
looking at the reports analysing the causes of 'disruptions' experienced in the
first half of 1957, 24 percent were attributed to problems with management
style; 38.1 percent were due to wage disputes; 24 percent were related to welfare
issues; 11.8 percent were caused by issues related to movement within factories, between factories and between regions; 6.1 percent were related to the
worker-trainee system; and 7.2 percent were related to the problems of temporary labourers.[127] Feng Chen concluded that 42 percent of disputes at this
time were caused by conflicts over wages, followed by 41 percent prompted
by welfare-related issues.[128] Authorities on the Chinese working class in the
Maoist period, such as Elizabeth Perry, have argued[129] that Chinese workers
made different sorts of demands to the 'normal' ones made by workers in capitalist countries. But we can see that the principle demands of Chinese workers
were precisely concerned with the cost of reproducing labour power under capitalism. The Chinese Communist Party were shocked by the widespread expressions of discontent that emerged in 1957 and quickly counterattacked with the
'Anti-Rightist Campaign' that began in July 1957. The central bureaucrats, having punished nearly two million on trumped-up charges of being rightists, took
this opportunity to lower wages in pursuit of the 'rational low wage system'.
This was far from a coincidence. The antagonistic relationship between accumulation and wages could now continue beyond 1957 and into the period of
the Great Leap Forward.

3   The Great Leap Forward and the Maoist-Style Free Labour Market

Lucien Bianco, in comparing the Stalinist industrialisation with the Maoist
one, came to an interesting conclusion: because Maoist China of 1949 was
more backward than the Soviet Union of 1928, the speed of industrialisation
ought to have been faster for China, whereas in fact it was slower in China.

---

126   Shen 2012, p. 131.
127   Gao A. 2013, p. 65. The total here comes to more than 100 percent because there is some
       overlap between categories.
128   Chen F. 2014, p. 498.
129   Perry 1994, quoted in Chen F. 2014, p. 498.

Bianco sees the Chinese bureaucrats as being more irrational than the Soviet ones.[130] However, military expenditures in the two countries reveal marked differences. Mike Kidron and Chris Harman analysed the contradictory relationship between high military expenditure and capital accumulation in their development of the permanent arms economy theory. While on the one hand the arms economy made postwar capital accumulation more stable, the burden of high military expenditure could also cause national competitiveness to lag in the long run. This meant that from the perspective of competition with other national capitals, the gradually increasing quantity of accumulated dead labour (particularly in department 1, but also in department 2) that could be used for production was growing less fast relative to the quantity of dead labour that could later be used for military expenditures. Meanwhile, the so-called Four Asian Tigers (South Korea, Taiwan, Singapore and Hong Kong) were able to grow faster than China because, in return for being militarily subordinate to the US, they were able to contain increases in military spending and focus on economic growth.

So, how large was military expenditure during the Mao period? Statistics are quite hard to come by, but those that we can find confirm a very high level of spending. For example, according to Mao's April 1956 speech 'On the ten major relationships', during the First Five-year Plan 'military and administrative spending' would occupy as much as 30 percent of total government spending.[131] However, as can be seen from Mao's speech, the understanding had already emerged that in order to develop a stronger national defence in the future it was necessary to temporarily reduce military spending in the present and pour everything into capital accumulation:

> We cannot do without the bomb. Then what is to be done about it? One reliable way is to cut military and administrative expenditures down to appropriate proportions and increase expenditures on economic construction. Only with the faster growth of economic construction can there be greater progress in defence construction. In the period of the First Five-Year Plan, military and administrative expenditures accounted for 30 percent of the total expenditures in the state budget. This proportion

---

130   Bianco 2007, p. 62.

131   This speech appears in the collection published in Hong Kong entitled 'Love Live the Thought of Mao Zedong' and was not included in the official collected works of Mao published by the Chinese government. The speech is available at: https://www.marxists.org/reference/archive/mao/selected-works/volume-5/mswv5_51.htm (Gipouloux 1986, note 10).

is much too high. In the period of the Second Five-year Plan, we must reduce it to around 20 percent, so that more funds can be released for building more factories and turning out more machines.[132]

State Planning Commission vice chief Bo Yibo also noted in his report of 30 August 1963 that: 'Because West Germany and Japan have limited defence budgets, they have more money to use for industrial development. These countries were able to construct comparatively strong basic industries'.[133] According to official statistics, the only time investment in defence industries (including defence research) fell below 10 percent of total industrial investment was in 1957–9, and in 1958 at the height of the Great Leap Forward it was a mere 5.1 percent.[134]

Cutting back on defence spending and loosening local discipline produced tremendous results. In 1958 alone, total investment was equivalent to 69 percent of investment in the entire First Five-year Plan and 63 percent of the fixed assets during the same period.[135] The percentage of total investment going to industrial investment rose from 52.6 percent in the First Five-year Plan to 63.2 per cent in 1958–9, while 'fixed capital construction' (*jiben jianshe*) rose from 71.7 percent to as much as 88 percent in 1958–9. The rate of investment outside of the state plan also rose from 10.4 percent (5.73 billion *yuan*) to 21.3 percent (13.03 billion *yuan*).[136] The absolute majority of investment was directed into heavy industry. But the imbalance across regions, sectors, and work units arising from competition between them put the brakes on expanded reproduction. Just as under 'normal' capitalism, the imbalance between sec-

---

132 Mao 1956. https://www.marxists.org/reference/archive/mao/selected-works/volume-5/mswv5_51.htm

133 Bo Yibo: Guanyu 1963 nian gongye, jiaotong jihua xiang zhongyang huibao tigang 薄一波：关于 1963 年工业，交通计划向中央汇报提纲 [Bo Yibo: report to the central government concerning the industry and transportation plan for 1963] ，1962. 10. 31, in Zhongguo shehui kexuewon he zhongyang dangan guan (2011b), p. 202.

134 Guomin jingji tongji tiyao (1949–1980 nian), ge guanli xitong touzi e (yi) 国民经济统计提要 （1949–1980 年, 各管理系统投资额（一）[National Economic Statistics Summary (1949–1980), investment in various management systems (1)], in Zhongguo shehui kexuewon he zhongyang dangan guan 2011b, p. 210.

135 Guojia tongji ju: Yijiuwuba nian quanguo gongye shengchan yikao dangnian jiben jianshe zengjia de chanzhi yu chanliang de qingkuang 国家统计局：一九五八年全国工业生产依靠当年基本建设增加的产值与产量的情况 [National Bureau of Statistics: the national industrial production relied on the increased output value and output of the fixed capital construction in 1958], 10 July 1959, in Zhongguo shehui kexuewon he zhongyang dangan guan 2011b, p. 806.

136 Zhongguo shehui kexuewon he zhongyang dangan guan 2011b, p. 809.

tors was worsened by over-investment, as was noted at the time: 'Due to our lax management, enterprises and basic construction work units ... are producing recklessly, purchasing recklessly, and ordering recklessly, leading to waste of capital and goods'.[137]

Despite this problem, if the level of investment could be enlarged and sustained, growth amidst imbalance would still have been possible for some time. However, growth came to a shuddering halt once the level of investment faltered. The rate of investment in large and medium-scale projects fell from 26.4 percent in 1957 to 9.8 percent in 1960. While the rate of profit was 35 RMB for every 100 during the First Five-Year Plan, it dropped from a high of 55 RMB in 1958 to 19 RMB the next year, and still further to 4 RMB in 1960.[138] The outcome of this was that production in 1961 collapsed by 30–40 percent compared to 1960, and only 10–20 percent of the original plan could be completed.[139] In the agricultural sector the situation was even more severe.[140]

What does it mean that the Chinese working class was being formed during the chaos of the Great Leap Forward? The official statistics tell us that the average wage of workers fell significantly during this period. The wage of state enterprise workers was frozen, and new entrants were employed as temporary workers on lower wages. The dream of Liu Shaoqi and the labour minister Mao Wenrui of expanding the army of temporary workers was actually realised under Mao's great experiment. However, all the other labour power-related metrics were off the planned targets. Ironically, while the Great Leap Forward is considered a departure from the norm even compared to the Soviet Union and other 'actually existing socialist' states, let alone capitalist states, it was precisely during this period that the CCP bureaucrats came closest to experiencing a level of labour flexibility that was closest to the ideal type of 'market capitalism'. This is even more paradoxical when you take into account the fact that the Chinese government had attempted to strengthen its control over labour power in the period immediately prior to the Great Leap Forward. But as this study pointed out earlier, so long as the bureaucrats sought to accumulate capital, there were limits to how far they could suppress the tendency of the Chinese working class to becoming free wage labourers.

In January 1958, restrictions on the migration of workers from the countryside under the *hukou* registration system were legally and institutionally strengthened. However, in reality the *hukou* system was weakened tremend-

---

137   Zhongguo shehui kexuewon he zhongyang dangan guan 2011b, p. 828.

138   Herrera & Long 2017, pp. 71–2.

139   Hu A. 2007, p. 385, table 4.

140   Hu A. 2007, p. 384.

ously during the Great Leap Forward.[141] For instance, the number of temporary residence permit holders in Tianjin grew from 74,000 in 1956 to 232,000 in 1958, and then declined again to 168,000 in 1959 and 73,000 in 1960.[142] How many workers were living in Tianjin additionally without any temporary residence permit is impossible to know. Factory managers in fact preferred peasants who could endure the punishing work hours and intense labour that the Great Leap Forward required of workers. Some reports suggest that around 6.6 percent of the peasants living in the region around Tianjin were officially hired to work in the city. But the vast majority worked without such a permit.[143] Official statistics reveal that nationally among 20 million new workers, 11 million had flowed into the cities from rural areas, and, of those, 8 million were temporary workers and 3 million were student trainees.[144] Since the pay of rural temporary workers was only half that of temporary workers from an urban background, hiring such a large number of rural temporary workers was a way for work units to save money from the wage bill by relying on a comparatively cheaper workforce.[145]

We can assume, however, that the real figures for rural to urban migration in this period must have been larger than those found in the official statistics. For example, a 1959 report on the problem of rural population movement used the expression 'speaking on the basis of incomplete statistics', indicating that the government did not have a clear idea of the scale of rural migration.[146] However, even looking only at the confirmed cases in the report, we can guess that the scale of migration must have been enormous. The report notes that where external labour forces were most needed for production-related construction in provinces like Xinjiang, Inner Mongolia, Gansu and Qinghai, 1.2 million migrated in.[147] According to a 1960 report entitled 'The problem of the free migration of the rural population', 2 million people had flowed into Inner Mongolia alone and over 60 percent of the 100,000 working at the Baotou Iron

---

141   Brown 2012, p. 51.

142   Brown 2012, p. 55.

143   Brown 2012, pp. 55~6.

144   Guojiā tongji ju: Xin zeng zhigong dui shichang de yali 国家统计局：新增职工对市场的压力 [National Bureau of Statistics: new employees caused pressure on market], 18 July 1959, in Zhongguo shehui kexuewon he zhongyang dangan guan 2011a, p. 194.

145   Zhongguo shehui kexuewon he zhongyang dangan guan 2011a, p. 194.

146   Neiwe bu dangzu guanyu nongcun renkou wailiu wenti de baogao 内务部党组关于农村人口外流问题的报告 [Report of the party committee at the Ministry of Internal Affairs on the outflow of rural population], 7 February 1959, in Zhongguo shehui kexuewon he zhongyang dangan guan 1998a, p. 227.

147   Zhongguo shehui kexuewon he zhongyang dangan guan 1998a, p. 227.

and Steel Complex were reportedly from outside the region.[148] In the case of Heilongjiang, the number of workers employed was double the original plan.[149]

We saw earlier how the bureaucrats sought to secure labour flexibility among the state enterprise workers during the First Five-year Plan through lay-offs. But that approach proved insufficient to meet the demand for labour and subsequent to 1955, work unit bureaucrats created consultative committees so as to put flexibilisation under bureaucratic control and cooperatively allocate state firm workers wherever the need arose. Even according to the evaluation of the bureaucrats themselves, this approach only achieved limited success. Then, during the explosive growth period of the Great Leap Forward, the pressure was such that it became necessary to secure workers by 'stealing' them from one's rivals rather than through negotiation, and reports of unauthorised cross-sector movement of skilled workers between state enterprises grew rapidly. The managers' methods for attracting workers from elsewhere were no different than those used by 'normal' capitalists.

For example, if we look at one of the cases in a labour ministry report warning of the unauthorised movement of workers, in Anhui Province, three skilled permanent workers moved from their workplace without permission to the Wuhan Iron and Steel Complex. Whereas their wages had previously been 91, 72 and 57 *yuan* per month, at their new workplace they earned 160, 140 and 120 *yuan* respectively. According to the same report, 'This sort of large-scale movement of labour between enterprises and between regions is happening not only among the newly established factories in the peripheral areas where workers and technicians are scarce, but also among the older enterprises in core areas'.[150] The competition between work units over workers was such that if managers tried to prevent them from leaving a workplace the workers would demand to be dismissed by the factory managers in the name of 'employment freedom'.[151]

A report that surveyed around 200 state enterprises in 10 cities between January and April 1960 found that some 8,500 people had moved workplaces (albeit this was based on 'incomplete statistics'). Another report from the same year, compiled by the party committee of the ACFTU and based on a survey

---

148   Laodong bu dangzu guanyu nongcun laodongli wailiu wenti gei zhongyang de baogao 劳动部党组关于农村劳动力外流问题给中央的报告 [Report from the Party committee at the Ministry of Labor to the Central Committee on the outflow of rural labor], 4th May 1960, in Zhongguo shehui kexuewon he zhongyang dangan guan 2011a, p. 228.

149   Zhongguo shehui kexuewon he zhongyang dangan guan 2011a, p. 229.

150   Zhongguo shehui kexuewon he zhongyang dangan guan 2011a, p. 230.

151   Dikötter, *Mao's Great Famine*, chapter 23.

of 206 state enterprises in 10 cities, including Beijing, entitled 'Report on the outflow of labour power from state enterprises' discovered 6,572 cases of persons moving without authorisation. In the case of Harbin city, in the period of January and April 1960 alone some 3.3 percent of the total labour force at 122 factories had moved workplaces without permission. The majority of them were student trainees and low level technical staff who had been employed since 1958, but they also included some technicians above the fourth grade.[152] This report also lists the reasons why workers changed their workplace and gave the most important reason as 'moving in order to get more money', which the authors saw as the pernicious influence of 'capitalist ideology'. The same report points out that relatively highly paid technicians commonly moved workplace because there was a demand for skilled labour at newly constructed factories.[153] Looking at reports from a variety of regions, there were a considerable number of workplaces among the state-owned factories where more than 15 percent of the workers had absconded and, among those, a significant number were skilled workers who formed the backbone of the workforce.

According to the same report, there was growing discontent among permanent workers at state enterprises because their wages remained very low due to the fact that the centre would not revise their pay grades, even when they had accrued considerable experience in their jobs. The workers claimed that they moved workplace because of the promise of higher wages, as the inflation caused by the Great Leap Forward meant they had had to reduce their consumption of vegetables while at the same time suffering due to housing shortages.[154] To make matters worse, the CCP bureaucrats discovered from a survey of four Beijing districts that right under their noses in the capital between January and June 1960 some 550 workers had received offers of higher wages and moved to new workplaces. One of these cases was particularly interesting: a glass factory proposed to workers at another factory who had been earning only 30 *yuan* per month that they would give them 120 *yuan* if they moved and even

---

152 Quan zong dangzu guanyu guoying qiye zhong laodongli wailiu qikngkuang de baogao
     全总党组关于国营企业中劳动力外流情况的报告 [Report of the party committee on the outflow of labor in state-owned enterprises], 15 July 1960, in Zhongguo shehui kexuewon he zhongyang dangan guan 2011a, p. 189.
153 Zhongguo shehui kexuewon he zhongyang dangan guan 2011a, p. 189.
154 Gu mu: Guanyu xunsu kefu gongren sizi li chang xianxiang he gonggu gongren duiwu de
     yijian 谷牧：关于迅速克服工人私自离厂现象和巩固工人队伍的意见 [Gu Mu: On speedily overcoming the phenomenon of workers leaving the factory and on consolidating the workers], in Zhongguo shehui kexuewon he zhongyang dangan guan 1998a, p. 192.

promised the workers that they would be able to deal with the problem of moving their *hukou* (household registrations).[155]

There were also cases in some regions and areas of work where the movement of skilled workers was actually the most common form of labour mobility. In the case of Heilongjiang Province, where demand for electricity workers was high due to the construction of so many new factories, more than 60 percent of new workers flowing out to other regions were workers with technical skills in the electrical power industry. In the case of state enterprises in Beijing and Harbin too, the workers leaving their jobs were newly employed permanent workers with high levels of skills and education. Naturally this ACFTU report criticised the workers who wanted to move workplace for higher wages as having 'an incorrect view of labour'. This unlicensed employment grew steadily to a huge scale. The industrial director of Jingdezhen City apparently recruited some 50 skilled workers at the National Science and Technology Innovation Convention and, not to be outsmarted, the deputy director of the labour bureau of the same city recruited 1,840 workers.[156] When the movement of state enterprise workers became too severe, the central government issued a critical directive, lamenting the 'mistake of luring away state enterprise workers by unjust means such as raising wages'.[157] This shows clearly that the 'immobility' of state enterprise workers in the Mao period was not a fixed phenomenon. Even at times when mobility was relatively stagnant, the principal cause was not some sort of peculiar characteristic of socialism, but can be found rather in key characteristics of China itself, such as the large quantity of surplus labour power and the fact that compared to the great majority of peasants and peasant migrants the workers had high incomes and good welfare. The fact that the wage freeze and abolition of bonuses during the Great Leap Forward partially smashed this presumption and led to increasing mobility even among the workers of existing state enterprises is important evidence for this.

Some central bureaucrats now began to think that the situation in China was identical to 'market capitalism' because the central control over residence permits and the movement of labour had collapsed. A 1958 report entitled 'A criticism of the phenomenon of workers' free movement', written by a Ministry of Industry official who had been sent out to the regions, urges that 'the state

---

155   Quan zong dangzu guanyu guoying qiye zhong laodongli wailiu qingkuang de baogao 全
      总党组关于国营企业中劳动力外流情况的报告 [Report of the party committee
      on the outflow of labour in state-owned enterprises], 15 July 1960, in Zhongguo shehui
      kexuewon he zhongyang dangan guan 2011a, p. 190.
156   Zhongguo shehui kexuewon he zhongyang dangan guan 2011a, p. 190.
157   Zhongguo shehui kexuewon he zhongyang dangan guan 2011a, p. 189.

ought to manage the labour force in a unified fashion, never leaving it to the free market to resolve the problem of labour'. The Ministry of Labour report uses very strong language, claiming that unlicensed movement of labour 'may alleviate the issue temporarily but a free labour market would surely open up the "gate of death"'.[158]

However, in the course of the Great Leap Forward it was no longer an assumption about the future but an established reality. In April 1959 the State Planning Commission complained that since control had been devolved, like investment, 'labour power is not being properly controlled'. It used the example of Sichuan Province, where control of labour power had been devolved to lower administrative work units with the result that 'we have no idea how labour power is being utilised throughout the province'.[159]

4   Chinese State Capitalism under Mao and the Question of Primitive Accumulation

One important problem not yet addressed in the formation of a capitalistic working class in the Maoist period is primitive accumulation. Left-wing scholars are broadly divided into two camps on this question. On the one hand there are those who believe that primitive accumulation did not occur in China at that time. On the other are those who see the primitive accumulation of this period as one of the 'achievements' of the CCP, but who nonetheless insist that this did not make China capitalist.

The former group tends to see primitive accumulation as a Weberian ideal-type narrowly defined by the British case that Marx cited in *Capital* Volume I, rather than as a universal precondition for capital accumulation. The extent to which primitive accumulation has taken place in a particular country is therefore measured by the extent to which peasants, deprived of livelihood

---

158   Laodong bu dangzu guanyu si zhao nongmin he wa yong zaizhie ren qingkuang xiang zhongyang de baogao 劳动部党组关于私招农民和 挖用 在职工人情况向中央 的报告 [The report of the party committee at the Ministry of Labour sent to the central committee: on the private recruitment of farmers and hoarding employees], 29 November 1958, in Zhongguo shehui kexuewon he zhongyang dangan guan 2011a, p. 168.

159   Guojia ji wei hui, guojia jianwei hui: Yijiuwujiu nian jīben jianshe xiane yishang shigong xiangmu di tiaozheng yijian 国家计委会，国家建委会：一九五九年基本建设限 额以上施工项目的调整意见 [National Planning Commission, National Construction Commission: Adjustments for construction projects above the fixed capital construction budget in1959], 8th April 1959, in Zhongguo shehui kexuewon he zhongyang dangan guan 2011b, p. 313.

via enclosure, have been transformed into wage labourers. Strictly applied, it would suggest, as Samir Amin has done, that even now China is not a capitalist state, let alone during the Maoist period. Amin contends that the formation of an urban working class on the basis of peasants being forced off the land through privatisation and their complete separation from the means of production did not occur in China. Because land did not become private property, he claims that the commodification of the means of production was incomplete. Amin insists that this shows that unlike the Soviet Union, in China the CCP achieved industrialisation while guaranteeing benefits for peasants.[160] Giovanni Arrighi similarly argued that China was not capitalist because proletarianisation had not taken place. More recently Gary Blank, basing himself on the arguments of political Marxists such as Robert Brenner, has maintained that China up to the present day has not been capitalist on similar grounds.[161]

In the case of the latter group, they tend to follow the periodisation of modern Chinese history set out by Hung Ho-Fung, who defines 1850–1980 as an era of primitive accumulation and points to the Mao period as the period of most intense capital accumulation. Hung argues that 'The price that the countryside was forced to pay under the collective agriculture system enabled rapid industrialization'.[162] Nonetheless, Hung still defines contemporary China as 'state socialism'. Wang Hui and Li Minqi, despite their various differences, come to the same conclusion.[163] This position can be summarised as: the Mao period was a period of primitive accumulation but not capitalist. It is thus a set of positions that divorce the concept of primitive accumulation from capitalism.

Mark Selden dealt with this problem in detail thirty years ago in his fascinating comparison of primitive accumulation in China and Taiwan. Selden, following Marx, argued that what allows capital accumulation societally is primitive accumulation, and at the heart of this are wage labourers and capital formation. After introducing research on the role played by price differentials between industrial goods and agricultural goods in the process of capital formation, Selden asserts there are more commonalities than differences on this point between Taiwan under Chiang and China under Mao. In both cases, landowners were sacrificed in land reforms, and the surplus generated by small landholding peasants was invested in urban industrialisation. In Taiwan, cap-

---

160   Amin 2013.
161   Blank 2015, chapter 3.
162   Hung H.F. 2015, p. 44.
163   Wang H. 2014, p. 138; Li M. 2012, chapter 2, p. 35.

ital formation took place via transferring agricultural surplus to manufacturing. Since agricultural markets stagnated and peasant earnings failed to grow, urban manufacturing was easily able to access cheap labour from the countryside without enclosure taking place.[164]

In the case of China, agricultural productivity increases depended on achieving the industrial development plan. However, while the First Five-year Plan anticipated that agricultural output would grow at an annual rate of 4.6 percent, it only achieved 1.7 percent per annum in 1953–4. This prompted the gradual strengthening of agricultural collectivisation through which agricultural surplus could be more efficiently concentrated in the hands of the state. The private selling of agricultural produce was criminalised and rural handicrafts were also collectivised.[165] Once the agricultural surplus was directly managed through collectivisation, Chinese industrial accumulation grew from 22.9 percent of GNP to 26.1 percent in 1955–6, and by 1959 it had reached 44 percent.[166] On the other hand, as the divergence between agriculture and manufacturing increased, peasants continuously migrated to cities and, just as in Taiwan, there was no problem in securing a supply of wage workers without enclosure.[167] Compared to those scholars who turn the cases discussed in *Capital* into doctrinaire models, Selden's analysis is very convincing. However, he derives a strange conclusion from this correct analysis. He does not see the great similarity between Taiwan and China as meaning that Mao's China was capitalist. While Selden presents a more persuasive analysis, he ends up with the same conclusion as Hung. However, Selden's frame of analysis is still very useful in understanding in greater detail both the urban-rural relationship during the Mao period and the process of primitive accumulation.

First, as Selden points out, securing a labour force for industrialisation did not require land enclosure. The difference in living standards between rural and urban areas continued throughout the Mao period, and meant that peasants were more than willing to become urban workers. There is a tendency to imagine Maoist China as a country of unimaginable equality by capitalist standards, but the difference in standards of living between urban and rural areas was similar to other developing nations and was actually worse than South Korea at the time. The lowest class accounted for 14–16 percent of gross income in China in the late 1960s while in South Korea it was 24 percent in the

---

164   Selden 1992.
165   Selden 1992, p. 115.
166   Selden 1992, p. 116.
167   Selden 1992, p. 123.

same period.[168] The standard of living for the majority of Chinese peasants during the 1953–78 period was lower than it had been in 1933.[169] Moving from the countryside to the city was considered an honour, and being employed in the city 'appeared to be even more spectacular than having a child going to college nowadays from the villagers' point of view'.[170]

The attraction of cities grew as the coercive work regime and pressure to fulfil quotas in the People's Communes[171] increased during the Great Leap Forward. According to one important case study on the rural area of Pingjiang during the Maoist period, some 20,000 peasants left the region in the second half of 1958 alone while another 30,000 left once the Great Leap Forward got underway. One local party official spoke frankly of the reasons for this exodus, saying, 'Why are the farmers leaving? We drove them to it by making their lives so miserable'.[172] The famine of the Great Leap Forward only accelerated a process that was already underway.

Second, Selden's analysis helps us understand that the curbing of class differentiation within rural areas under Mao had nothing to do with the socialist – or perhaps 'non-capitalist' – character of China. Instead, this was the result of surplus being extracted from rural areas in the process of capital formation. Mylene Gaulard also contended in her analysis of Chinese state capitalism that the prioritisation of heavy industry retarded other sectors, including agriculture.[173] Li Huaiyin likewise made a similar argument on the basis of a case study of production brigades.[174]

> The state's excessive extraction greatly impaired the team's ability of collective accumulation and impeded its investment in modern agricultural equipment. The average amount of 11,800 *yuan* that the state annually extracted from the team would have allowed the team to buy, for example, 7 walking tractors, or 15 water pumps, or 25 threshers, or 42,000 kilograms of chemical fertilizers. In actuality, however, with the limited amount of public accumulations, the team had only one tractor, one water pump,

---

168   Parish 1981, p. 41.
169   Bianco 2007, p. 361.
170   Li H. 2016, p. 389. Elizabeth Perry's research on the miners of Anyuan also reveals the same point: Perry 2012.
171   People's Communes (*renmin gongshe*) were the highest level of collective farm organisation in the countryside during the Mao period.
172   Gao A. 2013, p. 188.
173   Gaulard 2014, p. 219.
174   Production brigades constituted the middle level organisation of the collective farm system under Mao.

and one thresher, and consumed only about 1,500 kilograms of chemical fertilizers a year in most of 1970s. In other words, because of over-taxation by the state, the production team could only make minimal investments in modern inputs and maintain a 'simple reproduction' of the collective economy.[175]

This was not limited to China. South Korea also suppressed other sectors when developing heavy and chemical industries in the 1970s,[176] and of course North Korea did the same in the 1950s and 1960s, as is shown in Chapter 2 of this volume. This is an obvious outcome of backward states focusing what little capital they have at their disposal in a single sector. What was called 'equality' at the time can be explained in terms of what might be called Marxist common sense: 'Capital grows in one place to a huge mass in a single hand, because it has in another place been lost by many'.[177]

The size of the surplus originating from rural areas is controversial. According to research on this issue, estimates for the funds extracted between 1953 and 1978 due to price rural/urban differentials range between 600 billion and 800 billion RMB.[178] Another researcher has claimed that funds originating in 'unequal exchange between 1952–78 ... at one point reached 73.2 percent of the total value of movable assets belonging to state enterprises'.[179]

Third, Selden's argument can also be read as confirmation that the more effective exploitation of the urban working class was one of the most important reasons for the enforced sacrifice of the Chinese peasant class. This was in fact the main motivation for the abolition of rural markets in 1953 and the commencement of the state monopoly on agricultural produce (the compulsory purchase system). At a CCP meeting in October 1953 Chen Yun[180] made this point very sharply: 'Chen warned [about] what might transpire without a centralized system: prices would fluctuate, forcing wages up and damaging the First Five-Year Plan ...'. Mao Zedong was in complete agreement with this. However, since he needed to hide this reality, he 'ordered that "not one word" about the grain monopoly appear in newspapers'.[181]

---

175   Li H. 2009, p. 247.
176   Yi J. 2008, Chapter 2.
177   Marx, *Capital* vol 1. Chapter 25.
178   The figure of '600 billion RMB' is from Fazhan yanjiu suo zonghe keti zu 1987, while the figure of '800 billion RMB' from Xu X. 2002, chapter 7.
179   Yangsiyuan 2005.
180   Chen Yun (1905–1995) was at that time the head of the Central Finance and Economic Commission.
181   Brown 2012, pp. 34–5.

After making some similar observations about the Polish system during a similar period, one dissident intellectual in Poland made the following arguments:

> The system of draining surpluses by the reducing the market prices of produce from individual peasant farms (and, accordingly, limiting the consumption and investment power of rural population) is therefore a means of reducing expenditure for the purchase of labour power and the result of the class goal of production. In this way, the exploitation of the peasant is a result of the exploitation of the worker and is inseparably bound to production relationships prevailing in industry.[182]

This framework of analysis differs from previous modes of analysis that saw the urban working class as part of the privileged class, making possible a completely different interpretation of the class struggle strategy of Mao's China. It shows that it would have been possible for urban workers and rural peasants to unite in opposition to the bureaucratic system that subordinated their needs to capital accumulation.

Fourth, Selden's analysis hints that the reason labour productivity in the agricultural sector did not grow under Mao was closely connected to capital accumulation and not due to some non-capitalist peculiarities of Chinese society. As we have seen in the earlier analysis of the First Five-year Plan and the following period, industrial labour productivity grew continuously during the Mao period, just as in 'normal' capitalism. However, the same cannot be said for the total productivity of Chinese society, including agricultural productivity, and the CCP bureaucrats themselves understood this very well. For example, an article carried in the journal *Laodong* in 1958, with the title 'Wages and the total rate of productivity', aimed to justify the introduction of the 'rational low wage' system by arguing that the rate of wage increases for urban industrial workers should be tied to total productivity of society rather than industrial productivity.[183] Naturally this stagnating labour productivity or even declining agricultural productivity gives rise to doubts about whether China was actually capitalist at that time, or perhaps constituted some sort of bureaucratic collectivist society, as proposed by Robert Brenner.[184]

---

182   Kuron and Modzelewski 1982, p. 51.
183   Quoted in: Yamamoto 2000, p. 67.
184   Brenner 1991. (https://www.versobooks.com/blogs/2490-the-soviet-union-and-eastern-eu rope-the-roots-of-the-crisis)

However, as Philip Huang has repeatedly pointed out, while rural labour productivity remained low during the Mao period, land productivity actually grew continuously.[185] This was because in the absence of investment aimed at raising labour productivity, the central bureaucracy instead tried to extract as much surplus as possible from the land. The bureaucrats were faced with a contradiction. Considering that they were short of capital to invest in heavy industry they did not want to increase investment in agriculture, but they also knew that they had to increase agricultural production in order to feed the growing population of urban workers. In China, a country overflowing with surplus labour power, in the absence of additional investment, the only input that could be constantly increased was labour. Paradoxically, while the intensification of labour on given land resources might look at first sight like it was motivated by a non-capitalist mode of production, it actually produced the greatest increase in urban capital accumulation, accompanied by the rising technical/organic composition of capital in heavy industry.

Philip Huang's research on agriculture in southern China has shown that in the early 1950s the labour input per *mu*[186] of farming land was 30 days per year but by the late 1960s it had risen to as much as 100 days.[187] During the 1950s, the expansion of the collective farming system in stages, with the establishment of production teams, production brigades, and people's communes, was carried out with the aim of more effectively organising and concentrating agricultural labour. In a recent book analysing Mao's China through the framework of state capitalism, Elliot Liu has understood this process as the formal subsumption of labour to capital. This is a very important argument and provides a much better way of explaining the relationship between peasants and urban industrial development at that time than the assertion that they were actually 'modern serfs'. However, although formal subsumption means the beginning of capitalists' control over the labour process,[188] the Chinese state was not able to fully achieve formal subsumption because at that time it could not produce tractors on a large scale and thereby control agricultural surplus as the Soviet Union had done under Stalin. The CCP bureaucrats experienced constant problems in trying to control the labour process of the peasants. Thus, when planned targets were not met and the government bureaucrats frequently expressed their suspicions that the peasants were hiding grain, this actually reflected the weakness of their control over the agricultural labour process. The bureaucrats had

---

185   Huang 1990, chapter 9, p. 186.
186   A *mu* is a Chinese unit of land measurement equivalent to 666 m².
187   Huang P. 1990, pp. 231–2.
188   Callinicos 2014, pp. 201–3.

to rely on coercion in order to get the peasants to do work for which they had little drive. This is the reason why all the case studies that deal with the Great Leap Forward are full of reports of various kinds of violent incidents, including terrible beatings. Large-scale flood control works carried out by the state also had to rely more on the mobilisation of unpaid labour than mechanised methods.[189] In the region studied by Philip Huang, peasants had to spend more than 10 percent of their annual labour time on 'obligatory labour', that is, on state-led flood control works.[190] This also helps us to understand why in the process of establishing the People's Communes the Chinese state created communal canteens and creches on a large scale. By concentrating the time for eating they were able to secure more working hours and by 'liberating' women from domestic [reproductive] labour they could take control of more female labour power. The bureaucrats demanded that women stop caring so much about their children and focus instead on their work.[191] Of course, the focus on labour inputs was not simply a continuation of pre-capitalist agriculture. After the failure of the Great Leap Forward in particular, other inputs such as chemical fertilisers and tractors were expanded in order to increase agricultural production. However, in contrast to the situation in urban industry, this was not a way to replace human labour but a process that was carried out in conjunction with rising labour/land ratios.[192]

The labour-intensive character of Chinese capitalist development explains well the fateful relationship between the 'backyard furnaces' and the mass famine of the Great Leap Forward period. Labour inputs into agriculture became more and more important as time went on and so when agricultural labour was diverted to the construction and maintenance of backyard furnaces it meant that in many regions it was difficult to finish the harvest and agricultural products were left to rot in the fields.[193]

Finally, Selden demonstrates the possibility of universalising the Chinese experience of that time. He points out that developing industry by sacrificing agriculture in this way was a phenomenon that was repeated in a number of late developing industrial countries, including Taiwan, which is his main object of comparison with the PRC. In his recent book dealing broadly with the debate around the development of capitalism, Henry Heller has pointed out – similarly to Selden – that Japan after the Meiji Restoration, Taiwan and South Korea

---

189   Huang P. 1987, p. 232.
190   Huang P. 1987, p. 233.
191   MacFarquhar 1983, p. 105.
192   Huang P. 1987, p. 239.
193   MacFarquhar 1983.

all followed a similar pattern of development.[194] However, it is rather ironic that he did not include Mao's China in this list. Instead, Heller mistakenly introduces Maoism as an important tradition of Asian Marxism.[195]

We can draw two important conclusions from the analysis above. First, when it comes to analysing the working class of the Mao era, the 'privileged working class' and 'heterogeneous working class' theories are both barking up the wrong tree.

Second, the appearance of rural China at that time was not – as Samir Amin has suggested – a result of the fact that the CCP leaders were firmly opposed to enclosure, but rather one part of a single process brought about by the development of Chinese capitalism. It was a result of the fact that the CCP rulers were pursuing the mind-boggling aim of constructing a heavy industrial and military industrial base comparable with those of the United States and the Soviet Union in a country with a level of development comparable to Afghanistan in the 2000s. Fundamentally, we have to understand these two co-existing processes – on the one hand urban industry equipped with industrial facilities and, on the other, an agricultural system in which peasants were forced to work like serfs using essentially premodern farming techniques – as both subordinate to the capitalist totality.

5   State Capitalist Accumulation and the Pressure of International Competition

From the discussion so far, two things are clear. One is that the Chinese bureaucracy exploited the workers and the other is that in contrast to general common sense, Chinese workers, whether permanent or temporary, were under pressure from flexibilisation and increasing exploitation. But was this exploitation actually capitalist exploitation? While it looked similar in form, wasn't it actually different in terms of content? Surely the surplus extracted was not actually capitalist surplus value? Ultimately, this problem can be posed instead as the question of whether the concrete labour of the Chinese working class was converted to abstract labour and whether there was competitive pressure for this labour to correspond with internationally socially necessary average labour.

The Marxist economist Alfredo Saad-Filho gives the following explanation of the process of converting concrete labour to abstract labour and socially

---

194   Heller 2011, p. 151.
195   Heller 2011, p. 219.

necessary labour. He has proposed the three concepts of 'equalisation, syn-chronisation and homogenisation', explaining that:

> [t]he equalisation of labour and the determination of values and prices are the outcomes of a real process in three stages: first, individual labours are normalised across those producing the same kind of commodity; second, they are synchronised across those that have produced the same kind of commodity in the past or with distinct technologies; and, third, they are homogenised across the other types of labour as the commodity is equalised with ideal money.[196]

These three concepts are not to be understood as three stages but neither are they to be understood as being achieved instantaneously without reference to time, as in the models of mainstream economists. They should instead be understood as laws of tendency that take time to be realised and it is precisely international capitalist competition that enforces these tendencies.

If we are going to judge whether these tendencies were actually being real-ised during the Mao period then we need to examine a bit more closely some-thing that has been assumed throughout this chapter so far: the functioning of international capitalist competition on China in the 1950s and 1960s. Looking at the source texts concerning the 'rational low wage' system that was discussed earlier in this chapter, a fascinating expression is used. The use of the phrase 'there are definite constraints on the country's freedom of initiative' indicates that the Chinese state was not able to arbitrarily decide the ratio between cap-ital accumulation and wages, but did so under strict limitations. If you know anything at all about the aims of the central bureaucrats in the Mao period then you will know that the investment decisions of the core bureaucrats were strongly influenced by international geopolitical competition. The well-known Chinese economist Wen Tiejun, who was at one time Hu Jintao's economic advisor, put it this way:

> If later scholars simply analyse the Chinese economy in the 1960s without taking into consideration the influence of the geopolitical situation around China at that time, they will undoubtedly arrive at a negative assessment, even if they make use of Western micro-economic meth-ods.[197]

---

196   Saad-Filho 2002, p. 54.
197   Won T. 2016, p. 124.

This was just the same before the 1960s too, and if you look at the process by which the CCP was able to gain power, it is not surprising at all. Without the war against the Japanese or the ensuing Civil War, the Communists would not have been able to come to power, and the Korean War then pushed the new Chinese state right into the midst of geopolitical competition with the western bloc, led by the United States. Of course, a response to external competition (whether military competition or economic competition) can arise without necessarily forcing the adoption of capitalist industrialisation. External competition does not automatically give rise to the birth of capitalist relations of production within a state. Usually that requires a process whereby the massive bureaucratic apparatus known as the state makes capital accumulation its main aim and then intervenes deeply into the fabric of society in order to achieve that aim. Late nineteenth-century East Asia provides a good illustration of how different states responded quite differently to the intrusion of the Western imperialist powers. For example, towards the end of the Chosŏn Dynasty, when faced with attacks by the French and US navies, the Hŭngsŏn Taewon'gun, acting as regent, ordered the manufacture of weapons that were described in a 200-year-old Qing Dynasty military manual. Far from being focused on capital accumulation, the resources of the Chosŏn state continued to be used for projects that were intended to strengthen the symbolism of royal power, such as the extremely expensive rebuilding of royal palaces in the capital. Without fundamental changes to the taxation system, as had occurred after 1868 in Japan, the process of concentrating domestic surplus in the hands of the state in order to develop industry just did not occur in nineteenth-century Chosŏn.[198]

However, in China after 1949 the CCP bureaucrats behaved in a completely different way to these pre-capitalist bureaucrats. The geopolitical response of China during the Mao period was always to unflinchingly pursue a heavy industry-centred approach. In fact, an important motivation for China to participate in the Korean War was that it was a way for it to receive economic aid from the Soviet Union[199] and that aid was overwhelmingly focused on China's domestic military industry alongside the construction of heavy industries that could support it.

As we saw earlier, even in the midst of the great calamity of the Great Leap Forward, the government bureaucrats continued to push for higher labour productivity and the expansion of labour flexibility, and, interestingly we can also observe how they linked these efforts directly to national defence. For

---

198   Yŏn K. 2003, pp. 198–9.
199   Shen Z. 2013b, pp. 311–12.

example, in 1960 a report issued by the State Economic Commission stated that 'We absolutely must continue this movement, progressing stage by stage, in order to overcome our inferiority in national defence, in order to constantly raise the level of our country's technology, and in order to greatly increase our labour productivity'.[200] Again, in December 1960, the State Economic Commission pointed out that the aim of the technological innovation movement was to 'raise production while reducing the number of personnel [required]' and insisted that if China did not produce more with less workers it would fail to strengthen its national defences.[201]

The scope of comparison used by the Chinese state was broad. In one report, for example, the fuel efficiency and top speed of a Chinese-made truck – the Jiefang – was compared to equivalent overseas models and it was noted that the Chinese model required 7–8 litres per 100 kilometres while the foreign models could manage the same distance on only 5–6 litres. Likewise, the trucks produced in other countries had higher top speeds, managing 100 km/h, compared to a top speed of 65 km/h for the Jiefang.[202] In the case of labour productivity in the mining industry, while per capita production was 882 tons in China in 1962, it was 5,200 tons in the USA and 1,830 tons in the Soviet Union.[203] However, despite the very varied types of comparison contained in them, the conclusions of reports from this time were all the same: that the root of China's low labour productivity was the low level of mechanisation/automation in industry. As a result, despite various changes in policy from the time of the First Five-year Plan to the Adjustment Period and the construction of the Third Front, one

---

200 Zhonggong zhongyang pi zhuan guojia jingwei dangzu guanyu dangqian gongye jiaotong zhanxian shang jishu gexin, jishu geming yundong qingkuang de baogao, 中共中央批转国家经委党组关于当前工业交通战线上技术革新，技术革命运动情况的报告 [Approved by the Central Committee of the Communist Party of China, the report of the Party Committee at the State Economic Commission on the current technological innovations in the industrial transport front], 19 September 1960, in Zhongguo shehui kexuewon he zhongyang dangan guan 2011c, p. 405.

201 Guojia jingwei: Kaizhan jishu gexin, jishu gemìng yundong de gongzuo yaodian (caogao) 国家经委：开展技术革新，技术革命运动的工作要点 (草稿) [State Economic Commission: carrying out technological innovation, the main points of the technical revolutionary movement], in Zhongguo shehui kexuewon he zhongyang dangan guan 2011c, p. 409.

202 Guojia jingwei dangzu: Muqian woguo gongye jishu shuiping yu shijie liushi niandai xianjin jishu shuipìng de chaju 国家经委党组：目前我国工业技术水平与世界六十年代先进技术水平的差距 [National Economic and Trade Party Group: The gap between China's industrial technology and the world's advanced technology in the 1960s], 17th July 1963, in Zhongguo shehui kexuewon he zhongyang dangan guan 2011c, pp. 188.

203 Zhongguo shehui kexuewon he zhongyang dangan guan 2011c, p. 189.

thing that never changed was the bureaucrats' dogged pursuit of a higher ratio of mechanisation to labour power (in Marxist terms, a higher technical composition of capital). Another important case that illustrates this point is that of the metallurgical industry during the Adjustment Period, when the state sought to cut the number of workers by as much as 41 percent. This was considered necessary because of the gap with other countries: in the metal processing industry, the ratio of workers per machine in China was 11, compared to 3.5 in the Soviet Union and Britain and only two in the US and Japan. But there were also significant variations within China itself, such that in Shanghai the number of workers per machine was six, while in the northeastern region it was 14. Thus if the Chinese state wanted to reduce the ratio in other parts of the country to that existing in Shanghai it would have required reducing the size of the workforce by around 1.8 million workers.[204] As a result, from the viewpoint of the central government, the aim was clear: industry had to increase per capita productivity by raising the ratio of technology to workers and shift decisively from labour-intensive to capital-intensive.

These examples also show how comparisons of labour productivity and the technical composition of capital were important for setting economic targets. The main objects of comparison were not countries at similar levels of development to China but rather the principal Western countries and the Soviet Union; in other words, those countries decided China's geopolitical position and determined the international standard of labour productivity. For example, in 1960 the State Economic Commission produced a report that compared the level of development of basic industries in China with those in the US, the Soviet Union and Japan. It concluded that China's current level of development was on a par with the United States in 1900, the Soviet Union in 1934 and Japan in 1937. In its analysis of the technical gap between China and its rivals, the report showed that only 3 percent of lathe-based production was automated or semi-automated in China, compared to 6.5 percent in the Soviet Union by 1955. In terms of automation in the mining industry, the gap was again stressed in the report, noting that the US had already achieved an automation rate of 86.4 percent, while the Soviet Union had reached 52 percent and Britain 48.4 percent.[205] Finally, while the SEC report evaluated China's heavy industry as

---

204   Laodong bu: 1961–1963 Nian jingjian qu gong, jianshao chengzhen renkou de chubu anpai yijian 劳动部：1961–1963 年精简取工，减少城镇人口的初步安排意见 [Ministry of Labour: From 1961 to 1963, how to layoff workforces and reduce urban population, the initial assessment], 12 July 1961, in Zhongguo shehui kexuewon he zhongyang dangan guan 2011a, p. 201.

205   Guojia jingwei dangzu: Muqian woguo gongye jishu shuiping yu shijie liushi niandai

occupying approximately 8th or 9th position in the world, it continued to stress the discrepancies with other countries. Another report, released in August 1963, continued the pessimistic tone of earlier reports, noting that:

> If we are to talk about the level of our country's industrial technology in general, it is at the global level of the 1940s. In 1956 the Soviet Union helped us with the establishment of priority industries, but from the point of view of production technology they were mostly at the level of the 1940s, with only a minority of the industrial facilities based on the latest technology and some even being at 1930s levels ... When we look at our capabilities in product design and our labour productivity, we are only at 1940s levels.[206]

The reason for all these comparisons with the most powerful countries in the world was that they were competitors who influenced China geopolitically. The Chinese bureaucrats were being forced to compete not with countries at a similar level of development like Egypt or India but with the US, which had deployed the Seventh Fleet to Taiwan, and with its most important Asian ally, Japan. Thus their aim became to produce the same products as their Western capitalist competitors, to the same standard, using the same production methods and the same level of productivity. These sorts of comparisons were used in the formulation of targets for economic plans and came down to the level of individual work units and factories, expressed as the 12 items that each had to fulfil. These included not just the total quantity of output or the total value of output, but also the rate of increase in labour productivity.[207] These targets were based on the relevant competing sector, so that in military and heavy industries, for example, it meant reaching the average international socially necessary labour time. As China attempted to adjust the productivity of the concrete labour of its workers (in terms of mass of products and automation) to the level of its competitor countries, this acted as a form of intense pressure towards equalisation and synchronisation.

---

xianjin jishu shuiping de chaju 国家经委党组：目前我国工业技术水平与世界六十年代先进技术水平的差距 [National Economic and Trade Party Group: The gap between China's industrial technology and the world's advanced technology in the 1960s], 17 July 1963, in Zhongguo shehui kexuewon he zhongyang dangan guan 2011c, p. 190.

206 Guojia jingwei dui dangqian gongye shengchan shuiping de guji 国家经委对当前工业生产水平的估计 [The State Economic Commission's estimate of current industrial production levels], 30th August 1963, in Zhongguo shehui kexuewon he zhongyang dangan guan 2011c, p. 194.

207 Howe 1978, p. 31, table 17.

So far, the stage of comparison that presupposed equalisation stopped at the quantity and production technologies of commodities. But if the comparisons ended here then the equalisation and synchronisation of labour would have come to a halt. However, the labour of Chinese workers was also also compared using abstract numbers, by conversion to an 'imaginary currency', comparing labour in China with labour in Western countries by using monetary values expressed in international currency. China's participation in the international circulation of commodities at that time was quite limited.[208] However, as Isaak Rubin noted, in capitalism, before producers compare labour through money in the actual process of exchange, they have already equalised their products with a determined quantity of money ('a determined sum of value'), 'in consciousness'.[209] In the case of China, the comparison of these figures that passed across the desks of the planners was very important in the real world because they held the key to the country's fate. To take an example, in 1963 a report by the State Economic Commission compared the productivity of industrial workers in different countries by converting productivity to monetary values. According to this report, China in 1962 produced 1,800 *yuan* of added value per worker, which was only one-third of the added value produced by Japanese workers, one-quarter of that produced by Soviet workers, one-fifth of that produced by West German workers and barely one-twelfth of that produced by US workers.[210] The Chinese planners set 1960 and 1962 as their base years and then compared rates of industrial labour productivity between China and Western countries. They started by using each country's own currency and then made approximate conversions to Chinese *yuan*. Of course, errors might arise in this sort of calculation. However, more important than the accuracy of these comparisons is why the Chinese state made the effort to homogenise concrete labour through these comparisons and what the practical results of this were. One result was that even though China's heavy industry was not incorporated

---

208   However, the Chinese state did direct that exports should be increased, as long as they
          were at a level that did not harm the national defence and heavy-industry-first policy. This
          was because in order to import more high tech machinery for the construction of heavy
          industry, it was necessary to earn foreign currency. Duiwai maoyi gongzuo ershisi tiao 对
          外贸易工作二十四条 [24 clauses on foreign trade work], 3 March 1958, in Zhongguo
          shehui kexuewon he zhongyang dangan guan(2011d), pp. 6–8.
209   '[T]his equalization of labor carries with it a preliminary character "represented in con-
          sciousness"'. Rubin 1973, p. 70.
210   Guojia dui woguo dangqian gongye shengchan shuiping de guji 国家对我国当前工
          业生产水平的估计 [Comparing China's current industrial production level with other
          countries], 30th August 1963 in Zhongguo shehui kexuewon he zhongyang dangan guan
          2011c, pp. 190–4, p. 197.

into processes of international exchange, international competition was nearly always the decisive factor in how and where living and dead labour was put to use within China, regardless of the domestic needs of the country (neither the needs of the bureaucracy nor the people). Not only was the whole Chinese state subject to the international capitalist law of value, but the bureaucrats, in their enthusiastic participation in international competition, drove the formation of capitalist production processes within China. According to the *Cambridge History of China*, throughout the entirety of the Mao Zedong's rule, 'three quarters of investment was dedicated to producing machines that could produce more machines'.[211] The resemblance between this sentence and expressions used by Marx in *Capital* is truly striking.[212]

6 Conclusion: Taking a Longer View of Chinese Workers and State Capitalism

In this chapter we have seen how the Chinese Communist Party established a state capitalist regime of capital accumulation in the early years of Mao's rule. I have argued that the Chinese bureaucracy's drive to accumulate was driven by the pressure of geopolitical competition and that primitive accumulation took place through the establishment of the collective farming system. I have also shown how Chinese workers in industry were treated in similar ways to workers in other capitalist economies in order to maximise labour productivity and accumulation, using wage differentials, a gendered division of labour and a flexible workforce of permanent and temporary workers. We have seen how, in that process, proletarianisation took place on a mass scale. This process of class formation continued into the late Mao period and has continued since the beginning of reform and opening in 1978. In this conclusion therefore, I would like to expand the scope of the chapter somewhat in order to briefly address the question of continuities and breaks in the evolution of Chinese capitalism since the early twentieth century. Here I will address principally the question of continuity between workers under Chinese state capitalism during the Mao period and in the period of 'reform and opening' after 1978.

The Chinese intellectual Qian Liqun has argued for the concept of a 'Post-Mao Era'. This is because from his perspective there is no rupture between the

---

211 MacFarquhar and Fairbank (eds) 1991, p. 491.
212 'Accumulation for accumulation's sake, production for production's sake.' *Capital* vol. 1. Chapter 25.

Mao period and the subsequent period, a view that is well expressed in the following passage: 'Not only have the workers not been able to enjoy the fruits of the [last 60 years of] development, in fact their interests have been further encroached upon. This goes completely against the fundamental principles of socialism, so why does it keep happening in a country that calls itself socialist?'[213] Although when Chen analyses this continuity he does not include the socio-economic structure, his approach is still useful.

Of course, it is not only through state capitalism theory that one can find continuity between the Mao era and the era of 'reform and opening'. The idea that for one reason or another China is still not capitalist is actually quite widespread. However, if one doesn't understand the continuities through state capitalism theory then it is not possible to understand the changes since reform and opening properly.

For example, in the second edition of his book *Mao's China and After*, Maurice Meisner concluded that capitalism was developing in China in the 1980s and this would become an obstacle for the CCP.[214] Some Chinese Trotskyists based in Hong Kong also argued after the Tiananmen uprising that if the market opening continued the CCP 'would be swept away by the tide of capitalism'.[215] However, Chinese capitalism came into full bloom and thanks to that the CCP became stronger.

According to Barry Naughton, when various sorts of ideology are removed and one looks at the bureaucratic system of the Mao era simply from an economic standpoint, one arrives at the very simple reality that it was 'a system whose aim was to mobilise all resources for industrialisation'.[216] We would get closer to the essence of the matter if we replaced 'industrialisaton' with 'capital accumulation'. The CCP bureaucrats pursued reform and opening because they had realised the limits of a previous capital accumulation strategy focused on heavy industry and military spending, which had become an impediment to extracting the maximum amount of surplus value from workers. In addition, the fact there was a huge surplus population in the rural areas of China was becoming a bigger problem. As we saw earlier, CCP bureaucrats at the highest level had recognised the relationship between the permanent arms economy and Chinese capital accumulation themselves since the 1950s. And in fact it was only in the 1980s when the structure of geopolitical competition had changed that they were able to gradually pursue changes to Chinese capitalism. As a

---

213   Qian 2012, volume 2, p. 191.
214   Meisner 1986. See in particular the last chapter: 'China after Mao'.
215   Barrett 1996, p. 37. See: 'The tasks of revolutionary socialists at the current stage'.
216   Naughton 2006, p. 79.

result of these geopolitical changes and thanks to the improvements in relations with the US they were able to retreat partially from the heavy industry and military capital accumulation strategy of the past. However, this was simply a retreat from a particular accumulation strategy, not a retreat from capital accumulation itself. This is where we can locate the continuity between the Mao era and the post-Mao era. Despite the huge changes that have occurred since 1978, the Chinese working class in the post-Mao period demonstrates clear structural continuities with the working class of the Mao period because both are subordinated to capital accumulation.

As Wang Hui has pointed out in his preface to an important recent study of Chinese migrant workers by Lu Tu, the author intentionally does not apply the concept of 'working class' to migrant workers (*nongmin gong*).[217] This is because Lu believes that the workers of the past (by worker she automatically means state enterprise worker) and the 'new workers' of today are qualitatively different entities. While she thinks that Chinese workers in the past were in the social position of protagonists, today's workers (she uses the term *tagong*)[218] are simply in the position of being employed by someone. Likewise, in the preface to the book Wang Hui insists that the 'external environment' (including politics) was important in the formation of the Chinese working class and therefore the reason that the 'new workers' of today's China are unable to form themselves as subjects like the workers of the past is that the historical environment is different. These approaches to the problem have in common the fact that they are limited to analyses of politics and ideology.

There are also some who use an analysis of the socio-economic conditions of the working class to argue that there was a fundamental break between the Mao and post-Mao periods. Perhaps the most prominent version of this position centres around the 're-emergence of the labour market' theory. A jointly authored work by Pun Ngai, Beverly Silver and Lu Zhang, argues, for example, that 'the deepening commodification of labor since the mid-1990s has been accompanied by a rising tide of labor unrest in China'.[219] As we saw earlier in this chapter, beginning with the strikes of 1956–7, workers have continuously been struggling over the conditions under which they sell their labour. Furthermore, as Wen Tiejun has pointed out, the advance of migrant workers into the cities was not a simple result of the market but rather a joint enterprise of the central government and regional bureaucrats. As a result, the same

---

217   Lu T. 2017, pp. 59–60.
218   Literally, a worker employed by someone else.
219   Silver and Zhang 2009, pp. 174 5.

scholars describe workers in today's China using concepts such as 'partially proletarianised' or 'semi-proletarianised', but as we saw earlier in the discussion of
temporary workers in the Mao era, this is in no sense a new phenomenon. If
we look at the research of Lu Zhang, the Chinese automobile industry in fact
continued to use the Mao era temporary worker employment system right up
to the early-to-mid 1990s.[220] In other words, they continued to employ workers from rural areas with rural household registrations and pay them less than
workers with urban registrations.

The continuities for workers in these two periods do not end here. As we can
learn from the recent book dealing with Chinese workers' struggles, *China on
Strike*, various forms of coercion were still frequently being used in the 2000s,
including the use of company security or gangsters to force workers to meet
their production quotas or accept the level of their wages.[221] And even in the
2000s restrictions were still being imposed on the ability of workers to move
from one factory to another. Among the cases of strikes that are examined in
the book, there are those where workers wanted to resign from their posts but
were not permitted to by the factory, showing clearly that there continue to be a
variety of measures that limit the complete commodification of labour power.

The discrepancies between the legal ownership of businesses and the conditions of the working class also continue. Recently when a private steel company in China owned by a Taiwanese business was nationalised, workers' wages
were reduced and performance-based pay was introduced and workers went
on strike in protest. The *China Labour Bulletin* noted that it was 'ironic that
such a thing should happen after nationalisation in a country that proclaims
itself to be socialist', but if we look back over the cases we have examined in
this chapter, this doesn't seem at all surprising. Interestingly, in the same article, the *China Labour Bulletin* argued that the reason workers' conditions did
not improve after the nationalisation of the company was that 'they put developmentalism first in order to compete with Western countries', but there were
also frequent cases where the same sort of thing happened after nationalisation during the Mao era.

The demands for temporary workers to be made permanent also continue
as they did before. Recently a strike by nurses has raised the demand for equality, bringing to mind the struggles of temporary workers during the Cultural
Revolution.[222] This sort of continuity with the past exists because China is still

---

220   Zhang 2014, p. 67. It should be noted that Zhang herself does not recognise the structural
        continuity between the Mao and post-Mao periods.
221   Li, Friedman & Ren 2016.
222   China Labour Bulletin 2016, 'Nurses in Several Chinese Cities Strike over Low Pay and

a developing capitalist country, not because it is non-capitalist or because of certain historical legacies. The Xi Jinping government, famous for its so-called revival of Maoism, announced in March 2016 that it planned to lay off around five million workers at state enterprises.[223] If you were ignorant of the situation of workers during the Mao era this action might seem extremely paradoxical, but of course, as we have seen, the laying off of state workers was a hallmark of labour relations during Mao's time. Despite this, in today's China when faced with this sort of exploitation, it is Mao and his era that are raised most easily as an alternative. Of course, workers in the midst of their struggles will use various rhetorical means to give greater legitimacy to their struggle and they have the right to do so. Workers' struggles do not develop on the basis of a full and accurate understanding of their own position in society. In fact, it is often easier to find examples where they develop on the basis of the exact opposite. However, if the strategic perspectives of workers' struggles in China are limited to the Mao era or even make that period a key yardstick, then it can only be an obstacle to the development of those struggles.

Within this overall continuity, the Chinese working class has been steadily changing. Even in the case of Lu Zhang's outstanding research, she tends to imply that today's permanent workers are a legacy of socialism. However, Zhang's research on the labour process in China's automobile factories today provides an extremely important case study for understanding continuity and change. At Chinese joint-venture automobile plants, casual workers and permanent workers are doing the same work[224] and from the mid-1990s onwards the number of dispatched workers[225] began to increase rapidly in the industry. These workers were even cheaper than those with rural registrations because they didn't have to be paid any severance pay and they were extremely flexible. At its worst, in 2006 in some of the automobile enterprises, some 70 percent of casual workers were dispatched workers and within this group there were both rural-registered workers and urban-registered workers. Furthermore, as the general level of education increases in China, the gap between the skill levels of permanent skilled workers and other workers has been gradually decreasing. Even within the unevenness of the Chinese working class, a process

---

benefits', https://www.clb.org.hk/content/nurses-several-chinese-cities-strike-over-low-p ay-and-benefits [accessed August 2017]. For the struggles of temporary workers during the Cultural Revolution, see Li Xun 2015, vol. 1, chapter 16.

223   Reuters (1.3.2016), 'Exclusive: China to lay off five to six million workers, earmarks at east $23 billion.' http://uk.mobile.reuters.com/article/idUKKCN0W33DM?irpc=932

224   Zhang 2014, p. 219.

225   Dispatched workers are a type of agency workers who are common in present-day China.

of homogenisation has been going on. As a result, the numbers of workers with a rural *hukou* registration who actually think of themselves as urban citizens is increasing. As the media reports pointed out after the Honda strike of 2010, this has become a motivation for industrial struggle among the new younger generation of workers.[226] In a recent article William Hurst has argued that the equalisation of the Chinese working class is finally occurring. However, as we have seen earlier in the discussion of the flexibilisation of both temporary and permanent labour under Mao, the development of free wage labour and the homogenisation of the internal structure[227] of the Chinese working class are tendencies that have been continually in operation since the Mao period, despite the vicissitudes and precariousness of capital accumulation in a backward country.

Continuity in the conditions of the Chinese working class can also be found in the relationship between industrialisation and the countryside. Of course, the state's ability to intervene directly in the agricultural production process through the people's communes and production brigades was greatly weakened. But as we can see from Hung Ho-Fung's work, even in the 2000s rural areas were still playing the role of subsidising urban capital accumulation and this was exerting a huge influence on class differentiation in the countryside.[228] In addition, the question of who controls the land – the means of production – remains as one of the biggest issues, although it has changed in form over the years. While in the past, under the pretext of nationalisation, land was used to service capital accumulation without a penny being paid for it, today land is used to service capital accumulation under the rubric of 'development' without adequate compensation being paid to farmers.

Although there has been much change during the twentieth century history of the Chinese working class, there was no decisive break. Our conventional periodisation – Guomindang era – socialist era – era of rural migrant workers subordinated to global capitalism – is an arbitrary one. While the concrete patterns of labour-capital relations have changed over time, since the beginning of the twentieth century China has not been able to escape the fact that it has been part of the global capitalist system. The Chinese working class continues to change structurally and this opens up new prospects for workers' struggle and anti-capitalist alternatives that are completely different to those of Maoism and the theories influenced by it.

---

226   Hwang K. 2010.
227   This tendency does not imply that differences in wages and labour conditions have been eliminated.
228   Hung H. 2009b, p. 15, figure 6.

CHAPTER 4

State Capitalism and the Permanent War Economy in South Korea, 1950–72

Jeong Seongjin

1 Introduction

This chapter attempts to explain the rise of state capitalism in South Korea since the 1960s in terms of the effects of the permanent arms economy during the Korean War and the Vietnam War.[1]

First, this chapter argues that the Korean War period established three crucial structural characteristics of South Korean state capitalism. The first was broadly social and took the form of the establishment of a capitalist class structure. The second was mainly political, consolidating the Cold War regime, while the third was economic in character and took the form of the permanent arms economy.[2]

Second, this chapter also argues that the Vietnam War was not only crucial for the Korean economy to 'take-off' in the late 1960s and early 1970s through the operation of the permanent arms economy but also for internationalised state capitalism to be established in Korea.[3] Unlike the 'self-sufficient', or 'internally oriented' economy common to other cases of Third World state capitalism in the 1950s and 1960s, like India or North Korea, 'internationalised', or 'externally oriented' state capitalism is specific to the South Korean case. Indeed, it is one of the secrets of the success of South Korean state capitalism.

---

1 This chapter is revised from the author's previous work, Jeong 2000. An earlier version was presented at the workshop at SOAS in 2012. The author is thankful to Owen Miller for his invitation and encouraging comments. This work was supported by the Ministry of Education of the Republic of Korea and the National Research Foundation of Korea (NRF-2021S1A3A2A02096299).

2 For a discussion of the social structures of accumulation of Korean state capitalism, refer to Jeong (1997). The Korean War played a similar role to the American Civil War, which contributed to the development of American capitalism by fortifying the North's industrial hegemony through abolishing the slave labour plantation system in the South.

3 Considering this, it is quite strange that discussion of the 'Vietnam War' is almost absent in Amsden 1989, the representative work on the theory of the developmental state, or Seoul Institute for Social Sciences Economics Unit 1991, the textbook on modern Korean capitalism for the Korean left in the early 1990s, testifying to the predominance of the 'one-country' paradigm or the methodological nationalism among the contemporary Korean left.

This chapter emphasises the permanent arms economy in the geopolitical context of the Cold War as one of the most important causes of the rise and success of state capitalism in South Korea. While drawing upon previous studies of the relation between the Korean War, Vietnam War, and the Korean economy, especially Imura (1987; 1988a; 1988b; 1988c) and Park (1995), this chapter attempts to contribute to existing studies by explicitly applying the Marxist theories of state capitalism and permanent arms economy, originally developed by Cliff,[4] to the explanation of South Korea's rapid growth economy.[5] In existing works, Cliff's theory of state capitalism has usually been applied to the regimes of so-called 'actually existing socialism', not to the Western capitalist system. Additionally, the theory of permanent arms economy was conceived to explain the post-war boom in Western advanced capitalism, not the rapid economic growth of the Third World countries. This chapter attempts to show that the theories of state capitalism and the permanent arms economy can be combined and applied to explain high-speed capitalist development and its related contradictions in South Korea in the Cold War period.

2   Return to the Theory of State Capitalism

Considering that the theory of state capitalism was originally constructed in order to explain Western advanced capitalist countries, in a variant of the theory of 'state monopoly capitalism', or to analyse the former USSR, as in the work of Tony Cliff,[6] it may appear odd that the theory could also be applied to developing countries, like postcolonial South Korea of the 1950s–60s. However, it should be remembered that the theory of state capitalism was also the official theory employed by the Soviet Communist Party (CPSU) to describe some developing countries during 1950s–60s.[7] Indeed, the Soviet theory of state capitalism was received as the 'orthodox' Marxist theory of developing countries and was very influential among international left academics as late as the 1970s.[8] It dominated the research paradigm of radical scholars in Japan

---

4   Cliff 1974.
5   For recent discussion of the theories of state capitalism and permanent arms economy, refer to Harman 1984; 2010 and Pozo 2010.
6   Cliff 1974.
7   Clarkson 1978.
8   For the Soviet theory of state capitalism in the Third World, refer to Carlisle 1964, Petras 1976 and Clarkson 1978. For the Japanese debates on state capitalism in the Third World during the 1970s, refer to Honda 1970 and Ozaki (ed.) 1980.

and Korea who were working on developing countries during that period. The Soviet theory of state capitalism was originally developed after the death of Stalin to emphasise or justify the 'progressive' nature of some developing countries that had achieved political independence with the disintegration of colonialism after WWII. It described these countries as 'anti-imperialist' 'national democratic states', based on popular support from workers, peasants and the national bourgeoisie. It also viewed the social formation of some developing countries as a hybrid of 'modes of production', including state capitalism, private capitalism, petty commodity production etc, where the 'mode' of state capitalism played the hegemonic role.[9] It also emphasised the importance of the state sector, especially the nationalisation of a few key companies, in the transition to socialism. Indeed, it asserted that these 'national democratic states' were in the 'transition' process towards socialism, following the 'path of non-capitalist development'. In short, state capitalism was assumed to be the 'economic base' of the 'national democratic state'.

However, when some 'national democratic states' deserted their former 'non-alignment' line and took a pro-American, anti-Soviet position during the 1960s, Soviet ideologues withdrew their previous labelling of these countries as 'national democratic states', and began to criticise them as 'reactionary' 'bureaucratic capitalism', or 'neo-colonial', 'puppet regimes' of US imperialism. Hence the debates between those scholars who still argued for the 'progressiveness' of state capitalism, such as Rubinstein and Ozaki, and those who questioned it, such as Ghosh and Okakura. However, during these debates, the latter overwhelmed the former.[10] Moreover, with the increasing popularity of Latin American dependency theory from the 1970s, the Soviet theory of state capitalism appeared to merge with it, as can be seen in the phrase 'peripheral state capitalism'.[11] The Soviet theory of state capitalism had already been displaced by the rise of developmental state theory as the new research paradigm for developing countries, before it was totally discredited and forgotten, becoming a 'dead dog' with the fall of the USSR in 1991.[12] Considering this, it does not

---

9   In this regard, the Soviet theory of state capitalism could be seen as the application of Lenin's following description of post-1917 Russia as the hybrid of 'multi-formations': The following 'elements actually constitute the various socio-economic structures that exist in Russia at the present time. ... 1) patriarchal, i.e., to a considerable extent natural, peasant farming; 2) small commodity production ...; 3) private capitalism; 4) state capitalism; 5) socialism. Russia is so vast and so varied that all these different types of socio-economic structures are intermingled' (Lenin 1918, pp. 335–6).

10   Honda 1970.

11   Sakada 1992.

12   The Soviet theory of state capitalism, especially its 'neocolonial' version, like the theory of

seem strange that neither Johnson[13] nor Amsden,[14] founders of developmental state theory, mention or acknowledge the existence of the Soviet theory of state capitalism, although the latter predated the former and there exist important analytical and strategic similarities between two.

Compared to the theory of the developmental state, the Soviet theory of state capitalism appears analytically clumsy. The Soviet theory of state capitalism was more akin to an ideological instrument that served the geopolitical interests of the Soviet Union in the Third World than a scientific theory. While the aspects of state ownership or nationalisation were prioritised, concepts such as 'industrial policy', 'getting the price wrong', or 'export-led industrialisation', which are central to the theory of developmental state, are totally absent in the Soviet theory of state capitalism.

Does this mean that it is pointless to take a journey back from developmental state theory to the old theory of state capitalism? Not at all! First of all, besides the now discredited Soviet theory of state capitalism, there is another version of state capitalism theory which has strong roots in the classical Marxist tradition, and is most prominently represented by the work of Cliff. In the current academic ecology of development studies, where Marxist approaches seem to be almost extinct and the developmental state theory has established itself as the 'new normal' mainstream research paradigm, the old theory of state capitalism can provide valuable concepts and insights for Marxist development studies. Indeed, new demand for Marxist scholarship has arisen within development studies in order to fill the space on the left that has been vacated due to the rightward shift of developmental state theory. To meet this demand, Marxists have to move beyond counteracting the reformist Keynesian limits of developmental state theory and offer their own alternative research paradigm. For that, Marxists do not have to begin from scratch. The 'forgotten' theories of state capitalism could well provide useful clues for a new start. In fact, even the Soviet theory of state capitalism could be exploited if its 'rational kernel' is detached from its ideological distortions. Indeed, the Soviet theory has some merit in that it places central importance on class structure, as is seen in its theory of

---

'dependent state monopoly capitalism', was also popular among the South Korean left in the late 1980s. However, its popularity was very short-lived. In the face of the rapid development of independent capitalism in Korea as well as the collapse of 'actually existing socialism' after the late 1980s, many left Korean scholars had to drop the Soviet theory of state capitalism *in toto*. Some of them converted to the theory of 'medium developed capitalism', or developmental state theory later.

13   Johnson 1982.
14   Amsden 1989.

'multiple formations'. It also includes the transformative socialist perspective, though distorted, as its essential implication, which is totally absent in developmental state theory.

However, it is necessary not to repeat the shortcomings of the Soviet theory of state capitalism. First of all, its 'one country framework' or methodological nationalism should be rejected. Indeed, the Soviet theory of state capitalism is a strategy to build 'socialism in one country' for the Third World countries through the development of 'self-reliant' 'national' 'capitalism in one country'. This kind of 'one country framework' is incompatible with Marx,[15] who always conceived capitalism as well as socialism from the global viewpoint of 'world capitalism-world revolution'. To avoid the pitfall of the 'one country framework', an international dimension should be introduced to the Soviet theory of state capitalism. What is needed is to construct a theory of 'internationalised state capitalism'.

The legal fetishism of the Soviet theory, obvious in its 'progressive' version with its equation of state property with 'non-capitalism', and its catastrophism, characteristic of its 'neocolonial' version, must also be rejected. Indeed, between 'the path of non-capitalist development' and 'neocolonial bureaucratic capitalism', the third option, that is, the possibility of 'peripheral' state capitalism entering the 'centre' of the world system through the intensified accumulation of capital, is excluded a priori. Fortunately, Cliff's theory of state capitalism seems to provide important concepts that can overcome these limitations. Among them, the concept of geopolitical competition between 'many states' is crucial. Indeed, Cliff's original concept[16] of politico-military competition, or permanent arms economy, with its emphasis on the global dimension of state capitalism, which was used to define Stalinist Russia as state capitalism, can be applied to explain the rise of state capitalism in developing countries, like South Korea. Cliff's emphasis on the 'capitalist' nature of and capitalist 'development' in state capitalism could also provide the antidote to the legal fetishism and catastrophism of the Soviet theory of state capitalism. In short, a Marxist alternative to developmental state theory could be constructed and applied to development studies by critically reappropriating the 'rational' elements of older theories of state capitalism and permanent arms economy. This chapter attempts this in the case of postcolonial South Korea.

---

15   Marx 1973.
16   Cliff 1974.

3   The Korean War as the Foundational Moment for State Capitalism
     in Korea

Existing studies on the economic consequences of the Korean War largely con-
cur that they were negative for the accumulation of South Korean national
capital. They agree that the enormous physical and human destruction of the
war aggravated the already crippled state of the Korean economy caused by the
division of the Korean peninsula after liberation in 1945. It is also alleged that
the resulting dependent economic structure could not be sustained without US
aid. The few studies that have admitted the Korean War had positive economic
effects, such as Yook or Lee,[17] argued that the beneficiaries of the Korean War
were advanced capitalist countries, especially Japan, but not South Korea itself.
However, the common views regarding the economic effects of the Korean War
are problematic in that they are limited to the single country level. The development of Korean state capitalism can be explained only in the global context,
especially through the triangular geopolitical structure of East Asia. Although
the Korean War appears to have been destructive to the Korean economy when
viewed from a national scale, from an international perspective it actually functioned as the axis for high rates of capital accumulation in South Korea. The
Korean War provided the basis for the long boom in the advanced countries,
not only for the US but also for the post-war Japanese economic revival, by
establishing the East Asian Cold War regimes and the related US-Japan-Korea
permanent arms economy.

    Some existing studies do admit the positive effects of the Korean War on the
development of South Korean capitalism.[18] For example, Cumings[19] emphasised the positive effects of the land reform during the Korean War on the development of capitalism in South Korea, and found the secret of the extraordinary
rapid economic growth of Taiwan and Japan, in contrast to the chronic stagnation in Latin American countries, in the abolition of pre-capitalist property
relations, through the land reform in these two countries after WWII. Cumings
also indicated that capitalist development in South Korea should be viewed
in the regional context of East Asia.[20] Park also regarded the Korean War as

---

17   Yook 1959; Lee 1987.
18   Refer to Cumings 1984; Imura 1987; 1988a; 1988b; 1988c; Park 1990; Park 1993; Lee 1996; Jeong
      1995; Woo-Cumings 1998; Stubbs 1999; 2009; Johnson 2000; Pirie 2008; and Chang 2009.
19   Cumings 1984.
20   'Thus if there has been a miracle in East Asia, it has not occurred just since 1960s, it
      would be profoundly ahistorical to think that it did. ... A country-by-country approach

some sort of bourgeois revolution, in that it contributed to the realisation of the task of 'anti-feudal democratic revolution' through the eradication of semi-feudal landownership.[21] Sonn indicated that the crushing of the progressive workers' and peasants' movements that arose after Korea's liberation by the reactionaries during the Korean War and the establishment of a far-right anti-communist regime armed with an 'over-developed' state apparatus provided the social base for South Korea's repressive industrial relations, characterised by low wages, long working hours and high labour intensity.[22] Jeong showed that the Korean War contributed to the deconstruction of the remnants of the precapitalist social status system and related discrimination between nobles and lower people, while spurring the formation of an egalitarian civil consciousness.[23] Chang also argued that, 'It was during and after the Korean War that capitalist development in [South] Korea took shape. The Korean War produced a particular class composition, which consisted of the decomposed working class, critically declining landlord class, and an immediate alliance between the state and a few capitalists'.[24] Woo-Cumings emphasised the role of the Cold War in capitalist development in East Asia. 'The cold war in East Asia and American decisions connected to it has had strong influence on the industrial strategies of South Korea and Taiwan. ... The political economy of South Korea and Taiwan is thus inexplicable without the logic of a continuing mobilization for war'.[25] Stubbs also indicated that 'a complete analysis of the economic success of these [East and Southeast Asian] countries must take into account the sequence of wars that swept across East and Southeast Asia during the period of rapid economic development. Conventional explanations have to be combined with an understanding of the economic consequences of regional warfare and the preparation for war to fully appreciate the origins of

---

is incapable of accounting for the remarkably similar trajectories of Korea and Taiwan. ... Particularly important is the triangular structure of this arrangement: United States (core), Japan (semi-periphery), and Southeast Asia (periphery). This structure was clearly articulated in the deliberation leading up to the adoption of NSC 48/1 in late December 1949, a document so important that it might be called the NSC 68 for Asia. ... The first draft argued that the virtues of a 'triangular' trade between the United States, Japan, and Southeast Asia. ... I have also argued that industrial development in Japan, Korea, and Taiwan cannot be considered as an individual country phenomenon; instead, it is a regional phenomenon' (Cumings 1984, p. 3, p. 19, p. 38).

21   Park 1990.
22   Sonn 1991.
23   Jeong 1995.
24   Chang 2009, p. 90.
25   Woo-Cumings 1998, p. 319, p. 322.

the region's economic success. ... The location of East and Southeast Asia as a battle-ground in WWII and then in subsequent American attempts to contain Asian Communism, in terms of both interstate and insurgency wars, has provided a significant geostrategic context for rapid economic development'.[26] Pirie, meanwhile, noted that 'It is vital to study the broader regional and global context within which Korea was situated in the postwar period if we wish to develop a sophisticated, nuanced understanding of the Korean developmental state. ... Korea's integration into the global economy was shaped through its position within regional production structures and the Cold War geopolitical system'.[27]

However, the studies mentioned above did not resort to, or even mention, the theory of state capitalism and the permanent arms economy when they described the effects of the Korean War and the Vietnam War on South Korea's high rate of accumulation. In contrast, this chapter will explain the rise of capitalism in the Republic of Korea by explicitly considering the strong causal links between the permanent arms economy arising from the Korean and Vietnam Wars, state capitalism and rapid accumulation. As Stubbs indicated, 'a weak society', resulting from the events of WWII and its immediate aftermath, led to 'the rise of a relatively strong state' that was able to disable 'any concerted resistance' to it.[28] Also, 'the security situation' throughout East Asia placed social movements on the defensive and 'enhanced the state's autonomy'.[29] Moreover, war and the preparation for war gave strong impetus to the creation of a state apparatus and promoted the development of a powerful bureaucracy designed to mobilise all possible resources for the expansion of the military under the pretext of the threat from communism.[30] In short, the Cold War and the related permanent arms economy were crucial to the rise of state capitalism in East Asian countries, especially South Korea.

---

26   Stubbs 1999, p. 338.
27   Pirie 2008, p. 68.
28   Stubbs 2009, p. 6.
29   Stubbs 1999, p. 342. 'The genius of the states in South Korea and Taiwan – and Finland and Austria as well – was in harnessing real fears of attack and instability toward a remarkable development strategy. ... the cold war against their respective enemies continues to define the parameters of state action in these countries [South Korea and Taiwan], subsuming the development of social and economic institutions to exigencies of national survival. ... The existence for Taiwan and South Korea of enemies, as well as the ever present possibility of war, has continued to define the relationship of state to society' (Woo-Cumings 1998, p. 336; Woo-Cumings 1999, p. 10).
30   Stubbs 1999, pp. 340–1.

Tilly's aphorism that 'wars make states'[31] is especially pertinent in Korea. Indeed, wars and the threat of war have been crucial factors in the formation and development of the Korean state capitalism. The 'miracle' of the Korean developmental state would not have taken place without the operation of the permanent arms economy. Its main elements were the Korean War and related US aid in the 1950s, the Vietnam War and the turn to a strategy of export-led industrialization in the 1960s, and the defence-related heavy industrialization of the 1970s.[32]

World War II did not lead directly to the 'Golden Age' of post-war capitalism. While WWII brought the hope that the 1930s Great Depression could be overcome by the permanent arms economy, it ceased to function at the end of WWII. Moreover, the explosion of popular movements all over the world in the aftermath of the end of WWII threatened the very existence of capitalist social relations.[33] The 'Golden Age' of capitalism therefore did not begin with the end of WWII, but only with the re-starting of the permanent arms economy in combination with the smashing of popular anti-capitalist movements on a global scale. The 'Golden Age' was not pre-determined. Only the start of the Cold War made it possible to subdue popular struggles on a world scale and bring the permanent arms economy back into operation. The Cold War was formally launched with the Truman Doctrine in March 1947 and intensified with the Marshall Plan. However, the outbreak of the Korean War established it on a global scale. In this sense, the Korean War provided the pivotal moment for the postwar long boom by bringing the global permanent arms economy into operation. The Cold War regime helped the ruling classes of the Western and Eastern state capitalisms to repress the anti-systemic popular struggles in

---

31   Tilly 1985, p. 170.
32   In fact, heavy industrialisation from the 1970s was initiated by the need for military self-sufficiency and defence-related heavy industrialisation, occasioned by declining American fortunes in Vietnam, increasing North Korean guerrilla infiltration of South Korea, the Pueblo incident, the downing of the American EC-121 by the North Koreans, and the Nixon Doctrine (Woo-Cumings 1998, pp. 331–3). Johnson also noted that throughout the 1970s, 'Park continued to move the country toward an industrialisation that favored steel, shipbuilding, petrochemicals, and manufacturing rather than labor-intensive light industries. ... *Park's intention, not unlike that of the Stalinists in Eastern Europe, was to create the industrial foundation for South Korea's own national defense. ... Park had launched a program to build his own nuclear weapon*' (Johnson 2000, pp. 108–9. My emphasis).
33   'The extent of successful capitalist reconstruction achieved in Europe and Japan by early 1947 cannot be read off from indices for production or investment. ... The deep crisis which had gripped the system in the immediate aftermath of the war had yet to be resolved. In the spring of 1947 the capitalist class still faced enormous difficulties' (Armstrong et. al 1991, p. 67).

their countries. The US Congress passed the Taft-Hartley Bill, radically limiting trade union rights in 1947 when the Marshall Plan was announced. The power balance between labour and capital rapidly tipped in favour of the latter with the beginning of the Cold War, and especially after the Korean War, providing the social preconditions for the start of the 'Golden Age' of post-war capitalism.

The driver of the post-war permanent arms economy was US military expenditure. 'There was an unprecedented level of peacetime arms spending. It had been only a little over 1 percent of GNP in the United States before the war. Yet post-war "disarmament" left it at 4 percent in 1948, and it then shot up with the onset of the Cold War to over 13 percent in 1950–53, remaining between five and seven times the level of the inter-war years throughout the 1950s and 1960s. ... Arms expenditure, like "unproductive" expenditures, might be a deduction from profits in the short term, but in the long term it had the impact of reducing the funds available for further accumulation and so slowed the rise in the ratio of investment to the employed labor force (the "organic composition of capital"). ... The secret of the Western long boom of the 1940s, 1950s and 1960s lay in the way the national state could reduce the pressures leading to over-accumulation (by diverting a portion of capital into non-productive military channels)'.[34] In other words, military spending has functioned to counteract the tendency of the rate of profit to fall by containing the tendency of the organic composition of capital to rise. Indeed, the rate of profit of the advanced capitalist countries sustained its high level and did not show any tendency to fall during the 'Golden Age' after WWII. The average of the annual business net profit rate for seven advanced capitalist countries was 17.4 percent for 1952–5, 16.4 percent for 1956–60, and 17.9 percent for 1961–5.[35] Military expenditures in the Soviet Union and Eastern Europe, diverted from investment in productive industries, also contributed to counteracting the tendency of the rate of profit to fall by limiting the rise of the organic composition of capital. The post-war 'Golden Age' in the East as well as in the West would not have been possible without the operation of the permanent arms economy.

The cases of rapid economic growth in Japan and West Germany, contrasted to the decreasing competitiveness of US industries, are often cited as evidence to refute the theory of the permanent arms economy, in that they seemed to be based not on military expenditures but on enormous non-military civilian productive investments. However, the high economic growth rates of post-war Japanese and West German capitalism were possible only by free-riding

---

34   Harman 2009, pp. 166–8, p. 178.

35   Armstrong et al 1991, Table A2.

on the global permanent arms economy.[36] Indeed, Japanese growth crucially depended on the US-driven permanent arms economy. Japanese arms spending amounted to less than one percent of national product for a long time during the post-war period. Japan and Germany gained benefits from the high level of worldwide arms expenditure, especially by the United States, without having to sacrifice their own productive investment to pay for it. 'Had all countries had comparable levels of productive investment to that of the West Germans and Japanese there would have been a very rapidly rising global organic composition of capital and a downward trend in the rate of profit. ... *Non-military state capitalisms could only expand without crises because they operated within a world system containing a very large military state capitalism*'.[37] On this basis the cases of Japan and West Germany certainly do not provide counterfactual evidence against the theory of the permanent arms economy.

In fact, the outbreak of the Korean War in 1950 saved the US from falling into stagnation: 'pent-up consumer demand in the United States had largely disappeared by the end of 1947. ... Total business investment stagnated from early 1948. Profits peaked then too. By mid-1948 exports were 20 percent down on the previous year, despite emergency aid to Europe. In 1949 ... Business investment led the way down, declining by about 4 percent of GDP. ... Unemployment doubled to 7.6 percent. ... [But] the US economy revived on the expectation of hostilities in Korea'.[38] The rate of growth of US GNP was –1.9 percent in 1945, –19 percent in 1946, –2.8 percent in 1947, 3.9 percent in 1948, and 0 percent in 1949, before it jumped to 8.5 percent in 1950, the year of the Korean War, and as high as 10.3 percent in 1951.[39]

The Korean War also saved the Japanese economy from a severe recession after the 'Dodge Line'[40] and cleared inventories by as much as 100 to 150 billion yen thanks to special procurements and the related increase in exports.

---

36   Harman 1984, p. 94.
37   Harman 2009, pp. 198–9. My emphasis.
38   Armstrong et. al. 1991, pp. 106–8.
39   Economic Report of the President 1986, p. 253. 'The enormous increase in military spending boosted production considerably, simply by absorbing so many resources. The Korean War generated a dramatic commodities boom. Wool, rubber, tin, cotton and other basic commodities more or less trebled in price. ... Unemployment continued to fall in North America (to 3.2 percent in 1952, compared to 6.1 percent in 1950)' (Armstrong et. al. 1991, pp. 107–9). 'The outbreak of the Korean War came in the nick of time. The threatened crisis due to relative overproduction of consumer goods was averted and the dominance of the Permanent War Economy guaranteed' (Vance and Oakes 2008, p. 39).
40   The 'Dodge Line' refers to the Japanese economic policy for 'stabilisation and independence' recommended by Joseph Dodge, an American banker, who visited Japan in 1949 as a Special Adviser for US Occupation Forces in Japan to advise on the budget of the Japanese

TABLE 4.1   Japanese trade balance and Korean War special procurements (million dollars)

	1950	1951	1952	1953	1954	1955
Exports (A)	829	1,354	1,289	1,258	1,611	2,006
Imports (B)	886	1,645	1,701	2,050	2,041	2,061
Trade Balance (A)-(B)	−57	−292	−413	−792	−429	−54
Special Procurements	154	624	788	803	602	505

IMURA 1987, P. 317.

As Table 4.1 shows, the total amount of Japanese exports was 1.3 billion dollars during the Korean War, of which as much as 800 million dollars was accounted for by special procurements[41] for war. Japanese exports jumped by 61 percent in 1950, compared to the previous year, thanks to the global economic recovery driven by the Korean War.

The special procurements for the Korean War were mainly orders from the US military and related agencies to Japanese businesses for goods and services required for the Korean War. As is shown in Table 4.1, these special procurements rapidly increased from 1950, before decreasing in 1953, but maintained a level of 602 million dollars in 1954, making for a five-year total of 2.971 billion dollars. The major categories of goods for special procurements were arms, coal, gunny sacks, auto parts, and cotton while the main services procured were construction, auto repair, distribution, telegraphs, machine maintenance etc. The US allowed Japan to produce arms for the Korean War, though they were mostly gunpowder and ammunition, rather than advanced weapons. After the Korean War armistice was signed in July 1953, US special procurements from Japan sustained their high level, because US defence outlays in Asia continued to increase. The special procurements for one year after the Korean War were as large as 3.7 percent of Japan's 1950 GNP, playing a crucial role in stimulat-

---

government. The 'Dodge Line' sought to stabilise the economy and achieve fiscal soundness without American aid by setting a unitary exchange rate at one dollar to 360 yen.

41   According to Imura (1987), special procurements include the following categories: (a) US military purchase of goods and services in Japan for the Korean War. This is the special procurement of the Korean War in the narrow sense; (b) Purchases with the US defense account; (c) The personal consumption of US military personnel and their dependents in Japan; (d) Purchase made with the military and economic aid of the US Department of Defense or MSA fund in Japan. Category (d), called 'new special procurements', increased, compensating the decrease in category (a) after the Korean War armistice. Special procurements in the broad sense include categories (b) and (c) as well as (a).

ing the Japanese economy. The dollars acquired through special procurements for the Korean War amounted to 26.4 percent of Japan's total foreign exchange revenues in 1951 and 38.2 percent in 1953. They were thus the critical source of foreign exchange revenues. The Japanese foreign exchange reserve expanded to 1.122 billion dollars in 1952, from a mere 238 million dollars in 1949. Special procurements contributed to the increase of trade and production by making up for the trade deficits in Japan. While US aid made up for the trade deficits and helped Japan to import in excess of exports during the period from the surrender in 1945 to the 'Dodge Line' in 1949, special procurements played the same role with the phasing out of US aid to Japan after 1949. Increasing special procurements and related exports helped to clear the inventories and accelerate the increase of production in Japan. The Japanese mining and manufacturing production index exceeded its pre-war high in October 1950 and continued to increase to 104.6 in 1950 and 140 in 1952 (1934–6 set to 100). The exports of textiles, metal products and machinery increased rapidly after the Korea War. For example, steel exports increased from 32 million dollars in 1949 to 72 million dollars in 1950, and 259 million dollars in 1953. The rate of profit of Japanese businesses also increased thanks to the special procurements and increasing exports. During the Korean War wage increases were repressed and the prices of basic raw materials were limited, while the prices of exported goods and domestic industrial goods rose. As a result, the profit share of the Japanese corporate sector increased from 9 percent in 1948 to 15 percent in 1949, 22 percent in 1950, and 26 percent in 1951.[42] The Korean War brought such a big boom to the Japanese economy that it was called by contemporaries a 'kamikaze' (literally 'Divine Wind').[43] The expanded business profits in this period provided the source of the rationalisation investments for heavy industrialisation in the 1950s.

---

42 Armstrong et. al. 1991, p. 91.

43 Ichimada Hisato, President of Bank of Japan during the Korean War period, recollected that 'Japanese businesses were saved by the Korean War', and argued that 'with the execution of the Dodge Plan to control inflation and the US military special procurements due to the Korean War, the Japanese economy, hitherto distressed by bankruptcy, unemployment and lack of investment, suddenly entered a boom period. Textiles and metals were the goose that laid the golden eggs. Less than six months after the start of the Korean War, the prices of rayon, cotton yarn, silk, thin steel plate, and steel bars jumped by 3, 2, 1.8, 2.2, and 2.2 times respectively. ... Toyota automobile was also busy to meet the suddenly increasing orders for trucks. ... Without the Korean War, Toyota's success would not have been possible. ... Japan could recover its prewar level of economic activity and lay the foundation for the high economic growth after 1955 only through the windfall gains from the tragedy of the Korean peninsula' (Wada, 1999, pp. 241, 242, 243).

The economic beneficiaries of the Korean War were not confined to America and Japan, but extended to Germany. The Korean War boom began on a global scale from the summer of 1950. The German industrial production index jumped by 32.3 percent between March and December of 1950. The sudden, large increase in exports and domestic demand for a few months after the outbreak of the Korean War enabled the full-utilisation of capacities with the rush of orders to the investment goods industries in West Germany. 'The Korean boom provided the West German economy with a Keynesian stimulus just at a time when it was most needed and popular; as the boost did not come from government spending, all those negative crowding-out effects of an increase in public expenditure on domestic investment could be avoided'.[44] Thanks to the Korean War, the volume of German exports increased by about six times between 1948 and 1951 to regain its pre-war level. 'By 1952 the rate of accumulation had been levered up to 6 percent ... 3 times the rate in Germany's European rivals and twice that in the United States'.[45] The Korean War enabled the beginning of the German economic miracle. In the decade after the Korean War 'real GDP more than doubled and output per worker increased by almost 75 percent. ... the main pillars of the economic expansion in the period 1950–5 were exports and private investment, which, in real terms, grew by 17.5 percent and 12.4 percent p.a. respectively, much faster than private consumption (8.6 percent p.a.) and government expenditure (7.0 percent p.a.) ... a buoyant demand for West German goods on the world market drove firms into a very high rate of capital stock utilization ... this spurred the demand for new capital equipment, which further supported the expansion and thus led into a kind of virtuous circle. ... the Korean boom gave the West German economy an unexpected head start, which paved the way for a viable process of export-led expansion, above all of investment goods industries'.[46] If, as Brenner[47] has argued, the basic feature of the post-war 'Golden Age' was not so much the US boom itself as the Japanese and West German catch-up with the US economy, then the Korean War could well be registered as the foundation stone for the post-war 'Golden Age', because it jump-started the catch-up process. In general, the Korean War gave Japan an economic windfall comparable to the Marshall Plan.[48]

---

44   Giersch et. al. 1992, p. 62.
45   Armstrong et. al. 1991, p. 99.
46   Giersch et. al. 1992, p. 63, p. 273.
47   Brenner 2006.
48   Woo-Cumings 1999, p. 21.

TABLE 4.2   Korean economic growth in 1950s (%)

	All Industries	Agriculture etc	Manufacturing etc	Service
1954	6	7.7	16	1.2
1955	6.1	2.3	18	7.1
1956	1.3	−5.3	13.5	4.9
1957	8.8	8.6	14.8	6.8
1958	5.5	6.8	6.9	3.5
1959	4.4	−1.1	10.8	8
1960	2.3	−0.9	7.4	2.5
1961	4.2	16.2	4.2	−8.3
1962	3.5	−11	15.8	15.8
1954–59 Average	5.35	3.17	13.3	5.25

BANK OF KOREA, *NATIONAL INCOME IN KOREA, 1953–63*, 1965.

Park Hyun Chae's 'Theory of National Economy' described South Korea in the 1950s as experiencing a period of dependency and stagnation. However, this view should be rejected now. The growth rate of the South Korean economy of the 1950s was as high as that of the early 1960s, though lower than that of the late 1960s. As Table 4.2 shows, the annual average rate of growth of GNP for the period 1954–9 (5.35 percent), was almost the same as that for the period 1960–4 (5.5 percent). Moreover, the annual average growth rate of manufacturing for the period of 1954–9, 13 percent, was even higher than that for the period of 1960–4, at 9.4 percent. The Korean economic growth rate during the 1950s was no lower than those of many other countries in the Third World. Economic growth from the late 1960s in Korea was not a sudden event but the escalation of the steady growth of the 1950s. Moreover, the state capitalist development project had already been tried in the 1950s under the Syngman Rhee regime.[49] The aid which Syngman Rhee extorted from the US as his condition for accepting the Korean War armistice in 1953 played a crucial role in postcolonial reconstruction in South Korea. US economic aid to South Korea contributed to the country's high speed economic growth, just as the Marshall Plan laid the foundation for the reconstruction of capitalism in Europe.[50] The American aid to the

49   Lee 1996.
50   'From 1946 to 1976, the United States provided $12.6 billion in American economic and military aid to South Korea … combined with additional contributions from Japan and international financial institutions, the total gave South Korea in the midpoint year of

Korean government functioned to create the foundations for the development of state capitalism in Korea, as it was 'channeled through the state' and had given the Korean government 'a tremendous advantage when dealing with the major social players' in Korea.[51]

The basic components of internationalised state capitalism in South Korea are as follows.[52] First, during the Cold War, the United States tried to sustain the bourgeois regime in South Korea through military occupation, economic aid and permissive policies toward Korean exports into the United States. The US government usually regarded the political stability of an anti-Communist regime in South Korea as extremely important for US geopolitical interests. It frequently endorsed even military dictators who took power by coups d'etat. This strong political and economic backing for reactionary Korean governments helped maintain a political stability that contributed to economic growth.

Second, on the level of capital-labour relations, a one-sided subordination of labour to capital characterised postcolonial Korean state capitalism before the Great Workers' Struggles of 1987. This began with the elimination of the left during the Korean War and was reaffirmed by the military coup in 1961. Park Chung Hee arrested and jailed all the trade union leaders and replaced them with pro-government, pro-business gangs. Despite Western-style labour laws, unions were never allowed to function freely until 1987. In this oppressive era, workers were subjected to severe exploitation. Indeed, South Korea was notorious for having the longest working days in the world as late as the 1990s. The miraculously high and long economic growth in Korea can be traced to this subordination of labour and the strict discipline on the shop floor, maintained by the authoritarian state.

Third, as commonly noted by the developmental state theorists, Korean state capitalism is significant with its specific system of government subsidies and control of capital. After taking power in 1961, Park Chung Hee pursued strong state-directed industrialisation by nationalising commercial banks, launching extensive economic planning, and introducing a series of industrial policies. Park made an anti-Communist independent national economy his government's number one priority. For this, he largely copied Japanese economic policy during the colonial period. At the time the *chaebol* business con-

---

1960 a per capita assistance figure of $600 over three decades ... To put these figures in perspective, South Korean ... per capita GNP in 1965 was about $100 (in current dollars)' (Woo-Cumings 1998, pp. 328–9).

51   Stubbs, 2009, p. 11.
52   For more discussion, refer to Jeong 1997.

glomerates were too weak to resist the military dictatorship, and Park took control of them through industrial policy, especially directed credit. Park allocated credits and foreign loans only to those *chaebols* that met certain performance standards, such as a specified export target. The *chaebols* accumulated enormous capital in this process. The high economic growth in South Korea would have been impossible without this strong state-directed capital accumulation. It was largely due to 'getting prices wrong' by the strong government, as Amsden has argued.[53]

Fourth, on the international economic level, the Korean economy during the period 1961–87 was largely based on the trade triangle among Korea, the United States, and Japan. The Korean economy in this period is distinguished from other state capitalist Third World countries in that it was not only highly internationalised as an export-led economy but also had a specific niche in international trade due to its relations with the United States and Japan. After import substitution industrialisation (ISI) policies failed in the early 1960s, Park began to concentrate on increasing exports, which included the normalisation of relations with Japan and compliance with the United States to send troops to participate in the Vietnam War. From then on, the triangular trade developed. Korea began to import almost all its equipment and parts from Japan, processed them, and exported most of them to the United States. This trade pattern was one of the most powerful driving forces of Korean state capitalist accumulation in this period.

These components of internationalised state capitalism in Korea fitted remarkably well with each other and functioned fairly smoothly until the late 1980s, resulting in what came to be called the 'Korean economic miracle'.

4   The Vietnam War and the 'Take-off' of State Capitalism in South Korea

With the US bombing of North Vietnam in February 1965, the Vietnam War developed into an all-out war. The number of US soldiers deployed to Vietnam increased from 23,000 in February 1965 to 543,000 in April 1969, its highest

---

53   Amsden 1989. However, in Amsden's argument, the only actors are government and *chaebols*, while workers and the world market do not play any significant role. The crucial specificity of South Korea's economic success is located in the particular historical and geopolitical context of Northeast Asia, especially in the US-engineered Cold War, and in the extraordinary exploitation of workers, rather than in the differential degree of government discipline over capitalists.

TABLE 4.3   US military expenditures (billion dollars)

	Total federal outlays (A)	National defense (B)	Special Southeast Asia operations	B/A (%)
1949	40.6	13.1		32.3
1950	43.1	13.1		30.4
1951	45.8	22.5		49.1
1952	68	44		64.7
1953	76.8	50.4		65.6
1955	68.5	40.2		58.7
1960	92.2	45.9		49.8
1964	118.6	53.6		45.2
1965	118.4	49.6	0.1	41.9
1966	134.7	56.8	5.8	42.2
1967	158.3	70.1	20.1	44.3
1968	178.8	80.5	26.5	45
1969	184.6	81.2	28.8	44
1970	196.6	80.3	23.1	40.8
1965–70 Total	971.4	418.5	104.4	43.1

IMURA (1988A: 381)

point. As Table 4.3 shows, total US defence outlays jumped from 49.6 billion dollars in 1965 to 80.5 billion dollars in 1968, among which 'Southeast Asia Special Operation' related expenditures, namely Vietnam War expenses, skyrocketed from 0.1 billion dollars in 1965 to 28.8 billion dollars in 1969, totalling 104.4 billion dollars for the period 1965–70. The US government promoted the policy of 'Buy American' from the late 1960s, to contain the outflow of dollars due to US foreign military activities, demanding that US defence purchases be ordered from US businesses. America attempted to recycle US military expenditures in foreign countries, for example by forcing countries which received US military aid to purchase US-made arms. As a result, the drain of US defence expenditure began to decrease after 1967. Also, during the period of the Vietnam War, a large part of the increase in US defence expenditure was channelled to increase US domestic demand, especially in traditional defence businesses like ammunitions, clothes, vehicles, and foods, the spin-off effects of which are larger than the high-end defence industries, such as atomic missiles, generating a big increase in demand for industrial machines, steel, chemicals and so on. The Vietnam War-induced boom contributed to the realisation of full-employment, enabling wage increases, enhancement of work conditions, and the decreasing discrimination against women and black people in the US labour market.[54] The USA's annual average growth rate for the 1960s was 4.1 percent, much higher than that for the 1970s, at 2.8 percent, or for the 1980s at 2.6 percent. Also, the US unemployment rate for the 1960s was 4.6 percent, much lower than that for the 1970s at 6.1 percent, or for the 1980s at 7.2 percent. In addition, the annual average growth rate of US non-supervisory workers' average real wages was 1.4 percent, compared to minus 0.3 percent for the 1970s and minus 1 percent for the 1980s.

The Japanese economy experienced an unprecedented long economic boom during 1965–70, the main period of the Vietnam War. The annual average rate of growth of Japanese GNP during 1965–70 was 16.5 percent (11.8 percent in real terms). The period of 1965–70 is usually referred as the 'Second High Growth Period', preceded by the 'First High Growth Period' of 1955–61. If the Korean War special procurements were the foundation of the 'First High Growth Period' of 1955–61, the Vietnam War special procurements were behind the 'Second High Growth Period' of 1965–70. During the period of the Vietnam War, Japanese exports rapidly increased from 4.2 billion dollars in 1961 to 8.5 billion dollars in 1965, exceeded 10 billion dollars after 1967, and recorded 19.3 billion dollars in 1970, with a dazzling growth rate of 19.6 percent per annum for the period 1965 to 1970. As a result, Japanese trade balances turned from chronic deficits to surplus around 1965. The continuing expansion of exports was crucial to the Japanese 'Second High Growth Period' in 1965–70. Indeed, the large-scale investments in the advanced heavy industries, the driving force of the 'Second High Growth Period' after 1966, were made in the expectation that exports related to the Vietnam War would continue to increase. As Table 4.4 shows, Japanese exports to the US and 'Vietnam and neighbouring countries'[55] rapidly increased after 1965. The Japanese trade surplus with 'Vietnam and neighbouring countries' jumped after 1965, reaching 1.841 billion dollars in 1968 and 2.234 billion dollars in 1970. Moreover, Japanese trade balances with the US turned positive after 1965, recording a surplus of 868 million dollars in 1969. All these things would not have happened had Japan not been able to ride the Vietnam War-induced boom. The Vietnam War special procurements for Japan consisted of the purchases of goods and services by the US Forces in Japan as well as expenditures by the dependents of US Forces in Japan. According to

---

54   Baker et al. 1996.
55   'Vietnam and neighbouring countries' refers to countries and territories such as South
      Korea, Okinawa, Hong Kong, Taiwan, Philippines, Thailand and Vietnam.

TABLE 4.4   Japanese exports and imports by country (million dollars)

	US			Korea			Vietnam & neighbor countries		
	US exports	US imports	US balances	Korea exports	Korea imports	Korea balances	Vietnam & neighbor countries exports	Vietnam & neighbor countries imports	Vietnam & neighbor countries balances
1960	1,102	1,554	−452	100	19	81	785	368	417
1964	1,842	2,336	−495	109	42	67	1,116	637	479
1965	2,479	2,366	113	180	41	139	1,353	707	646
1968	4,087	3,527	560	603	102	501	2,784	943	1,841
1969	4,958	4,090	868	767	134	633	3,433	1,115	2,318
1970	5,940	5,560	380	818	229	589	3,636	1,402	2,234

IMURA (1988A: 389, 396)

TABLE 4.5   Japanese trade balance and Vietnam war special procurements (million dollars)

	1962	1963	1964	1965	1966	1967	1968	1969	1970
Exports(A)	4,861	5,391	6,704	8,332	9,641	10,231	12,751	15,679	18,969
Imports(B)	4,460	5,557	6,327	6,431	7,366	9,071	10,222	11,980	15,006
Trade Balance (A)-(B)	401	−166	377	1,901	2,275	1,160	2,529	3,699	3,963
Special Procurements	377	356	329	345	476	524	589	642	661

IMURA (1988A: 394)

Table 4.5, Vietnam War special procurements increased from 345 million dollars in 1965 to 661 million dollars in 1970. Vietnam War special procurements contributed significantly to Japanese economic growth as a major source of dollars, just as the Korean War special procurements had done previously. If the Japanese trade deficits with the US during the 'First High Growth Period' of 1955–61 were largely compensated by special procurements, the Vietnam War special procurements during the 'Second High Growth Period' of 1965–70 were the critical factor behind the net increase in Japanese foreign exchange reserves.

US military expenditures during the Vietnam War played the role of supplying dollars to 'Vietnam and neighbouring countries' which suffered from a lack of dollar reserves during the 1960s. In fact, Japan's trade surplus with 'Vietnam and neighbouring countries' rapidly increased after 1965, while the latter countries recorded large trade deficits, especially with Japan. What compensated

TABLE 4.6   Annual GNP Growth Rate in Korea (%)

	1960–69	1960–64	1965–69	1970
GNP	8.6	5.5	11.8	8.8
Manufacturing	16	9.4	22.5	18.3

Source: Bank of Korea, Economic Statistics Yearbook, 1971, 1978.

for the trade deficits of 'Vietnam and neighbouring countries', especially those with Japan, and sustained the Japanese exports parade was precisely US military expenditure. The big increase in Japanese exports to 'Vietnam and neighbouring countries' and the ballooning trade surplus with these countries was crucially indebted to the US injection of dollars into these countries by means of US military expenditures, which were recycled to Japan through the large increase in Japanese exports to these countries. On the other hand, 'Vietnam and neighbouring countries', especially South Korea, could embark on their own industrialisation projects with the dollars which were given to them by the US as compensation for cooperating with the US war campaign in Vietnam. The dollars were then recycled to Japan through increasing imports by these countries from Japan to purchase the machinery and raw materials for their industrialisation projects. In this respect, the Vietnam War was the crucial moment for the emergence of NICs in East Asia from 1970 onwards, especially in the case of South Korea.

If Korean economic growth during the 1960s is viewed separately in two halves, the annual average rate of growth of GNP for the second half (1965–9), 11.8 percent, was more than double that for the first half (1960–4), 5.5 percent, as Table 4.6 shows. This suggests that the Korean economic 'miracle' began in the late 1960s, rather than from the early 1960s. In its early phase it was hard to view Park Chung Hee's developmental strategy as a success. In fact, Park's First Five-Year Plan for Economic Development (1962–6) was copied from that of the preceding Chang Myeon government (1960–1) and was not so different from the common ISI plan. The First Five-Year Plan faced difficulties due to chronic inflation and lack of dollar reserves. Only by benefiting from the Vietnam War special procurements and normalisation of Korean-Japanese relations in 1965, in other words, only by 'internationalising' its state capitalism could the South Korean economy 'take-off' after the mid-1960s.[56] However, neoliberal economists usually argue that the failure of

---

56   'Much as Japan had started its postwar take-off with the Korean War, so Taiwan and South Korea were helped by the Vietnam War' (Woo-Cumings 1998, p. 329).

Park's trial of ISI in the early 1960s could be overcome by 'getting prices right' through the US AID structural adjustment programme during 1964–6. In other words, liberal economic reforms according to the US AID structural adjustment programme, such as devaluation and import liberalisation, provided the basis for South Korea's rapid economic growth by rectifying the skewed price system and establishing a neutral trade system through equalising export incentives with import incentives. In contrast, the developmental statists have argued that Park Chung Hee's early state-led developmental strategy was basically valid and continued without any fundamental break to the later export-oriented approaches. For example, Amsden argued that there was no significant liberal-istic revision of the developmental strategy around the mid-1960s.[57] However, the failure of Park Chung Hee's early ISI-type strategy is an undeniable fact. This does not mean we have to agree with the neoliberal economists' assertion that the early failure was overcome by liberal market reforms in the mid-1960s. What actually started South Korean rapid economic growth after the mid-1960s was the 'internationalisation' of state capitalism, where the permanent arms economy, founded by the Korean War and brought into full operation with the Vietnam War, played the crucial role. Indeed, the Korean government con-sciously utilised the Vietnam War special procurements for the 'take-off' of the Korean economy.

The deployment of the Republic of Korea Army to Vietnam started in Feb-ruary 1965. About 50,000 Korean soldiers were dispatched to the Vietnam War in the peak year of 1968, with a total deployment of 347,624 troops during the period 1964–75. According to the so-called 'Brown Memorandum' between Lee Dong-Won, Korean Minister of Diplomacy and Winthrop G. Brown, US Ambas-sador to Korea, the US government promised to provide the following benefits in exchange for the Korean government's troop deployment, in addition to mil-itary aid:[58] (1) Disbursement of expenses for maintaining the Korean troops in Vietnam directly into the Korean government budget in won; (2) Procurement of a substantial part of the goods and services for the USFK (US Forces in Korea) from Korean businesses; (3) Purchase of specific items for Korean, Vietnamese and other foreign countries' troops in Vietnam from Korean businesses; (4) Permission for Korean construction companies to bid for construction pro-jects in Vietnam. 'Particularly noteworthy [in the Brown Memorandum] were the use of the Agency for International Development (AID) and the assistance given to South Korean capitalists to profit from the war. Seldom have the links

---

57   Amsden 1989, pp. 64–70.
58   Baldwin 1975, pp. 7–8.

TABLE 4.7   The Vietnam war special procurements for Korea (million dollars)

	1965	1966	1967	1968	1969	1970	1971	1972	Total	Share (%)
Trade Balance	17.7	23.8	23.2	38	47.1	70.1	35.7	27.5	283.1	27.7
Exports	14.8	13.9	7.3	5.6	12.9	12.8	14.5	12.5	94.3	9.2
Military Procurements	2.8	9.9	15.9	32.4	34.2	57.3	21.2	15	188.8	18.5
Invisible Trade Balance	1.8	37.3	128.1	130.6	153.3	134.5	97.6	55.7	738.9	72.3
Military Services		8.3	35.5	46.1	55.3	52.3	26.5	9.2	233.2	22.8
Military Constructions		3.3	14.5	10.3	6.4	7.4	8.3	3.1	53.3	5.2
Military Remittances	1.8	15.5	31.4	31.4	33.9	30.6	32.3	26.8	201.5	19.7
Technicians Remittances		9.1	33.6	33.6	43.1	26.9	15.3	3.9	166.2	16.3
Special Compensation			4.6	4.6	10.8	15.2	13.9	12	65.3	6.4
Insurances		1.1	4.6	4.6	3.8	2.1	1.3	0.7	19.4	1.9
Total	19.5	61.1	151.3	168.6	200.4	204.6	133.3	83.2	1,022	100

PAK 1993, P. 19.

between AID/economic assistance, US military/political objectives, and the pursuit of war profits in the name of economic development been so explicitly revealed'.[59]

The Vietnam War provided the following 'take-off' inputs for the South Korean economy in the late 1960s. First, the special procurements for the Vietnam War, from US military expenditures for the war, provided the investment funds needed to start industrialisation. As Table 4.7 shows, South Korea earned about 200 million dollars per year in its peak years and 1.022 billion dollars in total for the period 1965–72 from Vietnam War special procurements, including remittances from deployed Korean soldiers. Korean exports to Vietnam increased from 17.7 million dollars in 1965 to 70 million dollars in 1970, making Vietnam the third largest export market for Korea. Exports to Vietnam made up 10.1 percent of Korea's total exports in 1965, 8.3 percent in 1968 and 8.4 percent in 1970. Table 4.7 also shows that the biggest item in the Vietnam War special procurements for Korea was the 'overseas allowances', remitted from Korean soldiers and technicians in Vietnam, amounting to 36 percent of total income from special procurements.[60] Besides the 'overseas allowances', the major form

59   Baldwin 1975, p. 7.
60   However, the combat compensation for South Korean soldiers deployed to Vietnam, called 'overseas allowances', were only one-sixth of those paid to American soldiers, and one-fifth of the Philippine or Thai soldiers' allowances. Moreover, the combat compens-

TABLE 4.8   Vietnam war special procurements and Korean economic growth (million dollars)

	Special Procurements (A)	GNP (B)	Exports (C)	Foreign exchange reserve (D)	Invisible trade balances (E)	A/B (%)	A/C (%)	A/D (%)	A/E (%)
1965	20	3,006	175	138	126	0.6	11.1	14.1	15.5
1966	61	3,671	250	236	238	1.7	24.4	25.9	25.6
1967	151	4,274	320	347	375	3.5	47.3	43.6	40.3
1968	169	5,226	455	388	425	3.2	37	43.5	39.7
1969	200	6,625	623	550	497	3	32.2	36.5	40.3
1970	205	7,834	835	584	491	2.6	24.5	35.1	41.7
1971	133	9,145	1,068	535	487	1.5	12.5	24.9	27.4
1972	83	10,254	1,624	694	579	0.8	5.1	12	14.4

PAK 1993, P. 39.

of US commercial assistance was the procurement of war supplies in Korea and construction/service contracts for South Korean firms in Vietnam.[61] According to Table 4.8, the Vietnam War special procurements increased every year, growing as a proportion of GNP from 0.6 percent in 1965, to 3.5 percent in 1967, and then falling back slightly to 3 percent in 1969. The Vietnam War special procurements were therefore as beneficial to the Korean economy as the Korean War special procurements were to the Japanese economy. Indeed, the total value of Vietnam War special procurements for the period 1965–72, 1.022 billion dollars, was larger than the capital provided to South Korea by Japan during this period, including the Claim Funds for Japanese colonial rule, which amounted to 800 million dollars.[62] The influx of dollars through the Vietnam War special procurements resolved the Korean economy's severe lack of dollars. In fact, the foreign exchange reserves of South Korea decreased from 205

---

ation for Korean soldiers deployed to Vietnam, mostly corporal or private first class, was the lowest among all the countries that dispatched soldiers, even lower than that of Vietnamese soldiers.

61   Baldwin 1975, p. 13.

62   The Claim Funds, provided by Japan to Korea, according to the Treaty on Basic Relations between Japan and the Republic of Korea, signed on 22 June 1965, to settle the problems in regard to property, claims for damages and economic cooperation, amounted to 800 million dollars, composed of 300 million dollars grant in economic aid, 200 million dollars in loans and 300 million dollars in loans for private trusts. The Park government used the Funds to construct the Pohang Iron and Steel Company (now POSCO), Soyang Dam, and the Kyŏngbu Express Way between Seoul and Pusan, among other projects.

million dollars in 1961 to 129 million dollars in 1964, threatening a currency crisis and the failure of the First Five Year Plan. With the Vietnam War special procurements, South Korea's foreign exchange reserves increased rapidly to 138 million dollars in 1965, 236 million dollars in 1966, 388 million dollars in 1966, and 584 million dollars in 1970. The Vietnam War special procurements were mainly composed of invisible trade revenues, such as soldiers' and technicians' salary remittances, rather than exports of goods. Table 4.7 shows that of the total 1.022 billion dollars of Vietnam War special procurements that flowed into South Korea, as much as 740 million dollars came from these invisible trade revenues.[63] The invisible trade revenues derived from the Vietnam War increased South Korea's foreign exchange reserves, thus providing the funds to import capital goods and raw materials badly needed for the industrialisation drive.[64] The influx of dollars through the Vietnam War special procurements were particularly timely, coming at the moment the South Korean economy slowed down due to decreasing American aid. These dollars were also crucial for the Korean economy's 'take-off' into high rates of economic growth from the late 1960s, that is, the rise of South Korea's particular form of state capitalism.

Second, with the escalation of the Vietnam War, South Korean exports, the driving force of the Korean economic 'miracle', grew in leaps and bounds. Indeed, the Vietnam War contributed to the successful switchover to export-oriented industrialisation in South Korea. Korean exports skyrocketed from 120 million dollars in 1964 to 1.624 billion dollars in 1972, thanks to an explosive increase in exports to the US. As a result, the US share of total Korean exports increased from about 20 percent in the early 1960s to 50.1 percent in 1969, while Japan's share decreased from about 40 percent in the early 1960s to about 20 percent after 1965. The major South Korean exports to the US were industrial goods, such as clothes, plywood, and electronics. As Table 4.3 shows, US military expenditure related with the Vietnam War, at over 25 billion dollars per year, provided a big boost to Korean exports. Total US imports began to increase rapidly with the escalation of the Vietnam War. The annual average rate of increase of US imports jumped from 5.6 percent for the period 1957–64 to 14.8 percent for the period 1965–72. As a result, total US imports increased

---

63   In Table 4.7, total = trade balance+invisible trade balance. In official trade statistics, the Korean soldiers' combat compensation, paid by the U.S. government, which was remitted to their family in Korea, was counted as an invisible trade revenue. The South Korean government forcibly held about 90 percent of the combat compensation from the soldiers and sent them to their families in Korea.

64   Sano 1992, p. 959.

from 18.7 billion dollars in 1964 to 55.6 billion dollars in 1972. In particular, US imports from South Korea increased at an annual rate of 47.5 percent for the period 1965–72. They increased by 21 times between 1964 and 1972, from 35.6 million dollars to 760 million dollars. The US market was not open to all developing countries. Although the US had taken measures to restrict imports of cotton and clothes from Korea, the US stopped applying the 'Buy American' policy with regard to South Korea after Korean troops were sent to the Vietnam War. Indeed, the 'Park-Johnson' summit in 1965 promised to increase US imports from South Korea as well as US military aid to the country.[65] Thanks to these measures, Korea could enter the US market more easily than other developing countries could. Third, US public loans to South Korea provided in return for its dispatch of troops to Vietnam eased the difficulties Korea faced in relation to attracting foreign capital in the mid-1960s. As Korea sent troops to the Vietnam War, the US began to provide public loans to Korea on the basis of the 'Brown Memorandum'. The US also pushed Japan to normalise its diplomatic relations with South Korea and asked European countries to strengthen their economic cooperation with Korea. As a result, foreign capital began to come to South Korea. Inbound foreign capital to South Korea from the 1950s to the early 1960s was mainly in the form of aid, and only partly loans or foreign direct investment. From the late 1960s, however, foreign loans to Korea increased rapidly, comprising up to three-quarters of all foreign capital. The amount of loans increased from a mere 142 million dollars total in the period 1959–65 to 218 million dollars in 1967, 430 million dollars in 1970, 737 million dollars in 1972, amounting to 3.08 billion dollars in total for 1966–72. Loans from the US increased particularly rapidly from the late 1960s, from a total of 74 million dollars for the period 1959–65 to 1.3 billion dollars for the period 1966–72, comprising 43 percent of all foreign loans. About half of the US loans were long-term and low interest, and mostly allocated to social infrastructure and core industries.

Fourth, US military aid, which increased with the deployment of the ROK Army to Vietnam, also eased the financing for economic growth by alleviat-

---

65   '(T)he United States was much less doctrinaire about economic arrangements in its satellites during the Cold War. In Japan and South Korea, its two main dependencies in East Asia, it insisted on the institution of private property and opposed any steps towards the nationalization of industry, but it tolerated land reform, state guidance of the economy, protectionism, mercantilism, and the cartelisation of industry as long as these methods produced economic growth and blunted the appeal of communism. ... It was not a process made available to the Latin American dependencies of the United States, because they were not of equal strategic importance in the Cold War' (Johnson 2000, pp. 95–6).

TABLE 4.9   Korean military expenditures and US military aid (million dollars)

	1966	1967	1968	1969	1970	1971	1972
Government Expenditures Total (A)	141	181	262	371	441	546	701
Military Expenditures (B)	41	50	65	84	102	135	174
US Military Aids (C)	57	73	110	146	104	208	212
B/A (%)	28.7	27.4	24.7	22.8	23.2	24.7	24.8
C/A (%)	40.4	40.3	41.8	39.4	23.7	38	

ECONOMIC PLANNING BOARD, KOREAN STATISTICS YEARBOOK, 1970, 1971.

ing the burden of defence expenses. As Table 4.9 shows, US military aid to Korea increased from 820 million dollars for the period 1961–5 to 1.68 billion dollars for the period 1966–70. The increase in US military aid allowed South Korea to limit its defence expenditure. In fact, US military aid to South Korea for the period 1966–72 amounted to 36.3 percent of total South Korean public expenditure. Thanks to this increase in US military aid, the ROK government was able to avoid increasing its own defence outlays, despite the heightened tensions with North Korea during this period due to the infiltration of North Korean commandos into Seoul or the Pueblo incident in 1968. In this regard, the government's active investment and lending, which is usually regarded as one of the most important policy tools of South Korean state capitalism, depended on the fiscal surplus generated by decreasing Korean defence expenses due to the rising US military aid to Korea during the Vietnam War.[66]

Fifth, the Vietnam War helped to establish the triangular trade pattern, one of the key components of South Korean state capitalism, in which Korea imported almost all its equipment and parts from Japan, processed them, and exported most of the products to the US. After the Vietnam War, the US share of imports to South Korea halved from about 50 percent in the early 1960s to about 20 percent in the 1970s, while Japan's share doubled from about 20 percent in the early 1960s to about 40 percent in the late 1960s. With the transition to export-led industrialisation from the late 1960s, the equipment and raw materials needed for the production of export goods began to be imported from Japan. The share of capital goods in total Korean imports from Japan increased from 26 percent for 1963–65 to 43 percent for 1966–9.

---

66   This situation contrasted directly with the situation North Korea faced, where its own 'self-reliant' state capitalist model was severely damaged by its rocketing defence expenditures in the 1960s.

5   Concluding Remarks

This chapter has aimed to connect the Korean War and the development of capitalism in Korea by examining the role of the Korean War in the establishment of capitalist class structure and the permanent arms economy. This approach differs fundamentally from the two contrasting approaches that currently dominate explanations of the South Korean economic 'miracle'. If the neoliberal free marketeers assert that South Korea's rapid economic growth was the result of Adam Smith's 'invisible hand', the developmental statists argue that it was accomplished by the 'visible hand', in other words, the government's interventions in the market through industrial policy, credit rationing, export subsidies and so on. As for the crisis of 1997 – the so-called 'IMF Crisis' – neoliberal free marketeers argue that it resulted from the *chaebol* system or crony capitalism that was fostered by the interventionist state. On the contrary, developmental statists argue that the crisis was caused by the weakening of the state under pressure from neoliberal globalization, especially the deregulation of transnational finance capital. If the neoliberal free marketeers' assertion simply does not fit with the reality of state capitalist development in Korea since the 1960s, the developmental statists' interpretation is problematic in that it neglects the class structure and contradictions inherent to capitalist development in Korea, and sometimes falls into apologetics for Park Chung Hee's authoritarian developmentalism. Moreover, both positions are blind to the specific class relations, the global geopolitical context and the closely related permanent arms economy on which South Korea's state capitalist development has been based.

This chapter stresses that in order to understand the rise of capitalism in South Korea and its high rate of accumulation it is necessary to focus on class dynamics in the global context, beyond the dichotomy of market vs. state. From this perspective the Korean War is situated at the origin of state capitalist development in Korea. The Korean War demobilised popular struggles and produced the repressive and dependent industrial relations that laid the foundations for high rates of capital accumulation from the 1960s onward. The Korean War also crucially helped to establish the Cold War regime and the US-Japan-Korea triangular military-security alliance, which constituted the geopolitical conditions for postcolonial state capitalist development in Korea. The Korean War special procurements contributed to ending the post-WWII recession and opening the post-war 'Golden Age' for the advanced countries. The global permanent arms economy, driven by the competitive arms production of the US and Russia, sustained the post-war long boom by providing counteracting forces to the tendency of the profit rate to fall as well as additional

effective demand. Indeed, capitalism lives by perennial massacre and destruction. The Korean War provided the crucial opportunity for defeated Japan to
recover, in particular by forcing the US to change its occupation policy from
democratic reform to securing the base for anticommunism in East Asia in
addition to the benefits Japan received from special procurements. The all-
out competitive drive for economic growth in East Asia under the pressure of
the Cold War was behind the successes of export-led industrialisation in some
countries, especially Japan and South Korea. The permanent arms economy of
the Korean War, marked by the establishment of capitalist class structure and
the Cold War regime, became fully operational with the Vietnam War in the late
1960s and functioned as a crucial component of the state capitalist social structure of accumulation, which sustained a 30-year long boom in South Korea.[67]
In fact, the high rate of state capitalist accumulation in South Korea was part of
the permanent arms economy in East Asia as a whole. If the rapid growth of the
Korean economy was not the automatic outcome of the free market, neither
can it be viewed as solely the achievement of the 'autonomous' state, as the
developmental statists have argued.[68] However, the permanent arms economy
in South Korea stopped functioning properly after the explosion of the June
Democratic Struggle in 1987 and the demise of the Soviet Union and Eastern
Bloc in 1989–91. The revival of organised labour after the 1987 struggle posed a
strong challenge to the repressive and super-exploitative labour regime established by South Korean state capitalism. In addition, the end of the Cold War
provided the US with an excuse to withdraw its policy of 'benign neglect' and
push for reform of the previous statist model, bringing neoliberal globalisation
to South Korea. The weakening of the permanent arms economy combined
with the exhaustion of the existing state capitalist social structure of accumulation culminated in the explosion of the crisis of 1997. Some commentators,
like Yang,[69] have argued that the conjuncture of state capitalism has passed
since the 1990s in South Korea, with the end of the Cold War and the acceleration of globalisation. Stubbs also indicated that 'The external facilitating
conditions began to change markedly during the 1980s. The Cold War became
less of a dominant factor in global affairs as the forces of globalization took

---

67 Jeong 1997.
68 Although existing econometric studies on military spending in Korea are split regarding
    its effects on economic growth, Moon and Hyun (1992) claim that South Korean milit-
    ary spending is positively associated with economic growth and that technological spin-
    offs from the defence sector have been a major catalyst in the transformation of Korean
    industry from labour-intensive to technology-intensive.
69 Yang 1993.

over. ... the downgrading of the threat from Asian communism reduced the need to maintain the massive military and police forces that had been found around East Asia up until the late 1980s'.[70] Are the days of state capitalism and the permanent arms economy over then? Probably not. Various signs suggest that elements of state capitalism are still a feature of the South Korean economy. After the global economic crisis of 2007–9, all the Korean presidents, from Lee Myung-bak to Yoon Suk-yeol, regardless of whether he or she is progressive or conservative, opted for more 'state capitalist' policies to cope with the ever deepening crisis.[71] The ramping up of geopolitical competition and the related arms economy among the rival states of Northeast Asia would also suggest that the days of state capitalism in South Korea are not yet over.

---

70   Stubbs 2009, p. 10.
71   According to Bremmer 2009, return to state capitalism becomes a new Zeitgeist of the world after the global economic crisis of 2007–9. Likewise refer to the cover story of *The Economist* (21–7 January 2012), titled 'The Rise of State Capitalism: The Emergence of the World's New Model'.

CHAPTER 5

China's State-Permeated Capitalism: a Global Political Economy Perspective

Tobias ten Brink

1   Introduction

In this chapter, I offer readers a rough guide to China's political economy in the 2000s and early 2010s. As is by now well-known, this continent-sized economy has gone through an extraordinary boom of historic proportions. Yet what kind of political economy the People's Republic of China (PRC) has actually evolved into is still a matter of debate.

Because China has developed a political economy that resembles socio-economic developments in capitalist systems, I synthesise in the following, insights from Comparative Political Economy (CPE) and International Political Economy (IPE) into what might be called a Global Political Economy perspective in order to understand the nature of China's Post-Maoist economy.

To describe China as a capitalist society (more specifically, as a special type of capitalism) has only become common practice in the last few years in Western research on the country. For a long time, by referring either to elite-centred theories of totalitarianism or cultural(ist) explanations, authors tended to analyse China as a unique case hardly comparable with other systems ('China is China is China'). Although China scholars had introduced Western social science and economics theories, such as institutionalism, since the beginning of the reform period under Deng Xiaoping, to describe China as capitalist was still a rare exception until the 2000s.[1] From then on, when describing economic transformation processes in China, authors tended to take one of two common positions. Many used the dynamics of the reform policies as an argument to underline the 'capitalist-socialist' or 'hybrid' character of the system.[2] Not unlike the official position of the Chinese leadership, they viewed the existence of a state-controlled 'socialist market economy' and the dominant role of the Chinese Communist Party (CCP) as signs that the People's Republic

---

1   On the history of Western research into China see ten Brink 2012a.
2   See Arrighi 2007, Li 2008, Sigley 2006, Itoh 2003, Wu 2005.

contains relatively intact foundations of a non-capitalist society. An opposing viewpoint analysed the growing importance of private firms as an expression of a restructuring of China, with liberal traits similar to those of processes in other capitalist systems,[3] sometimes leading to untimely predictions about China's democratisation.[4]

My analysis sees the People's Republic of China as having developed a distinct form of capitalism. The Chinese system has undergone an unprecedented transformation from a so-called planned economy which, in reality, was characterised by plan anarchy,[5] to a strongly market-oriented system while exhibiting a degree of continuity in its political and social institutions. But although the Chinese model will have vestiges of a bureaucratic economy, a ruling communist party, and late industrial development for a long time to come, it cannot be equated with a simple hybrid that combines 'capitalist' and 'socialist' principles. That would only be possible if one defined these terms quite narrowly and viewed socialism, like the current Chinese leadership does, as a form of modernisation and as pursuing economic growth by any means deemed necessary, and capitalism as a mere synonym for markets.

For this reason, I draw on theories in CPE and IPE and include the work of China scholars who have stressed the need to engage in cross-national comparisons and thus have begun to study China as a new form of state or state-led capitalism.[6] However, in contrast both to liberal observers who do not distinguish contemporary Chinese state capitalism thoroughly from older varieties[7] and to developmental state theorists (for a critique, see Lee in this volume), I analyse China's political economy as a novel, variegated form of a state-*permeated* capitalism. Its activity is based on close, competition-driven operations between

---

3   See Hart-Landsberg and Burkett 2005; Wilson 2007; Witt 2010.

4   See Rowen 2007.

5   See ten Brink 2013a, Chapter 11, for a reconstruction of the historical transformation of Mao's command economy into a modernised, i.e. domestically competition-driven, state-permeated form of capitalism. I thereby make a strong argument for important continuities of the Chinese economy over the course of the second half of the twentieth century, such as a 'proto-capitalist' planning anarchy and heterogeneous state and party institutions. This runs counter to conventional wisdom that sees a radical rupture in the late 1970s. I also explain the movement away from Maoist planning as part of a gradual, yet crisis-driven process of institutional change that was interwoven with global waves of (liberal) reforms from the 1970s on.

6   See Chu 2010; Fligstein and Zhang 2011; Kennedy 2011; McNally 2007, and 2012; Nee and Opper 2007.

7   *The Economist* 2012.

various state and domestic business coalitions at the national and sub-national level (which are frequently integrated into global value chains), not solely by an all-powerful, centralised steering bureaucracy.

In the following sections, first, a definition, or rather a working definition that suits the purpose of this chapter, of capitalism is derived which is based on five key dimensions of capitalist systems. Second, in the main part of the chapter these five dimensions are applied to China and utilised to synthesise the nature of China's capitalism. Rather than proving China's 'capitalist-socialist' nature, I conclude that the concept of a variegated state-permeated form of capitalism more accurately captures the country's growth dynamics as well as socio-economic instabilities.

2   Five Dimensions of Capitalism(s)

Within Chinese society one can find several peculiarly shaped characteristic attributes of capitalist 'socialisation'. These include: the systemic requirement for extended accumulation and innovation for the sake of profit maximisation, the development of production based on pragmatic motives, and, on the level of social and intersubjective relations, alienation, powerlessness and individualisation processes that force people into competition with one another. A sharp orientation towards growth and competition combines with an assertive national 'upgrading' focus that includes proactive state promotion and support of outward foreign direct investment.

Drawing on both Comparative and International Political Economy (CPE and IPE) scholarship, I seek to combine important insights of both perspectives to form a Global Political Economy approach.[8] IPE scholars are concerned with the analysis of global capitalism as an economic world order, its development over time, especially (neo)liberalisation tendencies from the 1970s on and its crisis tendencies, and how this affects economic and political actors. Through this emphasis on structures and change, an IPE perspective sometimes neglects the specific national conditions, constellations and path dependencies and thereby is not able to fully explain developments in individual economies. By contrast, CPE scholars emphasise the national diversity of economic systems and institutional arrangements that govern economic life in these countries. CPE thereby identifies different 'varieties', 'models' or 'variegations' of

---

8   See for instance Coates 2005; Jessop and Sum 2006; Streeck 2010. Also see ten Brink 2013a, Chapter I.

capitalist economic coordination (e.g. liberal, coordinated, dependent or state-permeated capitalisms)[9] and analyses their path dependency and persistence (despite neoliberalisation) over time. But through a frequently static national focus, a CPE perspective tends to underplay the degree of change that is often induced through the forces of global capitalism.

With a focus on three main actors that effect socio-economic development in modern capitalist societies – state institutions, firms, and workers (and their various internal as well as external relationships) – an approach can be formulated that distinguishes between five dimensions of capitalist systems in general – whose mixture ratios in turn bring forth different concrete historical variants of capitalism. Since, as will be shown below, China indicates that the world economy was able to impose its driving forces even onto this special case, although only to a certain degree, this underlines the need to use the concept of an *internationally variegated capitalist world system* to explain the economic development of China. China's political economy has to be analysed against the background of common characteristics in global capitalism and, in a further step, against its prevailing phase-specific characteristics such as liberalisation and transnationalisation of production, but without denying its internal specifics. According to this perception, the level of the overarching 'commonalities' of (global) capitalism and its phase-specific characteristics should not lead to losing sight of the 'diversity' between and within capitalisms. Thus, a Global Political Economy perspective is required precisely so as to study individual capitalisms.

Five dimensions that offer a general conceptualisation of key elements of capitalism with leeway for concrete variation – in which state institutions, firms, and workers play a role – include:

(1) *competitive relationships between companies and the crisis-prone nature of capitalist dynamics*: The systemic requirement for extended accumulation and innovation in capitalist economies is achieved through competition between companies. This process of competition-driven accumulation generates an unsynchronised, combined and crisis-prone dynamism. The study of the specific institutional conditions and relationships between companies under which the drive to accumulate prevails – in the case of China, for instance, the distinctive political framework of entrepreneurial activity, i.e. private-public forms of company organisation within a variety of production regimes – is one of the foundations of research on capitalism(s).

---

9   See May et al. 2013.

(2) *a hierarchical division of labour, distinct labour systems and intermediary institutions that are labour-inclusive or not*: Social stratification, in particular the vertical class polarisation between those with and without wealth and the social structural conflict this creates, is another precondition of capitalist dynamics. As will be shown with respect to China, the wage-labour relationship and the development of 'quasi-corporatist' labour relations entail specific balances of class forces, ownership and control structures that are crucial in determining the participation of actors in the processes of decision-making, planning and control over production, distribution and consumption.

(3) *the significance of money and of specific financial systems*: Money is a basic medium of socialisation in the capitalist mode of production. The circulation of industrial capital, for instance, gains its characteristic elasticity from the mechanisms of credit. At the same time capitalist actors or the state, when it acquires its material resources in the form of money, are subject to monetary restrictions. As is shown with respect to China's financial architecture, a Global Political Economy perspective additionally has to come to grips with a variety of financial systems, since the role and significance of banking, equity and other forms of finance capital as well as the amount of state control in banks and capital markets diverge between capitalisms.

(4) *the embedding of individual national economies in worldwide economic and political structures*: Particular capitalist systems can only be adequately analysed against the background of their integration in global economic, political and other intersocietal relations which place enormous constraints on their freedom of action. The need to differentiate between various types of capitalism is rooted in the acknowledgement that there is a spatiotemporal unevenness between the major sub-systems of the world economy. The internationally variegated capitalist world system is made up of a network of capitalisms, along national and regional lines, which differ but are linked and which undergo permanent processes of differentiation and adaptation. As can be shown, China is a case of enormous interest in this respect.

(5) *the state as a relatively autonomous political agency with a monopoly of power and coercion*: Contrary to economistic theories the state in capitalist systems per se attempts to guarantee a number of social, legal and infrastructural integrative and adaptive functions which make it possible to sustain a capitalist economy in the first place. 'Economics' and 'politics' thus form a network of structural interdependencies, which holds true even for 'neoliberal' economies. Not only are companies depend-

ent on their respective state authorities, the existence of the state is also contingent on successful dealings within the national economy. National political mechanisms are structurally dependent on successful accumulation within national borders. This manifests itself also in the necessity for governments to generate tax incomes. In order to be able to distinguish between different economic policies, varying degrees and forms of state intervention must be taken into account.[10] Furthermore, as can clearly be observed in China, state intervention and state ownership can be one of many forms of particularistic control and the exercise of economic and political power under capitalism.

In what follows, I attempt to demonstrate two things: On the one hand, that these five dimensions when applied to China show that the country has indeed developed the basic institutions and interest alignments characteristic of capitalist societies as an outcome of the interplay of domestic and international developments. On the other hand, these five dimensions can also serve as a means to identify the *specific* institutional arrangements and power alignments that have emerged in China. The Chinese variety of capitalism is characterised by intimate connections between state and private actors on different administrative levels which give rise to the notion of a state-*permeated* capitalism in opposition to older varieties of state capitalism[11] as well as to more liberal forms of capitalism.

In the next section, I begin this inquiry by looking into the dynamics of the party-state. Because of the special importance of a dynamic-authoritarian form of governance in the economic sphere, I deal with the state and state-business relations first. I then present distinctive forms of private-public company organisation. After outlining a fragmented type of quasi-corporatism in work relations, I discuss some key features of the state-permeated financial system. I then describe China's integration into the world economy, into East Asia, and into further transnational relations, as China became the most attractive production location in the world, benefitting from several 'lucky' external coincidences. All in all, I show how the specific combination of these five dimensions leads to a distinctive form of capitalism. In this way it is also shown, that, although China emerged as a major 'winner' of the worldwide economic rebal-

---

10   In reality the crisscross of areas of government responsibility and its underlying institutional characteristics are the basis for distinct political systems (such as liberal democracy or, in the case of China, a non-liberal form of governmentality, the 'party-state').

11   By older varieties of state capitalism, I refer for instance to the classical Japanese or Korean developmental state or to Stalinist varieties of command economies.

ancing in the wake of the 2008/09 global economic crisis, the continuity of its trajectory is threatened by the crisis-prone processes of global capitalism and also by a tendency toward internal economic and social crises.

A short disclaimer: note that in the following, this chapter for the most part does not investigate the ideational manifestations generated by the logic and nature of capitalism in China. Moreover, not all institutional bases, societal contexts and socio-cultural factors that contribute to China's state-permeated capitalism could be considered. In addition, space restrictions and the aim of providing a comprehensible rough guide compel this chapter to serve as a schematic snapshot rather than a dynamic and integrated analysis.[12]

3 The Party-State and the Economy

As is argued above, in capitalist systems the interactions between economic and political actors form a network characterised by structural interdependencies. Government actions play a constitutive role in shaping economic processes. China illustrates this in great detail. Thus, the political economy of China has to be analysed against the broader background of the politics of the central state, intra-regional competition and state entrepreneurialism.

3.1 Chinese Multi-Level-Governance

The movement away from Maoist planning occurred as part of a gradual, yet crises-driven process of institutional change. This entailed the transition from a bureaucratic, authoritarian-developmental dictatorship to a regionalised state-capitalist arrangement in which domestic competition played an increasing role.[13] Facing the ruin of the Cultural Revolution, there was a growing acceptance within important factions of the Chinese power elite that whatever policies would increase national output had a valid place. The reform process was initiated for the survival of the party-state, not ideological principle. It resulted in a process fought out in a crises-driven 'trial and error' mode which led to a huge success of experimentation with markets and entrepreneurialism. This

---

12 A much broader analysis of the trajectory and current evolution of China's economy as well as on conceptual tools to analyse Chinese capitalism can be found in ten Brink 2013a.

13 In classical Maoism, the state competed with other states (geopolitically) but tried (often unsuccessfully, as the term 'plan anarchy' indicates) to suppress domestic economic competition. It also restricted an opening up of the economy.

tentative constellation of 'crossing the river by groping for stones' paved the way for the resilience of the party-state as well as its adaptability.[14]

China's party-state is not a monolith. At present, the authoritarian Chinese state is trying to come to grips with the basic contradictions of the mode of accumulation in a rearticulated manner. A remarkable combination of central and decentralised power constitutes a fragmented system of multi-level-governance. It is thus impossible to understand the Chinese economy without reference to the diverse political fragmentation below the level of the central state.

Political institutions in China provide the basic framework for accumulation – an administrative structure that supplies order (administration, jurisdiction, security), an economic infrastructure (such as the transport system or communication) plus other arrangements for instance in labour relations. Disintegration tendencies, for example those that arose after the Asian crisis from 1997 on and the privatisation of numerous State Owned Enterprises (SOEs), were met by the central government with macro-economic Keynesian-like interventions. Even more extensive economic programmes applied as a consequence of the 2008 world economic crisis had a similar function.[15]

Although mainland China resembles East Asian states such as Japan or South Korea in several development policy terms – it fulfilled for instance a similar functional developmental role in raising investment and thereby fostering structural change during the phase when the economy had the highest growth prospects – it also differs in several ways. First, the territory of the PRC is much larger than that of other East Asian states, and thus a more fragmented and heterogeneous system exists: The coexistence of twenty-two provinces, five autonomous regions, four municipalities with the status of a province (Beijing, Shanghai, Tianjin, Chongqing) and two special administrative regions (Macao, Hong Kong) has led to the development of a disparate picture. Second, the industrial development of China started later. The PRC developed its economy in a phase of advanced transnationalisation after the 1970s which coincided with an opportunity structure that led to a comparatively strong opening of the economy. Third, the economy was more based on planned-economy elements than its East Asian competitors, who favoured administrative guidance.

Compared with liberal or coordinated varieties of capitalism, the government is much more openly focusing on state intervention. It influenced the

---

14   See Saich 2004.
15   Naughton 2011.

direction the transformation would take through market entry regulation and modified tax and credit granting policies. Several waves of bureaucratic restructuring led to attempts to create supraministerial institutions. But it was not until 2003 that the idea of establishing a body based on the Japanese Ministry of International Trade and Industry (MITI, now METI) could be put into effect. The reorganised National Development and Reform Commission (NDRC) is now a hub in the organisation of industrial development.[16]

Further, in contrast to more dependent capitalisms in the Global South, the Chinese party-state proved to be a strong negotiation partner vis-à-vis foreign firms and states. Based on its state apparatuses, the size of China's domestic market, and the lucrative investment climate, which makes the country attractive for Western multinationals, China did not have to 'sell-out'. State managers accordingly do not have to give in to the demands of foreign multinationals. In this way, they only *selectively* opened the economy, for instance for technological modernisation through foreign multinationals, and protected their national currency.

In all of this, elements of an economisation of the state sector and the party can be detected, in the course of which economic cost-income calculations were introduced over the past decades as part of an internal rationalisation process. The major corporate reforms of 1994, the establishment of new organisational standards and the weakening of direct party and government controls over independent company boards did initially limit the powers of state authorities but resulted nonetheless in a form of modernisation that is by no means without any control through government bodies (e.g. through the holding of shares in listed companies).

3.2   Competition-Driven Governance

Because national policy is often masked by the decisions of provincial governments and other subnational authorities and as central policy directives are often not applied uniformly, state intervention Chinese style could possibly better be defined by the expression 'diffuse' state capitalist developmentalism.[17] What Western CPE scholars would potentially call productive incoherence in effect delineates some of the peculiarities of China and maybe one of its competitive advantages.

In the 1980s, the redistributive functions of the state were initially concentrated on the subnational political levels. Since then, subnational admin-

---

16   Yang 2004.
17   McNally and Chu 2006, p. 54.

istrations, especially in the coastal areas, have mostly pursued successful economic strategies by stimulating economic efficiency in their territories by means of supervision of and direct intervention in companies.[18] This also includes subnational governments allowing local enterprises for instance to violate national labour laws and standards. Driven by internal competition of subnational bodies vying with each other to attract investors, growth dynamics have been initiated – in the absence of 'disturbing factors' such as a vibrant civil society.[19]

Government officials or state managers in this capitalism without liberal-democratic institutions thereby often substitute for entrepreneurship. Since they are subject to *competitive* pressures,[20] the capacities involved in the accumulation activities of local political institutions have a lot in common with private capitalist companies. Therefore, counter-juxtaposed concepts of state and private actors do not bring much clarification in the case of China. The opposite is the case, as for instance the legal form – private versus state property – does not determine the scope of budget constraints on actors in the economy in the customarily assumed dichotomy of soft budget constraints for state companies versus hard budget constraints for private enterprises. As Walder wrote some time ago, the 'analysis of soft budget constraints usually proceeds as if there is only one owner in the economy, 'the state', although in fact [in China] there potentially are as many owners of public enterprises as there are government jurisdictions'.[21]

Yet, forced by this *internal competition* (i.e. between local governments) and the realities of economic regionalisation, not only dynamic economic developments but also trends towards over-investment and doubling of capital expenditure have been initiated. As is revealed in the next section, there is almost no classical top-down control in large parts of the economy anymore. This also means that nowadays, regulatory chaos is prevalent as new regulatory bodies have often been layered upon old administrative agencies.

---

18   Nee and Opper 2007.
19   The emergence of a changed power configuration between industry and government is manifest in a new kind of competition setup: 'Previously, citizens competed to enter officials' patronage networks. ..., now officials also compete with each other for links to larger private companies, with successful ones becoming shareholders and managers' (Wank 1999, p. 198). This results in semi-autonomous network communities of political and private actors whose economic development concepts are relatively independent of central government bodies.
20   On the role of competition and competitive pressures under capitalism, see ten Brink 2014, pp. 42–4, 50–4; and Heinrich 2003.
21   Walder 1995, p. 268.

All in all, the background of a fragmented, competition-driven form of multi-level-governance should not lead to any premature conclusion that the central state has become weaker. Whereas the first phase of reform from 1978 on saw the scope of central government influence being cut back, the second phase of reform that started in the 1990s included wide-ranging attempts by the central state to (re)gain a greater scope for action. The central government did not only convert to capitalist growth policies, ideals of individual entrepreneurialism and active support to privatising SOEs. There was and still is another role of the central state that should not be underestimated, namely the provision of an overarching institutional architecture which accommodates competition. Despite the fact that experimentation procedures are delegated to local authorities, the central administration in Beijing plays an indispensable role in universalising local innovations, thereby providing coordination in the Chinese policy cycle. Again, recently, in reaction to the global slump, the state leadership re-emphasised centralisation.

Finally, an analysis of capitalism in China should include the role of the CCP. The dual structure of party and government in which ideally the party determines the political direction to be implemented by the administrative bodies of government has proved to be astonishingly flexible. Although centrifugal forces are at work within the power elite, its relative homogeneity provided enough scope for the transition to an entrepreneurial state and for the initiation and implementation of new policies.

In today's China the party with its 70 million members acts as a kind of catch-all party of capitalist modernisation that attempts to control social transition – while still functioning as a channel for the power elite. Of the around 40 million people officially described as cadre who work in the public service, the military or the party and whose status is secured by privileges, the absolute majority are party members.[22]

Regarding the role of the CCP in economic governance, it has remained important in SOE governance via key personnel decisions and other forms of party control. Additionally, although local governments can act quite autonomously from central government institutions, the Communist Party has retained a strong influence. In this sense, 'economic development concepts' are continuously shaped by central party bodies, though local interpretations make a difference. In the 2000s a partial withdrawal of the CCP from the legislative process and everyday administrative activities could be observed. The growing

---

22   Shambaugh 2009.

importance of the People's Congresses, including at the provincial level, thus reflects to a certain degree a process of societal pluralisation and local autonomy that is in turn linked to the regionalisation of the country. The CCP can thus increasingly be termed a 'reactively influential' party that retains its viability in an authoritarian, consultative way.

In the terminology of critical IPE, in the 2000s, the Chinese power elites were capable of transforming their former dominance into what Gramsci calls *hegemony*, a more consensual and legitimised form of rule, forming and consolidating a historical bloc by including the urban middle classes and intellectuals. The question is therefore not so much how the party is driven back by marketisation tendencies, but rather how the party has contributed to the emergence of a new form of capitalism and will continue to do so.

4 Thickly Embedded Capitalists: Company Organisation in China

The accumulation drive in China is achieved in an environment where economic rights of disposition and control have been shifted from state authorities to the management of numerous individual companies. This process reconfigured the structurally interdependent relations between economic actors and those with political power. But currently China is neither 'free' nor 'competitive' in the classic sense, it is governed by a 'mixed economy' system of formal and informal relations – a corporate culture that is referred to as 'red capitalism'.[23]

Although a refurbished form of state enterprise is dominant at the level of central government, in particular at the subnational level 'private-public' economic regimes gained significance. The figures for 2006 (with no big trend change afterwards) suggest a share of industrial output by SOEs of 31.2 per cent, while the share of private companies has risen to 37.2 per cent and the share of foreign-funded private enterprises, including investment from Hong Kong, Macau and Taiwan, amounts to 31.6 per cent.[24]

In contrast to older forms of state capitalism and developmental states, there is neither a classical top-down control prevalent nor is there a single guiding enterprise model in China, such as there is with the *chaebol* in South Korea. New forms of profit-oriented and competition-driven enterprises have emerged that are mostly listed, yet often dominated by state block-share-

---

23 Dickson 2007.
24 Chen and Wang 2010, pp. 45–50. Thus, in what follows, it should not be forgotten that Foreign Invested Enterprises (FIEs) from Taiwan, Hong Kong and many OECD-countries play a very important role in China's business sector.

holders. At the 'top tier',[25] refurbished SOEs continue to retain their influence, especially in sectors such as petrochemicals, telecommunications or electricity. Many of the large, centrally controlled state enterprises were drawn
together from 2003 on under the new State Asset Supervision and Administration Commission (SASAC) and have preferential access to state controlled
capital resources such as loans, land and subsidies.[26] On the central level,
SASAC administers government holdings and supervises around 100 of the
biggest national firms. The quasi-trustee control of the SASAC as well as that
of regional SASACs that are dispersed all over the country hence does not
correspond to that of a classic planning authority into which companies pay
money.

In the 'middle tier' where no natural monopolies and less strategic concerns
exist – such as machinery, automobiles, chemicals, electronics as well as in cutting edge environmental, energy, and other 'Strategic Emerging Industries' –
direct state ownership has been weakened. SOEs were thereby complemen-
ted by big public-private hybrids such as Huawei and private firms such as
Geely.[27] Nowadays, large non-state firms are also seen as 'national champions'
by state managers. Beneath those two dominant tiers, a great variety of small
and medium (mostly private) firms exist – for instance in light manufacturing,
and in export-oriented sectors.

The rapid expansion of the official private sector was driven by private
formations of companies from below along with reform from above (e.g. the
restructuring of SOEs) and external influences including foreign direct investment and the acceptance of East Asian and Western business models. Especially at the subnational level, enterprises owned by cities or urban districts
have been wholly or partially privatised. However, because of their close connections to state authorities many of those Collectively Owned Enterprises
(COEs) and Privately Owned Enterprises (POEs) cannot be regarded as classic private enterprises in the liberal sense.[28] They often continue to incorporate state shareholders or private shareholders who are embedded in the local
party-state. Private property remains embedded in the local political scene, as
demonstrated in the case of 'management buy-outs' by party and state functionaries. In the 1990s, many former political cadres chose the path of red
capitalism, an option made possible inter alia in a clause of the Corporations

---

25   Pearson 2011.
26   Li and Xia 2008.
27   This picture still abstracts too much since there exists immense diversity between indus-
     trial sectors (see Lüthje et al. 2013).
28   See ten Brink 2012b.

Act of 1994 that permitted the reforming of 'public' companies as private 'limited liability companies'.

For this reason it seems sensible to speak of a *unity in diversity*, of a heterogeneous assortment of company forms and production regimes assembled as it were under a state capitalist apparatus. According to empirical studies, the transformation processes amounted to an alliance between economic and political power elites and were also manifested as many people simultaneously occupied multiple positions in the political and economic sector. Entrepreneurs state in surveys that economic advantages and connections to the political sphere are the main reasons for joining the party.[29] They are also often appointed to institutions like the National People's Congress or its local equivalents.

At the empirical level this phenomenon is often referred to using a Chinese term meaning relationship: *guanxi*. The country is seen as a *'guanxi* society' where a predominance of an extremely personalised form of interaction and reciprocity tempered with self-interest dictate economic activity. From an economic perspective, *guanxi* interaction is sometimes seen as compensation for the historic absence of a regulative basis for market interaction: It facilitates reaction to market signals and technology transfer. However, the networks of private enterprises, local government officials and party cadres also produce access to political support, from county authorities, for instance. Conversely companies gain information about planned political reforms. What is involved here are microstructures of competition-driven state-permeated capitalism in which 'private' and 'state' actors (ultimately defined by the state) are bound together on several levels.[30] The *guanxi* networks lend the Chinese economy a high degree of particularised coordination in the sense that it occurs within the confines of a competitive society where a variety of local networks and alliances compete with each other. At the same time the networks act as local links or intermediaries to the global economy, often through the investment and business dealings of overseas Chinese. Therefore, as part of the growing monetisation of social relations, these private-public alliances do not, as assumed by neo-classical economists, constitute a gradual transition to a 'pure' market but are themselves to be regarded as a form of 'marketisation'. Although – following the privatisation of soes and coes in the 2000s – local governments may today be less involved in influencing economic decisions directly, the commercial

---

29   Dickson 2007, pp. 841–2; Tsai 2007.
30   There is no strict dividing line between recognised *guanxi* practice and corruption punishable by law.

rationality is virtually synonymous with an ongoing development and cultivation of personal relations with local district bodies who have the resources to promote business.

5   Fragmented Quasi-Corporatism: Chinese Labour Relations

Despite huge regional differences, differing ways of organising work as well as a marked development and prosperity gap between town and country, relevant characteristics of urban labour relations can still be identified as resulting from the greatest transformation in history of rural to industrial labour.[31]

China's industrial structure is a product of its gradual transformation into a party-state mediated, class-divided society.[32] The remodelling of labour relations was and still is generally based on fragmented regulation and a huge segmentation and segregation of the labour force which resulted in a low wage regime that resembles a neoliberal utopia: 'The Party state has created a rough approximation of the neoliberal ideal whereby a disorganised mass of individuals is forced to confront the hegemonic power of state and capital *as individuals*'.[33] In the following, the four main actors in China's labour system are described.

– *State actors*: In the area of labour relations the partial withdrawal of direct state intervention is accompanied by a tendency to more indirect political influencing – the juridification of work relations. Moreover, the state has established industrial consultation by tripartite bodies at different administrational levels, consisting of the relevant state institutions, the trade unions and the employers' associations.[34] The objective clearly lies in the institutionalisation of statutory and regulatory norms governing wage labour. The basis for this is the Labour Law passed in 1994, a number of subsequent regulations and the Labour Contract Law of 2008 that set the parameters for employment contracts. (Yet, at the local level, the state only selectively enforces labour regulations, while serving as the authority of last resort when strikes and other forms of resistance emerge.) At the same

---

31   See Friedman and Lee 2010, and ten Brink 2013a, Chapter III, for an overview of this transformation. Since the 1980s, approximately 250 million Chinese from rural provinces have migrated to China's cities and urban areas.

32   So 2005.

33   Friedman and Lee 2010, p. 530. Western MNCs producing in China are also part of the hegemonic power bloc workers are confronted with.

34   Shao et al. 2011.

time, against the background of the erosion of the factory-based system of social security (*danwei*), the central government is attempting to cushion the effects of the polarisation of society by setting up a social security system based on Western and East Asian models. Additionally, increased efforts by the state to cover the rising demand for higher skilled labour by increasing education expenditures can be detected.

– *The employers as a conscious collective*: The employers control key economic resources and frequently possess – and this applies not only to the managers of SOEs – political influence. The employers' associations, some of which existed prior to 1979 (like the All China Federation of Industry and Commerce), act as lobbyists and could develop their own expansion dynamics. The employers have developed 'a remarkable awareness of common interests and positions' on many issues and are acting collectively, in the practical sense of the word, regardless of many differences in opinion, mentality and conduct.[35]

– *Trade unions*: The All China Federation of Trade Unions (ACFTU) with its around 200 million members is officially the largest union in the world, although it cannot be regarded as a free trade union since it is largely controlled by the CCP and does not function as an independent advocate for wage earners. However, the ACFTU is the sole national trade union organisation formally represented with its subdivisions at nearly all levels in provinces, local districts and firms. Overall, unionisation at the company level dominates. Trade union leaders are usually also administrative functionaries in the companies and they normally act as tools of co-management.

– *Employees as underrepresented agents of countervailing power*: In many industrial sectors basic wages are currently only 50 per cent of total wages. The payment of overtime and bonuses to supplement wages is evidence of the wage earners' weak negotiating position. Although independent trade unions have so far not been able to form in China, collective forms of conflict are not without importance. In addition to possibilities of complaint, new forms of resistance have developed and the number of social protests (demonstrations, riots, and strikes) rose significantly in recent years.[36] Therefore, the implementation of the Labour Contract Law is dependent on social pressure and is partially evident in successful lawsuits, for instance on the back payment of wages.

---

35   Chang et al. 2008, p. 11.
36   CLB 2011.

Two conclusions can be drawn from this: The first is that the regulation of labour relations in China is concentrated at the level of individual companies. This localisation of industrial relations, which fragments the representation of the interests of the workforce, does not run counter to the party-state's stake in national competitiveness. Different types of production regimes, a massive segmentation and flexibilisation of employment, low base wages, long working hours that are often in violation of existing legal standards, but also huge wage differentials between employees and the missing mobilisation capacity of trade unions opened a huge 'space' of opportunities for (but were also the result of) private entrepreneurial 'experiments'. When confronted with group interests of entrepreneurs, the state occasionally assumes the role of a balancing element; this conforms with a fundamental state responsibility in capitalist societies – and should not be misinterpreted as a relic of 'socialism'.[37]

The second point is that short of downright inordinateness, a quasi-corporatism came into existence with the state establishing industrial consultation by tripartite bodies. Meanwhile, in China a collective representation of worker interests that is typical of most developed capitalist systems is lacking. Therefore, the corporatist structures remain fragmented and incomplete. As trade unions have not become independent from the CCP, a fourth party is in practice added to the usual tripartite corporatism – a working class with minimal union representation. Nevertheless, the working population, albeit largely outside the existing consultation systems, is influential through their own initiatives and opposition. A widespread series of strikes in the summer of 2010 has even been interpreted as the harbinger of the end of the Chinese model of labour subordination in the not-so-distant future.[38]

6   The State-Permeated Financial System

Because of the strategic role of government, developments in the financial sector object against the notion of a simple adaptation of a liberal model. In China, the logic of 'finance-driven accumulation' has not become prevalent,

---

37   Note, as an example, the central government's mediating role in the public discussions leading up to the Labour Contract Law, in which it had to balance against more liberal concepts of labour regulation by e.g. large enterprise groups, or its comparably permissive stance toward the strike movement in the summer of 2010.

38   Butollo and ten Brink 2012. As a result, a new trend is embodied by forces in the ACFTU (e.g. in Guangdong) that aim for more independence and a strengthening of trade union power to represent workers.

even though some preconditions for this were created in the form of stock markets and the conversion of many state enterprises into shareholder companies. Yet, it would also be erroneous to depict the financial sector as a realm of purely policy-driven activity, in which economic rationality, and thus capitalist imperatives, are lacking. By pointing to the decisive role of state institutions, and/or a continuous struggle for power among a number of 'factions', authors tend to characterise it as something outside the 'normal' world of financial markets.[39] But this approach uses an ideal-typical understanding of a functioning liberal financial system as a blueprint, and it tends to understand the behaviour of financial sector actors as governed by invariable self-preservation motives.[40]

In my view, China now has nearly all the institutions and interest alignments of Western finance systems, yet they are bound into a *specific* structure.[41] For instance, the characteristics of both enterprises as well as financial institutions create a system of incentives in which stock market capitalisation plays a minor role in the investment regime. Investments are mainly raised by way of internal savings and bank loans. This also implies that Chinese firms are relatively independent from short-term volatilities on global capital markets as well as from profit expectations by international investors.

Up to the present day, financing through bank loans is more common than through the capital market. The banking system is made up of coexisting central state commercial banks, semi-governmental and municipal banks, independent banks and credit cooperatives. State banks act as the main financing sources of economic growth although a number of firms on the fringe strongly rely on informal sources. At the centre is the People's Bank of China that has determined monetary policy since the mid-1980s, controlled exchange rates and supplied commercial banks with credit. Today, modelled on the Federal Reserve Bank of the United States, it has several regional offices and many provincial and local branches. The largest commercial banks currently listed grew during the 1980s from the substructures of a central bank complex that existed before 1978. In addition to the biggest state banks and other state controlled 'policy banks', many commercial, mainly listed banks have started to assert themselves.[42]

---

39   See Shih 2008.
40   See Gruin 2013, for an alternative approach to the Chinese financial system.
41   Naughton 2007, pp. 449–81. See Zysman 1983, as early evidence for a variety of Western financial systems.
42   Up into the 2000s the banking system in the PRC has not been as strongly profit-oriented as in a liberalised monetary economy. It financed loss-making state enterprises, for instance, together with their social security systems. The granting of loans was also rationed for

The Chinese stock market, with the big stock exchanges in Shanghai and Shenzhen, encouraged the restructuring of SOEs as it opened up new avenues of capital procurement with new shareholders. But, in general, its significance lies well below banking. Moreover, a solid integration in global finance markets can so far not be detected. The low proportion of assets held by foreigners is an indicator for this. Further, the Chinese government has learned from the 1997/98 Asian crisis and state control of capital movements and exchange rates is to be upheld.

Overall, state permeation, often in the form of and through competing local alliances, remains a defining characteristic of China's financial sector. Dominated by a state-led banking sector, it has served the Chinese growth strategy well in the 2000s in actively allocating capital towards investment and export sectors. This also meant that although the economy has been integrated into global product markets, the financial sector largely was not, and thus remained relatively independent from external credit. Partly because of its peculiar structure, the financial sector has come through the global banking crisis relatively well. However, this state-permeated system also creates considerable problems. What once proved capable of managing macro-economic dynamics against the background of China's special role in the world economy (see next section) is now creating obstacles against correcting the imbalances that developed as a result of China's growth strategy.[43] Whereas in Western economies private banks sometimes refused to lend money, China has to deal with the economic consequences of its highly expansionary credit policy. In 2008/09, the government used two main instruments to come to grips with the global slump: First, the huge investment stimulus relied on the structure of the CCP, whose political hierarchy 'was used to mobilise local governments to quickly ramp up investment projects'; second, it was 'the financial system – especially the state-owned banks – which was ordered to provide credit to finance these investment projects'.[44] As a result, since 2010 problems of bad loans and over-investment emerged that cannot be easily confined. A housing bubble in urban housing markets indicates these problems.

----

a long period. Ultimately the loan plan was replaced by a 'loan recommendation' that gives the commercial banks more room to manoeuvre without substantially limiting the political power of the central bank.

43   See Gruin 2013. This is not to say that China's financial system did not go through crises before. On the contrary, its gradual change over time was largely crises-driven (on the effects of the 1990s financial dysfunctions, see Yang 2004, pp. 81–94).

44   Naughton 2010b.

7   Lucky Coincidences: China in the Global Economy

Although China's financial system is not integrated into global financial circuits to a large degree, the fact that one-third of *industrial* output in China is in fact produced by foreign-funded private enterprises reveals the importance of analysing China in a global context. The current situation in the PRC is marked by the efforts of the political leadership to mitigate the contradictory effects of capitalist modernisation, typically justified with the objective of a 'harmonious society'. These strategies are, however, masked in many different ways by global and East Asian economic dynamics as well as the influence of economic and political actors who are not directly dependent on the Chinese party and state leadership or that are difficult to influence.

According to recent IPE literature, Chinese integration into global, East Asian and other transnational economic relations and power structures has led to a fragile but dynamic balance of power between mainland Chinese, overseas Chinese and foreign economic engagement.[45] The relative success of economic reorganisation in China is thus partly due to favourable external opportunity structures.

From the 1970s on, the development of the global economy has been marked by a trend to considerable disparities that allowed some countries to achieve significant GDP growth, despite generally low average growth rates in comparison with the preceding post-1945 period. In this constellation, China was able to prosper as its economy was in a favourable internal starting position, was able to grow at the expense of other countries and benefited both from the situation in East Asia and from other 'lucky' coincidences related to an increasing over-accumulation of capital in the North.

Paradoxically, China's dynamic reform path originated at a time when the prolonged post-war boom period was coming to an end. In contrast to other 'state socialist' societies, China profited from the onset of the 'globalisation' phase in the 1970s. Indeed, the global signs of stagnation in the real economy from the early 1970s on put more pressure on the Soviet Union and its vassals than on China: 'The fact that socialism fell when world manufacturing

---

45   Reference can be made to a number of debates analysing the ascent of China in the context of restructuring of the global economy and hegemonic structures (see Breslin 2007; Hung 2009; Zweig and Chen 2007). A study of the economic (and political) intervention of Chinese actors in global processes can also uncover elements that help define Chinese capitalism; these are not looked into at this point. An analysis of China's inclusion in transnational production networks that boosted the importance of the 're-export economy' and led to a greater dependence on world markets also helps understand China's economy.

already suffered from excess capacity contributed to the destruction of the productive capacities of former socialist economies. This is much less the case in China ..., where the agrarian sector remained dominant through the whole socialist epoch'.[46] In the late 1970s, China was still under-industrialised and could exploit this constellation, while profiting additionally from its socio-geographical situation.

The further development of the Chinese 'miracle' can only be explained with reference to external factors. Foreign direct investments (FDI) and their attendant export orientation are an important element here. Geographical factors and good timing also favoured economic growth. As an investment location, China was in the immediate vicinity of an East Asian growth region and the networks of the overseas Chinese.[47] This favourable setting was to prove useful in solving problematic situations that threatened to jeopardise growth from the 1980s on. While Western and Japanese entrepreneurs were still criticising the investment climate in China, overseas Chinese were able to become the key source of FDI during the first phase of economic reforms thanks to their familiarity with Chinese customs and language. To some extent the capital of overseas Chinese also eased the way for the much bigger wave of other foreign investments from the 1990s on. As a result of the Asian Crisis of 1997/98, and through the Dotcom Crisis in 2001, transnational production networks (above all in the electronics industry) began to shift their orientation more and more towards the Chinese mainland.

As an emerging economy in which an export-orientated model became established, China benefited from the 1990s on from another special global economic constellation. The old centres showed a lower investment ratio: 'the industrial countries are now accumulating at a slower rate than the world as a whole ... The baton of 'super-accumulator' was passed ... to China in the 1990s. In the early 2000s the growth of capital stock in China could easily be 12 per cent or more'.[48] The two engines of the world economy since the mid-1990s,

---

46   King and Szelényi 2005, p. 209.

47   The regional environment, meaning the East Asian growth and integration process and the internal Asian trade and production chains, were a decisive external factor in China's successful integration into world markets. In this process, a special link was forged between parts of coastal China, Hong Kong and Taiwan. At the latest from the late 1990s on, a transnational economic region – the 'China Circle' – could be identified. As time passed, the networks of overseas Chinese merged with those of mainland China.

48   Glyn 2006, pp. 86–7. Authors who single out low labour costs as 'pull factors' for FDI to explain China's successful rise (Lardy 2002, p. 61) overlook a fundamental 'push factor' for risky investments – an over-accumulation of capital at times classified as a capital investment crisis in the traditional production centres. Additionally, it is not only low labour

the USA and, to a lesser extent, China achieved growth via two different, complementary and mutually dependent paths. Whereas in the USA large chunks
of GDP growth consisted of (debt-financed) consumption rather than investments, the Chinese boom was a mirror image of that in the USA. The Chinese
boom can be explained by a very high rate of investment and relatively low
consumption. The relative importance of investments continued to grow from
around 30 percent of GDP in the early 1990s to nearly 40 percent after 2000.
Large amounts of liquid assets in the North secured the supply of investments
and stoked the boom even further. In this situation, the old centres as end buyers of Chinese exports played a key role. The growing investment-consumption
gap has increased its reliance on exports. The end of the consumer boom in
the USA and other countries was therefore bound to trigger a crisis in those
Chinese sectors geared to the consumer market.

The fact that China became the most attractive production location in the
world at precisely the moment when real accumulation in the old centres was
slowing down, is an indication of something that has been underestimated in
both liberal marketisation success stories[49] as well as in a state-centred scen-
ario with the Chinese Leviathan as a clever, forward-looking force that shapes
the economy: namely the role of unintentional, contingent developments in an
anarchic global economic system – developments that may yield more negative
effects for China in the future.

8   State Capitalism, Chinese Style: Summary and Perspectives

With the help of a Global Political Economy perspective, it is possible to
depict the kind of political economy that has actually emerged in the PRC.
For the want of a more suitable term, China was described as a new form of
competition-driven state-permeated – and, more precisely, since there exists
enormous heterogeneity in the Chinese political economy – variegated capitalism. The increasing significance of market institutions in economic life is by
now indisputable, and in labour relations, the party state, hand in hand with
Western multinationals, has produced a rough approximation of neoliberal
ideals. However, even if the PRC is an essential part of a world economy organ-

---

costs that count, but also the quality of 'human capital'. As foreign chambers of commerce
put it, in comparison to other emerging countries China 'offers a workforce that is relatively well-educated, hardworking, eager to learn skills, and reliable. This combination is
hard to beat' (AmCham 2005, p. 24).

49   See Huang 2008.

ised by neoliberal precepts, it retains a specific character. The process of capitalist development in China should therefore not be analysed in narrow terms
of a linear progression towards liberal market capitalism. The extent of state
interventionism in corporate governance inside the firm, the state's assistance
in the firm's external transactions, as well as the role of the CCP make for a special form of capitalist modernisation with a communist 'façade'. Furthermore,
as China's response to the global crisis has up to now [early 2013] been comparatively successful, the power elite believes that this success justifies their
economic system, their strategy of both market mechanisms and macroeco-
nomic instruments as well as many of their other industrial and administrative
policies.

The peculiarities of the Chinese system include a competition-driven system of multi-level-governance and a dynamic state dirigisme, a special form
of heterogeneous private-public corporate organisation, a fragmented type of
quasi-corporatism in labour relations, and a state-permeated financial system. To this, China's selective integration into global economic, East Asian
and other transnational relations has to be added, which has led to a fragile
balance of power between mainland Chinese, overseas Chinese and foreign
economic engagement. Rather than proving its 'capitalist-socialist' character,
China's variegated capitalist arrangement points to the reality of a complex set
of competition-driven relationships between 'private' and 'public' actors and
between various vertical and horizontal decision-making structures – a setup
that, so far, has been kept in check by central power elites as the authority of
last resort in moments of crises.

Is this, then, the beginning of a Chinese century? Or, moreover, can we
assume a new state-capitalist phase of global capitalism in which China acts
as the role model? Clearly, from a critical viewpoint, and against Western commentators who are in the grip of 'Sinomania',[50] this is a question too early to
answer. Indeed, liberal forms of capitalism are in crisis and there is evidence
that other large emerging economies such as India and Brazil are trying to
emulate some of the ingredients of China's 'success story'. And, given that current growth trends continue and that the rise of several other large emerging
economies goes on, liberal hegemony might be challenged in the not so dis-
tant future. Yet, it should be kept in mind that China's apparently unstoppable
rise is confronted with severe *challenges* that should be addressed in future
research.[51] I will therefore end by hinting at topics that are interesting with

50   Jacques 2009.
51   See, as an example, ten Brink 2013b, and the 2013 special issue on Rebalancing China's
      economy in the *Journal of Current Chinese Affairs* (Volume 42).

respect to research on China and state capitalism. As was only barely touched upon in this chapter, the continuity of the Chinese trajectory is threatened by the crisis-prone processes of global capitalism and the tendency for internal crises to develop. In particular, the government faces the obstacles of a continuing dependence on exports. It therefore aims to make the transition from export-driven growth to a more domestically-centred model based on internal consumption. Government strategies of industrial restructuring in the wake of the global downturn addressed some of these problems, but the huge stimulus plans and the related re-organisation of industrial assets also accelerated over-accumulation due to their massive bias towards fixed capital formation. Thus, analysing both socio-economic imbalances and the limits of the state's capacity to regulate the economy represent interesting fields for future studies.

In addition to the conflict 'between the needs to draw down liquidity and reduce inflationary pressures, on the one hand, and the enormous economic and political commitments already made to investment projects, on the other',[52] *societal polarisation* endangers stability. Trapped between public promises of social justice and the enduring belief in low wages as a competitive advantage, governmental crisis management oscillates between social appeasement and world-market oriented restructuring. Thus, analyses of Chinese labour relations and resistance by the new Chinese working class that might challenge the hegemony of the post-Maoist power elites clearly also are among the most interesting future research areas.

At the moment [early 2013], China's economic development looks extremely bright, mostly because other capitalist powers look so miserable. While this fact challenges liberal marketisation success stories and state-centric theories, it also indicates that China is irreversibly enmeshed in a capitalist world economy still struggling with the ramifications of the global slump.

---

52   Naughton 2010.

CHAPTER 6

Developmental State Theory and Chinese Capitalism: a Critical Review

Lee Jeong-goo

1   Introduction

China has recorded astonishing economic growth since the economic reforms and open door policy that began in 1978. This achievement has raised two questions for China specialists. The first is what the dynamics generating this high economic growth are. The second is whether China can overtake the US as the economic and political influence of the US decreases globally. The second issue particularly reflects the expectation that the Chinese economic growth model can replace the US neoliberal economic development model – the so called Washington Consensus – since China has become the world's second largest trading nation, recorded a huge trade surplus and now has the highest foreign exchange reserves in the world.

The two questions are closely related. If the high economic growth of China has not been generated from the neo-classical economic development model (expansion of the market, deregulation, small government, opening markets etc), it illustrates the possibility that the Chinese model can supplant Anglo-Saxon capitalism. The perspective of the US economy contrasts with the Chinese economy because the US has suffered from a twin deficit and was at the epicenter of the 2007 8 economic crisis. Joshua Ramo's 'Beijing Consensus' clearly presents the aforementioned expectation.[1] A growing interest in academia concerning the Chinese model also reflects this expectation.[2]

The economic crisis that began in 2007 has had a certain impact on the Chinese economy, but the Chinese model still enjoys some popularity and there are still demands for the generalisation of the Chinese economic experience and its diffusion to other countries. Fewsmith argued that the debate on the Chinese model was a recurrence of the 1990s debate on whether China was a socialist or capitalist country. He also claimed that the debate was about

---

1   Ramo 2004.
2   Chŏn 2008; Chang 2011.

the particularity of Chinese civilization.[3] The Chinese model has also attracted much attention in China. For example, Pan Wei, a professor at Beijing University, argued that the China Model was not only successful but also that it represented a renaissance of Chinese traditional culture.[4] He interestingly argued that the rule of law was separable from democracy and that it was actually necessary to separate the two. He pointed out that China accepted the former but did not accommodate the latter, an argument that may come from the perception that China has succeeded in economic development at the expense of democracy.

When applied to the Chinese case, Developmental State Theory (DST) also implies that it is the country's particular political arrangement – an authoritarian regime with a one-party state system, controlled by the Communist Party of China (CPC) – that has enabled it to achieve economic development. A critical Marxist examination of this influential hypothesis is therefore much needed.

This chapter will provide such a critical review of the application of Developmental State Theory to China. In the following section the general characteristics and origins of the theory are illustrated and its application to Newly Industrializing Countries (NICS) is examined. The subsequent section reviews previous works that have applied the theory to China while section 4 explains the problems found in this literature in terms of the relation between the state and capital, the state's industrial policy and the state's foreign economic policy. This will demonstrate how the theory is unable to fully explain the economic growth of China and the NICs in East Asia. Finally, this chapter will introduce alternative explanations for Chinese economic growth that avoid the weaknesses of Developmental State Theory.

2   The Developmental State Theory and the Newly Industrializing Countries (NICs) in East Asia

The modern notion of 'development' goes back to the German Historical School of the late nineteenth and early twentieth centuries. When faced with comparatively advanced England and France, Gerschenkron argued that there was an 'advantage of backwardness' in economic development. The common strategy of these thinkers was that they sought protection for their economies

---

3   Fewsmith 2011.
4   Pan 2010.

from advanced capitalist countries that demanded free trade and open markets.[5]

After World War II, Latin American countries pursued economic development through an import-substitution industrialisation policy, but the policy failed when it was faced with the debt crisis of the early 1980s. A belief that the role of the state must be minimised and market forces allowed free rein has proliferated since the late 1980s, coinciding with the end of the Cold War. This belief is usually called neoliberalism.

The emergence of the Newly Industrialising Countries (NICs) was a challenge to mainstream economics. At first, neoliberal economists claimed that the development of the NICs came from unrestricted market power.[6] However, the classic research on the role of the Ministry of International Trade and Industry (MITI) in Japanese economic development by Chalmers Johnson and other studies by Alice H. Amsden, Robert Wade and Peter Evans emphasised the strategic role of states in directing the processes of industrialisation and modernisation.[7] Developmental State Theory has gained popularity and discussions about the theory have been boosted by these authors. Even the World Bank, which previously advocated the free market and small government, has acknowledged the role of states in economic development and improving the living standards in the countries of East Asia.[8]

Developmental State Theory has gained a certain historical momentum because it argues that different paths of economic development other than neoliberal orthodox doctrine are possible and it is distinguished from the standpoint that considers the state to be a non-economic institution. Governments usually intervene in economies throughout fiscal and monetary policies and also deploy trade policies and foreign exchange policies in order to protect their own industries and markets. Nevertheless, all states can't be reduced to the developmental state. The developmental state has the following distinctive characteristics.

The first characteristic is that the developmental state is accompanied by strong economic-political elites or decision makers who have the power and authority to carry out economic development, improving living standards and eliminating technological gaps. These elites sometimes appeal to nationalism to achieve economic development.

---

5   Gerschenkron 1966.
6   Balassa et al 1982.
7   Johnson 1982; Amsden 1989; Wade 1990; Evans 1995.
8   World Bank 1993.

The second characteristic is that it has a competent and authoritarian state apparatus which can assist the elites. The state apparatus's technical management skills can direct and promote socioeconomic development. The MITI in Japan, the Economy Planning Board (EPB) of South Korea and the Council for Economic Planning and Development (CEPD) of Taiwan are good examples.

The third characteristic is the fact that these elites and state apparatuses have relative autonomy from certain other interest groups within society. This enables the developmental state to carry out the imperative of economic development without depending on capital or labour. Evans used the term 'embedded autonomy' to explain that the developmental state is more efficient in economic development than other types of state. He argued that 'It is an autonomy embedded in a concrete set of social ties which bind the state to society and provide institutionalised channels for the continual negotiation and renegotiation of goals and policies'.[9]

The fourth characteristic of the developmental state is its tendency toward an authoritarian political system which oppresses political rights, civil rights and civil society organisations. Developmental state theorists believe that there is not much relation between economic development and democracy, while neoliberal economists insist that economic development will bring democracy and good government.

The characteristics of the developmental state can be summarised many other ways and definitions of Developmental State Theory vary according to authors.[10] In this sense, Stubbs has pointed out that 'the concept of the DS still has currency. ... Much depends on how the DS is defined'. He continued that 'the narrower the definition, the easier it is to pronounce the death of the DS. The broader the definition the more aspects of the original construction can be located in contemporary societies around East Asia'.[11]

Developmental State Theory has faced both theoretical and empirical challenges since the 1990s. One argument is that all states, including developmental states, have been constrained or limited in their roles due to the continual spread and deepening of globalisation.[12] Others have argued that the developmental state no longer worked after the East Asian crisis in 1997 and that these states, which were unable to make artificial interventions and strategic industrial policies under the influence of globalisation and neoliberalism,

---

9   Evans 1992, p. 163.
10   Yun 2006, pp. 45–68; Pak 2008, pp. 17–38.
11   Stubbs 2009, p. 17.
12   Cerny 1997.

had become regulatory states.[13] The advocates of Developmental State Theory argued against those challenges, claiming that the role of the state in the neoliberal era was rather transformed than diminished and that states played a role in economic recovery after the East Asian crisis in spite of the fact that the NICs followed neoliberal policies.[14]

Linda Weiss in particular has argued against the claim that globalisation weakened the power of the state and has insisted that Japan responded to globalisation with the regional integration of production in Asia. She pointed out that a hierarchical order had been constructed through the integration process and that this demonstrated the strong capacity of the state to transform itself. As a result, she expected that the nation state's power would actually increase in the neoliberal era.[15]

Hayashi also shared the idea that the developmental state was still valid. He wrote that 'the developmental state is a model of state-led industrialization for developing countries, where the market mechanism is underdeveloped or the market itself does not exist. The underdevelopment (or non-existence) of the market means that the market does not signal which industries should grow or disappear. Under the circumstances, the government should be more proactive than just leaving all economic activity to the market: the government should identify which industries should be targeted and actually promote those industries. However, the means to promote particular industries do not have to equate to trade protectionism. Southeast Asian countries have implemented state-led industrialisation by utilising MNCs, and have been successfully upgrading their economic structure through FDI. Their experience provides an important insight when considering future strategies that today's developing countries could pursue'.[16]

Wong argued that even though the existing developmental state is not adequate in the era of neoliberal globalisation and the role of the state in East Asia has thus changed, East Asian states are still developmental states if one applies a broad definition of development. He noted that the restructuring of the existing developmental state does not mean obsolescence and states with a developmental orientation continue to play an important role in economic, social and political development in East Asia.[17] He particularly suggested that the new role of the developmental state is not limited to industrial policies

---

13   Kim 1999.
14   Weiss 2002, pp. 110–18.
15   Weiss 2002, p. 309.
16   Hayashi 2010, p. 62.
17   Wong 2004, p. 357.

but has been expanded creatively to R&D policies, social welfare reforms, and economic policy more generally. According to him, 'the state still matters in economic development – how it matters has changed considerably'.[18]

Mark Beeson rejected the hypothesis that the developmental states are converging on a US-style capitalism. He pointed out that 'For all the attention the globalization phenomenon receives, one of the most striking paradoxes it highlights is the persistence of highly distinctive forms of economic organization, despite apparently ubiquitous 'external' competitive pressures'.[19] He emphasised that it was important to understand that the developmental states have developed based on a distinctive class structure which was established through struggles and compromises in the past under the particular historical environment in East Asia and to understand that it could persist because it satisfied and promoted the needs and interest of the strongest agents, the state and the capitalists. Beeson did not advocate the developmental state as strongly as Wong, but argued that it can still be influential due to 'path dependence', despite the fact that it is no longer appropriate or effective.[20]

There are of course many more debates and discussions on developmental state theory. However, this paper will focus on whether this theory, which emerged from the attempt to explain the economic development of the East Asian NICS, can also be applied to China.

3   Expanded Application: China

Many experts on China have introduced new terms in order to explain the reforms and economic development that began in the late 1970s. For example, terms like 'entrepreneurial state', 'corporatist state', 'regulatory state', 'dual development state', 'market-facilitating state', 'rent-seeking state' have been introduced into the academic vocabulary.

There are two reasons why such varied terms have sprung up to explain Chinese economic development. The first reason is that China is such a big country, with its large central government and 31 regional governments. All these governments are agents of reform and economic development. This creates a situation in which directly opposite economic policies can sometimes co-exist in the same country. In this sense, there is an argument that it is difficult to generalise China's experience using a single term. The second reason,

---

18   Wong 2004, p. 357.
19   Beeson 2001, p. 488.
20   Beeson 2001, p. 489.

stemming from the first, is that decision-making institutions are decentralised. Since the ministries of the central government compete with one other for their own economic achievements and the introduction of the *fangquan rangli* (the decentralisation of power and transfer of profits) policy, decision-making units have become diffuse and policies varied.

Gordon White pioneered the application of Developmental State Theory to the Chinese case. He believed that DST could be applied to socialist countries and he classified socialist countries into the following three categories. The first was those countries that had achieved mature socialist development such as China. The second category included those countries at the stage of proto-industrialisation like Nicaragua and Angola. The third category covered countries in between the two such as Cuba and Vietnam.[21] He also argued that China was a typical reformist developmental state when it pursued its reform and opening policy.[22] His argument, however, did not get much support or attention since most developmental state theorists believed that DST is better applied to capitalist countries than socialist countries. States, they believed, can regulate the market for economic development but states should not deny the market mechanism and private property rights. The countries which White classified as socialist have since started market reforms and the concept of the socialist developmental state has therefore lost its ideological significance.

Mark Blecher, Vivienne Shue and Jean Oi have studied the role of regional government in economic development during the 1980s, when the reform and opening policy was still in its early stages.[23] Vivienne Shue created new terms like the 'entrepreneurial state' and the 'regulatory state'. According to her, the entrepreneurial state is an entity not only directly engaged in production but also in establishing new enterprises and providing financial support to enterprises in order to increase their competitiveness.[24] Jean Oi used the new term 'local corporatist state' to denote a form of decentralised developmental state.[25] She argued that local government officials promoted regional economic development by supporting township and village enterprises, providing them with resources and technology and sometimes redistributing resources. In this local corporatist state model, the regional government officials became economic agents. Oi distinguished two forms of the industrialisation process in rural China. Under the corporative form the regional government officials acted like

---

21   White 1984, pp. 111–14.
22   White and Wade 1988, p. 19.
23   Blecher 1991; Blecher and Shue 1996; Oi 1995.
24   Shue 1995.
25   Oi 1995, p. 1139.

managers providing resources, while under the littoral form private firms were established by capital from overseas Chinese.

Jane Duckett studied cases of real estate development and the city commerce department of Tianjin city government. These cases showed that certain departments of the regional government sought to profit and competed with each other through the creation of new businesses and the investment of public funds. Individual departments of the city government or the regional government, however, were not likely to be independent profit-making units because these institutions could be closed down by the city government or the regional government.[26]

In a broad sense, the entrepreneurial state might be a part of the developmental state since the state is a major economic agent with an entrepreneurial orientation. But the entrepreneurial state is different to the developmental state because it does not share certain characteristic elements of the developmental state such as a collective vision for economic development, the existence of an elite who pursue this vision, the state's capacity to control economic development and a unified single state which can integrate the interests of the whole of society.

There are two contrasting views on this issue. On the one hand, there is the opinion that China is not a developmental state any more because not only the central government but also the 31 regional governments can deploy independent economic policies and have independent economic interests thanks to the policy of decentralisation since the 1980s. On the other hand, there is an argument that China is still a developmental state in spite of its decentralised governance structure. Ming Xia introduced a new term, the 'dual developmental state', in order to explain the new power relations between the central government and the regional governments and also the relationship between administrative institutions and legislative institutions.[27]

There has been much discussion comparing different Newly Industrialised Countries (NICs) and comparing the NICs with China. Baek Seung-Wook pointed out that China shared more elements of the developmental state than Southeast Asian countries. According to him, China had some different characteristics when compared with the Southeast Asian countries. For example, the greater importance of state-owned enterprises, a non state-owned sector developed by the state's market creation policy (or a dual system of state-owned enterprises and non state-owned enterprises) and the export-oriented

---

26   Duckett 1998.
27   Ming 2000, pp. 21–6.

industrialisation of the non state-owned sector are among them.[28] He also indicated that China and Southeast Asian countries shared certain similarities in terms of the finance system centred on banks. He argued that this system was different to Japan's Main Banking System and South Korea's diversification trend with the development of the *chaebol* conglomerates.[29] Yun Sang-Woo also pointed out the role of the Chinese state as a developmental state which initiated a marketisation drive providing the motivation for growth while the coordination of economic and institutional elements was the most important single factor for economic growth in China.[30]

Both Baek and Yun raised the question of whether China would maintain the characteristics of a developmental state after its entry into the WTO in 2001.[31] Baek foresaw that China would retain several important characteristics of the developmental state rather than seek to pursue the Anglo-Saxon model with the liberalisation of capital markets.[32]

Alongside the argument that the state's power has been weakened under the influence of neoliberal globalisation, there is an argument that DST has become an obsolete concept. It is argued that both China and Japan are no longer developmental states because China is undergoing a neoliberal structural adjustment process and Japan is in the midst of a long depression. On the contrary, some scholars still believe that East Asian countries including China and Japan are developmental states. For example, Mark Beeson, who compared the experience of China and Japan, suggested that it was premature to argue that the developmental state was not functioning in Japan despite the reforms of its state-led development model. Furthermore, he argued that China followed Japan's early experience after the war and embraced elements of neomercantilism and state interventionism.[33]

Zheng Yongnian concluded his study on how the Chinese state had changed in the globalisation era by pointing out that globalisation had brought serious problems to China but it was coping with the problems with ideological and institutional flexibility.[34]

After this review of some of the many attempts to apply DST to China let us now turn to a critical discussion of whether the theory is actually applicable to China.

---

28   Baek 2005, pp. 493–5; Baek 2008, pp. 264–5.
29   Baek 2008, pp. 265–6.
30   Yun 2006, p. 304.
31   Baek 2008, pp. 267–8; Yun 2006, pp. 299–303.
32   Baek 2008, pp. 269–71.
33   Beeson 2009, pp. 22–7.
34   Zheng 2004, p. xvii.

4   Critical Review of the Application of DST to China

The key arguments around the application of DST to China will be examined in terms of the relationship between state and capital, the state's industrial policy, and the state's foreign policy.

4.1   The Relationship between State and Capital

In DST, the state is a key agent which is beyond the interests of the various groups within society and coordinates and integrates the interests of these groups. In this sense, the state is not only an independent organisation but also an autonomous organisation. Skocpol argued that the state 'conceived as organizations claiming control over territories and people may formulate and pursue goals that are not simply reflective of the demands or interests of social groups, classes, or society'.[35]

Rueschemeyer and Evans argued that the state bureaucracy had a specific perspective distinguished from the ruling class with its private ownership since the state bureaucracy structurally did not have a short-term interest in profit. This distinctive perspective could be produced from their specific training and therefore the state tended to represent itself ideologically as the protector of universal interests.[36] Skocpol, Rueschemeyer and Evans considered that the state was separate and independent from the interests of various social groups. This meant that the economic, political, ideological spheres were reconstructed according to national state's interests. For them, therefore, the concept of 'bringing the state back in' as a key agent of development is crucial.

The state played a key role in Chinese economic development. China's economic policy in the 1980s was to maintain the state-owned sector while allowing the development of private firms in non state-owned sectors. Naughton described this strategy as 'growing out of the plan'.[37] The non state-owned sector grew rapidly and soon accounted for a huge share of the total economy. When the Chinese state integrated the Chinese economy into the world market by initiating the opening policy, attracting FDI and so on, the private sector was the main beneficiary. But the state-owned sector still accounts for a considerable proportion of the economy. The state-owned sector maintains the key role in heavy chemical, steel, energy, and raw materials industries and also has an important share in fixed capital investment, gross domestic production,

---

35   Skocpol 1985, p. 9.
36   Rueschemeyer and Evans 1985, p. 53.
37   Naughton 1996.

and the total number of employees. This dual system of state sector and non-state sector has therefore been highlighted as an important characteristic of the Chinese economy since the 1990s.[38]

The *zhuada fangxiao* (抓大放小, grasping the large enterprise and letting go the small enterprise) strategy, which was decided at the 5th plenary session of the 14th CPC central committee meeting in 1995, is considered to be a policy of privatising state-owned enterprises (SOEs); however, it was actually a policy for strengthening SOEs. Peter Noland pointed out that the policy is a strategy to promote large enterprises and neglect small companies in order to survive in a competitive global marketplace. Jiang Zemin, general secretary of the Communist Party of China emphasised at the 15th national congress of the CPC that it would try its best to reform state-owned enterprises through good management for big enterprises and a more flexible policy for small and medium-size enterprises.[39] In other words, the policy means privatisation for uncompetitive small and medium-size enterprises and more state support for big enterprises.

The State-owned Assets Supervision and Administration Commission (SASAC), which is a part of the State Council, has initiated the privatisation of medium and large SOEs. SASAC is selling off the state's shares in SOEs but it still owns two-thirds of the total shares of the listed companies and controls key industries and public utilities like munitions, energy, and natural resources industries. Yongnian Zheng pointed out that the main strategy for the reform of SOEs is the establishment of huge industrial conglomerates similar to Korean *chaebol*.[40]

The restructuring of the state-owned sector in China from the 1990s onward, however, has become distinctly more neoliberal than developmental, with the establishment of market-oriented policies like the corporation law, mass lay-offs, and welfare reductions. This shows that the state not only plays a role as a collective capitalist but also plays the role of providing institutional support and convenience for foreign and private capital.

Private corporations have increased rapidly since the reform and opening policy and the Chinese bourgeoisie has constructed a collective identity since the middle of the 1990s.[41] Successful businessmen and women have been elected as members of the National People's Congress and legislated or amended laws on their own behalf. Furthermore, the capitalist class has promoted its interests through its connections with the CPC and clever manoeuv-

38   Baek 2008, pp. 250–51.
39   Noland 2002, pp. 38–9.
40   Zheng 2004, p. 105.
41   Dickson 2003, p. 163.

ring deployed by the major business associations. Dickson presented two interesting results by comparing businessmen who used to be central government officers and businessmen with other social backgrounds. The first finding was that there was no evidence for the unofficial connection between state bureaucrats and industrial elites in China, which is one of the key elements of the 'embedded autonomy' defined by Evans.[42] Party officials and government officials did not come from the same schools and did not share the same experience. He even pointed out that businessmen who used to be party officials were losing their connection with the party.[43] The second finding was that the state's influence on the economy in general was shrinking, while the influence of private businessmen was expanding. Jiang Zemin's announcement that he would open the CPC's doors to private businessmen and businesswomen on 21 July 2001 demonstrated that their power and influence had become much stronger. The Chinese government therefore could not realise its intention of making selective interventions in the accumulation process of industrial capital. The continuous suspicion of private businessmen towards the state's policy also showed that private businessmen did not much trust state policy.[44]

With its reform and opening policy the Chinese government provided bases and spaces for the establishment and development of private enterprises after 1978. Thus private enterprises could grow thanks to the government's support. The fact that the role of the Chinese state in China's economic development was so significant seems to demonstrate that DST is applicable to China. However, there is one big difference. As mentioned above, the state in DST leads the whole of society with its strong power but does not replace capital itself. However, the Chinese state took on the role of collective capitalist and acted as such on its own behalf rather than as a developmental state with relative autonomy. The fact that the Chinese state acted as a collective capitalist could explain why the state tried to control the economy (this is the reason why developmental state theorists present China as a developmental state) and at the same time played the role of regulatory state or predatory state by establishing a market economy, strengthening a single regulatory institution, and cutting welfare. The Chinese government has been exposed to competition with private and foreign capital since the beginning of the 2000s – after

---

42   Evans does believes that unofficial connections are important, however. He wrote that 'states are connected to "economic elites" or "the capitalist class" via ties to particular firms and individuals. The success or failure of transformative projects depends on how they jibe with the strategies of particular firms' (Evans 1995, p. 20).

43   Dickson 2003, pp. 44–5.

44   Dickson 2003, pp. 107–14, pp. 161–2.

China entered the WTO in 2001 – and could not achieve the same control over private capital it had in the 1990s.[45]

4.2   Analysis of the State

In DST the state is an entity with an imperative to carry out economic development, acting entirely in the collective interests of the whole society, rather than that of particular social groups or individual state bureaucrats. Evans, therefore, argued that the actions of the state could not be reduced to a simple aggregate of individual motivations. He argued that the decisions of state bureaucrats depended on the institutional context, which had a complex interactional form arising from history and embedded in the social structure. The institutional context was an actual entity that preceded individual interest.[46]

Evans thought that the relative autonomy of the state depended on a split in the ruling class and pressure from the ruled class.[47] He did therefore not treat the state as a hierarchical construction with unitary interests. The internal structure of the state and the class structure of society were the main elements influencing the relative autonomy of the state in his argument. He also pointed out the conditions under which the state could overcome these influences, which were a collaborative and cohesive bureaucratic mechanism and relative autonomy from the ruling class.[48]

It is, however, difficult to discover such a cohesive group of bureaucrats sharing unitary interests in the case of China. Kenneth Lieberthal described this situation as 'fragmented authoritarianism'. He pointed out that the central government's decisions were not consistent and unified owing to the division of the decision-making processes of the different departments and competition between departments and between leaders who had different political, ideological and military backgrounds.[49] Futhermore, Shue argued that Chinese political leaders sought to secure their legitimacy by providing stable conditions for economic development and prosperity.[50] This foundation for the state may be rather more unstable and weaker than the revolutionary zeal that existed before 1978, for example during the Cultural Revolution.

Zheng Yongnian paid attention to the role of the SETC (State Economic and Trade Commission) established by Zhu Rongji in 1993. The SETC was

---

45   Howell 2006, p. 285.
46   Evans 1995, p. 28.
47   Rueschemeyer and Evans 1985, p. 63.
48   Rueschemeyer and Evans 1985, p. 67.
49   Lieberthal 1992, pp. 1–30.
50   Shue 2004, pp. 24–30.

a key department of the Chinese government for controlling the domestic market. But as Zheng pointed out, even the SETC was unable to substantially influence the economy because of frequent leadership and organisational changes.[51]

Weiss recognised that the state's concerted policy orientation, strong will and capacity for achieving its goals did not actually reveal themselves in developmental states. She pointed out that the arguments of existing developmental state theorists were not consistent with actual historical cases and the unilateralism of the state could be a weakness rather than an advantage for development. She argued that the issue was 'whether the state is able to use its autonomy to consult and to elicit consensus and cooperation from the private sector'.[52] She suggested the paradoxical term 'governed interdependence' which combined both distance and a close relationship between the state and the capitalist class, arguing that both corporation and disconnection were necessary.[53]

The term 'governed interdependence' reflects a fundamental contradiction of DST. It is not possible for the state to maintain its distance from capital. The term 'governed interdependence', however, still implies that there is a distance between state and capital. It is highly questionable whether the Chinese state maintains distance between itself and capital since China's state-owned sector is the biggest among the so-called developmental states. At the same time, the state, as collective capital, faces competition with both domestic and foreign private capital.

A conclusion can be drawn from this discussion. A cohesive and unitary state does not exist in China. Rather, there exist conflicts and contradictions of interests inside the Chinese state. The Chinese bureaucracy historically has not shared a unitary ideology and single political-economic goal. The state bureaucrats and people who are in charge of industries compete with each other in order to achieve higher positions and greater influence.[54] Multilateral and multi-layered interests inside the Chinese state are expressed through internal competition between bureaucrats.

4.3   The Relation between Central and Regional Government

Central government is a major driving force for economic development in the general argument of DST. DST therefore focuses on the decision-making bodies

---

51   Zheng 2004, pp. 103–8.
52   Weiss 1995, p. 595.
53   Weiss 1995, p. 604.
54   Solinger 1984, p. 36.

of the central government or on national political leaders. This is not the case for China where the regional government enjoys a certain level of autonomy in making economic policies and sometimes does not follow central government decisions. The regional government, like the central government, is not a homogeneous economic agent and internal cohesiveness, which is a key characteristic of DST, is not assured.

Chinese regional governments have had considerable authority over important decisions since the decentralisation process began in the early 1980s. Regional governments can mobilise huge public funds and also hold significant off-budget funds as well as budgets from the central government. Some rich regional governments like Shanghai, Guangdong and Tianjin can also mobilise foreign loans and levies, meaning that their financial dependence on the central government is relatively low.

The weakness of the decentralisation strategy is that it makes it difficult for the central government to enforce state policies consistently and to allocate resources to different regions.[55] Tsai pointed out that regional governments displayed various attitudes to the private sector, from active promotion and collaboration to hindrance and antagonism.[56] Ming even introduced the term 'dual developmental state', pointing out that not only the elites in the central government but also the elites in the regional governments harboured desires for economic development.[57]

The argument that China is not a developmental state because its administrative structure has a federal character stands against the argument that China is still a developmental state in spite of this federalism. Montinola and others have pointed out that central government policy faced substantial constraints because of federalism. On the contrary, Cai and Treisman claimed that it is a developmental state despite its federal governance structure. They argued that the Chinese state was very centralised and powerful and that important reforms, which provided the basis for the current economic development, had been introduced in the 1970s and 1980s before the decentralisation process started.[58]

Chai and Treisman's argument, however, does not correspond with certain facts, like the widening gap between different provinces and economic sectors after the opening of the market. The real estate boom, which was promoted by the regional governments, has decreased the efficiency of economic

---

55   Breslin 1996, p. 690.
56   Tsai 2004.
57   Ming 2000, pp. 136–77.
58   Cai and Treisman 2006, pp. 505–35.

resource allocation in China and has emerged as one of the serious risk factors for the Chinese economy. Localism in China actually constrains the control of the central government over regional governments and therefore decreases the efficiency of resource allocation. It also escalates competition among the regional governments and maintains the large socio-economic gaps between different regions.

4.4   *Guanxi Capitalism*

One of the key elements in Developmental State Theory is the role played by an ideology of social cohesion provided by political elites within the central government. The social cohesion ideology in China appears, on the one hand, as an emphasis on economic development and on the other as a form of nationalism. As social inequality has deepened, the argument that economic development compensated for the lack of democracy has become less convincing. Discontent among Chinese society's have-nots, such as peasants and workers, has increased since the gap between the rich and poor began to widen in the 2000s. Nationalist ideology is also a double-edged sword. There were huge anti-US demonstrations in China after NATO bombed Yugoslavia and the Chinese embassy in Belgrade was hit. However, when the anti-US protesters began to express their discontent with the Chinese government and the CPC the government used force to suppress them. This revealed that in conditions where social discontent was widespread, social cohesion could be destroyed suddenly by chance events.

The legitimacy of the developmental state can be achieved not only by economic development itself but also by shared expectations of economic development benefiting the majority of the population. If improvements in living standards are not guaranteed, the ideology of economic development will not function effectively. Thus the poor conditions of education and healthcare in some regions have prevented the ideology of social cohesion from working and former leaders Hu Jintao and Wen Jiabao had to promote the slogan of 'harmonious society' as a supplementary ideology.

Corruption within the CPC and the government apparatus have also been a key factor undermining the legitimacy of the state. A potential 'corporate coherence',[59] which can be created by unofficial networks of CPC members, can be easily subordinated to personal interests when strong discipline does not exist in the CPC. Situations in which personal interest takes priority over the public interest have been exposed by the chronic structural corruption

---

59   Evans 1992, p. 163.

within the Chinese state apparatus. This contradicts the DST argument that the government of the developmental state is able and authoritative but comparatively free from particularised interests. Evans pointed out that the developmental states in Japan and South Korea could be successful because these states had 'embedded autonomies'.[60] But in contrast to them China lacks this element.

According to research carried out by the Chinese Academy of Social Science, which is a body of the State Council of the People's Republic of China and the Central Party School of the Communist Party of China, among the 3,320 people who had property of more than 100 million *yuan*, 2,932 were children of high ranking officials of the CPC or the government.[61] C.A. McNally pointed out that the *guanxi* network was still an important element for the success of private enterprises in spite of institutional changes.[62] Those unofficial networks are the main channels of corruption.[63]

4.5   *Industrial Policy*

Developmental State Theory considers industrial policy to be a key form of state intervention in economic development. The goal of industrial policy is strengthening international competitiveness and pursuing export-oriented industrialisation. Wade stressed that it aimed 'to use national policies to promote industrial investment within national boundaries, and to channel more of this investment into industries whose growth is important for the economy's future growth'[64] while Evans argued that 'state involvement is a given. The appropriate question is not "how much" but "what kind"'.[65] The industrial policy of a developmental state depends on whether companies or industries can meet the (global) standard of the marketplace by themselves. State industrial policy has faced many restrictions in the era of globalisation and neoliberalism. It is recognised in heterodox economics therefore that state and capital are complementary rather than conflictual, in contrast to the market imperfection approach. There are, however, still some problems. For industrial policy, it is necessary to consider diversification, complexity, and historical context while technical development, financial sector support to industry, market expansion, upskilling, restriction or promotion of competition, and impact on

---

60   Evans 1992, p. 163.
61   Bardhan 2010.
62   McNally et al 2007, p. 2.
63   Minxin 2011, pp. 268–73, pp. 313–18.
64   Wade 1990, p. 350.
65   Evans 1995, p. 10.

foreign trade must all be taken into account too. However, in reality no state actually considers all of those elements when deciding policy.[66]

Hausmann and Rodrik's argument, however, is virtually impossible to sustain for two reasons. The first reason is that the state, according to this argument, grasps all the potential needs of the economic base and provides all existing and potential standards and rules. To do so, the state must completely control financial, managerial, and political processes. This is simply impossible. The second reason is that the state can't know the list of areas in which it wants to intervene in advance. Institutions and the market develop hand in hand and new trade develops new markets and institutions, creating transaction costs and other related issues. Considering this situation, the practicality of DST is rather doubtful.

The definition of the developmental state's industrial policy is also problematic. This is because non-developmental states also seek to implement industrial policy. For example, Lazonick and O'Sullivan, who study US and UK enterprises, argue that the US is a developmental state since the US and UK states allocate resources in order to boost the growth of private enterprises.[67] This clearly demonstrates that DST is suffering from conceptual inflation. Thus the definition of industrial policy within DST becomes important. Chang Ha-Joon defines it as 'a policy intended to affect particular industries to achieve outcomes that are perceived by the state to be efficient for the economy as a whole'.[68]

There are three dimensions of industrial policy. One is the horizontal policy which impacts on industries in general such as trade, competition, and innovation. The second dimension is vertical policy which aims at certain sectors. The last is structural policy that seeks to make structural changes in economic activities. Examining China's industrial policy using these three dimensions, vertical policy focusing on restructuring of the government-owned sector was the main policy from the beginning of the reform and opening policy up to 1993. This was followed by horizontal policy with the introduction of corporation law and changes in the governance structure of state-owned enterprises which had an influence on industry in general. Vertical policy like the privatisation of small and medium size public enterprises and strengthening the competitiveness of large and medium size enterprises was also deployed during this period. Industrial policy has therefore pursued steady structural changes since the reform and opening policy was first introduced. Baek Seung-Wook has also pointed

---

66   Hausmann and Rodrik 2006.
67   Lazonick and O'sullivan 1997, p. 22.
68   Chang 1993.

out that China's industrial policy put more weight on industrial restructuring rather than privatisation and downsizing.[69]

China's industrial policy has been pushed through because of the need for structural adjustment in order to respond to the decreasing competitiveness of state-owned enterprises. But it has not been well established because it is not promoted as planned.[70] Baek Seung-Wook was therefore unable to confirm that China's industrial policy is actually that of a developmental state even though China has generally followed the industrial policy of a developmental state.[71]

China entered the WTO in 2001 and was incorporated into the stream of globalisation. This has certainly brought about changes in China's industrial policy. After entering the WTO, China can no longer utilise certain policies such as export subsidies, import tariffs and the inflow of foreign capital, especially hedge funds, has made it more difficult to achieve its financial policy goals (intervention on interest rates and exchange rates). It is, however, too premature to announce that the Chinese state has totally surrendered to the world market or to external pressure. On the one hand, there are still industrial sectors which the state controls and in which it tries to boost competitiveness. It can be said that a developmental state-style industrial policy is applied to these sectors. On the other hand, there are sectors where the pressure of the world market is stronger than the state's supervision or control. In other words, those sectors dominated by private enterprises. This multifaceted character demonstrates that the dynamics at work within the contemporary Chinese economy cannot be accounted for by a single developmental state style industrial policy.

5 Alternative Explanations for the Chinese Economic Growth

There are many critical studies on DST and specifically of the argument that China is a developmental state.[72] Critics of this argument have mainly pointed out that China has a decentralised system and does not have strong central government leadership, as has been noted above.

There are, however, more important elements.

(1) The state is not a relatively autonomous institution but a means of capital accumulation and takes part in accumulating capital by itself. When the state

---

69   Baek 2008, p. 260.
70   Baek 2008, pp. 260–1.
71   Baek 2008, pp. 259–64.
72   Breslin 1996; Hart-Landsberg and Burkett 2001; Howell 2006; Radice 2008; Fine 2012.

accumulates capital by itself, it means the state functions as a form of collective capital. There is competition not only between the state sector represented by state-owned enterprises and the private sector represented by foreign-funded enterprises but also between capitals in each sector. This competition forces the state to function for the sake of capital, not for society in general, as the developmental state theorists claim.

(2) The Chinese state is not a neoliberal state since it intervenes for economic development and to strengthen regulation when it thinks it is needed. Also the Chinese state controls much of the economy. Nevertheless it is different from the idealised developmental state because its capacity and power is subordinated to competition among domestic and foreign capitals.

(3) State and capital are bound together by structural interdependence. Economic development helps to strengthen the state by increasing tax revenue. A strong and authoritarian state suppresses social forces which can encroach on the interests of capital.

(4) The degree of conflation and collusion between state and capital is decided externally by pressure from competition within world capitalism and internally by the relative strength of classes in society (particularly the working class and peasant class). In the case of China, the pressure to survive within world capitalism has determined national policies such as the People's Communes, the Great Leap Forward and the Reform and Opening policy that began in 1978.

Chinese political economy has a multi-faceted character not because of the country's huge territory or political decentralisation but due to the various and complex forms taken by the relationship between state and capital. This is not specific to China but a general character of the capitalist state. The state sector is an essential feature of contemporary capitalism. The state is a gigantic consumer and leverages this purchasing power for other policies. As mentioned previously, the state conducts capital-friendly policies by providing an economic and social base for economic development. The state is also a huge industry by itself and closely related with industry through industrial policy. This character is well established in China which has a dual structure encompassing a state-owned sector and a private sector.

There is, however, still one question to be answered. If China's economic development has not been caused by the state-led development argued for by DST, and the role of the state is not the most important factor, then what is behind China's rapid development?

The keys to the success of the Chinese economy differ according to the period one examines. From 1978 to 1993, the key elements were the expansion of the domestic market; the growth of township-village enterprises using surplus labour in rural areas and orienting themselves towards domestic niche markets; and the growth of private firms (including the self-employed private firm) in a market economy which was allowed by the state. The main elements between 1994 and the early 2000s were an improvement in the competitiveness of state-owned enterprises and foreign direct investment. From the early 2000s onward, the main factor has been the process of integrating the Chinese economy into global production networks. In particular, the rapid increase of FDI from 1993 has been combined with cheap (former peasant) labour to transform China into an export-oriented economy.

After China transformed itself into an export-oriented economy, it has shown some dominant characteristics. Chinese industry imports parts and components from other parts of Asia and assembles complete products. It then ships these products to places like the US and EU for final consumption. China is therefore not only the new 'workshop of the world' but also provides huge market for other countries in Asia.[73]

China's current account surplus from exports has been spent on buying US government bonds. Therefore, dollars flow from the US to China and then from China back to the US. This money flow is based on the circulation of goods.[74]

China's economic development, particularly after 1993, has been due to the fact that it could occupy a niche within changing global production networks. This in turn was partly due to the existence domestically of large numbers of peasant labourers and an authoritarian political system which is friendly to capital but hostile to labour.

Two characteristics have appeared in China's economic development process since the reform and opening policy was introduced. One is that investment (gross capital formation) has been maintained at a very high level, accounting for almost 40 percent of GDP,[75] and the other is that China's industrial finance is heavily dependent on banks. More than 80 percent of business finance is provided by banks. The five biggest state-owned banks dominate most of this business finance.[76]

The Chinese economy has faced international and domestic competition and pressure since it pushed through its opening policy. As a result of the intro-

---

73   Ahearne et al 2006; Haltmaier et al 2007.
74   Hart-Landsberg and Burkett 2005, pp. 99–108.
75   Naughton 2011, p. 189.
76   Naughton 2011, p. 412, p. 607.

duction of the market and liberalisation, it has had to internationalise domestic enterprises and accept the deregulation process. In this sense, Hart-Landsberg and Burkett argued that the DST theorists 'have generally supported the neoliberal view that working class opposition to "labor market flexibility" is a major obstacle to successful restructuring'. As an example, they cited Ha-Joon Chang's view, although 'he dresses it up with utopian appeals for non-existent capital-labor collaboration'.[77]

6   Conclusion

This chapter has critically examined the Developmental State Theory and its application to China. It has suggested the argument that China is a developmental state is not adequate when one examines the characteristics of the Chinese state, the relation between the central government and regional governments and the state's industrial policy. In particular, it points out that DST regards the state as an institution with relative autonomy and this explanation cannot properly comprehend that the Chinese state also takes on the role of collective capitalist.

It also argues that the rapid economic development of China has been generated by various important elements such as the increase of FDI, transformation into an export-oriented economy and the provision of labour by rural migrant workers rather than the developmental state.

This chapter certainly does not deny the important role of the state in the economic development of China and NICs in East Asia but it is critical of the argument that these states are developmental states. Furthermore, this chapter has argued implicitly that incorporation into global capitalism and the discovery of a niche market position through export-oriented economies are more important factors in the economic development of these states.

---

77   Hart-Landsberg and Burkett 2001, p. 422.

CHAPTER 7

Historical Dynamics and the History of Capitalism and State Capitalism

Michael Haynes

The relationship of 'state' and 'capital' is one of the most controversial issues in the social sciences in general and on the left in particular. Are 'state' and 'capital' exclusive things or do they merge into forms of 'state capitalism' as a normal and inevitable part of the functioning of capitalism as a whole? In this chapter I want to return to some of the big themes set out by Miller and Dale in their introduction and to push the argument forwards in the light of the contributions that have followed, which have explored the ways in which this relationship has developed in the two Koreas and China. In the first part I bring together some big themes and data to help contextualise the discussion. In the second part I briefly set out some key areas where existing theoretical discussion is weak because it fails to address the elements that have played a key role in the accounts here. The third part then concludes by reviewing some of the characteristics of the success of the East Asian cases and the limits to it being replicated.

1 Capitalism and the Competition of States

Capitalism exists as a global economy made up of competing companies and competing states. This simple and seemingly uncontroversial statement hides a key problem. What is the relationship between the interstate system and capitalism as a whole? Many theorists and historians have treated this relationship as contingent, with the inter-state system preceding the development of capitalism. The contributors to this book share the view that the inter-state state system develops *within* capitalism and that the state itself is not only a support for private capital but can itself play the role of state capitalist.

In the English language the word state is a complex one. Here we are immediately interested in two aspects. The first is the idea of a state as a well defined territory which is both independent and separate from other states similarly defined. Such states are a product of the modern era. Before this, in some parts of the world few of the constituent elements of statehood were in existence.

TABLE 7.1   Number of members of the League of Nations
             1920–1940 and United Nations 1945–2011[a]

1920	42	1960	99
1930	54[*]	1970	127
1940	44[*]	1980	154
1945	51	1990	159
1950	60	2000	189

a   League of Nations Data compiled by author from contempor-
    ary lists. * indicates numbers reduced by withdrawals so actual
    state numbers higher. United Nations numbers from http://
    www.un.org/en/sections/member-states/growth-united-nat
    ions-membership-1945-present/index.html

In other parts, great 'Empires', the seeming ancestors of some of today's states, may have existed but they did not function in the same way as modern states. In still other parts such as Europe, sovereignty and authority was shared or 'parcellised' between competing centres of authority and lands not unified territorially. The history of the modern state as a territorial concept is much more recent than we imagine. So too is the history of a territorialised interstate system. It begins to arise in the sixteenth and seventeenth centuries as capitalism develops in Europe. The history of actual states is more recent still. Counting states is hard because much depends on definitions. It is clear that the development of capitalism in Europe led, for a time, to the consolidation of a smaller number of larger states. Around 1870 there were only some 40 or so states in the sense that we are using the term here. From the First World War we can use membership of the League of Nations (although its membership was reduced by withdrawals as well as annexation) and then later United Nations membership as an indicator for the numbers of states in the global system. This data is set out in Table 7.1. It shows how the numbers of states grew in the twentieth century linked to the internal break up of 'imperial' states and decolonisation. The inter-state system is not, as those like Charles Tilly, Michael Mann and Nigel Harris and others continue to argue, logically and historically prior to capitalism but something which develops as part of the capitalist system. But we must also recognise that the theoretical and historical elaboration of this argument is still underdeveloped.[1] A first central fact in the history of capitalism

---

1   Barker 1978.

for us is therefore that it exists as a world of many competing states as well as competing private capitals.

We can also think of a 'state' in a second way, in terms of a bureaucratic apparatus of power and authority which then rules over the state as territory. It is the state in this sense which is the basis of law, order and regulation and which creates the internal conditions within which capitalism functions. To do this it must tax and spend. It is the taxing and spending state too that supplies key elements needed for the system to function which are not profitable for individual capitals to supply (although they may try for a time to do so). This includes infrastructure, education, health and welfare provision etc. It is the state that also provides overall 'national' direction especially in terms of economic policy and regional and global competition. It is the state that protects the territorially based interests of 'its' capital from other states and projects its own power outwards to widen its sphere of interest and expand the power of its 'national' capitals. And it is this state which can direct production and distribution and take it over if the circumstances are require it. Our measures of what these states do are also imperfect. The crudest one is to take the amount of expenditure that flows through the state. Figures for early capitalism are few. In the emerging capitalist states of sixteenth century Western Europe, state expenditure (and income) struggled to get beyond 5 percent of output. In the seventeenth and eighteenth centuries it rose above five percent and could go much higher in conflicts. Table 7.2 shows how this measure has grown since the 1870s for a sample of advanced states and the shares in some individual ones.

The second central fact in the history of capitalism therefore seems to be that 'the state' is a major fact of life for everyone and, allowing for war-time surges, its importance has grown over time even in economies that cannot be thought of as late developers or possibly non-capitalist actors as some, but not the contributors here, argue the USSR, China and North Korea were or still are.

There is a third central fact in the history of capitalism that is central to the arguments of this book and that is the way in which it has created such enormous economic inequalities, and therefore also power inequalities, between states (we cannot discuss here the no less important issue of inequalities *within* states, though some are discussed by the contributors in their chapters). Again the huge inequalities that exist – what is sometimes called 'divergence big time' – are a product of capitalism. If we look at the world around 1500 then the differences between the most advanced regions were more qualitative than quantitative. How big the quantitative gaps were remains contentious. Some even claim that if we look at a Europe-China comparison then China (or parts of it) was on a par with Europe (or parts of it) until perhaps as late as 1800. The important thing for us is that when the *qualitative* shifts that created

TABLE 7.2   General government expenditure as a percentage of GDP[a]

	Average advanced countries	UK	USA	France	Germany	Sweden	Japan
c1870	10.8	9.4	7.3	12.6	10.0	5.7	8.8
1913	13.1	12.7	7.5	17.0	14.8	10.4	8.3
1920	19.6	26.2	12.1	27.6	25.0	10.9	14.8
1937	23.8	30.0	19.7	29.0	34.1	16.5	25.4
1960	28.0	32.2	27.0	34.6	32.4	31.0	17.5
1980	41.9	43.0	31.4	46.1	47.9	60.1	32.0
1990	43.9	39.9	32.8	49.8	45.1	59.1	31.3
2000	39.2	35.4	33.7	51.4	44.7	53.4	–
2010	42.4	47.5	42.9	56.5	47.3	50.8	39.6
2015	41.4	42.2	37.6	56.6	43.8	49.6	39.6

a   Tanzi & L. Schuknecht 2000, pp. 6–7 for data 1870–1990. Their average is for 14 states. OECD database for data 2000–2015. The average is for 9–10 of the states counted in the previous years since not all the earlier sample is covered.

the basics of capitalism had worked through, they enabled the development of industrialisation, which exploded the *quantitative* differences. These differences allowed the European powers and the US to mould the world in their interests through formal and informal colonialism. Although the mainstream 'neo-classical' or 'neo-liberal' tradition in economic history continues to insist that this happened because of the benefit of the free enterprise, this was far from the only element. Looked at from the other side what struck many contemporaries was both what Marx called 'the cheap power of … commodities' battering down all Chinese walls and the mobilisation, albeit at much lower levels, of state power to assist this. Integration and subordination often needed real artillery. Marx understood this but so did writers like Friedrich List and, later, Gustav Schmoller. Schmoller wrote that

> It was clearly those governments which understood how to put the weight of their fleets and their admiralties, the apparatus of customs, laws and navigation laws, with rapidity, boldness and clear purpose at the service of the economic interests of the nation and the state which obtained their lead in the struggle and the riches of industrial prosperity.[2]

---

2   Quoted, Briggs, ed. 1970, p. 33.

It is telling to recall the influence of opium in Asia and its role in globalising capitalism. To generate income for British rule in India, opium was exported eastwards on a large scale. When the Chinese state tried to limit its sale, the British responded with two opium wars in 1839–42 and 1856–60. The Chinese authorities were humiliated, territory was lost and China opened up even more to narco-imperialism. Estimates of the numbers in China who were opium consumers vary enormously. Early on opium had been for elite consumption but gradually the 'market' widened as the trade took off from the 1820s. In the 1830s there may have been 3 million users. By the 1900s it was many times that – estimates vary between 3 and 10 percent of the population with perhaps 20 percent plus of adult males and 3–4 percent plus of females being addicts. At this point people in China were consuming 85–95 percent of the world's opium supply – probably three to four times the global supply today.[3]

The result was that as the most advanced states went forwards, those being integrated as colonies or semi-colonies were remoulded, developing unevenly and often stagnating or even going backwards. Paul Bairoch's 'heroic' estimates of world manufacturing output have still not been superseded. He estimated that in 1830, the advanced 'developed' countries had some 40 percent of manufacturing output. By 1914 they had over 90 percent. In 1750 the per capita level of industrialisation of China, based on its handcraft industries, had been 80 percent of the UK level. By 1860 it was 6 percent and in 1913 only 3 percent. Traditional handicraft and artisan industries were increasingly marginalised as the share of modern factory industries grew. Britain led the way with the share of these industries growing from 32–40 percent in 1830 to 72–80 percent by 1913. In the 'Third World' (including Japan at this point) it was only in the very late nineteenth century, in some places and not without significant problems, that the share of new technology industries began to rise from around 1–3 percent in 1880 to 10–19 percent in the more successful cases. It was still virtually non-existent in many other places.[4]

Where states had sufficient autonomy to act (obviously not in the formal colonies) their governments had to try to mobilise resources to halt the slide and to look to reforms that might encourage a degree of modernisation and economic growth. The contradictions this could create were sometimes explosive as in Tsarist Russia, the Ottoman Empire and China.

The 'state' had to play a much more important role than it appeared to have done in the early industrialisation of the more advanced countries. The process

---

3 United Nations Office on Drugs and Crime 2008, *passim*.
4 Author's calculations from Bairoch 1982.

of 'catching up' had to be different from that of starting out. This was at the heart of the arguments of Alexander Gerschenkron about late development in Europe that are noted by Miller and Dale. It was also a key part of the rise of Japan. Paul Kennedy writes that

> Japan had to be modernised not because individual entrepreneurs wished it, but because the 'state' needed it … The state encouraged the creation of a railway network, telegraphs, and shipping lines, it worked in conjunction with emerging Japanese entrepreneurs to develop heavy industry. Iron, steel, and shipbuilding, as well as to modernise textile production. Government subsidies were employed to benefit exporters, to encourage shipping, to get a new industry set up. Behind all this lay the impressive policy commitment to realise the national slogan *fukoku kyōhei* (rich country with a strong army).[5]

This applied more widely and more so in the inter-war years and the first great 'systemic' crisis of capitalism

> Anglo-Saxon theories of the market, the individual and liberalism were judged inappropriate and downright harmful. Celal Bayar, Turkey's Minister of Economy, stated to the Grand National Assembly in 1936, 'I cannot even pronounce liberalism, this word is foreign to me … we want to establish the principles of a government-controlled economy, and we are leading towards these new principles'.[6]

The idea of the state as capitalist therefore predates arguments about whether this is a better way to characterise the so-called 'socialist' states, especially after the degeneration of the Russian Revolution and the rise of Stalinism that Miller and Dale discuss. State capitalism began to seem like a part of the normal functioning of capitalism as a global system. But before World War II, of the more backward states, it was Japan and Russia under Stalin which seemed to be successful in terms of mobilising resources for competitive growth. Beyond them the evidence of success was limited,

> There was then for a considerable time no newcomers to the industrial scene. With the doubtful exception of Manchuria, China, India and prob-

---

5   Kennedy 1988, p. 266.
6   Quoted Waterbury 1999, p. 329.

ably Argentina and Brazil, the countries in which industrialisation had not taken root before 1900, showed no development in that direction in the following decades either, until the end of the Second World War. It was as if the world industrialisation process had run out of steam, or alternatively, as if the countries that remained backward after 1900 lacked too many conditions to make the jump over the ever higher threshold.[7]

This brings us to the final element we wish to stress that seems to follow logically both from this analysis and the preceding chapters. This is the role of military competition and war in capitalism and state capitalist development. As with the arguments about the inter-state system, many theorists argue that war reflects some transcendent logic.[8] Whether or not humans have always fought is not a debate we can enter into here. We are interested in the specific multiplicity of characteristics within capitalism that create the situation where it can only exist as a system in which the potential for conflict is general and endemic – globally, regionally and locally.

Capitalism is a divided system both economically and politically. It is a competitive system with no overarching order. The 'international' in political terms is what states agree or the most powerful states impose. It is an expansionist system. Each unit has to defend its own while also looking for influence beyond both formal (colonialism) and informal. It is an unequal system where different states and capitals have different degrees of power, different interests and different reach. And it is a dynamic system which is likely to be unstable in the long run. The inequalities of power can lead some states to appear to impose periods of imperial peace – either on their own (the Pax Britannica, the Pax Americana) or in sullen stand-offs (the Cold War) – but in each case any velvet glove hides an iron first that on occasion will be employed aggressively. But as the relative balance of economic power shifts then so also do challengers arise, and the capacity to maintain hegemony come under pressure. Power and the capacity to deploy it is also affected by technological change. Over time this has allowed the more advanced states to generate, to adapt a common phrase, more 'bucks to invest in bangs'. In turn they have also got more 'bangs for the bucks' they spend. Once we integrate division, competition, expansion, inequality and dynamism into our analysis it becomes easier to see the extent to which force is ever present in the economic system. It is there symbolically and it is there in terms of its real deployment.

---

7 Pollard 1990, pp. 87–8.
8 In Charles Tilly's widely quoted formulation, 'war made the state and the state made war'. Tilly 1975, p. 42.

TABLE 7.3   Military Spending of the main western capitalist powers as a percentage of GDP[a]

	1870–1913	1920–1938	1960	1970	1989	2000	2016
USA	0.7	1.2	8.9	7.9	5.5	2.9	3.2
UK	2.6	3.0	6.5	4.8	3.6	2.2	1.8
France	3.7	4.3	6.3	4.2	3.4	2.5	2.3
Germany	2.6	3.3	4.0	3.5	2.7	1.4	1.2

a   Data for 1870–1970 from M. Harrison 2014; for 1989–2016 from Stockholm International Peace
Research Institute database.

Adam Smith famously wrote in the *Wealth of Nations* that 'defence, however,
is of much more importance than opulence'.[9] It is true that some liberals
abhorred particular wars – Cobden and Bright in Britain, for example – but
all supported the idea of national 'defence' and, on occasion, 'national offence'.

> It is mainly our system of Free Trade which gives our country the greatest
> commerce per head of population of any country of the world, and this
> enables and requires us to maintain the largest merchant fleet and navy
> …

said one British commentator in the nineteenth century. Who? None other
than Stanley Jevons, otherwise known as one of the fathers of modern economic theory.[10] A century on this idea was echoed by Thomas Friedman in his
celebration of the way that globalisation had become bound up with US military power:

> the hidden hand of the market will never work without the hidden fist.
> Macdonald's cannot flourish without McDonnell Douglas. And the hid-
> den fist that keeps the world safe for Silicon Valley technologies to flourish
> is called the US Army, Air Force, Navy and Marine Corps.[11]

Table 7.3 sets out some selected data from several advanced Western powers to
illustrate some of the shifts in the level of military spending in the last century
and a half, including the Cold War period so crucial in this book. The centrality

---

9   Smith 1910, p. 338.
10   Quoted in Jordan 1974.
11   Friedman 1999, p. 464.

of different types of military spending to developments in the East Asian case and its sometimes paradoxical effects play a key role in some of the discussions here, and not least that of Seongjin Jeong.

Since the end of the Cold War the resources devoted to military expenditure, globally and in the most advanced countries, have fallen but not as much as supporters of the idea of peaceful globalisation hoped. More recently there has been pressure to increase spending again. This comes both from the USA and its potential challengers. As the world's greatest power, the USA, on one estimate, seems to have participated in roughly the same percentage of bilateral conflicts (some 10 percent) pre, during and post the Cold War era.[12]

How common and extensive are the conflicts that occur? This partly depends on definitions. One database of 'Militarised Interstate Disputes' distinguishes between five types of conflicts. Those that involve no threat of force, the threat of force, the deployment of force, the use of force, and war – which it arbitrarily defines as involving 1,000 or more battle deaths (which excludes quite a lot of conflicts as wars). 'Armed conflicts' in these lesser terms are commonplace. War too is still frequent. There is a small industry collecting data and trying to measure the numbers of wars, their participants, scale and number of fatalities. This data is used to try to identify long-run patterns and trends with sharply differing results depending on how it is done.[13] The squabbles this produces are unhelpful in that they distract us from understanding how the patterns of war depend on time and place as capitalism itself changes. The wars of its origin are not the same as the wars of its maturity; nor are the wars of colonisation the same as wars of decolonisation and so on.[14]

When big wars like World War I and II, or huge military stand-offs like the Cold War, do occur they can suck in huge resources and so change the functioning of capitalism in ways that undercut simple views of what capitalism is. In the UK, for example, from 1916 the Ministry of Munitions integrated business and the state. Lloyd George said of his time as Minster of Munitions that those who ran this system 'between them ... touched the industrial life of the country and of the Empire at every point. All the means of production, distribution and exchange were at their command'.[15] There is some exaggeration here but not so much. Then, as the Second World War was developing, E.H. Carr wrote, in a piece published on 1 September 1939, that

---

12   Harrison and Wolf 2012, p. 1062.
13   See, as an example, the debates generated by Harrison and Wolf or the work of Steven Pinker.
14   See, for example: Mann 2018.
15   Lloyd George 1938, p. 150.

TABLE 7.4   Military outlays as a percentage of national income 1939–44[a]

	1939	1940	1941	1942	1943	1944
Current Prices						
USA	1	2	11	31	42	42
UK	15	44	53	52	55	53
Germany	23	40	52	64	70	
Italy	8	12	23	22	21	
Japan	22	22	27	33	43	76
Constant Prices						
USSR	–	17	28	61	61	53

a   Broadberry and Harrison 2008.

> the whole world is moving in the same direction, and … the resemblances
> in the economic structure of Soviet, Fascist and democratic countries are
> rapidly becoming quite as striking as the differences between them.[16]

Just over a year later he wrote in an anonymous leader in *The Times* that in
Britain,

> in 1940 the manufacturer forgoes profits, the worker forgoes trade union
> restrictions on the conditions of employment, the consumer forgoes lux-
> uries and lends to the Government to finance expenditure for which no
> material return is asked or expected.[17]

Table 7.4 shows not state expenditure but military outlays for some of the lead
participants in World War II.

We see here the extraordinary scale of the commitment. We see too how capitalist competition transforms itself and how, in total war, the state reshapes the
competition of private capitals into the organised competition of militarised
state capitals.

16   Quoted in Haslam 1999, p. 75.
17   Quoted in Haslam 1999, p. 90.

2   Putting the Jigsaw Together: Capitalist Competition and the Forms
      of the State

How do we begin to combine these pieces of the jigsaw with the analysis of
capitalism as an 'economic system'? Marx was a propagandist, a commentator,
journalist and a theorist. In the former capacity he discussed capitalism as he
saw it in all its complexity. As a theorist he tried to pare down his argument to
get at the essence of capitalism in terms of exploitation, value, price and profit
etc. It was always his intention to build this up into a more complex account in
successive volumes of *Capital*. His wider work makes it absolutely clear that all
of the things we have talked of would figure in his analysis. But he did not sys-
tematise them. This was left to those who followed, including those who began
to develop the theory of imperialism that captured some of the elements we
have discussed. Not least here were Lenin and Bukharin, although others like
Rudolph Hilferding and Rosa Luxemburg made major contributions. But they
too were often writing under the pressure of the moment and the fate of their
work and insights became bound up with the fate of the Russian Revolution
both politically and theoretically.

The degeneration of the Russian Revolution acted to block the development
of these ideas – both on the left and the right. As Miller and Dale argue, in the
late nineteenth century parts of the left, including parts of the reformist left,
began to link the idea of socialism with state ownership. Those on the radical
left were always more ambiguous about if not hostile to this. This connection
of socialism to state property, to nationalisation and planning came to be consolidated in Russia from 1928 onwards. It was taken up globally by the larger
part of the left that wanted to see in Russia, even if only in the most corrupt and
degenerate forms, some embodiment of the future. Reducing socialism to state
property and planning necessarily then reduced capitalism to private property
and the market. This led to the idea that what mattered was the internal relations within states and that there were even two or more global systems in
place. The result was, and to an extent still is, a significant degree of theoretical impoverishment.

The idea of a capitalism as a globalising system, although rediscovered in
parts by 'world system' theorists, has still not been placed at the centre of discussion as it should be. The nature of societies is too often reduced to descriptive labelling in terms of abstract categories which are taken to be self-evident.
As Miller and Dale point out, one of these is 'wage labour', another is 'property'.
Commentators have then struggled to make sense of the things that we have
discussed. Their logic leads them to see many of the key issues as tangential to
capitalism rather than bound up with its essence. Larry Neal, for example, one

of the editors of the *Cambridge History of Capitalism* (two collective volumes which are largely an historical defence of capitalism against its past and present critics), defines capitalism as a system based on 1. private property rights, 2. enforceable contracts, 3. markets with prices responsive to supply and demand, and 4. supportive governments.[18] Lists like this are so arbitrary, restrictive and their components so vague that one does not know whether to cry in despair or laugh as it leads some contributors who take it seriously to declare all the 'bad stuff' non-capitalist. Whether in their right-wing forms, as with Neal, or left-wing forms when espoused by Marxists, these approaches then become empirically impoverishing. There is less incentive to try to pierce the world of appearances and to look at how forms change and things come to acquire new content. Hopefully the detailed chapters here, and their empirical content, show that re-engaging theoretically with these big problems is the productive way forward empirically too. But it is worth spelling out at least some of the implications of this.

The first is that capitalism must be analysed as a dynamic mode of production. This dynamism is *extensive* in the sense that the logic of capitalism forces it outwards to encompass the whole world. In the process it has, as this book has shown, pulled in the East Asia region and led to Japan, the two Koreas and China becoming capitalist states and to different degrees (least of all for North Korea) global players in a system no longer as dominated by the USA and European powers. This dynamism is also *intensive*. One aspect of this is *quantitative* – the long-run expansion of accumulation and output and its ups and downs. Another is the dynamism of forms. Capitalism is continually changing and adapting as it develops so that reducing it to a set of simple categories makes no sense. What is really necessary is to understand how forms can and do change and the dynamic that runs through them – a task which is both theoretical and empirical.

Central here is an understanding both of the role of competition as a driving force and the way that this moulds not simply commodity production and the narrowly economic but the much wider set of realities and the elements – including the state military production that they require. As Miller and Dale say, there have been too few attempts to theorise fully the variety of forms of competition including the role of force within it. Even those who stress the centrality of free labour often do not seem to understand the degree to which the labour market has been underpinned, and remains underpinned, by significant degrees of non-economic coercion. Just as force is central to capitalist

---

18   Neal 2014, p. 2.

inter-state competition, so it also stands in the background of 'free labour' and, in certain circumstances, forced labour has displaced more formally free labour within capitalism, as can be seen in parts of the stories told here.[19]

The flipside to failure to allow for and analyse the variety of forms is what has been called 'the fetishism of commodity fetishism'. This is the approach that dwells on commodity production and exchange – it is the Marxist version of the conventional obsession with markets. But the things that function as commodities (including labour), the way they function, and the values they 'contain' are mediated in numerous different ways from those we theorise when we strip capitalism down to its bare essentials. This is more obvious when the producer and consumer is the state. It is especially obvious in the production of military goods. As Mark Harrison puts it,

> military-technical innovation is subsidised. Pre-contract lobbying and collusion, among firms and between buyer and seller, and post-contract renegotiation are normal. These [are] standard features of capitalist defence markets.[20]

But reflection should show that this is just as evident in 'private capital'. 'Commodity production' now often takes place across borders but in production chains within the same companies. Making sense of commodity production, exchange and values when things move within the same companies is complex. Somewhere between 35 and 50 percent of merchandise trade is said to be intra-company trade. Imparting meaning and value to the exchange of services as intangibles is even more complex. Foreign direct investment too is often internal to companies whose operations span borders. Some 65–75 percent of technology transfer is said to be transfers within companies. Even defining intra-firm trade becomes a problem when illusions of the dispersion of control are created.[21] This is one of the reasons why it is hard to distinguish between what some call intra-company trade and 'arms-length' trade. Indeed, even the idea of 'arms length' reflects the sense that the degree of separation between buyer and seller that is often imagined to constitute a true market exchange is less than might appear. While firms may have outsourced, the extent to which they remain in control of their power may not have diminished. This is particularly important when looking at the role of Western capital abroad including in places like China. Nolan and Zhang stress that in global

---

19   Barker 2009.
20   Harrison 2014.
21   Lanz and Miroidot 2011.

supply chains power lies with what they call 'system integrators'. This power cannot be captured simply by looking at firm assets or turnover. 'The "commanding heights" of the world economy are almost entirely occupied by firms from high income countries, whose principal customers are the global middle class'.[22]

New mediations are also created by the growth of tax havens. One-quarter of global wealth is said to be held in tax havens and one-third of global GDP is produced in small island economies. Of course, this is the world of appearance, of the conjuring tricks of accountants and lawyers. To explore what is really happening we have to understand why these layers are important as well as what happens when we peel them away to get at what is underneath. The same applies when we find that as much as half of global banking assets are seemingly located in tax havens, one-third of foreign direct investment flows from them and one-half of global trade ostensibly passes through them.[23] Overlapping with this problem too is that of the considerable amount of criminalised and semi-criminalised production and exchange that is inherent to global capitalism. Guns, body parts, drugs, diamonds, precious metals, stolen knowledge, stolen capital, forced labour, slave labour, pornography, the list goes on. Are these a negation of the ideas of commodity production and value? Of course not. Value formation and exchange is there. But are they, and the conditions under which they are produced and exchanged, a reflection of simple commodity production and commodity exchange, of value and the like? Of course not too. They are much more complex.

This applies too when we turn to the issue of the state. In the 1980s the phrase 'bringing the state back in' became popular but there has still been a reluctance to bring it back in terms of the idea of 'state capitalism'. Too often the state is simply taken as given. In the next decades the issue then became one of whether 'the state' was being 'rolled back'. But do we even know in these terms what the state is?

The juxtaposition of private and state is not a distinction founded in the analysis of social relations and the dynamic of capitalism. It is a formal legal one. But it is the state which is the foundation of law. Without the state there can be no 'private property' and, given that a key aspect of the definition of the modern state is its monopoly of the means of force, there can be no institution to 'protect' and 'defend' private property. If taken seriously the legalistic approach would require us to become experts in the circular reasoning of the

---

22   Nolan and Zhang Jin 2010.
23   See for example Shaxson 2011 and also the work of the Tax Justice Network.

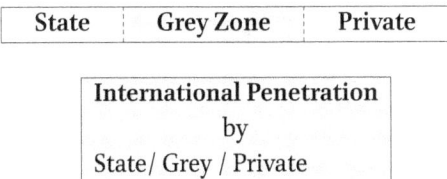

FIGURE 7.1   State/ Private Forms within an Economy

jurisprudence of property law. Worse, the tendency to imagine that the categories of 'private' and 'state' are simple and self-evident has prevented people from analysing a crucial part of how capitalism generates hybrid forms.

Instead of thinking of capitalism as having two sectors – a private and state one – it is better to think of there being three – a private, state and a grey zone between – each of which can themselves be penetrated by similarly located 'capital' from the outside. A simple view of this is shown in Figure 7.1. Note that the borders between what we are calling the grey zone and the private and state sectors are porous and malleable.

This is no small point. In his discussion of China, Tobias ten Brink brings out the complexity of ownership and control issues there. As he stresses, understanding this requires an appreciation of the specifics of development in China and its location in the global system. But wherever we look we find aspects of hybridity too. One of the problems with the political attack on neo-liberal privatisation in the advanced countries is that it has distracted us from seeing how much of the supposed shift to the private sector is in reality a shift into this grey zone of hybridity.

The consequence of this is that just as it is hard to map the boundaries of the firm, so it is also hard to map the contours of the state. What is in the state and what is not in it is hard even for the statisticians to grasp. Some elements of this, such as what counts as public sector debt and what does not, are more widely known. However, the scale of the problem is less appreciated. Who really owns the banks if they are too big to fail? What about the railways in an advanced state like the UK – are they state or private? UK statisticians might define some operators as private but these might be state-owned operators in other countries – either way the services they offer cannot be discontinued. What about the Channel tunnel – is it classified the same way in the UK and France? Are universities in the UK part of the state? They are largely financed by students who are in turn financed by the state. They are ruled, regulated, measured and inspected by quasi-state institutions. But technically they now fall outside the state for measurement purposes. What about the NHS? Where do its many parts fit in any classification? The complexities are such they we can only alert readers to them, not simply as classificatory problems but also as reflections of the real complexity of private and state forms.[24] This has always existed. The problem is that the scale of the grey zone has grown in recent decades. In the UK, for example, one group of researchers estimated that by 2007 at least 1.7 million people were excluded from state employment figures but were effectively part of the 'para-state'. Adding up employment in the state and the para-state gave them a quite different picture of state employment in Britain. It rose consistently, if unevenly, from 20.8 percent in 1978 to 23.1 percent in 1987, 23.3 percent in 1997 and 25.3 percent in 2008.[25]

But if the borders are porous and the result is a hybridity of forms then what happens to the idea of the autonomy of the state? The state is commonly tied to private interests in numerous ways. The grey zone can be used by private interests to trap and plunder the state and, through it, society in different ways. It can become an exercise in what conventional economists call rent-seeking where profits are privatised and grabbed by different sections of the capitalist class and risks socialised. It can also work the other way. The state can rise above the competing interests of private capitals and either subsume the major part of production or use its influence in the grey zone as the means through which a lever can be pulled from the centre. The state in these terms can become 'a state capitalist' or what the conventional literature calls a 'development state' and this idea has been central to much discussion of East Asian capitalisms.

The idea of the 'development state' has been attractive because it seems to contrast with the logic of the Washington consensus and the mantras of the market. But Jeong-Goo Lee points to some of the problems in this discussion. In particular, development state theorists have failed to give enough attention to the state as a class institution and failed to deal adequately with the role of repression and exploitation. In posing the problem as one of either the market or the development state they have also failed to explore how both are alienated forms generating different degrees of coherence and inco-

---

24   This grey zone has a formal intermediate sector called NPISH by the statisticians. This stands for 'non-profit institutions serving households'. The standard definition of these (here from Eurostat) is 'private, non-market producers which are separate legal entities. Their main resources, apart from those derived from occasional sales, are derived from voluntary contributions in cash or in kind from households in their capacity as consumers, from payments made by general governments, and from property income'. Operationalising this definition is a nightmare in terms of classification. But the grey zone extends far beyond this as the example of the banks or the UK railways show.

25   Froud et al 2011, p. 18.

herence. Alongside the anarchy of the market there can also be the anarchy of the plan or the planlessness of the plan. Not the least of the reasons for using the term state capitalism is that it confronts in its name the theoretical problems that the seemingly more neutral term 'development state' sidesteps.

'State capitalism' has worked both in the sense of coming into existence as a more coherent form and driving development forward through increasing the rate of accumulation and directing labour to different ends. But full-bloodied state capitalism is *not* the norm. The default condition is one where those aspiring to lead a state which drives development forward are as likely to be restrained and hindered by the social forces around them. Despite the attempt to rehabilitate Tsarism in Russia, the developmentalists there before 1914 were much less successful than those in the USSR under Stalin. Internal divisions within the government and state, and within the ruling class, meant that consistent policies that might have pushed the economy forward more were not pursued. The paradox of the Russian Revolution and the Civil War was that the old ruling class was destroyed but the state reconfigured. As the revolution degenerated further in the 1920s a new ruling class came to the fore with Stalin at its head. From 1928–9 onwards accumulation and economic development were then able to be driven forward heedless of the cost and with the Gulag as the reward for those who opposed it and who saw socialism as being something else other than state-driven development.

In understanding these different possibilities and outcomes we need therefore to have a much more focused analysis of the ways in which the global and local class relations interact. Miller and Dale note this in their introduction and the chapters that have followed discuss many aspects of this. Elements of state capitalism have been, are and will be always part of the capitalist system. They have grown over time. But the circumstances in which more full-blooded versions of state capitalism develop whether in peace or war or this part of the globe or that are always specific to time, place and global circumstances, as has been shown here.

3   Global Capitalism and the Changing Development Space: East Asia and beyond?

How then should we assess the recent past performance and potential of these East Asian states? Figure 7.2 gives us some sense of this. The figure plots output per head in these states against that of the USA which is assumed to be 100 for each year. These figures, in purchasing power parities, are drawn from what is

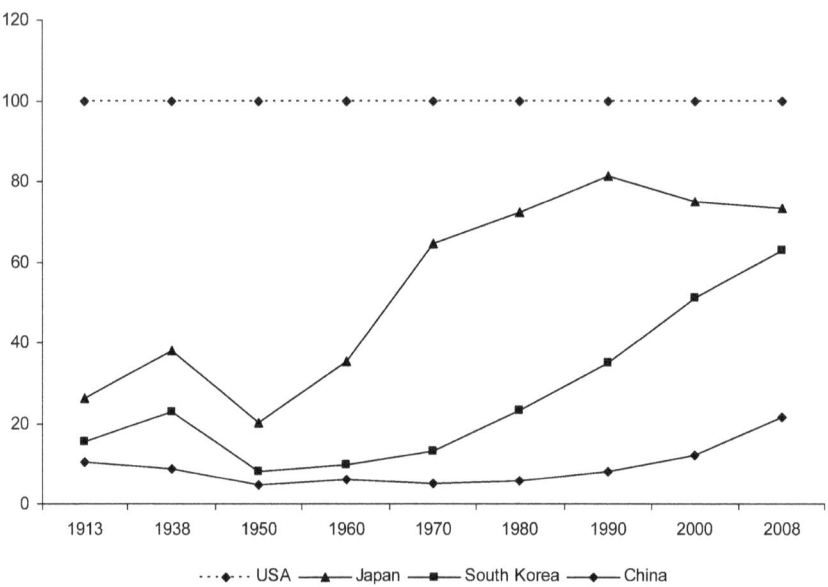

FIGURE 7.2 Output per head of Japan, South Korea and China as a percentage of the US level
1913–2008
Note: Maddison database, University of Groningen.

called the Maddison data set.[26] All economic data are problematic and some
of the data here may be more problematic than others but they are the best we
have. Maddison's figures for North Korea are some of the weakest in the whole
data set and are not used here. The others may be imperfect in their detail but
this is unlikely to change the bigger picture. The reader should note that the
data for 1913 presents low figures for China that not all accept. But this would
only serve to make the fall in the next century the greater. More important for
us is the pattern since 1950. We can see here how impressive the performance
of Japan and South Korea have been in closing the gap with the USA as the
most advanced large capitalist economy. The pattern in China, encompassing
the pre- and post-Mao periods, shows both the progress made but also the gap
that still exists.

---

26   It is important to note that measuring output in exchange rates reflects the ability to
      command resources externally. Measuring it on the basis of purchasing power parities
      reflects the ability to command resources internally. For the most advanced states the
      differences are sight. For less advanced states purchasing power parity calculations will
      make their levels of output and development appear higher than calculations in exchange
      rates.

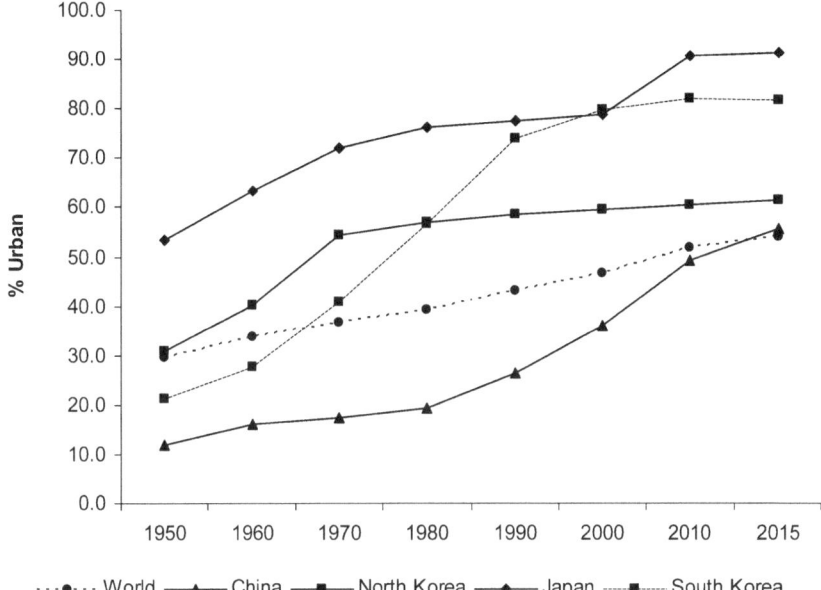

FIGURE 7.3 Growth of urban share in selected countries 1950–2015
Note: Data from United Nations, *World Urbanisation Prospects 2018 database*.

Figure 7.3 shows the internal transformations using urbanisation data which reflect both the social transformation and the creation of working classes in these societies. Again there are cautions over the data but the big picture is clear. There have been, and are continuing to be in China, huge urban transformations.

Why is catch up growth so fast when it is successful? The basic answer is twofold. Firstly it is emulative. It operates by borrowing what is known. This borrowing may be unofficial or official but catch-up states tend to generate – at least in the very early stages of their growth – little new knowledge themselves. The second is that major gains can be made from the urbanisation shown in Figure 7.3. This moves people from less productive labour in the countryside to more productive labour in the towns. Both emulation and structural change are dynamic drivers. They were evident in the history of the USSR and Japan as they are evident in the accounts here of the Koreas and China.[27] If, additionally, as has been shown here, progress was supported in different ways by the Cold War situation and the neglected subsidies and transfers that benefited especially Japan and South Korea, then the results become even more remarkable.

---

27   See Young 1995.

But possible successes can be easily disrupted as the case of North Korea shows. The trajectories shown in Figures 7.2 and 7.3, for all the doubts about data quality, are telling. The cases of Japan and South Korea are unusual in that their surges have been sustained. Even when successful the gains that emerge from emulation and structural change weaken over time for two very obvious reasons. First, the more advanced the economies become, the less scope there is for emulation and the more they must generate innovation within. This is much more complex in terms of the resources it needs and the degree of direction it can be given by the state. It is one thing to direct a catching up process towards what is known, it is quite another to try to 'plan' and 'direct' capital towards an unknown future. The second is that, beyond a certain point, the transfer of resources and especially labour from the countryside must slow. The catch-up patterns evident in Figure 7.3 come therefore to have something of an S shape, slow to take off, then fast and then slowing.

Japan has been by far the most successful example of catch-up. So successful was it that in the 1980s, for a time, people projected its growth forward suggesting that soon the productiveness of Japanese capitalism would outshine the rest. It did not happen. Growth slowed and a mountain of problems emerged. But still Japan has moved forward and sustained its position as an advanced economy, belying those who flipped to a more pessimistic view. South Korea is behind Japan but it too may be as successful in the long run. Inevitably there remains unevenness but those in most advanced parts of South Korean capitalism seem to have a sense of the need to focus how to shift the production structure of firms and the economy upwards. Clearly there is a successful learning experience that they can draw on (Japan) and failure (North Korea). Nevertheless, the US Conference Board productivity databases suggest that in 2017 GDP output per hour worked was only 65 percent of the US level for Japan and 51 percent for South Korea.[28]

China, as can be seen, is much lower down the curve still. Its size gives it huge weight in the global economy much as happened with the USSR in the Cold War. Unlike the USSR it will almost certainly become the world's biggest economy. This is in no small part because of its billion plus population. At a per capita level it still has a long way to go. This means that there is still scope for more emulation and more structural change. How far it has to go is an important question. The distance can be seen not only in crude GDP per head figures (its GDP per hour calculations are much less reliable but much lower than those for South Korea) but also in the structure of the economy. In 2016 two Amer-

---

28   The Conference Board, *Total Economy Database*, Summary Tables, March 2018.

ican commentators published a short account seeking to downplay China's potential and US fears.[29] During the Trump presidency such arguments seemed unheard, but they carry some force for us. It is not simply that there are vast areas that are still rural but that most advanced sectors are often still focusing on processing. Half of China's exports consist of processed goods that involve parts often drawn from elsewhere. The iPhone, as everyone should know, is not 'made in China' but 'assembled in China'. China is not yet generating much new knowledge its own. (Patent statistics which are often quoted seem to be inflated and of limited significance). In the years 1990–2015 scientists in the US won 114 Nobel prizes, those in China two. This weakness plays out in the military sphere. Like the USSR before it, China has a large military in terms of numbers but its technology is weaker. In fact it is even weaker today than that of Russia. 'China still cannot mass produce high-performance aircraft engines, despite the immense resources it has throwing at the effort, and relies instead on second-rate Russian models'. China's R&D spend, and its quality, is not insignificant but still dwarfed by that of more advanced states. In the case of military R&D the gap is enormous. In 2012, the US spent $79bn on this whereas China seems to have spent around one-thirteenth of this amount. The authors claim with some force that China is likely to be a more impressive economic power than a military one. Even here it cannot try to command the global economy in the same way that firms and states in the US or Europe can. The Chinese leadership too is claimed to be a learning leadership. But the question of whether the leadership can continue to push China forward is one we must leave to readers to judge.

Our concluding points must be rather different. The contexts in which the changes in these East Asian states occurred and the detailed discussions in the previous chapters can be thought of in terms of the idea of a global development space. This space determines the balance of opportunities and constraints for development. At the end of the Second World War this development space seemed to be almost non-existent, save for that part exploited by Japan and the Soviet bloc. Pessimism continued long after. But gradually, and not least for the East Asian states discussed here, the opportunities seemed to be greater than the constraints if states could mobilise 'internally' to interact positively with a more dynamic external economic and geo-political environment.

The nature of any development space therefore changes over time – this is what we would expect given our emphasis on the contradictory dynamism of

29   Brooks and Wohlforth 2016.

Global Ecological Constraints

Production Structures			Geo Political Conditions/ Constraints
National/ International Supply chains/ Product space Competitive power FDI technology transfer	←→	←→	War Cold War Peace Friend/foe Arms Aid Technology transfers
		National Policies	
Global Macro Economic Conditions Economic growth Debt Financial crisis	←→	←→	**Policy Constraints** (a) IFIS : IMF WB WTO [TRIMS] TRIPS GATTS etc (b) **Alliances and organisations** NATO, Comecon etc (c) **Regional economic groupings**

Global Ecological Constraints

FIGURE 7.4   The development space broadly conceptualised

capitalism. But this also means that it is foolish to suggest that because a policy worked in the 1990s when the development space had a particular form then they could have worked a half century earlier when the space was quite different. The same applies if we project this idea forward to other states. But what is the development space?

The idea of the development space has usually been thought of in very narrow terms. Here we want to widen it. Figure 7.4 tries to set out some of the bigger elements involved, with a view to capturing the key ones at work since the 1950s and those which are likely to be in play in the foreseeable future.

In our conceptualisation the development space is constrained by global ecological limits. In the past these have been considered to be of limited significance. This is no longer the case. The very successes of East Asian capitalism in generating growth have added to the global resource strain and the problems of pollution and global warming. And since capitalist growth is a competitive process, further development implies even greater strains as the most advanced move forward and the less advanced try to catch up with a moving target. In this sense the capitalist and state capitalist growth model seems to be unsustainable at the global level.[30]

Within these ecological constraints the nature of global production structures then play a key role. Change here has been a crucial element in opening up the space for the East Asian countries (excluding North Korea) to develop an export-led model of growth and not least through the shift in manufacturing production away from the advanced economies as they have moved more into services. This space too is not unlimited and it is contested. Attempts are continually being made to reduce the space by enclosing, for example, the movement of ideas and intellectual property. Then we have the changing geopolitical constraints that have figured prominently in these accounts. The Cold War had an enormous influence but the balance of opportunities and constraints varied as the contrasting experience of the states discussed shows. When the Cold War ended, conflicts and tensions did not disappear but re-emerged in new ways. The idea of the end of history, magnanimous Marshall Plan style gestures in which the richer capitalist powers helped out poorer ones, proved to be fleeting dreams. Global macro-economic conditions changed and are changing. We now live in a much more unstable world where local and general crises seem to be becoming more common. Then we have the battle over policy constraints and the way that this is played out in the global institutions, alliances and regional organisations. This has been the focus of most of the discussion about a development space, but as can be seen here it is one aspect of a much more complex set of relations.

This leads us to our final reflection. This is the extent to which the economic successes of 'state capitalism' in the East Asian cases, the goods that flow from them, and the resources they suck in, might be contributing to a closing of the development space elsewhere. We know that over time the nature of world trade has shifted in two crucial ways. Firstly, merchandise trade – which consists of agricultural goods, fuels and mining products, and manufactured products – has diminished in importance as trade in services has grown. For

---

30   See, for example, the projections in Haynes and Husan 2000.

TABLE 7.5   Percentage distribution of global merchandise exports 1948–2016[a]

	USA	Europe	Asia	in which Japan	South Korea	China	Sub Sahara Africa
1948	28.1	35.1	14.0	0.4	na	0.9	7.3
1953	24.8	39.4	13.4	1.3	na	1.2	6.5
1963	19.9	47.8	12.5	3.5	na	1.3	5.7
1973	17.3	50.9	14.9	6.4	na	1.0	4.8
1983	16.8	43.5	19.1	8.0	na	1.2	4.5
1993	17.9	45.3	26.0	9.8	na	2.5	2.5
2003	15.8	45.9	26.1	6.4	na	5.9	2.4
2016	14.2	38.4	34.0	4.2	3.1	13.6	2.2

a   World Trade Organisation 2017, p. 100.

the advanced countries it is commercial services trade that is now the more important. The second is the disaggregation of production into long supply chains. An understanding of the changing pattern of merchandise trade has to reflect these elements. Table 7.5 shows how the distribution of world merchandise exports has shifted in the period covered by this book.

We see here the rise of Japan, South Korea and China and the ways in which the relative shares of the USA and Europe have moved.

Table 7.6 shows the weight of manufactured goods in total merchandise trade. We can see how this weight has been high throughout the post-war years for the high income countries and the UK as an example. We also see the rising shares for Japan, South Korea and China.

The weight of these East Asian economies in the global system is now significant. Because of its huge size, that is especially the case for China. Its very recent growth seems to swamp all others – giving the illusion that here has been major progress across 'the poor world', 'the developing world', etc. In these terms there is now no longer a 'Third World'.

But take China out of these calculations – take it out of the BRICS too – and the situation looks rather different. The final columns in Table 7.5 and 7.6 show the rather different experience of Sub Saharan Africa. We see here how the share of Sub Saharan Africa in global merchandise trade has continually diminished since 1948. We see too that while the East Asian economies have surged, the share of manufactured goods trade in the trade of Sub Saharan Africa has been flat for the last decades. The figures for Sub Saharan Africa are themselves

TABLE 7.6   Manufactured exports as a percentage of merchandise exports[31]

	High Income	UK	Japan	South Korea	China	Sub Saharan Africa
1965	64.5	81.0	90.6	59.3	–	
1970	68.9	80.1	92.5	76.5	–	9.1[*]
1980	68.2	71.5	94.7	89.5	–	–
1990	74.1	79.1	95.9	93.5	65.6	–
2000	74.5	75.7	93.9	90.7	88.2	25.5
2010	69.2	68.4	89.0	89.0	93.6	22.6
2014	67.2	73.8	88.2	86.8	94.0	23.9

inflated by the role of South Africa. Take that economy out and the situation looks far worse. The story or stories of recent developments in Africa can be traced elsewhere.[32]

What is interesting to us here is that it is an example of the ways in which the stories told here of the East Asian economies are themselves changing global dynamics. This is so not only in terms of their relations with the world's most powerful states but also some of the poorest. Today the focus is on China or at least the China beyond the Cold War context that marked its outward political vision before the 1990s. Yet just as other capitalist states that have been involved in catch up have also been expansionist at the same time so the same is true of the East Asian states too. Japan before 1945 is too well known to need comment. But it is worth reminding readers that there is a more recent history of Japan, South Korea and even North Korea in seeking influence much further away including in Africa.

Today in Africa the Chinese leadership is now presenting itself as a friend. China is bringing goods, ideas and capital without, it claims, the strings of the former colonial powers and the United States. The scale of its activity is exciting much more attention than the activities of Japan and South Korea. Still it is far from clear that the overall effect is positive. Producers in Africa have not only to face the competition of the producers in the US and Europe but East Asian goods and Chinese goods in particular. These outcompete 'African' goods. They narrow the production possibilities there. And why would China's motives be

31   Compiled by author from World Bank World Economic Indicators.
32   Ayuba and Haynes 2017.

unsullied? Whether as private, state or private-state hybrids, capitals, and the capitalists in charge, be they American, British, Japanese, Korean, or Chinese, are always opportunists – seeking to expand where they can and change the world in their interests rather than those of their own populations or the global population as a whole.

Looking Forward

The promise of capitalism has always been limitless expansion. But we know that there are very real limits. Development has always been uneven and it continues to be so. The unevenness is not fixed but what is possible is always structured by time and in space. The East Asian cases examined here show that in the late twentieth century more possibilities opened up than had existed earlier. 'Development states' were able to make use of them. But to write as if these states were neutral forces working benignly for all is to miss the real nature of the social relations on which they are based. No less false is to try to generalise from their experience to possibilities across the globe. It is false because the specific opportunities and possibilities available to them were, and are, not available to all. It is false because the fallacy of composition still remains. You cannot develop the whole world on the basis of export-led growth. In these terms something has to give if within these states and beyond them the possibilities of a different kind of system are to be realised.

But this search for a better way of doing things, a post-capitalist alternative, is the more necessary still because we now understand too that capitalism cannot be a system of infinite expansion saved by techno-fixes to its problems. The very successes of the East Asian countries have exposed the extent to which we live on one planet with a very finite availability of resources and a very finite atmosphere. Projecting the East Asian cases forward as the way to the future, even if we ignore all the arguments made about their real nature in this book, answers neither the needs of the present nor the very immediate future.

Glossary of Terms in East Asian Languages

baogongzhi (Ch) 包工制　contract labour system

danwei (Ch) 单位　'work unit', the basic unit of organisation in the industrial system of the People's Republic of China. Terms used in North Korea with similar meanings include *pŭrigada* 브리가다 [from the Russian бригада] and *chag'ŏppan* 작업반.

fangquan rangli (Ch) 放权让利　the decentralisation of power and transfer of profits

fukoku kyōhei (Ja) 富国強兵　'wealthy country, strong army' – a central slogan of Meiji period Japan

guanxi (Ch) 关系　network of relationships, usually between the state bureaucracy and businesspeople

gudinggong (Ch) 固定工　permanent worker

hetonggong (Ch) 合同工　contract worker

hukou (Ch) 户口　household registration system in the People's Republic of China

jiben jianshe (Ch) 基本建设　fixed capital construction

jiegu 解雇 (Ch)　dismissal from a post

jijianzhi (Ch) 计件制　term for piece rate wages system in the PRC

jingjian 精简 (Ch)　lay-offs

nengjin nengchu (Ch) 能进能出　free movement of workers, literally: ability to enter and exit [a workplace]

nongmin gong (Ch) 农民工　a 'peasant-worker', or in other words an industrial worker who has recently migrated from the countryside

renmin gongshe (Ch) 人民公社　'people's commune' – the term used for collective farms in the PRC

togŭpche (Ko) 都給制　term for piece rate wages system in the DPRK

xuetuzhi (Ch) 學徒制　apprenticeship system

zaibatsu (Ja) / *chaebŏl* (Ko) 財閥　a large industrial conglomerate, usually family owned

zengchan jieyue (Ch) / *chŭngsan chŏryak* (Ko) 增产节约　a slogan of the rapid industrialisation period in both the PRC and DPRK: 'increase production, conserve resources'

zhuada fangxiao (Ch) 抓大放小　'grasping the large enterprise and letting go the small enterprise'

Bibliography 1: References in English and Other European Languages

Ahearne, A et al. 2006, 'Flying Geese or sitting Ducks: China's Impact on the Trading Fortunes of other Asian Economies', Board of Governors of the Federal Reserve System, *International Finance Discussion Papers*, No. 887.

AmCham (American Chamber of Commerce) 2005, *American Business in China. 2005 White Paper*, Beijing: The American Chamber of Commerce.

Amin, Samir 2013, 'China 2013', *Monthly Review* 64:10. https://monthlyreview.org/2013/03/01/china-2013/.

Amsden, Alice H 1989, *Asia's Next Giant: South Korea and Late Industrialisation*, New York: Oxford University Press.

Anievas, Alex and Kerem Nisancioglu 2015, *How the West Came to Rule*. London: Pluto Press.

Anita Chan 2016, *China's Workers Under Assault: Exploitation and Abuse in a Globalizing Economy*, Routledge.

Armstrong, Charles 2004, *The North Korean Revolution, 1945–1950*, Ithaca: Cornell University Press.

Armstrong, P., Glyn, A. and Harrison J. 1991, *Capitalism since 1945*, Oxford: Blackwell.

Arrighi, Giovanni 1994, *The Long Twentieth Century*, London: Verso.

Arrighi, Giovanni 2007, *Adam Smith in Beijing: Lineages of the 21st Century*, London: Verso.

Ayuba, Keziah, and Mike Haynes 2017, 'Business and economics in Africa – one story or many?' International Journal of Management Concepts and Philosophy 10,1: 54–72.

Baek, Seung-Wook 2005, 'Does China Follow 'the East Asian Development Model'?' *Journal of Comtemporary Asia* 35:4, 485–98.

Bairoch, Paul 1982, 'International industrialisation levels from 1750–1980', Journal of European Economic History, 11:1: 269–310.

Baker, D., Pollin, R. and Zahrt, E. 1996, 'The Vietnam War and the Political Economy of Full Employment', *Challenge*, May–June.

Balassa, B. in association with J. Berlinski et al. 1982, *Development Strategies in Semi-industrial Economics*, Johns Hopkins University Press for the World Bank.

Baldwin, F. 1975, *America's Rented Troops: South Koreans In Vietnam*, BCAS.

Banaji, Jairus 1977, 'Modes of Production in a Materialist Conception of History', *Capital & Class* 1:3.

Banaji, Jairus 2011, *Theory As History: Essays on Modes of Production and Exploitation*, Chicago: Haymarket Books.

Bardhan, Pranab 2010, 'The Paradigm of Capitalism under a Developmental State: Does It Fit China and India?' *Singapore Economic Review* 55:2, 243–51.

Barker, Colin 1978, 'A note on the theory of capitalist states', Capital & Class, 2.1:118–26.

Barker, Colin 1978, 'The State as Capital', *International Socialism* 2:1, 16–42.

Barker, Colin 1982, 'The Origins and Significance of the Meiji Restoration'. http://www .marxists.de/fareast/barker/

Barker, Colin 1998, 'Industrialism, Capitalism, Value, Force and States: Some Theoretical Remarks', unpublished conference paper. https://sites.google.com/site/colinbarkers ite/5---publications-and-papers-1996-2000

Barker, Colin 1999–2000, 'Military competition *qua* competition', notes sent to Emma Bircham. https://sites.google.com/site/colinbarkersite/5---publications-and-papers -1996-2000

Barker, Colin 2009, 'Industrialism, capitalism, force and states: some theoretical and historical issues', International Journal of Management Concepts and Philosophy 3,4: 313–31.

Barrett, Thomas 1996, *China, Marxism, and democracy: selections from October review*, Humanities Press.

Barry J. Naughton 2007, *The Chinese Economy: Transitions and Growth*, The MIT Press.

Beeson, Mark 2001, 'Globalization, Governance and the Political-Economy of Public Policy Reform in East Asia', *Governance: An International Journal of Policy and Administration* 14:4, 481–502.

Bernstein, Henry 2013, 'Historical Materialism and Agrarian History', *Journal of Agrarian Change* 13:2, 310–29.

Bian, Morris L. 2005, *The Making of the State Enterprise System in Modern China: The Dynamics of Institutional Change*, Cambridge MA: Harvard University Press.

Bianco, Lucien 2014, *La récidive: Révolution russe, révolution chinoise*, Paris: Editions Gallimard.

Binns, Pete 1975, 'The Theory of State Capitalism', *International Socialism* 1:74, 20–5. http://www.marxists.org/history/etol/writers/binns/1975/01/statecap.htm

Blank, Garry 2015, *Is the East Still Red?* Winchester: Zero Books.

Blecher, M 1991, 'Development State, Entrepreneurial State: The Political Economy of Socialist Reform in Xinji Municipality and Guanghan County', in Gordon White (ed.) *The Chinese State in the Era of Economic Reform: The Road to Crisis*, 265–94. Basingstoke: Macmillan.

Blecher, M. 2008, 'Into Space: The Local Developmental State, Capitalist Transition and the Political Economy of Urban Planning in Xinji', *City*, 12:2, 171–82.

Blecher, Marc and Vivienne Shue 1996, *Tethered Deer: Government and Economy in a Chinese County*, Stanford. CA: Stanford University Press.

Bonwetsch, Bernd 1997, 'Stalin, the Red Army, and the "Great Patriotic War"', in Moshe

Lewin and Ian Kershaw, eds, *Stalinism and Nazism; Dictatorships in Comparison*, Cambridge: Cambridge University Press.

Bremmer, I. 2010, *The End of the Free Market: Who Wins the War Between States and Corporations*, Portfolio/Penguin.

Brenner, Robert 1991, 'The Soviet Union and Eastern Europe – The Roots of the Crisis', *Against the Current* March/April. https://www.versobooks.com/blogs/2490-the-sovi et-union-and-eastern-europe-the-roots-of-the-crisis

Brenner, Robert 2006, *The Economics of Global Turbulence*, London: Verso.

Breslin, Shaun 2007, *China and the Global Political Economy*, Basingstoke: Palgrave-Macmillan.

Breslin, Shaun G 1996, 'China: developmental state or dysfunctional development?' *Third World Quarterly*, 17:4, 689–706.

Briggs, Asa 1970, *The Nineteenth Century. The Contradictions of Progress*, London: Thames and Hudson.

Broadberry, Stephen and Mark Harrison 2008, 'Economics of the World Ears' in *The New Palgrave Dictionary of Economics*, edited by Steven Dulauf and Lawrence Blume. London: Palgrave Macmillan.

Brooks, Stephen G., and William C. Wohlforth 2016, 'The once and future superpower. Why China won't overtake the United States', *Foreign Affairs*, 95, 91–104.

Brown, Jeremy 2012, *City versus Countryside in Mao's China: Negotiating the Divide*, New York: Cambridge University Press.

Bukharin, Nikolai 1982 [1916], 'Toward a Theory of the Imperialist State', in *Selected Writings on the State and the Transition to Socialism*, Nottingham: Spokesman.

Burnham, Peter 1995, 'State and market in international political economy: Towards a Marxian alternative', *Studies in Marxism*, 2.

Butollo, Florian and Tobias ten Brink 2012, 'Challenging the Atomization of Discontent. Patterns of Migrant-Worker Protest in China during the Series of Strikes in 2010', *Critical Asian Studies*, 44:3, 419–40.

Cai, Hongbin and Daniel Treisman 2006, 'Did Government Decentralization Cause China's Economic Miracle?' *World Politics*, 58:4, 505–35.

Cai, Yongshun 2006, *State and Laid-Off Workers in Reform China: The Silence and Collective Action of the Retrenched*, Abingdon: Routledge.

Callinicos, Alex 2014, *Deciphering Capital: Marx's Capital and Its Destiny*, London: Bookmarks.

Carlisle, Donald S. 1964, 'The Changing Soviet Perception of the Development Process in the Afro-Asian World', *Midwest Journal of Political Science* 8:4, 385–407.

Central Statistical Board Under the State Planning Commission of the D.P.R.K. 1961, *Statistical Returns of National Economy of the Democratic People's Republic of Korea (1946–1960)*, Pyongyang: Foreign Languages Publishing House.

Cerny, Philip G 1997, 'Paradoxes of the Competition State: The Dynamics of Political Globalisation', *Government and Opposition*, 32:2, 251–74.

Chan, Anita 2015, *China's Workers Under Assault: Exploitation and Abuse in a Globalizing Economy*, Abingdon: Routledge.

Chan, Ming K. 2002, 'Realpolitik and legacy of labor activism and popular mobilization in 1920s Greater Canton', in Mechthild Leutner (ed), *The Chinese revolution in the 1920s: between triumph and disaster*, Abingdon: Routledge.

Chang, D. 2009, *Capitalist Development in Korea: Labour, Capital and the Myth of the Developmental State*, London: Routledge.

Chang, H-J 1993, *The Political Economy of Industrial Policy*, London: Macmillan.

Chang, Kai, Boy Lüthje and Luo Siqi 2008, *Die Transformation der Arbeitsbeziehungen in China und ihre Besonderheiten*, unpublished manuscript, Düsseldorf: Hans-Boeckler-Foundation.

Chattopadhyay 1994, *The Marxian Concept of Capital and the Soviet Experience*, Westport: Praeger.

Chen, Feng 2013, 'Against the State: Labor Protests in China in the 1950s', *Modern China* 40:5, 488–518.

Chen, Jiagui and Qin Wang 2010, 'The Reform, Opening, and Development of China's Industrial Economy', in *Transforming the Chinese Economy*, edited by Cai Fang, Leiden: Brill, 39–83.

Chan, Chris King-chi 2012, *The Challenge of Labour in China: Strikes and the Changing Labour Regime in Global Factories*, Abingdon: Routledge.

Chu, Yin-Wah (ed.) 2010, *Chinese Capitalisms: Historical Emergence and Political Implications*, Houndmills: Palgrave Macmillan.

Chuang Collective (ed.) 2016, *Chuang 1*, AK Press Distribution.

Chung, Joseph Sang-hoon 1972, 'North Korea's 'Seven Year Plan' (1961–70): Economic Performance and Reforms', *Asian Survey*, 12:6, 527–45.

CIA National Foreign Assessment Center 1978, 'Korea: The Economic Race Between the North and the South', Washington D.C.: The Center.

Ciliga, Ante 1940, *The Russian Enigma*, London: The Labour Book Service.

Clarkson, Stephen. 1978, *The Soviet Theory of Development: India and the Third World in Marxist-Leninist Scholarship*, Toronto: University of Toronto Press.

CLB (China Labour Bulletin) 2011, *Unity is Strength. The Workers' Movement in China 2009–2011*, Hong Kong: China Labour Bulletin.

Cliff, Tony 1948, *The Nature of Stalinist Russia*, internal document of the British Revolutionary Communist Party (1944–1949).

Cliff, Tony 1963, 'Permanent Revolution', *International Socialism* 1:12. https://www.marxists.org/archive/cliff/works/1963/xx/permrev.htm

Cliff, Tony 1964, *Russia: A Marxist Analysis*, London: International Socialism.

Cliff, Tony 1974 [1955], *State Capitalism in Russia*, London: Pluto.

Coates, David (ed.) 2005, *Varieties of Capitalism, Varieties of Approaches*, Basingstoke: Palgrave Macmillan.

Crawcour, E. Sydney 1997, 'Industrialization and technological change, 1885–1920', in Yamamura Kozo (ed.), *The Economic Emergence of Modern Japan*, Cambridge: Cambridge University Press.

Cumings, Bruce 1982, 'Corporatism in North Korea', *The Journal of Korean Studies* 4, 269–94.

Cumings, Bruce 1984, 'The Origins and Development of the Northeast Asian Political Economy: Industrial Sectors, Product Cycles, and Political Consequences', *International Organization*, 38:1.

Dale, Gareth 2004, *Between State Capitalism and Globalisation: The Collapse of the East German Economy*, Bern: Peter Lang.

Davidson, Neil 2012, 'The Necessity of Multiple Nation-States for Capital', *Rethinking Marxism* 24:1, 26–46.

Derr, Arius M. and Robert Kelly 2018, 'Kim Jong-un's Inner Circle', Centre for International Governance Innovation. https://www.cigionline.org/articles/north-korean -elite-behind-kim-jong-un

Dickson, Bruce J 2003. *Red Capitalists in China: The Party, Private Entrepreneurs and Prospects for Political Change*, Cambridge: Cambridge University Press.

Dickson, Bruce J. 2007, 'Integrating Wealth and Power in China: The Communist Party's Embrace of the Private Sector', *The China Quarterly*, 192, 827–54.

Dikotter, Frank 2010, *Mao's great famine: the history of China's most devastating catastrophe, 1958–1962*, London: Bloomsbury.

Duckett, Jane 1998, *The Entrepreneurial State in China: Real Estate and Commerce Departments in Reform Era Tianjin*. London: Routledge.

Dunayevskaya, Raya 1958, *Marxism and Freedom: from 1776 until today*, New York: Bookman Associates.

Eberstadt and Banister 1992, *The Population of North Korea*, Berkeley: Institute of East Asian Studies.

Economist 2012, 'The Rise of State Capitalism. The Emerging World's New Model', *The Economist*, January 21st–27th.

Engels, Friedrich 1894 [1878], *Herrn Eugen Dührings Umwälzung der Wissenschaft*, Stuttgart: Dietz.

Engels, Friedrich and Karl Marx 1848, *Manifesto of the Communist Party*. https://www .marxists.org/archive/marx/works/1848/communist-manifesto/

Evans, Peter 1992, 'The State as Problem and Solution: Embedded Autonomy and Structural Change', Stephen Haggard and R.R. Kaufman (eds), *The Politics of Economic Adjustment*, Princeton University Press. 139–81.

Evans, Peter 1995, *Embedded Autonomy*, Princeton University Press.

Evans, Peter, Dietrich Rueschemeyer and Theda Skocpol (eds.) 1985, *Bringing the State Back In*, Cambridge: Cambridge University Press.

Fallows, James M. 1994, *Looking at the Sun: The Rise of the New East Asian Economic and Political System*, New York: Pantheon Books.

Fernandez, Neil 1997, *Capitalism and Class Struggle in the USSR: A Marxist Theory*, Aldershot: Ashgate.

Fewsmith, Joseph 2011, 'Debating "the China Model"', *China Leadership Monitor*, 35, 1–7.

Filtzer, Donald A. 2002a [1986], *Soviet Workers and De-Stalinization: The Consolidation of the Modern System of Soviet Production Relations 1953–1964*, Cambridge: Cambridge University Press.

Filtzer, Donald A. 2002b, *Soviet Workers and Late Stalinism: Labour and the Restoration of the Stalinist System after World War II*, Cambridge: Cambridge University Press.

Fine, Ben 2012, 'Locating the Developmental State and Industrial and Social Policy after the Crisis'. mimeo.

Fligstein, Neil and Zhang Jianjun 2011, 'A New Agenda for Research on the Trajectory of Chinese Capitalism', *Management and Organization Review*, 7, 1: 39–62.

Frazier, Mark 2002, *The making of the Chinese industrial workplace: state, revolution, and labor management*, Cambridge: Cambridge University Press

Friedman, Eli and Ching Kwan Lee 2010, 'Remaking the World of Chinese Labour: A 30-Year Retrospective', *British Journal of Industrial Relations*, 48, 3: 507–33.

Friedman, Thomas 1999, *The Lexus and the Olive Tree*, London: Harper Collins.

Froud, Julie, Sukdhev Johal, John Law, Adam Leaver, and Karel Williams 2011, 'Rebalancing the economy (or buyer's remorse)', CRESC, University of Manchester.

Gabriel, Resnick & Wolff 2011, 'What Happened To Chinese Communism: The Transition From State Feudalism To State Capitalism', in Pollard 2011, *State Capitalism, Contentious Politics and Large-Scale Social Change*, Leiden: Brill.

Gaulard, Mylène 2014, *Karl Marx à Pékin – Les racines de la crise en Chine capitaliste*, Paris: Demopolis.

Giersch, H., Paque, K-H. and Schmieding, H. 1992, *The Fading Miracle: Four Decades of Market Economy in Germany*, Cambridge: Cambridge University Press.

Gipouloux, François 1986, *Les Cent Fleurs à l'usine: agitation ouvrière et crise du modèle soviétique en Chine, 1956–1957*, Paris: Éditions de l'École des hautes études en sciences sociales.

Gluckstein, Donny 2012, *A People's History of the Second World War: Resistance Versus Empire*, London: Pluto Press.

Gluckstein, Ygael [Tony Cliff] 1957, *Mao's China: Economic and Political Survey*, London: George Allen & Unwin Ltd.

Glyn, Andrew 2006, *Capitalism Unleashed: Finance, Globalization, and Welfare*, Oxford: Oxford University Press.

Gold, Thomas B. (ed) 2009, *Laid-Off Workers in a Workers' State: Unemployment with Chinese Characteristics*, Springer.

Goodkind, West and Johnson 2011, 'A Reassessment of Mortality in North Korea, 1993–2008', Paper presented at the annual meeting of the Population Association of America, April 2011.

Gordon, Andrew 2003, *A Modern History of Japan: From Tokugawa Times to the Present*, Oxford: Oxford University Press.

Gruin, Julian 2013, 'Asset or Liability? The Role of the Financial System in the Political Economy of China's Rebalancing', *Journal of Current Chinese Affairs*, 42, 4: 73–104.

Haltmaier, J et al. 2007, 'The Role of China in Asia: Engine, Conduit, or Steamroller?' Board of Governors of the Federal Reserve System, *International Finance Discussion Papers*, No. 904.

Harman, C. 1984, *Explaining the Crisis: A Marxist Reappraisal*, London: Bookmarks.

Harman, C. 2009, *Zombie Capitalism: Global Crisis and the Relevance of Marx*, London: Bookmarks.

Harman, Chris 1991, 'The state and capitalism today', *International Socialism* 2:51, 3–54. www.marxists.org/archive/harman/1991/xx/statcap.htm

Harris, Nigel 1978, *The Mandate of Heaven: Marx and Mao in Modern China*, Quartet Books.

Harris, Nigel 2017 [1971], *Selected Essays of Nigel Harris: From National Liberation to Globalisation*, Leiden: Brill.

Harrison, Mark and Nikolaus Wolf 2012, 'The frequency of wars', *Economic History Review*, 65, 3: 1055–1076.

Harrison, Mark 2014, 'Capitalism at war', in The Cambridge History of Capitalism vol. 1, edited by Larry Neal, Cambridge: Cambridge University Press.

Hart-Landsberg, Martin 1998, *Korea: division, reunification, and U.S. foreign policy*, New York: Monthly Review Press.

Hart-Landsberg, Martin and Paul Burkett 2001, 'Economic Crisis and Restructuring in South Korea: Beyond the Free Market-Statist Debate', *Critical Asian Studies*, 33:3, 403–30.

Hart-Landsberg, Martin and Paul Burkett 2005, *China and Socialism. Market Reforms and Class Struggle*, New York: Monthly Review Press.

Haslam, Jonathan 1999, *The Vices of Integrity. E.H. Carr 1892–1982*, London: Verso.

Hausmann, Ricardo and Dani Rodrik 2006, 'Doomed to Choose: Industrial Policy as Predicament', paper prepared for the first Blue Sky seminar organized by the Center for International Development, Harvard University, September.

Hayashi, Shigeko 2010, 'The Developmental State in the Era of Globalization: Beyond the Northeast Asian Model of Political Economy', *The Pacific Review* 23:1, 45–69.

Haynes Michael and Rumy Husan 2000, 'National inequality and the catch-up period: some growth alone scenarios', *Journal of Economic Issues*, 34:3, 693–705.

Haynes, Michael 1983, 'Capitalism in Marx's time and ours', *International Socialism*, 2:57.

Haynes, Mike 1985, *Nikolai Bukharin and the Transition from Capitalism to Socialism*, Croom Helm.

Heinrich, Michael 2003, *Die Wissenschaft vom Wert*, Münster: Westfälisches Dampfboot.

Heller, Henry 2011, *The Birth of Capitalism: A 21st Century Perspective*. London: Pluto Press.

Herrera, Rémy & Zhiming Long 2017, 'Capital accumulation, profit rates and cycles in China from 1952 to 2014', *Journal of Innovation Economics & Management*, no. 23.

Hershatter, Gail 1993, *The Workers of Tianjin, 1900–1949*, Stanford: Stanford University Press.

Honig, Emily 1992, *Sisters and Strangers: Women in the Shanghai Cotton Mills, 1919–1949*, Stanford: Stanford University Press.

Hoston, Germaine 1986, *Marxism and the Crisis of Development in Prewar Japan*. Princeton: Princeton University Press.

Howard, Joshua H. 2004, *Workers at War: Labor in China's Arsenals, 1937–1953*, Stanford: Stanford University Press.

Howe, Christopher 1973, *Wage Patterns and Wage Policy in Modern China 1919–1972*, Cambridge: Cambridge University Press.

Howe, Christopher 1978, *China's Economy: A Basic Guide*, Basic Books.

Howe, Christopher and Walker, Kenneth R. 2016 [1990], *The Foundations of the Chinese Planned Economy: A Documentary Survey, 1953–65*, Springer.

Howell, Jude 2006, 'Reflections on the Chinese State', *Development and Change*, 37:2, 273–97.

Huang, Philip 1990, *The Peasant Family and Rural Development in the Yangzi Delta, 1350–1988*, Stanford University Press.

Huang, Yasheng 2008, *Capitalism with Chinese Characteristics. Entrepreneurship and the State*, New York: Cambridge University Press.

Huinink, Johannes and Karl Ulrich Mayer 1993, 'Lebensverläufe im Wandel der DDR-Gesellschaft', in Hans Joas and Martin Kohli, eds, *Der Zusammenbruch der DDR*, Frankfurt/Main: Suhrkamp.

Hung, Ho-fung (ed.) 2009a, *China and the Transformation of Global Capitalism*, Baltimore: The Johns Hopkins University Press.

Hung, Ho-fung 2009b, 'America's Head Servant? The PRC's Dilemma in the Global Crisis', *New Left Review*, 60. https://newleftreview.org/II/60/ho-fung-hung-america-s-head-servant

Hung, Ho-fung 2015, *The China Boom: Why China Will Not Rule the World*, New York: Columbia University Press.

Hurst, William 2009, *The Chinese Worker after Socialism*, Cambridge: Cambridge University Press.

Hurst, William 2015, Chinese Labor Divided, *Dissent*, Spring 2015. https://www.dissentmagazine.org/article/chinese-labor-divided

Hwang Su-kyoung 2016, *Korea's Grievous War*, Philadelphia: University of Pennsylvania Press.

Isaacs, Harold 2010 [1951], *The Tragedy of the Chinese Revolution*, Chicago: Haymarket.

Itoh, Makoto 2003, 'Sozialistische Marktwirtschaft und der chinesische Weg', *Supplement der Zeitschrift Sozialismus*, 7–8/2003.

Jacques, Martin 2009, *When China Rules the World: The End of the Western World and the Birth of a New Global Order*, New York: The Penguin Press.

James, C.L.R., Raya Dunayevskaya and Grace Lee Boggs 1950, *State Capitalism and World Revolution*, Chicago: Charles H. Kerr Publishing Company (1986 edition).

Jeong Seongjin 1997, 'The Social Structure of Accumulation in South Korea: Upgrading or Crumbling?', *Review of Radical Political Economics*, 29:4.

Jessop, Bob and Sum Ngai-Ling 2006, *Beyond the Regulation Approach: Putting Capitalist Economies in Their Place*, Cheltenham: Edward Elgar.

Johnson, C. 1999, 'The Developmental State: Odyssey of a Concept', in Meredith Woo-Cumings (ed). *The Developmental State*, Cornell University, 32–60.

Johnson, Chalmers 1982, *MITI and the Japanese Miracle: The Growth of Industrial Policy, 1925–1975*. Stanford, CA: Stanford University Press.

Johnson, Chalmers 2000, *Blowback: The Costs and Consequences of American Empire*, An Owl Book.

Jordan, H.S. Gerald 1974, 'Pensions not Dreadnoughts: the Radicals and naval retrenchment' in A.J.A. Morris (ed), *Edwardian Radicalism 1900–1914. Some Aspects of British Radicalism*, Abingdon: Routledge, 162–79.

Kennedy, Paul 1988, *The Rise and Fall of the Great Powers. Economic Change and Military Conflict from 1500–2000*, London: Unwin Hyman.

Kennedy, Scott (ed.) 2011, *Beyond the Middle Kingdom: Comparative Perspectives on China's Capitalist Transformation*, Stanford, CA: Stanford University Press.

Kidron, Michael 1967, 'A Permanent Arms Economy', *International Socialism* 1:28, 8–12. https://www.marxists.org/archive/kidron/works/1967/xx/permarms.htm

Kidron, Michael 1970, *Western Capitalism Since the War*, Harmondsworth: Penguin Books.

Kidron, Mike n.d., *The Presence of the Future*, unpublished manuscript.

Kim Hyung-A 2004, *Korea's Development under Park Chung Hee: Rapid Industrialization, 1961–1979*, London: RoutledgeCurzon.

Kim Il Sung 1971, 'On some theoretical problems of the socialist economy', in *Selected Writings of Kim Il Sung: Revolution and Socialist Construction in Korea*. New York: International Publishers.

Kim, Suzy 2014, *Everyday Life in the North Korean Revolution*, Ithaca: Cornell University Press.

King, Lawrence P. and Iván Szelényi 2005, 'Post-Communist Economic Systems', in *The Handbook of Economic Sociology*, edited by Neil J. Smelser and Richard Swedberg, Princeton: Princeton University Press, 205–29.

Kocka, Jürgen 2016, *Capitalism: A Short History*, Princeton: Princeton University Press.

Koestler, Arthur 1945, *The Yogi and the Commissar, and other essays*, London: Jonathan Cape.

Kurlantzick, Joshua 2012, 'The Rise of Innovative State Capitalism', *Business Week*, June. http://www.businessweek.com/articles/2012-06-28/the-rise-of-innovative-state-capitalism

Kuron J and Modzelewski, K. A 1967, *Revolutionary Socialist Manifesto (An Open Letter to the Party)*. https://www.marxists.org/history/etol/newspape/isj/1967/no028/kuron.htm

Lacher, Hannes 2006, *Beyond Globalization: Capitalism, Territoriality and the International Relations of Modernity*, Abingdon: Routledge.

Lampland, Martha 1995, *The Object of Labour: Commodification in Socialist Hungary*. Chicago: University of Chicago Press.

Lampland, Martha 2016, *The Value of Labor: The Science of Commodification in Hungary, 1920–1956*, Chicago: University of Chicago Press.

Lange, Oskar 1969, 'The Role of Planning in Socialist Economy', in Morris Bornstein, ed., *Comparative Economic Systems*, Homewood, IL: Richard Irwin.

Lankov, Andrei 2002, *From Stalin to Kim Il Sung: The Formation of North Korea, 1945–1960*, Rutgers University Press.

Lankov, Andrei 2013, *The Real North Korea: Life and Politics in the Failed Stalinist Utopia*, Oxford University Press.

Lankov, Andrei 2014, 'Low-profile Capitalism: The Emergence of the New Merchant/Entrepreneurial Class in Post-Famine North Korea', in Park Kyung-Ae and Scott Snyder, *North Korea in Transition: Politics, economy, and society*, Lanham: Rowman & Littlefield.

Lanz, Rainer and Sebastian Miroudot 2011, 'Intra-Firm Trade, Patterns, Determinants and Policy Implications', OECD Trade Policy Papers no. 114, OECD Publishing, Paris.

Lardy, Nicholas R. 2002, *Integrating China into the Global Economy*, Washington: Brookings.

Lazonick, W. and M. O'Sullivan 1997, 'Finance and industrial development', *Financial History Review* No. 4. 7–29.

Lee, Ching Kwan 2007, *Against the law: labor protests in China's rustbelt and sunbelt*, Berkeley: University of California Press.

Lenin, Vladimir 1919, 'Report Of The Central Committee'. https://www.marxists.org/archive/lenin/works/1919/rcp8th/02.htm

Lenin, Vladimir 1977 [1918], 'Left-Wing' Childishness and the Petty-Bourgeois Mentality', *Collected Works*, Vol. 27, Moscow: Progress Publishers, 323–354.

Lewin, Moshe 1985, *The Making of the Soviet System*, London: Methuen.

Li, Huaiyin 2009, *Village China Under Socialism and Reform: A Micro-History, 1948–2008*, Stanford: Stanford University Press.

Li, Huaiyin 2016, 'Worker Performance in State-Owned Factories in Maoist China: A Reinterpretation', *Modern China* 42:4, 377–414.

Li, Huaiyin 2017, 'Everyday Power Relations in State Firms in Socialist China: A Reexamination', *Modern China* 43:3, 288–321.

Li, Minqi 2016, *China and the Twenty-first-Century Crisis*, London: Pluto Press.

Li, Shaomin and Jun Xia 2008, 'The Roles and Performance of State Firms and Non-State Firms in China's Economic Transition', *World Development*, 36, 1: 39–54.

Li, Xiaoxi 2008, '30 Years of Reform Transforms China Beyond Recognition', *China Economist*, 16, 9–10: 84–94.

Li, Zhongjin, Eli Friedman and Hao Ren 2016, *China on Strike: Narratives of Workers' Resistance*, Chicago: Haymarket Books.

Lieberthal, Kenneth G 1992, 'Introduction: The 'Fragmented Authoritarianism' Model and its Limitations', Kenneth G. Lieberthal and David M. Lampton (eds.). *Bureaucracy, Politics, and Decision Making in Post-Mao China*. Berkeley, Calif.: University of California Press, 1–30.

Liu, Elliott 2016, *Maoism and the Chinese Revolution: A Critical Introduction*, Oakland: PM Press.

Lloyd George, David 1938, War Memoirs of Lloyd George, vol. 1, London: Odhams.

Lu, Ming and Yiran Xia 2016, 'Migration in the People's Republic of China', *ADBI Working Paper* 593. https://www.adb.org/publications/migration-people-republic-china/

Lu, Xiaobo 1997, *Danwei: The Changing Chinese Workplace in Historical and Comparative Perspective*, M.E. Sharpe.

Lüthje, Boy, Luo Siqi and Hao Zhang 2013, *Socio-economic transformation and industrial relations in China*, Frankfurt: Campus.

MacFarquhar, Roderick 1983, *The Origins of the Cultural Revolution – 2. The Great Leap Forward, 1958–1960*, Columbia University Press.

MacFarquhar, Roderick and John K. Fairbank 1991, *The Cambridge History of China, vol. 15, Part 2. Revolutions within the Chinese Revolution, 1966–1982*, Cambridge: Cambridge University Press.

Mann, Michael 2018, 'Have wars and violence declined?', *Theory and Society* 47:1, 37–60.

Mao Zedong 2007, *On Practice and Contradiction*, (Introduction by Slavoj Žižek), London: Verso Books.

Marx, Karl 1858, *Theories of Surplus Value*. https://www.marxists.org/archive/marx/works/1863/theories-surplus-value/cho8.htm

Marx, Karl 1875, *Kritik des Gothaer Programms*. www.marxists.org/deutsch/archiv/marx-engels/1875/kritik/randglos.htm

Marx, Karl 1990, *Capital*, Vol. 1, Harmondsworth: Penguin.

Marx, Karl 1993 [1857], *Grundrisse: Foundations of the Critique of Political Economy*, London: Penguin.

May, Christian, Andreas Nölke and Tobias ten Brink 2013, ‚Institutionelle Determinanten des Aufstiegs großer Schwellenländer: Eine global-politökonomische Erweiterung der Vergleichenden Kapitalismusforschung, *Politische Vierteljahresschrift*, Sonderheft 48: 67–94.

McNally, Christopher A. 2007, *China's Emergent Political Economy: Capitalism in the Dragons's Lair*, London: Routledge.

McNally, Christopher A. 2012, 'Sino-Capitalism: China's Reemergence and the International Political Economy', *World Politics* 64:4, 741–76.

McNally, Christopher A. and Yin-Wah Chu 2006, 'Exploring Capitalist Development in Greater China: A Synthesis', *Asian Perspective* 30:2, 31–64.

McNally, Christopher, Hong Guo and Guangwie Hu 2007, 'Entrepreneurship and Political Guanxi Networks in China's Private Sector', *East-West Center Working Papers* No. 19, Aug 2007.

Meisner, Maurice 1986, *Mao's China and after: a history of the People's Republic*, New York: Free Press.

Miller, Owen 2016, 'War, the State and the Formation of the North Korean Industrial Working Class'. *Third World Quarterly* 37:10, 1901–1920.

Ming, Xia 2000, *The Dual Developmental State: Development strategy and institutional arrangements for China's transition*. Aldershot: Ashgate.

Montinola, Gabriella, Yingyi Qian and Barry R. Weingast 1995, 'Federalism, Chinese Style: The Political Basis for Economic Success in China', *World Politics* 48:1, 50–81.

Moon, C. and Hyun I. 1992, 'Muddling through Security, Growth and Welfare: The Political Economy of Defense Spending in South Korea', in Steve Chan and Alex Mint (eds.) *Defense, Welfare and Growth: Perspectives and Evidence*, Routledge.

Moon, Seungsook 2005, *Militarized Modernity and Gendered Citizenship in South Korea*, Durham: Duke University Press.

Moore, Jason 2014, *Capitalism in the Web of Life: Ecology and the Accumulation of Capital*, London: Verso Books.

Morris-Suzuki, Tessa 1989, *A History of Japanese Economic Thought*, Abingdon: Routledge.

Myers, Brian 2010, *The Cleanest Race: How North Koreans See Themselves and Why it Matters*. New York: Melville House.

Nagel, Sarah 2012, 'Staatskapitalismus goes global', PROKLA, 169(4), 641–57.

Nakamura Takafusa 1999, 'The Japanese war economy as a 'planned' economy'. In Eric Pauer (ed.) *Japan's War Economy*, Abingdon: Routledge.

Naughton, Barry 1988, 'The Third Front: Defence Industrialization in the Chinese Interior', *The China Quarterly* 115, 351–86.

Naughton, Barry 1996, *Growing out of the plan*. Cambridge: Cambridge University Press.

Naughton, Barry 2007, *The Chinese Economy: Transitions and Growth*, Cambridge, MA: MIT Press.

Naughton, Barry 2010, The Policy Challenges of Post-Stimulus Growth. http://www
.globalasia.org/print.php?c=e287 (accessed 16 October 2010).

Naughton, Barry 2011, 'China's Economic Policy Today: The New State Activism', *Euras-
ian Geography and Economics*, 52, 3: 313–29.

Naughton, Barry 2015, '*Danwei*: The Economic Foundations of a Unique Institution', In
Lu Xiaobo and Elizabeth J. Perry, *Danwei: the changing Chinese workplace in historical and comparative perspective*, Abingdon: Routledge.

Neal, Larry 2014, 'Introduction', The Cambridge History of Capitalism vol. 1, edited by
Larry Neal, Cambridge: Cambridge University Press.

Nee, Victor and Sonja Opper 2007, 'On Politicized Capitalism', in *On Capitalism*, edited
by Victor Nee and Richard Swedberg, Stanford, CA: Stanford University Press, 93–
127.

Nolan, Peter 2001, *China and World Economy*, Basingstoke: Palgrave.

Nolan Peter and Jin Zhang 2010, 'Global competition after the financial crisis', New Left
Review 64, 97–108.

Nove, Alec 1992, *An Economic History of the USSR, 1917–1991*, Harmondsworth: Penguin.

Oi, Jean 1995, 'The Role of the Local State in China's Transitional Economy', *The China
Quarterly* 144, 1132–49.

Palmer, Brandon 2013, *Fighting for the Enemy: Koreans in Japan's War, 1937–1945*, Seattle:
University of Washington Press.

Pan, Wei 2010, 'Western System Versus Chinese System', The University of Nottingham
China Policy Institute *Briefing Series*, issue 61.

Parish, William 1981, 'Egalitarianism in Chinese Society', *Problems of Communism*,
January–February 1981.

Park, Inho 2017, 'The Creation of the North Korean Market System', Seoul: Daily NK.

Patrick Murray 2000, 'Marx's 'Truly Social' Labour Theory of Value: Part 1, Abstract
Labour in Marxian Value Theory', *Historical Materialism* 6:1, pp. 27–66.

Pearson, Margaret M. 2011, 'Variety Within and Without: The Political Economy of
Chinese Regulation', in *Beyond the Middle Kingdom*, edited by Scott Kennedy, Stanford, CA: Stanford University Press, 25–43.

Perry, Elizabeth J. 1994, *Shanghai on Strike: The Politics of Chinese Labor*, Stanford University Press.

Perry, Elizabeth J. 1997, *Proletarian Power: Shanghai in the Cultural Revolution*, Boulder:
Westview Press.

Perry, Elizabeth J. 2005, *Patrolling the Revolution: Worker Militias, Citizenship, and the
Modern Chinese State*, Lanham: Rowman & Littlefield.

Perry, Elizabeth J. 2012, *Anyuan: Mining China's revolutionary tradition*, Berkeley: University of California Press.

Petras, J. 1976, 'State Capitalism and the Third World', *Journal of Contemporary Asia*,
6:4, 432–43.

Pirie, Ian 2008, *The Korean Developmental State: From Dirigisme to Neo-liberalism*, London: Routledge.

Pollard, Sidney 1990, *Typology of Industrialisation Processes in the Nineteenth Century*, London: Harwood Academic Publishers.

Pollard, Vincent Kelly (ed.) 2011, *State Capitalism, Contentious Politics and Large-Scale Social Change*, Leiden: Brill.

Pollard, Vincent Kelly 2011, 'State Capitalist Analysis – Before the Russian Revolution, in Reaction to Stalin's Consolidation of Power, and after the Cold War', in Pollard (ed.), *State Capitalism, Contentious Politics and Large-Scale Social Change*, Leiden: Brill.

Pozo-Martin, Gonzalo 2010. 'Reassessing the permanent arms economy', *International Socialism*, 2:127.

Pun, Ngai 2016, *Migrant Labor in China: Post-Socialist Transformations*, Cambridge: Polity Press.

Radice, Hugo 2008, 'The Developmental State under Global Neoliberalism', *Third World Quarterly* 29:6, 153–74.

Ramo, Joshua. C 2004, *The Beijing Consensus*. London: The Foreign Policy Centre.

Reiman, Michal 1987, *The Birth of Stalinism: The USSR on the Eve of the 'Second Revolution'*, Indiana University Press.

Resnick, Stephen A., Richard D. Wolff 2002, *Class Theory and History: Capitalism and Communism in the USSR*, Hove: Psychology Press.

Robinson, Joan V. 1965, 'Korea, 1964: Economic Miracle', *Monthly Review* 16:9, 541–9.

Rosenberg, Justin 1994, *The Empire of Civil Society*, London: Verso.

Rosenberg, Justin 2006, 'Why is There No International Historical Sociology?', *European Journal of International Relations*, 12:3.

Rowen, Henry S. 2007, 'When Will the Chinese People Be Free?', *Journal of Democracy*, 18, 3: 38–52.

Rubin, Isaak 1973 [1928], *Essays on Marx's Theory of Value*, Montreal: Black Rose Books.

Rueschemeyer, Dietrich and Peter Evans 1985, 'The State and Economic Transformation: Toward an Analysis of the Conditions Underlying Effective Intervention', Peter Evans, Dietrich Rueschemeyer and Theda Skocpol (eds), *Bringing the State Back In*. Cambridge: Cambridge University Press, 44–77.

Saad Filho, Alfredo 2002, *The Value of Marx: Political Economy for Contemporary Capitalism*, Abingdon: Routledge.

Saich, Tony 2004, *Governance and Politics of China*, Houndmills: Palgrave.

Sanchez-Sibony, Oscar 2014, *Red Globalization: The Political Economy of the Soviet Cold War from Stalin to Krushchev*, Cambridge: Cambridge University Press.

Sapir, Jacques 1997, 'The Economics of War in the Soviet Union During World War II', in Moshe Lewin and Ian Kershaw (eds) *Stalinism and Nazism; Dictatorships in Comparison*, Cambridge: Cambridge University Press.

Satya Gabriel, Stephen A. Resnick and Richard D. Wolff 2012, 'What Happened To

Chinese Communism: The Transition From State Feudalism To State Capitalism', in Pollard, Vincent (ed), *State Capitalism, Contentious Politics and Large-Scale Social Change*, Chicago: Haymarket Books.

Selden, Mark 1992, *The Political Economy of Chinese Development*, Abingdon: Routledge. (Original article published in *World Development* 14 in 1986).

Serge, Victor 2017, *Year One of the Russian Revolution*, Chicago: Haymarket Books.

Shambaugh, David 2009, *China's Communist Party: Atrophy and Adaptation*, Berkeley: University of California Press.

Shao, Sijun, Chris Nyland and Cherrie Jiuhua Zhu 2011, 'Tripartite Consultation: An Emergent Form of Governance Shaping Employment Relations in China', *Industrial Relations Journal*, 42, 4: 358–74.

Shaxson, Nicholas 2011, *Treasure Islands: Tax Havens and the Men Who Stole the World*, London: Macmillan.

Shen, Zhihua 2012, *Mao, Stalin and the Korean War: Trilateral Communist Relations in the 1950s*, Abingdon: Routledge.

Shih, Victor 2008, *Factions and Finance in China. Elite Conflict and Inflation*, New York: Cambridge University Press.

Shue, Vivienne 1995, 'State Sprawl: The Regulatory State and Social Life in a Small Chinese City', Deborah S. Davis, Richard Kraus, Barry Naughton and Elizabeth J. Perry (eds.). *Urban Spaces in Contemporary China*, Cambridge: Cambridge University Press and Woodrow Wilson Center Press. 90–112.

Shue, Vivienne 2004, 'Legitimacy Crisis in China?' P.H. Gries and S. Rosen (eds.). *State and Society in 21st Century China: Crisis, Contention and Legitimation*, New York and London: RoutledgeCurzon, 24–49.

Sigley, Gary 2006, 'Chinese Governmentalities: Government, Governance and the Socialist Market Economy', *Economy and Society*, 35, 4: 487–508.

Silver, Beverly J. and Zhang, Lu 2009, 'China as an Emerging Epicenter of World Labor Unrest', in: Ho-fung Hung (ed), *China and the Transformation of Global Capitalism*, Baltimore: The Johns Hopkins University Press.

Skocpol, Theda 1985, 'Bringing the State Back in: Strategies of Analysis in Current Research', Peter Evans, Dietrich Rueschemeyer and Theda Skocpol (eds.), *Bringing the State Back In*. Cambridge: Cambridge University Press. 3–37.

Smith, Adam 1910 [1776], The Wealth of Nations, Volume 1, London: J.M. Dent.

So, Alvin Y. 2005, 'Beyond the logic of capital and the polarization model', *Critical Asian Studies*, 37, 3: 481–94.

Solinger, Dorothy J 1984, *Chinese Business Under Socialism*, University of California Press.

Streeck, Wolfgang 2010, 'E Pluribus Unum? Varieties and Commonalities of Capitalism', MPIfG Discussion Paper, Max Planck Institute for the Study of Societies. http://www.mpifg.de/pu/mpifg_dp/dp10-12.pdf (accessed 9 January 2011).

Stubbs, Richard 1999, 'War and Economic Development: Export-Oriented Industrialization in East and Southeast Asia', *Comparative Politics*, April 1999, 337–55.

Stubbs, Richard 2009, 'What ever happened to the East Asian Developmental State? The unfolding debate', *The Pacific Review*, 22:1, 1–22.

Suh, Daesook 1988, *Kim Il Sung, the North Korean Leader*, New York: Columbia University Press.

Tanzi, Vito and Ludger Schuknecht 2000, *Public Spending in the Twentieth Century. A Global Perspective*, Cambridge: Cambridge University Press.

ten Brink, Tobias 2012a, 'Kontinuität und Wandel: China in der westlichen Chinaforschung', *Geographische Revue*, 14, 2: 36–52.

ten Brink, Tobias 2012b, 'Perspectives on the Development of the Private Business Sector in China', *China – An International Journal*, 10, 3: 1–19.

ten Brink, Tobias 2013a, *Chinas Kapitalismus. Entstehung, Verlauf, Paradoxien*, Frankfurt: Campus.

ten Brink, Tobias 2013b, 'Paradoxes of Prosperity in China's New Capitalism', *Journal of Current Chinese Affairs*, 42, 4: 17–44.

ten Brink, Tobias 2014, *Global Political Economy and the Modern State System*, Leiden, Boston: Brill.

The Economist 2012, 'Special Report: State Capitalism, The Visible Hand', *The Economist*, 21 Jan, 3–18.

The Economist 2012, 'The Rise of State Capitalism: The Emerging World's New Model', 21–7 January.

Tilly, C. 1985, 'War Making and State Making as Organized Crime', in P. Evans, D. Rueschemeyer and T. Skocpol (eds.), *Bringing the State Back In*, Cambridge University Press, 169–91.

Tilly, Charles, 1975, 'Reflections on the history of European state making' in *The Formation of National States in Western Europe*, edited by Charles Tilly, Princeton: Princeton University Press.

Trotsky, Leon 1931 [1906], *Results and Prospects*, www.marxists.org/archive/trotsky/1931/tpr/rp01.htm

Trotsky, Leon 1971, *1905*, Harmondsworth: Penguin.

Trotsky, Leon 1972 [1937], *The Revolution Betrayed*, New York: Pathfinder Press.

Trotsky, Leon, *Leon Trotsky's Collected Writings on China*. https://www.marxists.org/archive/trotsky/china/index.htm

Tsai, Kellee S 2004, *Back-Alley Banking: Private Entrepreneurs in China*. Ithaca, NY, and London: Cornell University Press.

Tsai, Kellee S. 2007, *Capitalism without Democracy: The Private Sector in Contemporary China*, Ithaca: Cornell University Press.

United Nations 2018, *United Nations World Urbanisation Prospects 2018*. https://population.un.org/wup/Country-Profiles/

United Nations Office on Drugs and Crime 2008, A Century of International Drug Control, Geneva, United Nations.

Van der Linden, Marcel 2007. *Western Marxism and the Soviet Union*. Leiden: Brill.

Van der Linden, Marcel and Karl Heinz Roth 2014, *Beyond Marx, Theorising the Global Labour Relations of the Twenty-First Century*, Historical Materialism Book Series, Volume: 56, Leiden: Brill.

Van Der Pijl, Kees 1993, 'Soviet Socialism and Passive Revolution', in Stephen Gill (ed.), *Gramsci, Historical Materialism and International Relations*, Cambridge: Cambridge University Press.

Van Der Pijl, Kees 1995, 'The Second Glorious Revolution; Globalizing Elites and Historical Change', in Björn Hettne, *International Political Economy*, Halifax: Fernwood.

Van Der Pijl, Kees 1998, *Transnational Classes and International Relations*, London: Routledge.

Van Ree, Erik 1989, 'The Limits of Juche: North Korea's dependence on Soviet industrial aid, 1953–76', *Journal of Communist Studies*, 5:1, 50–73.

Vance, T. and Oakes, W. 2008, The Permanent War Economy, Center for Socialist History.

Vance, T.N. 1951, 'The Permanent War Economy', *New International*, 17:1–6. https://www.marxists.org/history/etol/writers/vance/1951/permwar/index.htm

Wade, Robert 1990, *Governing the Market: Economic Theory and the Role of Government in East Asian Industrialization*, Princeton University Press.

Walder, Andrew G. 1995, 'Local Governments as Industrial Firms: An Organizational Analysis of China's Transitional Economy', *American Journal of Sociology*, 101, 2: 263–301.

Walder, Andrew G. and Jean C. Oi 1999, 'Property Rights in the Chinese Economy: Contours of the Process of Change', Jean C. Oi and Andrew G. Walder (ed.), *Property Rights and Economic Reform in China*, California: Stanford University Press.

Walder, Andrew G. 2015, *China under Mao: a revolution derailed*, Cambridge MA: Harvard University Press.

Walker, Gavin 2016, *The Sublime Perversion of Capital: Marxist Theory and the Politics of History in Modern Japan*, Durham: Duke University Press.

Wang Hui 2014, *China from Empire to Nation-State*, translated by Michael Gibbs Hill, Cambridge MA: Harvard University Press.

Wank, David L. 1999, *Commodifying Communism: Business, Trust, and Politics in a Chinese City*, Cambridge: Cambridge University Press.

Waterbury, John 1999, 'The long gestation and brief triumph of import-substituting industrialisation', World Development, 27, 2: 323–41.

Weiss, Linda 1995, 'Governed Interdependence: Rethinking the Government-Business Relationship in East Asia', *The Pacific Review*, 8, 4: 589–616.

Weiss, Linda 1998, *The Myth of the Powerless State*, Ithaca: Cornell University Press.

Wendt, Alexander and Michael Barnett 1993, 'Dependent State Formation and Third World Militarization', *Review of International Studies* 19:4, 321–47.

Werner, Jake 2012, 'Global Fordism in 1950s urban China', *Frontiers of History in China*, 7:3.

White, Gordon 1984, 'Developmental States and Socialist Industrialisation in the Third World', *Journal of Development Studies*, 21:1, 97–120.

White, Gordon and Robert Wade 1988, 'Developmental States and Markets in East Asia: An Introduction', Gordon White (ed.). *Developmental States in East Asia*, Basingstoke: Macmillan Press. 1–29.

Wilson, Jeanne 2007, 'China's Transformation towards Capitalism', in *Varieties of Capitalism in Post-Communist Countries*, edited by David Lane and Martin Myant, Houndmills: Palgrave, 239–57.

Witt, Michael A. 2010, *China: What Variety of Capitalism?* http://www.insead.edu/facult yresearch/research/doc.cfm?did=46188 (accessed 15 December 2010).

Wolf, Martin 2010, 'How China must change if it is to sustain its ascent', *Financial Times*, 22 September, p. 15.

Wong, Joshep 2004, 'The Adaptive Developmental State in East Asia', *Journal of East Asian Studies*, 4:3, 345–62.

Woo-Cumings, M. 1998, 'National Security and the Rise of the Developmental State in South Korea and Taiwan', in Henry S. Rowen, ed., Behind East Asian Growth: The Political and Social Foundations of Prosperity, Routledge: 319–337.

Woo-Cumings, M. 1999, 'Introduction: Chalmers Johnson and the Politics of Nationalism and Development', in Meredith Woo-Cumings ed. *The Developmental State*, Itahca: Cornell University Press, 1–31.

Woo, Jung-en [Meredith Woo-Cumings] 1991, *Race to the Swift: State and Finance in Korean Industrialization*, New York: Columbia University Press.

World Bank 1993, *The East Asian Miracle: Economic Growth and Public Policy*. Oxford University Press.

World Trade Organisation 2017, World Trade Statistical Review 2017, Geneva, WTO.

Wright, Andrew 1997, 'On Holloway', unpublished notes.

Wu, Jinglian 2005, *Understanding and Interpreting Chinese Economic Reform*, Singapore: Thomson.

Wu, Yiching 2015, *The Cultural Revolution at the Margins: Chinese Socialism in Crisis*, Cambridge MA: Harvard University Press.

Yang, Dali L. 2004, *Remaking the Chinese Leviathan: Market Transition and the Politics of Governance in China*, Stanford: Stanford University Press.

Yi, Jonghyun 2008, *The Korean Retailing Sector since the 1970s: Government, Consumers and the Rise & Fall of the Department Store*, Phd thesis, Department of Economic History of the London School of Economics and Political Science.

Young, Alwyn 1995, 'The tyranny of numbers: confronting the statistical realities of the East Asian growth experience', *The Quarterly Journal of Economics*, 110, 3: 641–80.

Zander, Ernst 1974, *Kommunismus und Leistungsprinzip*, Heidelberg: Sauer.

Zhang, Lu 2014, *Inside China's Automobile Factories: the politics of labour and worker resistance*, New York: Cambridge University Press.

Zheng Chaolin and Gregor Benton 1997, *An Oppositionist for Life: memoirs of the Chinese revolutionary Zheng Chaolin*, Humanities Press.

Zheng, Chaolin 2022, *Selected Writings*, edited by Gregor Benton and John Sexton, Leiden: Brill.

Zheng, Yongnian 2004, *Globalization and State Transformation in China*. Cambridge: Cambridge University Press.

Žižek, Slavoj 2007, 'Introduction', in Mao Tse-Tung, *On Practice and Contradiction*, London: Verso.

Zweig, David and Chen Zhimin (eds.) 2007, *China's Reforms and International Political Economy*, London: Routledge.

Zysman, John 1983, *Government, Markets, and Growth. Financial Systems and the Politics of Industrial Change*, Ithaca: Cornell University Press.

Bibliography II: References in East Asian Languages

Primary Sources

Volumes published by the Chinese Academy of Social Sciences and the Central Archives (中国社会科学院和中央档案馆)

Zhonghua renmin gongheguo jīngji dangan ziliao xuanbian 1949–52 中华人民共和国经济档案资料选编 1949–52 [Selected economic archives of the People's Republic of China 1949–52]

Gongye juan 工业卷 (1996) [Volume on Industry]

Jiben jianshe touzi he jianzhu juan 基本建设投资和建筑卷 (1989) [Volume on Basic Construction investment and Construction]

Jiaotong tongxun juan 交通通讯卷 (1996) [Volume on Transportation and Communication]

Jinrong juan 金融卷 (1996) [Volume on Finance]

Laodong gongzi he zhigong fuli juan 劳动工资和职工福利卷 (1994) [Volume on Labor wages and employee benefits]

Zhonghua renmin gongheguo jīngji dangan ziliao xuanbian 1953–57 中华人民共和国经济档案资料选编 1953–57 [Selected economic archives of the People's Republic of China 1953–1957]

Zonghe juan 综合卷 (1998) [Summary volume]

Cazheng juan 财政卷 (2000) [Volume on Government finance]

Gongye juan 工业卷 (1998) [Volume on Industry]

Guding zi chan touzi he jianzhu ye juan 固定资产投资和建筑业卷 (1998) [Volume on Fixed Assets Investment and Construction industry]

Jiaotong tongxun juan 交通通讯卷 (1998) [Volume on Transportation and Communication]

Jinrong juan 金融卷 (2000) [Volume on Finance]

Laodong gonzi he zhigong baoxian fuli zuan 劳动工资和职工保险福利卷 (1998) [Volume on Labor wage and employee insurance benefits]

Nongye juan 农业卷 (1999) [Volume on Agriculture]

Shangye juan 商业卷 (2000) [Volume on Commerce]

Zhonghua renmin gongheguo jīngji dangan ziliao xuanbian 1958–65 中华人民共和国经济档案资料选编 1958–65 [Selected economic archives of the People's Republic of China 1958–65].

Zonghe juan 综合卷 (2011) [Summary volume]

Guding zi chan touzi he jianzhu ye juan 固定资产投资与建筑业卷 (2011) [Volume on Fixed Assets Investment and Construction]

Shangye juan 商业卷 (2011) [Volume on commerce]

Cazheng juan 财政卷 (2011) [Volume on Government finance]

劳动就业和收入分配卷 (2011) [Laodong jiuye he shaoru fenpei juan, Volume on Labor Employment and Income Distribution]

Jinrong juan 金融卷 (2011) [Volume on Finance]

Gongye juan 工业卷 (2011) [Volume on Industry]

Jiaotong tongxun juan 交通通讯卷 (2011) [Volume on Transportation and communication]

Nongye juan 农业卷 (2011) [Volume on Agriculture]

Duiwai maoyi juan 对外贸易卷 (2011) [Volume on Foreign Trade]

Secondary Sources

Chinese Language

Fazhan yanjiusuo zonghe ketizu 发展研究所综合课题组 1987, 'Nongmin, shichang he zhidu chuangxin' 农民, 市场和制度创新, *Jingji yanjiu* 经济研究, 1987, no. 1.

Gao Aidi 高爱娣 2008, *Zhongguo gongren yundong shi* 中国工人运动史 [The history of the Chinese workers' movement], Beijing: Zhongguo laodong shehui baozhang chubanshe.

Gao Aidi 高爱娣 2013, *Gongyunshi lun* 工运史论 [A study of the history of the workers' movement], Beijing: Guangming ribao chubanshe. http://cdmd.cnki.com.cn/Article/CDMD-10052-2005066805.htm

Hu Angang 胡鞍钢 2007, *Zhongguo zhengzhi jingji shi lun, 1949–1976* 中国政治经济史论 1949–76 [The Political and Economic History of China, 1949–76], Beijing: Tsinghua University press.

Li Dajia 李達嘉 2015, *Shangren yu gongchan geming 1919–27* 商人與共產革命 1919–27, [Capitalists and communist revolution, 1919–27], Taibei Shi: Zhongyang yanjiuyuan jindaishi yanjiusuo.

Li Sishen 李思慎 2009, *Li lisan houbansheng, shang/xia* 李立三後半生, 上/下 [Li Lisan, the second half of his life, two vols.], Hong Kong: Dashan Culture Publishing Co., Ltd.

Li Xun 李遜 2015, *Geming zaofan niandai: shanghai wenge yundongshi gao* 革命造反年代: 上海文革運動史稿 I & II [The age of revolution and rebellion: history of the Cultural Revolution in Shanghai], Hong Kong: Oxford University Press (China).

Lu Tu 吕途 2013, *Zhongguo xin gongren: Mishi yu jueqi* 中国新工人: 迷失与崛起 平装 [New Chinese workers: lost and rising], Beijing: Falu chubanshe.

Qian Liqun 錢理群 2012, *Mao Zedong shidai he hou Mao Zedong shidai* 毛澤東時代和後毛澤東時代 (1949–2009), [Mao Zedong era and post-Mao Zedong era (1949–2009)], Taibei shi: Lianjing chuban.

Qian Liqun 錢理群 2007, *Jujue yiwang: '1957 Nian xue' yanjiu biji* 拒絕遺忘: '1957 年學' 研究筆記, 牛津大學出版社 [Refuse to forget: '1957 studies' research notes], Hong Kong: Oxford University Press (China).

Shen Zhihua 沈志華 2013a, *Chuzai shizilu koude xuanze 1956–7* 處在十字路口的選擇 1956–7 年的中國, Guangzhou: Guangdong renmin chubanshe.

Shen Zhihua 沈志華 2013b, *Chaoxian zhanzheng zaitan* 朝鮮戰爭再探, Hong Kong: Sanlian shudian.

Sun Zijian 孙自俭 2013, *Minguo shichi tielu gongren qunti yanjiu 1912–37* 民国时期铁路工人群体研究 (1912–37), [Research on Railway Workers Groups in Republican China], Zhengzhou: Zhengzhou daxue chubanshe.

Wang Yongzhen 王永玺 2013, *Zhongguo gongren yundong shi yanjiu* 中国工人运动史研究 [Research on the history of Chinese workers' movement], Beijing: Zhongguo Gongren Chubanshe.

Won Tiejun 温铁军 2013, *Baci weiji: zhongguo de zhenshi jingyan 1949–2009* 八次危机: 中国的真实经验 (1949–2009), Beijing: Dongfang chubanshe.

Yang Siyuan 杨思远 2005, *Zhongguo nongmin gong de zhengzhi jingji xue kaocha* 中国农民工的政治经济学考察 [A political economic study of China's peasant migrant workers], PhD. Dissertation, Minzu University of China.

Zhang Jingru 張靜如 2011, *Zhongguo dangdai shehui shi. Di i juan*, 中國當代社會史. 第 1 卷, 1949–1956, [Chinese Contemporary Social History Volume 1], Changsha: Hunan Renmin chubanshe.

Korean Language

Ch'oe Chongt'ae 최종태, Kim Kangsik 김강식 2003, *Pukhan ui nodong kwa illyŏk kwalli* 북한 노동과 인력 관리 [Management of labour and manpower in North Korea], Seoul: SNU Press.

Ch'oe Chunggŭk 최중극 1992, *Widaehan choguk haebang chŏnjaeng kwa chŏnsi kyŏngje* 위대한 조국 해방 전쟁과 전시 경제 [The great fatherland liberation war and the wartime economy], Pyŏngyang: Sahoe kwahak ch'ulp'ansa.

Chang Yunmi 장윤미 2011. 'A study on the Chinese Model' *Contemporary China Studies* Vol. 13. No. 1. 75–116.

Chŏn Hyŏnsu 전현수 1999, 'Sanŏp ŭi kugyuhwa wa inminkyŏngje ŭi kyehoekhwa: kong'ŏp ŭl chungsimŭro' '산업의 국유화와 인민경제의 계획화: 공업을 중심으로' [The nationalisation of industry and the planification of the people's economy: focusing on industry.], *Hyŏndae pukhan yŏn'gu* 2:1.

Chŏn Ingap 전인갑 2002, (20 segi chŏnban'gi) Sanghae sahoe ŭi chiyŏkchuŭi wa no-dongja (20세기 선반기) 上海社會의 地域主義와 勞動者 [(The first half of the 20th century) Regionalism and the working class in Shanghai Society], Seoul: SNU Press.

Chŏn Sŏng-hŭng 전성흥 2008, *Chungguk model ŭi tŭngjang kwa ŭimi* 중국모델의 등장과 의미 [The rise of the Chinese model and its consequences], Chŏn Sŏng-hŭng (ed.) *Chungguk model ron*, Seoul: Buk'i Ch'ulp'ansa.

Chŏn Yongsik 전용식 1958, 'Urinara kwadogi kyŏngje palchŏn ŭi t'ŭksŏng' '우리나라 과도기 경제발전의 특성' [The character of our country's transitional economic development], in *Chosŏn minjujuŭi inmin konghwaguk ch'anggŏn 10chunyŏn kinyŏm ronmunjip: Urinara esŏ ŭi sahoejuŭi kyŏngje kŏnsŏl*, Pyŏngyang: Kwahagwon ch'ulp'ansa.

Chŏng Chinsang 정진상 1995, 'Haebang chikhu sahoe sinbunje yuje ŭi haech'e' '해방직후 사회신분제 유제의 해체' [Deconstruction of the Remnants of Pre-Modern Social Status System after the Liberation in Korea], *Sahoe kwahak yŏn'gu* 사회과학연구 13:1.

Chŏng Sŏngjin [Jeong Seongjin] 정성진 2000, 'Han'guk chŏnjaeng, pet'ŭnam chŏnjaeng kwa yŏnggu kunbi kyŏngje' '한국전쟁, 베트남 전쟁과 영구군비경제' ['The Korean War, the Vietnam War and the Permanent War Economy'], *Kyŏngje wa sahoe* 경제와 사회, no. 46.

Chosŏn Minjujuŭi Inmin Konghwaguk Naegak Pŏpgyu Chŏngni Wiwŏnhoe 조선 민주주의 인민 공화국 내각 법규 정리 위원회 1961, *Chosŏn Minjujuŭi Inmin Konghwaguk Pŏpgyujip*, vols 1–4 조선 민주주의 인민 공화국 법규집 [DPRK Penal Code 1961], Pyongyang: Kungnip Ch'ulp'ansa.

Chosŏn rodongdang chung'ang wiwonhoe tangryŏksa yŏn'guso 1989 [1979], Chosŏn rodongdang ryaksa 2. Seoul: Tolbegae.

Chungang Ilbo T'ŭkpyŏl Ch'wijaeban 중앙일보특별취재반 1992, *Pirok Chosŏn minju juŭi inmin konghwaguk* 秘錄조선민주주의인민공화국 [Secret records of the DPRK], Seoul: Chungang Ilbosa.

Hwang Kyŏngchin 황경진 2010, Chungguk sinsedae nongmingong ui kibon hyŏnhwang gwa t'ŭkching 중국신세대농민공의 기본현황과 특징 [The current situation and characteristics of the new generation of peasant workers in China], *Kukche nodong p'ŭrip'ŭ* 국제노동프리프 [International Labor Brief], December 2010.

Kim Hakchun 김학준1995, *Pukhan 50-nyŏnsa* 북한 50년사 [Fifty Years of North Korean History], Seoul: Tonga Publishing.

Kim Hwangil 김황일 1953, 'Inmin kyŏngje ŭi pokku kŏnsŏl e issŏsŏ rodong kyegŭp ŭi yŏkhal' '인민경제의 복구 건설에 있어서 로동계급의 역할' [The role of the working class in the recovery and construction of the people's economy], *Inmin* 인민, 1953.9, 64–72.

Kim Il Sung 김일성 1970, *Sahoe juŭi kyŏngje kwalli munje e taehayŏ*, vol 3 사회주의 경제관리 문제에 대하여 [On the problems of socialist economic management], Pyŏngyang: Chosŏn nodongdang ch'ulp'ansa.

Kim Il Sung 김일성 1979~98, *Chŏjakchip* 저작집 [Works], 50 vols., Pyŏngyang: Chosŏn nodongdang ch'ulp'ansa.

Kim Il Sung 김일성 1981 [1961], 'Modŭn him ŭl yŏsŏt kae koji ŭi chŏmnyŏng ŭl wihayŏ'

모든 힘을 여섯 개 고지의 점령을 위하여 [All efforts towards the achievement of our six goals] in: *Kim Il Sung chŏjakchip 15*, Pyŏngyang: Chosŏn nodongdang ch'ulp'ansa.

Kim Il 김일 1998, 'Chosŏn minjujuŭi inmin konghwaguk inmin kyŏngje palchŏn 6 kaenyŏn kyehoek e taehayŏ', in *Chosŏn rodongdang taehoe charyo chip*, vol. 3, Kukt'o t'ongilwŏn.

Kim Songbo 김성보 1995, 'Pukhan ŭi t'oji kaehyŏk kwa nongch'on kyech'ŭng kusŏng pyŏnhwa' '북한의 토지개혁과 농촌 계층 구성 변화', *Tongbang hakchi* 동방학지 87, 63.

Kim Sŏngbo 김성보 et al. 2004, *Pukhan hyŏndaesa*, [Modern history of North Korea], Seoul: Ungjin.

Kim Yŏnch'ŏl 김연철 2001, *Pukhan ui sanŏphwa wa kyŏngje chŏngch'aek* 북한의 산업화 와 경제정책 [Industrialisation and economic policy in North Korea], Seoul: Yŏksa pipy'ŏngsa.

Kim Yŏnch'ŏl 2012 [1998], '1950 nyŏndae pukhan ŭi nodong chŏngch'aek kwa nodongja', [North Korean labour policy and workers in the 1950s]. In: Yoksa munje yon'guso (ed.), *1950 nyondae nambukhan sont'aek kwa kulchol*, Seoul: Yoksa pip'yongsa.

Kim Yuntae 김윤태 1999, *Tong asia palchŏn kukka wa chiguhwa* 동아시아 발전국가와 지구화 [The Developmental State in East Asia and Globalization], *Korean Sociology* 한국사회학, 33:1, 83–102.

Kwon O-yun 1997, 'Pukhan sahoe juŭi ch'eje esŏ ŭi nodongdongwon sudan kwa kŭ pyŏnhwa e kwanhan yŏn'gu' '북한 사회주의 체제에서의 노동동원수단과 그 변화에 관한 연구' [A study on the changing methods of labour mobilisation in the North Korean socialist system], *Kungmin yulli yŏn'gu* 국민윤리연구 37.

Kwon O-yun 2004, 'Haebanghu nodong chohap ŭrosŏ pukhan chigŏp tongmaeng ŭi sŏnggyŏk pyŏnhwa (1945–1950)' 해방후 노동 조합으로서 *Pukhan yŏn'gu hakhoebo* 8.1.

Nam Ch'unhwa 남춘화 1957, 'Hyŏn sigi issŏsŏ nongsanmul sumae kagyŏk chejŏng kwa kwallyon toen myŏt kaji munje', *Kyŏngje kŏnsŏl* 경제건설, 1957.11, 72–5.

Paek Sŭng-uk [Baek Seung-Wook] 백승욱 2008, *Segyehwa ŭi kyŏnggye e sŏn chungguk* 세계화의 경계에 선 중국 [China on the border of the Globalization], Seoul: Changbi Ch'ulp'ansa.

Pak Hyŏnch'ae. 박현채 1990, '한국전쟁과 한국 경제의 전개' ['The Korean War and the Evolution of the Korean Economy'], *Hyŏndae saehoe* 현대사회, no. 36.

Pak Ŭn-hong 박은홍 2008, *Tong asia ŭi chŏnhwan: palchŏn kukka rŭl nŏmŏ* 동아시아의 전환: 발전국가를 넘어 [The Transformation of the East Asia: Beyond the Developmental State], Seoul: Arche Publishing.

Pei Minxin 2011, *Pulhwaksilhan chungguk ŭi mirae* 불확실한 중국의 미래 [China's uncertain future], Hwang Sŏng-don trans. Seoul: Chaekmirae Publishing.

Ri Chongdŭk 리종득 1955, 'Kiŏpso tongnip ch'aesanje ŭi ŭiŭi wa jjaehŭ tŭresŏŭi kŭ ŭi chŏg'yong mit kanghwa taech'aek' 기업소 독립 채산제의 의의와 째흐들에서의 ㄱ

의 적용 및 강화 대책 [The significance of the self-financing enterprise accounting system and the policy of implementing and strengthening it], *Inmin* 인민, 1955.3.

Seoul Institute for Social Sciences Economics Unit 서울사회과학연구소 경제분과 1991, 한국에서의 자본주의 발전 [The Development of Capitalism in Korea], Seoul: Sae-Gill Publishing.

Sŏ Hwi 서휘 1956, 'Che 3ch'a tangdaehoe kyŏlchŏng silhaeng ŭl wihan chigŏp tongmaeng tanch'e ŭi kwaŏp', *Rodong sinmun* 로동신문, 21.6.1956.

Sŏ Taesuk [Suh Dae-sook] 서대숙 1989, *Kim Il Sung: Pukhan ŭi chidoja* 김일성: 북한의 지도자, translated by Sŏ Chusŏk, Seoul: Ch'ŏnggye Yŏn'guso.

Sŏ Tongman 서동만 2005, *Pukchosŏn sahoechuŭi ch'eje sŏllipsa* 북조선 사회주의 체제 설립사, [A history of the establishment of the North Korean socialist system], Seoul: Sŏnin.

Son Hoch'ŏl 손호철 1991, 'Hanguk chŏnjaeng kwa ideollogi chihyŏng: kukka, chibae yŏnhap, ideollogi' '한국전쟁과 이데올로기 지형: 국가, 지배연합, 이데올로기' ['The Korean War and Contour of Ideologies: State, Ruling Coalition and Ideology'], in: The Institute for Far Eastern Studies at Kyungnam University 경남대학교 극동문제 연구소 (ed.), 한국전쟁과 남북한 사회의 구조적 변화 [The Korean War and Structural Changes of Societies in North and South Korea].

Wada Haruki 和田春樹 1999, *Hanguk Chŏnjaeng* 한국전쟁 [The Korean War], Seoul: Changjak kwa pibyŏngsa.

Yang Munsu 양문수 2003, '1970 nyŏndae pukhan kyŏngje wa changgi ch'imch'e mek'ŏnijŭm ŭi hyŏngsŏng' '1970년대 북한 경제와 장기 침체 메커니즘의 형성 [The North Korean economy in the 1970s and the formation of the mechanism of long-term stagnation]', *Hyŏndae Pukhan yŏn'gu* 6:1.

Yang Munsu 양문수 2001, *Pukhan kyŏngje ŭi kujo: kyongje kaebal kwa ch'imch'e ui mek'ŏnijŭm* 북한 경제의 구조: 경제 개발과 침체의 메커니즘 [The structure of the North Korean economy: the mechanisms of economic development and stagnation]. Seoul: SNU Press.

Yang Ujin 양우진 1993, 'Hyŏndae Han'guk chabonjuŭi palchŏn kwajŏng yŏn'gu' '현대 한국자본주의 발전과정 연구' [A Study on the Development of Capitalism in Post-War Korea: Focusing on the Consolidation and Decay of the State Capitalism Conjuncture], PhD. Dissertation in Economics, Seoul National University. (English title as printed on the cover of the dissertation).

Yi Chongsŏk 이종석 2011, *Pukhan ui yŏksa 2: chuch'e sasang kwa yuil ch'eje 1960–1994* [History of North Korea vol. 2: Juche thought and the monolithic system], Seoul: Yŏksa pip'yŏngsa.

Yi Pyŏngch'ŏn 이병천 1996, '냉전분단체제와 권위주의적 자본주의 산업화: 한국' [Regime The Cold War division system and authoritarian capitalist industrialization in South Korea], *Sahoe kyŏngje p'yongnon* 사회경제평론, no. 7.

Yi Sŏngbong 이성봉 2004, '1960 nyŏndae pukhan ŭi nodong chŏngch'aek kwa punbae',

[North Korea's labour policy and distribution in the 1960s], in: *Pukhan hyŏndaesa* 1, Seoul: Hanul.

Yi Sŭnghyŏn 이승현 2004, '1960 nyŏndae pukhan ŭi kwŏllyŏk kujo chaep'yŏn kwa yuil sasang ŭi taedu: chehanjŏk tawŏnsŏng esŏ yuil ch'ejero', in: *Pukhan hyŏndaesa* 1, Seoul: Hanul.

Yi T'aesŏp 이태섭 2009, 북한의 경제위기와 체제변화 *Pukhan ŭi kyŏngje wigi wa ch'eje pyŏnhwa* [North Korea's economic crisis and systemic change], Seoul: Sŏnin.

Yi Taegŭn. 이대근 1987, Han'guk chŏnjaeng kwa 1950nyŏndae ŭi chabon ch'ukchŏk 한국전쟁과 1950년대의 자본축적 [The Korean War and capital accumulation in the 1950s], Seoul: Kkachi Books.

Yŏn Kapsu 연갑수 2003, *Taewŏn'gun Chipkwŏn'gi puguk kangbyŏng chŏngch'aek yŏn'gu*, 대원군집권기 부국강병정책 연구, [Research on the 'Prosperous Country, Strong Army' policy during the rule of the Taewŏn'gun], Seoul: SNU Press.

Yuk Chisu 육지수 1959, 'Han'guk ŭro put'ŏ ŭi muyŏk p'ung: 6.25ka segye kyŏngje e kkich'in yŏnghyang' '한국으로부터의 무역풍: 6.25가 세계경제에 끼친 영향' [Trade Wind from Korea: The Effect of the Korean War on the World Economy], *Sasanggye* 사상계, June 1959.

Yun Sang-u 윤상우 2006, *Tong asia palchŏn ŭi sahoehak* 동아시아 발전의 사회학 [Sociology of the development in the East Asia], Seoul: Nanam ch'ulp'an.

Japanese Language

Furusawa Kenji 古澤賢治 1993, *Chugoku keizai no rekishiteki tenkai* 中國經濟の歷史的展開 [The Historical Development of the Chinese Economy], Kyoto: Minerva Shobo.

Honda Kenkichi. 本多健吉 1970, *Teikaihotsu keizairon no kōzō* 低開發經濟論の構造 [Structure of the Theory of Underdeveloped Economies], Tokyo: Shinhyoronsha.

Imura Kiyoko 井村喜代子 1987, '1949-nen aki Chōsen sensō to gōri-ka tōshi' '1949 年秋-朝鮮戰爭と合理化投資' (上) [Autumn of 1949: Korean War and Restructuring Investment, Part I], *Mita Journal of Economics* 三田學會雜誌, 80:4.

Imura Kiyoko 井村喜代子 1988a, 'Betonamu sensō to kōdo seichō no saigen, hatan (I)' 'ベトナム戰爭と高度成長の再現. 破綻' (上) [The Vietnam War, the Return of High Growth and Its End, Part I], *Mita Journal of Economics* 三田學會雜誌, 81:3.

Imura Kiyoko 井村喜代子 1988b, 'Betonamu sensō to kōdo seichō no saigen, hatan (II)' 'ベトナム戰爭と高度成長の再現. 破綻' (下) [Vietnam War and Return of High Growth and Its End, Part II], *Mita Journal of Economics* 三田學會雜誌, 81:4.

Imura Kiyoko 井村喜代子 1988c, '1949 年秋-朝鮮戰爭と合理化投資' (下) [Autumn of 1949: Korean War and Restructuring Investment, Part II], *Mita Journal of Economics* 三田學會雜誌, 81:1.

Ozaki Hikosaki 尾崎彦朔 ed. 1980, *Daisan sekai to kokka shihonshugi* 第三世界と國家資本主義 [The Third World and State Capitalism], Tokyo: Tokyo University Press.

Pak Kǔnho 朴根好 1993, *Kankoku no keizai hatten to Betonamu sensō* 韓國の 經濟發展とベトナム戰爭 [Korean Economic Development and the Vietnam War], Tokyo: Ochanomizu Shobo.

Sakata Mikio. 坂田幹男 1992, 'Kankoku kokuka shihon shugi no dōyō to saihen: 'Shūhen-bu fo – do shugi' no kiki ka 'shūhen-bu kokuka shihon shugi' no saishū kyokumen ka' '韓國國家資本主義の動搖と再編: '周邊部フォ-ド主義' の危機カ '周邊部 國家資本主義'の最終局面カ' [Turbulence and Reconfiguration of Korean State Capitalism: Crisis of 'Peripheral Fordism' or the Final Stage of 'Peripheral State Capitalism'], *Keizai hyoron* 經濟評論, 41:2: 2–22.

Sano Koji 佐野孝治 1992, 'Kankoku keizai e no Betonamu sensō no eikyō' '韓國經濟へのベトナム戰爭の影響' [The Effects of the Vietnam War on the Korean Economy], *Keio Journal of Economics* 三田學會雜誌, 84:4, 945–972.

Yamamoto Tsuneo 山本恒人 2000, *Gendai chūgoku no rodo keizai: 1949–2000: goriteki teichinkintai' kara gendai rodo shijō e* 現代中國の勞動經濟: 1949–2000: 「合理的低賃金制」から現代勞動市場へ [Labour economy of Modern China 1949–2000: From 'reasonable low wage system' to modern labour market], Tokyo: Sodosha.

Yi Jongwon 李鍾元 1996, *Higashi ajia reisen to kanmi kankei* 東アジア冷戰と韓美關係, [The East Asian Cold War and US-Korea Relations], Tokyo: Tokyo University Press.

Index